PROCESS AND REALITY

Corrected Edition

PROCESS AND REALITY

AN ESSAY IN COSMOLOGY

GIFFORD LECTURES DELIVERED IN THE UNIVERSITY
OF EDINBURGH DURING THE SESSION 1927–28

BY

ALFRED NORTH WHITEHEAD

F.R.S., Sc.D. (Cambridge), Hon. D.Sc. (Manchester),
Hon. LL.D. (St. Andrews), Hon. D.Sc. (Wisconsin),
Hon. Sc.D. (Harvard and Yale)

CORRECTED EDITION

EDITED BY

DAVID RAY GRIFFIN

AND

DONALD W. SHERBURNE

THE FREE PRESS

A Division of Macmillan Publishing Co., Inc.
NEW YORK
Collier Macmillan Publishers
LONDON

The Free Press
A Division of Macmillan Publishing Co., Inc.
866 Third Avenue, New York, N.Y. 10022

Collier Macmillan Canada, Ltd.

First Free Press Paperback Edition 1979

Library of Congress Catalog Card Number: 77-90011

Printed in the United States of America

Paperbound printing number

2 3 4 5 6 7 8 9 10

Casebound printing number

1 2 3 4 5 6 7 8 9 10

Library of Congress Cataloging in Publication Data

Whitehead, Alfred North, 1861-1947.
    Process and reality.

    (Gifford lectures; 1927-28)
    Includes index.
    1. Cosmology--Addresses, essays, lectures.
2. Science--Philosophy--Addresses, essays, lectures.
3. Organism (Philosophy)--Addresses, essays, lectures.
I. Griffin, David   II. Sherburne, Donald W.
III. Title. IV. Series.
BD511.W5 1978   113   77-90011
ISBN 0-02-934580-4
ISBN 0-02-934570-7 pbk.

EDITORS' PREFACE

Process and Reality, Whitehead's *magnum opus*, is one of the major philosophical works of the modern world, and an extensive body of secondary literature has developed around it. Yet surely no significant philosophical book has appeared in the last two centuries in nearly so deplorable a condition as has this one, with its many hundreds of errors and with over three hundred discrepancies between the American (Macmillan) and the English (Cambridge) editions, which appeared in different formats with divergent paginations. The work itself is highly technical and far from easy to understand, and in many passages the errors in those editions were such as to compound the difficulties. The need for a corrected edition has been keenly felt for many decades.

The principles to be used in deciding what sorts of corrections ought to be introduced into a new edition of *Process and Reality* are not, however, immediately obvious. Settling upon these principles requires that one take into account the attitude toward book production exhibited by Whitehead, the probable history of the production of this volume, and the two original editions of the text as they compare with each other and with other books by Whitehead. We will discuss these various factors to provide background in terms of which the reader can understand the rationale for the editorial decisions we have made.

Whitehead did not spend much of his own time on the routine tasks associated with book production. Professor Raphael Demos was a young colleague of Whitehead on the Harvard faculty at the time, 1925, of the publication of *Science and the Modern World*. Demos worked over the manuscript editorially, read the proofs, and did the Index for that volume. The final sentence of Whitehead's Preface reads: "My most grateful thanks are due to my colleague Mr. Raphael Demos for reading the proofs and for the suggestion of many improvements in expression." After retiring from Harvard in the early 1960's, Demos became for four years a colleague at Vanderbilt University of Professor Sherburne and shared with him his personal observations concerning Whitehead's indifference to the production process.

Bertrand Russell [1] provides further evidence of Whitehead's sense of priorities when he reports that Whitehead, in response to Russell's com-

---

[1] *Portraits from Memory* (New York: Simon and Schuster, 1956), p. 104.

plaint that he had not answered a letter, "justified himself by saying that if he answered letters, he would have no time for original work." Russell found this justification "complete and unanswerable."

In 1929, when *Process and Reality* was in production, the same sense of priorities was operative. Whitehead was sixty-eight years old, and he still had major projects maturing in his mind: *Adventures of Ideas, Modes of Thought*, and numerous articles and lectures were still to come. "Original work," fortunately, continued to take precedence in his life over humdrum details and trivia. Unfortunately, however, 1929 found Demos in England (working with Russell). As best we can determine at this time, no one with both a familiarity with Whitehead's thought and an eye for detail undertook to shepherd *Process and Reality* through the production process —Demos, in particular, was never aware that anyone else from the philosophical community had worked on the manuscript or proofs. Whitehead's only personal acknowledgment in the Preface is to "the constant encouragement and counsel which I owe to my wife."

An examination of the available evidence, including the discrepancies between the two original editions and the types of errors they contained, has led us to the following reconstruction of the production process and of the origin of some of the types of errors.

First, to some extent in conjunction with the preparation of his Gifford Lectures and to some extent as an expansion and revision of them,[2] Whitehead prepared a hand-written manuscript. Many of the errors in the final product, such as incorrect references, misquoted poetry, other faulty quotations, faulty and inconsistent punctuation, and some of the wrong and missing words, surely originated at this stage and were due to Whitehead's lack of attention to details. In addition, the inconsistencies in formal matters were undoubtedly due in part to the fact that the manuscript was quite lengthy and was written over a period of at least a year and a half.

Second, a typist (possibly at Macmillan) prepared a typed copy for the printer. The errors that crept into the manuscript at this stage seem to include, besides the usual sorts of typographical errors, misreadings of Whitehead's somewhat difficult hand.[3] For example, the flourish initiating Whitehead's capital "H" was sometimes transcribed as a "T," so that "His" came out "This," and "Here" came out "There." Also, not only the regular mistranscription of *"Monadology"* as *"Monodology,"* but also other mistranscriptions, such as "transmuted" for "transmitted" and "goal" for "goad," probably occurred at this stage. (Professor Victor Lowe

[2] See Victor Lowe, "Whitehead's Gifford Lectures," *The Southern Journal of Philosophy*, Vol. 7, No. 4 (Winter, 1969–70), 329–38.

[3] For samples of his handwriting, see the letters published in *Alfred North Whitehead: Essays on His Philosophy*, ed. George L. Kline (New York: Prentice–Hall, 1963), p. 197; and *The Philosophy of Alfred North Whitehead*, ed. Paul Arthur Schilpp, 2nd ed. (New York: Tudor Publishing, 1951), pp. 664–65.

has reported an incident which, whether or not it involved a misreading of Whitehead's handwriting, provided—as Lowe says—a bad omen for what would happen to the book: "On April 11, 1928, Kemp Smith received this cable from Whitehead: TITLE GIFFORD LECTURES IS PROCESS AND REALITY SYLLOBUS FOLLOWING SHORTLY BY MAIL WHITCHCAD."[4])

Third, it appears that Macmillan set type first and that Cambridge set its edition a bit later, using either a copy of the typed manuscript or, more likely, a copy of Macmillan's proofsheets. There are a large number of errors which the two editions had in common, a large number in the Macmillan edition which were not in the Cambridge edition, and some few in the latter which were not in the former. Their distribution and their character suggest the following observations: Macmillan provided poor proofreading; the Cambridge editor did a much more rigorous job of catching typographical errors; the Cambridge editor also initiated certain sorts of editorial changes, which primarily involved punctuation, though these were not consistently applied throughout the entire text; finally, the types of errors unique to the Cambridge edition seem not to be due to carelessness, but to deliberate attempts to make the text more intelligible—attempts which fell short of their goal because the Cambridge editor did not understand Whitehead's technical concepts.

There is independent evidence that Whitehead himself saw proofs. Lowe has published a letter from Whitehead to his son, dated August 12, 1929, which reads in part: "At last I have got through with my Gifford Lectures—final proofs corrected, Index Printed, and the last corrections put in." [5] The deplorable state of the text, plus Whitehead's lack of enthusiasm for this sort of work, make it virtually certain that he did not do much careful proofreading. Lowe reports [6] that Whitehead, after discussions with C. I. Lewis, decided to change the adjectival form of "category" from "categorical" to "categoreal" and made this change throughout the galleys. We strongly suspect that Whitehead's work on the proofs was limited for the most part to very particular, specific corrections of this sort.

It would have been useful in the preparation of this corrected edition to have had Whitehead's manuscript and/or typescript. Unfortunately, all efforts to locate them have been unsuccessful—both are probably no longer extant. We do have some corrections, additions, and marginalia which Whitehead himself added to his Cambridge and Macmillan copies. In addition there is a one-page list entitled "Misprints" (evidently given to Whitehead by someone else) with an endorsement in Whitehead's handwriting: "Corrections all inserted." This data was given to us by Lowe, who is writing the authorized biography of Whitehead and has been given access to family materials, and to whom we express our deep appreciation.

[4] Lowe, *op. cit.*, 334, fn. 14.
[5] *Ibid.*, 338.
[6] *Ibid.*, fn. 19; as Lowe reports, he received this information from H. N. Lee.

Finally, in 1966 Lowe was allowed by Mrs. Henry Copley Greene to see a typescript of Part V, which was inscribed: "Rosalind Greene with his love From Alfred Whitehead Oct. 12, 1928." This typescript had some corrections in Whitehead's hand on it; Lowe reports that, with one exception, the published texts contained these corrections (e.g., the capitalization of 'Creature' and 'Itself' in the last paragraph).

It was on the basis of the above evidence and interpretations that we arrived at the principles that guided our editorial work in regard to both the more trivial and the more significant issues.

The most difficult and debatable editorial decisions had to be made, ironically, concerning relatively trivial matters, especially those involving punctuation. We tried to steer a middle course between two unacceptable extremes.

On the one hand, the editors of a "corrected edition" might have introduced into the text *all* the changes which they would have suggested to a still-living author. The obvious problem with this alternative is that, since the author is no longer living, he would have no chance to veto these "improvements" as being inconsistent with his own meaning or stylistic preferences.

On the other hand, to avoid this problem the editors might have decided to remove only the most obvious and egregious errors, otherwise leaving the text as it was. One problem with this alternative is that this important work would again be published without benefit of the kind of careful editorial work Whitehead had every right to expect—work which the Cambridge editor began but did not carry out consistently. Another problem is that there are over three hundred divergencies between the two original editions. In these places it is impossible simply to leave the text as it was— a choice must be made. And clearly, in most of these places the Cambridge punctuation is preferable and must be followed—it would be totally irresponsible to revert to Macmillan's punctuation. But once Cambridge's punctuation has been followed in these places, the question arises, How could one justify accepting Cambridge's improvements in these instances and yet not make similar improvements in parallel passages?

Accordingly, in trying to steer a middle course between these two extremes we decided that the most responsible plan of action would be to take the changes introduced by the Cambridge editor (which, of course, were made during Whitehead's life-time and could have been vetoed in his personal copies) as precedents for the kinds of changes to be carried out consistently. A prime example is provided by the fact that Cambridge deleted many, but not all, of the commas which often appeared between the subject and the verb in Macmillan. However, we left some other questionable practices (e.g., the frequent use of a semicolon where grammatical rules would call for a comma) as they were, primarily because Cambridge did not provide sufficient precedents for changes, even though we would ourselves have suggested changes to Whitehead had we been editing this book in 1929.

Working within these guidelines, the editors have sought to produce a text that is free not only of the hundreds of blatant errors found in the original, especially in the Macmillan edition, but also free of many of the minor sorts of inconsistencies recognized and addressed to some extent by the Cambridge editor.

It is in the matter of the more significant corrections involving word changes that editors must guard against the possibility that interpretative bias might lead to textual distortions. There were three factors which helped us guard against this possibility. First, we drew heavily upon a substantial amount of previous work, coordinated by Sherburne, in which the suggested corrigenda lists of six scholars were collated and then circulated among eight scholars for opinions and observations. The publication of the results of these discussions,[7] plus the lengthy discussions that preceded and followed it, have established a consensus view about many items which provided guidance. Second, in their own work the two editors approach Whitehead's thought from different perspectives and focus their work around different sorts of interests. Third, we used the principle that no changes would be introduced into the text unless they were endorsed by *both* editors.

We note, finally, that there can be no purely mechanical guidelines to guarantee objectivity and prevent distortion. Ultimately, editors must rely upon their own judgment, their knowledge of their texts, and their common sense. Recognizing this, we accept full responsibility for the decisions we have made.

Besides the issues discussed above, there were other editorial decisions to be made. There were substantial differences of format between the two original editions. Cambridge had a detailed Table of Contents at the beginning of the book, whereas Macmillan had only a brief listing of major divisions at the beginning with the detailed materials spread throughout the book as "Abstracts" prior to each of the five major Parts of the volume. Primarily because it is a nuisance to locate the various sections of this analytic Table of Contents in Macmillan, we have followed Cambridge in this matter. We have also followed the Cambridge edition in setting off some quotations and have let it guide us in regard to the question as to which quotations to set off (the Macmillan edition did not even set off page-length items).

Since most of the secondary literature on *Process and Reality* gives page references to the Macmillan edition, we considered very seriously the possibility of retaining its pagination in this new edition. For several technical

---

[7] Donald W. Sherburne, "Corrigenda for *Process and Reality*," in Kline, ed., *op. cit.*, pp. 200–207.

reasons this proved impractical. Consequently, we have inserted in this text, in brackets, the page numbers of the Macmillan edition, except in the Table of Contents.

In regard to certain minor differences between the texts, some of which reflect American vs. British conventions, we have followed Macmillan. Examples are putting periods and commas inside the quotation marks, numbering the footnotes consecutively within each chapter rather than on each page, and writing "Section" instead of using the symbol "§."

Except for those matters, which simply reflect different conventions, we have left a record of all of the changes which we have made. That is, in the Editors' Notes at the back of the book we have indicated all the divergencies (or, in a few cases, *types* of divergencies) from both original editions, no matter how trivial, thereby giving interested scholars access to both previous readings through this corrected edition. We have indicated in the text, by means of single and double obelisks († and ‡), the places where these divergencies occur. The more exact meaning of these symbols, plus that of the single and double asterisks, is explained in the introductory statement to the Editors' Notes.

The original editions had woefully inadequate Indexes. For this volume, Griffin has prepared a totally new, enormously expanded Index. Sincere thanks are due to Professor Marjorie Suchocki, who correlated the Index items to the pagination in this new edition, and to Professor Bernard M. Loomer, who many years ago prepared an expanded Index which was made available to other scholars.

One other edition of *Process and Reality* has appeared which has not yet been mentioned. In 1969, The Free Press published a paperback edition. It should in no way be confused with the present corrected edition, published by the same company. The 1969 edition did not incorporate the corrigenda which had been published by Sherburne; it added some new errors of its own; it introduced yet another pagination without indicating the previous standard pagination; and it did not contain a new Index. We wish to commend The Free Press for now publishing this corrected edition.

We acknowledge most gratefully the support of the Vanderbilt University Research Council, which provided Sherburne with travel funds and released time to work on this project. We are also deeply indebted to the Center for Process Studies, which has supported this project extensively, and in turn to both the Claremont Graduate School and the School of Theology at Claremont, which give support to the Center. Finally, we express our warm appreciation to Rebecca Parker Beyer, who was a great help in comparing texts and reading proofs.

David Ray Griffin
Center for Process Studies

Donald W. Sherburne
Vanderbilt University

PREFACE

[v]* THESE lectures are based upon a recurrence to that phase of philosophic thought which began with Descartes and ended with Hume. The philosophic scheme which they endeavour to explain is termed the 'Philosophy of Organism.' There is no doctrine put forward which cannot cite in its defence some explicit statement of one of this group of thinkers, or of one of the two founders of all Western thought, Plato and Aristotle. But the philosophy of organism is apt to emphasize just those elements in the writings of these masters which subsequent systematizers have put aside. The writer who most fully anticipated the main positions of the philosophy of organism is John Locke in his *Essay*, especially [1] in its later books.

The lectures are divided into five parts. In the first part, the method is explained, and the† scheme of ideas, in terms of which the cosmology is to be framed, is stated summarily.

In the second part,‡ an endeavour is made to exhibit this scheme as adequate for the interpretation of the ideas and problems which form the complex texture of civilized thought. Apart from such an investigation the summary statement of Part I is practically unintelligible. Thus Part II at once gives meaning to the verbal phrases of the scheme by their use in discussion, and shows the power of the scheme to put the various elements of our experience into a consistent relation to each other. In order to obtain a reasonably complete account of human experience considered in relation to the philosophical [vi] problems which naturally arise, the group of philosophers and scientists belonging to the seventeenth and eighteenth centuries has been considered, in particular Descartes, Newton, Locke, Hume, Kant. Any one of these writers is one-sided in his presentation of the groundwork of experience; but as a whole they give a general presentation which dominates the development of subsequent philosophy. I started the investigation with the expectation of being occupied with the exposition of the divergencies from every member of this group. But a careful examination of their exact statements disclosed that in the main the philosophy of organism is a recurrence to pre-Kantian modes of thought. These philosophers were perplexed by the inconsistent presuppositions underlying their inherited modes of expression. In so far as they, or their

---

[1] Cf. *An Essay Concerning Human Understanding*, Bk. IV, Ch. VI, Sect. 11.*

successors, have endeavoured to be rigidly systematic, the tendency has been to abandon just those elements in their thought upon which the philosophy of organism bases itself. An endeavour has been made to point out the exact points of agreement and of disagreement.

In the second part, the discussions of modern thought have been confined to the most general notions of physics and biology, with a careful avoidance of all detail. Also, it must be one of the motives of a complete cosmology to construct a system of ideas which brings† the aesthetic, moral, and religious interests into relation with those concepts of the world which have their origin in natural science.

In the third and fourth parts, the cosmological scheme is developed in terms of its own categoreal notions, and without much regard to other systems of thought. For example, in Part II there is a chapter on the 'Extensive Continuum,' which is largely concerned with the notions of Descartes and Newton, compared with the way in which the organic philosophy must interpret this feature of the world. But in Part IV, this question is treated from the point of view of developing the detailed method [vii] in which the philosophy of organism establishes the theory of this problem. It must be thoroughly understood that the theme of these lectures is not a detached consideration of various traditional philosophical problems which acquire urgency in certain traditional systems of thought. The lectures are intended to state a condensed scheme of cosmological ideas, to develop their meaning by confrontation with the various topics of experience, and finally to elaborate an adequate cosmology in terms of which all particular topics find their† interconnections. Thus the unity of treatment is to be looked for in the gradual development of the scheme, in meaning and in relevance, and not in the successive treatment of particular topics. For example, the doctrines of time, of space, of perception, and of causality are recurred to again and again, as the cosmology develops. In each recurrence, these topics throw some new light on the scheme, or receive some new elucidation. At the end, in so far as the enterprise has been successful, there should be no problem of space-time, or of epistemology, or of causality, left over for discussion. The scheme should have developed all those generic notions adequate for the expression of any possible interconnection of things.

Among the contemporary schools of thought, my obligations to the English and American Realists are obvious. In this connection, I should like especially to mention Professor T. P. Nunn, of the University of London. His anticipations, in the *Proceedings of the Aristotelian Society*, of some of the doctrines of recent Realism, do not appear to be sufficiently well known.

I am also greatly indebted to Bergson, William James, and John Dewey. One of my preoccupations has been to rescue their type of thought from the charge of anti-intellectualism, which rightly or wrongly has been associated with it. Finally, though throughout the main body of the work I am in sharp disagreement with Bradley, the final outcome is after all not so greatly different. I am particularly indebted to his chapter on the nature [viii] of experience, which appears in his *Essays on Truth and Reality*. His insistence on 'feeling' is very consonant with my own conclusions. This whole metaphysical position is an implicit repudiation of the doctrine of 'vacuous actuality.'

The fifth part is concerned with the final interpretation of the ultimate way in which the cosmological problem is to be conceived. It answers the question, What does it all come to? In this part, the approximation to Bradley is evident. Indeed, if this cosmology be deemed successful, it becomes natural at this point to ask whether the type of thought involved be not a transformation of some main doctrines of Absolute Idealism onto a realistic basis.

These lectures will be best understood by noting the following list of prevalent habits of thought, which are repudiated, in so far as concerns their influence on philosophy:

(i) The distrust of speculative philosophy.

(ii) The trust in language as an adequate expression of propositions.

(iii) The mode of philosophical thought which implies, and is implied by, the faculty-psychology.

(iv) The subject-predicate form of expression.

(v) The sensationalist doctrine of perception.

(vi) The doctrine of vacuous actuality.

(vii) The Kantian doctrine of the objective world as a theoretical construct from purely subjective experience.

(viii) Arbitrary deductions in *ex absurdo* arguments.

(ix) Belief that logical inconsistencies can indicate anything else than some antecedent errors.

By reason of its ready acceptance of some, or all, of these nine myths and fallacious procedures, much nineteenth-century philosophy excludes itself from relevance to the ordinary stubborn facts of daily life.

The positive doctrine of these lectures is concerned with the becoming, the being, and the relatedness of 'actual entities.' An 'actual entity' is a *res vera* in the [ix] Cartesian sense of that term;[2] it is a Cartesian 'substance,' and not an Aristotelian 'primary substance.' But Descartes retained in his metaphysical doctrine the Aristotelian dominance of the category of 'quality' over that of 'relatedness.' In these lectures 'relatedness' is dominant over 'quality.' All relatedness has its foundation in the relatedness of actualities; and such relatedness is wholly concerned with the appropriation of the dead by the living—that is to say, with 'objective immortality' whereby what is divested of its own living immediacy becomes

---

[2] I derive my comprehension of this element in Descartes' thought from Professor Gilson of the Sorbonne. I believe that he is the first to insist on its importance. He is, of course, not responsible for the use made of the notion in these lectures.

a real component in other living immediacies of becoming. This is the doctrine that the creative advance of the world is the becoming, the perishing, and the objective immortalities of those things which jointly constitute *stubborn fact*.

The history of philosophy discloses two cosmologies which at different periods have dominated European thought, Plato's *Timaeus*,[3] and the cosmology of the seventeenth century, whose chief authors were Galileo, Descartes, Newton, Locke. In attempting an enterprise of the same kind, it is wise to follow the clue that perhaps the true solution consists in a fusion of the two previous schemes, with modifications demanded by self-consistency and the advance of knowledge. The cosmology explained in these lectures has been framed in accordance with this reliance on the positive value of the philosophical tradition. One test of success is adequacy in the comprehension of the variety of experience within the limits of one scheme of ideas. The endeavour to satisfy this condition is illustrated by comparing Chapters III, VII, and X of Part II, respectively entitled 'The Order of Nature,' 'The Subjectivist Principle,' and 'Process,' with Chapter [x] V of Part III, entitled 'The Higher Phases of Experience,' and with Chapter V of Part IV, entitled 'Measurement,' and with Chapter II of Part V, entitled 'God and the† World.' These chapters should be recognizable as the legitimate outcome of the one scheme of ideas stated in the second chapter of Part I.

In these lectures I have endeavoured to compress the material derived from years of meditation. In putting out these results, four strong impressions dominate my mind: First, that the movement of historical, and philosophical, criticism of detached questions, which on the whole has dominated the last two centuries, has done its work, and requires to be supplemented by a more sustained effort of constructive thought. Secondly, that the true method of philosophical construction is to frame a scheme of ideas, the best that one can, and unflinchingly to explore the interpretation of experience in terms of that scheme. Thirdly, that all constructive thought, on the various special topics of scientific interest, is dominated by some such scheme, unacknowledged, but no less influential in guiding the imagination. The importance of philosophy lies in its sustained effort to make such schemes explicit, and thereby capable of criticism and improvement.

There remains the final reflection, how shallow, puny, and imperfect are efforts to sound the depths in the nature of things. In philosophical discussion, the merest hint of dogmatic certainty as to finality of statement is an exhibition of folly.

In the expansion of these lectures to the dimensions of the present book,

---

[3] I regret that Professor A. E. Taylor's *Commentary on Plato's Timaeus* was only published after this work was prepared for the press. Thus, with the exception of one small reference, no use could be made of it. I am very greatly indebted to Professor Taylor's other writings.

I have been greatly indebted to the critical difficulties suggested by the members of my Harvard classes. Also this work would never have been written without the constant encouragement and counsel which I owe to my wife.

A. N. W.

Harvard University
January, 1929

CONTENTS

PART I
THE SPECULATIVE SCHEME

PART II

DISCUSSIONS AND APPLICATIONS

SECTION

IV. Higher Phases of Microscopic Concrescence.

V. Summary.

PART III
THE THEORY OF PREHENSIONS

I. Genetic and Morphological Analysis; Genetic Consideration is Analysis of the Concrescence, the Actual Entity *Formaliter*; Morphological Analysis is Analysis of the Actual Entity as Concrete, Spatialized, *Objectivé*.†

II. Finite Truth, Division into Prehensions; Succession of Phases, Integral Prehensions in Formation; Five Factors: Subject, Initial Data, Elimination, Objective Datum, Subjective Form; Feeling is Determinate.

III. Feeling Cannot be Abstracted from Its Subject; Subject, Aim at the Feeler, Final Cause, *Causa Sui*.

IV. Categories of Subjective Unity, of Objective Identity, of Objective Diversity.

V. Category of Subjective Unity; The One Subject is the Final End Conditioning Each Feeling, Episode in Self-Production; Pre-established Harmony, Self-Consistency of a Proposition, Subjective Aim; Category of Objective Identity, One Thing has one Rôle, No Duplicity, One Ground of Incompatibility; Category of Objective Diversity, No Diverse Elements with Identity of Function, Another Ground of Incompatibility.

VI. World as a Transmitting Medium; Explanation; Negative Prehensions, with Subjective Forms.

VII. Application of the Categories.

VIII. Application (*continued*).†

IX. Nexūs.

X. Subjective Forms; Classification of Feelings According to Data; Simple Physical Feelings, Conceptual Feelings, Transmuted Feelings; Subjective Forms not Determined by Data, Conditioned by Them.

XI. Subjective Form, Qualitative Pattern, Quantitative Pattern; Intensity; Audition of Sound.

XII. Prehensions not Atomic, Mutual Sensitivity; Indefinite Number of Prehensions; Prehensions as Components in the Satisfaction and Their Genetic Growth; Justification of the

SECTION

III. Application of First Categoreal Obligation; Supplementary Phase Arising from Conceptual Origination; Application of Fourth and Fifth Categoreal Obligations; Conceptual Reversion; Ground of Identity, Aim at Contrast.

IV. Transmutation; Feeling a Nexus as One, Transmuted Physical Feeling; Rôle of Impartial Conceptual Feeling in Transmutation, Category of Transmutation, Further Explanations; Conceptual Feelings Modifying Physical Feelings; Negative Prehensions Important.

V. Subjective Harmony, the Seventh Categoreal Obligation.

I. Consciousness, Propositional Feelings, Not Necessarily Conscious; Propositional Feeling is Product of Integration of Physical Feeling with a Conceptual Feeling; Eternal Objects Tell no Tales of Actual Occasions, Propositions are Tales That *Might be†* *Told* of Logical Subjects; Proposition, True or False, Tells no Tales about Itself, Awaits Reasons; Conceptual Feeling Provides Predicative Pattern, Physical Feeling Provides Logical Subjects, Integration; Indication of Logical Subjects, Element of Givenness Required for Truth and Falsehood.

II. Proposition not Necessarily Judged, Propositional Feelings not Necessarily Conscious; New Propositions Arise; Possible Percipient Subjects within the 'Scope of a Proposition.'

III. Origination of Propositional Feeling, Four (or Five) Stages, Indicative Feeling, Physical Recognition, Predicative Pattern (Predicate), Predicative Feeling; Propositional Feeling Integral of Indicative and Predicative Feelings.

IV. Subjective Forms of Propositional Feelings, Dependent on Phases of Origination; Case of Identity of Indicative Feeling with the Physical Recognition, Perceptive Feelings;† Case of Diversity, Imaginative Feelings; Distinction not Necessarily Sharp-Cut; The Species of Perceptive Feelings: Authentic, Direct Authentic, Indirect Authentic, Unauthentic; Tied Imagination.

V. Imaginative Feelings, Indicative Feeling and Physical Recognition Diverse, Free Imagination; Subjective Form Depends on Origination, Valuation rather than Consciousness; Lure to Creative Emergence; Criticism of Physical Feelings, Truth, Critical Conditions.

VI. Language, Its Function;† Origination of the Necessary Train of Feelings.

PART IV
THE THEORY OF EXTENSION

PART V
FINAL INTERPRETATION

SECTION

PART I
THE SPECULATIVE SCHEME

CHAPTER I

SPECULATIVE PHILOSOPHY

SECTION I

[4] THIS course of lectures is designed as an essay in Speculative Philosophy. Its first task must be to define 'speculative philosophy,' and to defend it as a method productive of important knowledge.

Speculative Philosophy is the endeavour to frame a coherent, logical, necessary system of general ideas in terms of which every element of our experience can be interpreted. By this notion of 'interpretation' I mean that everything of which we are conscious, as enjoyed, perceived, willed, or thought, shall have the character of a particular instance of the general scheme. Thus the philosophical scheme should be coherent, logical, and, in respect to its interpretation, applicable and adequate. Here 'applicable' means that some items of experience are thus interpretable, and 'adequate' means that there are no items incapable of such interpretation.

[5] 'Coherence,' as here employed, means that the fundamental ideas, in terms of which the scheme is developed, presuppose each other so that in isolation they are meaningless. This requirement does not mean that they are definable in terms of each other; it means that what is indefinable in one such notion cannot be abstracted from its relevance to the other notions. It is the ideal of speculative philosophy that its fundamental notions shall not seem capable of abstraction from each other. In other words, it is presupposed that no entity can be conceived in complete abstraction from the system of the universe, and that it is the business of speculative philosophy to exhibit this truth. This character is its coherence.

The term 'logical' has its ordinary meaning, including 'logical' consistency, or lack of contradiction, the definition of constructs in logical terms, the exemplification of general logical notions in specific instances, and the principles of inference. It will be observed that logical notions must themselves find their places in the scheme of philosophic notions.

It will also be noticed that this ideal of speculative philosophy has its rational side and its empirical side. The rational side is expressed by the terms 'coherent' and 'logical.' The empirical side is expressed by the terms 'applicable' and 'adequate.' But the two sides are bound together by clearing away an ambiguity which remains in the previous explanation of the term 'adequate.' The adequacy of the scheme over every item does not mean adequacy over such items as happen to have been considered. It

3

means that the texture of observed experience, as illustrating the philosophic scheme, is such that all related experience must exhibit the same texture. Thus the philosophic scheme should be 'necessary,' in the sense of bearing in itself its own warrant of universality throughout all experience, provided that we confine ourselves to that which communicates with immediate matter of fact. But what does not so communicate is [6] unknowable, and the unknowable is unknown; [1] and so this universality defined by 'communication' can suffice.

pantheism

This doctrine of necessity in universality means that there is an essence to the universe which forbids relationships beyond itself, as a violation of its rationality. Speculative philosophy seeks that essence.

SECTION II

Philosophers can never hope finally to formulate these metaphysical first principles. Weakness of insight and deficiencies of language stand in the way inexorably. Words and phrases must be stretched towards a generality foreign to their ordinary usage; and however such elements of language be stabilized as technicalities, they remain metaphors mutely appealing for an imaginative leap.

There is no first principle which is in itself unknowable, not to be captured by a flash of insight. But, putting aside the difficulties of language, deficiency in imaginative penetration forbids progress in any form other than that of an asymptotic approach to a scheme of principles, only definable in terms of the ideal which they should satisfy.

The difficulty has its seat in the empirical side of philosophy. Our datum is the actual world, including ourselves; and this actual world spreads itself for observation in the guise of the topic of our immediate experience. The elucidation of immediate experience is the sole justification for any thought; and the starting-point‡ for thought is the analytic observation of components of this experience. But we are not conscious of any clear-cut complete analysis of immediate experience, in terms of the various details which comprise its definiteness. We habitually observe by the method of difference. Sometimes we see an elephant, and sometimes we do not. The result is that an elephant, when present, is noticed. [7] Facility of observation depends on the fact that the object observed is important when present, and sometimes is absent.

The metaphysical first principles can never fail of exemplification. We can never catch the actual world taking a holiday from their sway. Thus, for the discovery of metaphysics, the method of pinning down thought to the strict systematization of detailed discrimination, already effected by antecedent observation, breaks down. This collapse of the method of rigid empiricism is not confined to metaphysics. It occurs whenever we seek the

---

[1] This doctrine is a paradox. Indulging in a species of false modesty, 'cautious' philosophers undertake its definition.

larger generalities. In natural science this rigid method is the Baconian method of induction, a method which, if consistently pursued, would have left science where it found it. What Bacon omitted was the play of a free imagination, controlled by the requirements of coherence and logic. The true method of discovery is like the flight of an aeroplane. It starts from the ground of particular observation; it makes a flight in the thin air of imaginative generalization; and it again lands for renewed observation rendered acute by rational interpretation. The reason for the success of this method of imaginative rationalization is that, when the method of difference fails, factors which are constantly present may yet be observed under the influence of imaginative thought. Such thought supplies the differences which the direct observation lacks. It can even play with inconsistency; and can thus throw light on the consistent, and persistent, elements in experience by comparison with what in imagination is inconsistent with them. The negative judgment is the peak of mentality. But the conditions for the success of imaginative construction must be rigidly adhered to. In the first place, this construction must have its origin in the generalization of particular factors discerned in particular topics of human interest; for example, in physics, or in physiology, or in psychology, or in aesthetics, or in ethical beliefs, or in sociology, or in languages conceived as storehouses of human experience. In [8] this way the prime requisite, that anyhow there shall be some important application, is secured. The success of the imaginative experiment is always to be tested by the applicability of its results beyond the restricted locus from which it originated. In default of such extended application, a generalization started from physics, for example, remains merely an alternative expression of notions applicable to physics. The partially successful philosophic generalization will, if derived from physics, find applications in fields of experience beyond physics. It will enlighten observation in those remote fields, so that general principles can be discerned as in process of illustration, which in the absence of the imaginative generalization are obscured by their persistent exemplification.

Thus the first requisite is to proceed by the method of generalization so that certainly there is some application; and the test of some success is application beyond the immediate origin. In other words, some synoptic vision has been gained.

In this description of philosophic method, the term 'philosophic generalization' has meant 'the utilization of specific notions, applying to a restricted group of facts, for the divination of the generic notions which apply to all facts.'

In its use of this method natural science has shown a curious mixture of rationalism and irrationalism. Its prevalent tone of thought has been ardently rationalistic within its own borders, and dogmatically irrational beyond those borders. In practice such an attitude tends to become a dogmatic denial that there are any factors in the world not fully expressible in terms of its own primary notions devoid of further generalization. Such a denial is the self-denial of thought.

The second condition for the success of imaginative construction is unflinching pursuit of the two rationalistic ideals, coherence and logical perfection.

Logical perfection does not here require any detailed [9] explanation. An example of its importance is afforded by the rôle of mathematics in the restricted field of natural science. The history of mathematics exhibits the generalization of special notions observed in particular instances. In any branches of mathematics, the notions presuppose each other. It is a remarkable characteristic of the history of thought that branches of mathematics,† developed under the pure imaginative impulse, thus controlled, finally receive their important application. Time may be wanted. Conic sections had to wait for eighteen hundred years. In more recent years, the theory of probability, the theory of tensors, the theory of matrices are cases in point.

The requirement of coherence is the great preservative of rationalistic sanity. But the validity of its criticism is not always admitted. If we consider philosophical controversies, we shall find that disputants tend to require coherence from their adversaries, and to grant dispensations to themselves. It has been remarked that a system of philosophy is never refuted; it is only abandoned. The reason is that logical contradictions, except as temporary slips of the mind—plentiful, though temporary—are the most gratuitous of errors; and usually they are trivial. Thus, after criticism, systems do not exhibit mere illogicalities. They suffer from inadequacy and incoherence. Failure to include some obvious elements of experience in the scope of the system is met by boldly denying the facts. Also while a philosophical system retains any charm of novelty, it enjoys a plenary indulgence for its failures in coherence. But after a system has acquired orthodoxy, and is taught with authority, it receives a sharper criticism. Its denials and its incoherences are found intolerable, and a reaction sets in.

Incoherence is the arbitrary disconnection of first principles. In modern philosophy Descartes' two kinds of substance, corporeal and mental, illustrate incoherence. There is, in Descartes' philosophy, no reason why there should not be a one-substance world, only corporeal, or [10] a one-substance world, only mental. According to Descartes, a substantial individual 'requires nothing but itself in order to exist.' Thus this system makes a virtue of its incoherence. But,† on the other hand, the facts seem connected, while Descartes' system does not; for example, in the treatment of the body-mind problem. The Cartesian system obviously says something that is true. But its notions are too abstract to penetrate into the nature of things.

†

The attraction of Spinoza's philosophy lies in its modification of Descartes' position into greater coherence. He starts with one substance, *causa sui,* and considers its essential attributes and its individualized modes, i.e., the *'affectiones substantiae.'* The gap in the system is the arbitrary introduction of the 'modes.' And yet, a multiplicity of modes is a fixed requisite, if the scheme is to retain any direct relevance to the many occasions in the experienced world.

The philosophy of organism is closely allied to Spinoza's scheme of thought. But it differs by the abandonment of the subject-predicate forms of thought, so far as concerns the presupposition that this form is a direct embodiment of the most ultimate characterization of fact. The result is that the 'substance-quality' concept is avoided; and that morphological description is replaced by description of dynamic process. Also Spinoza's 'modes' now become the sheer actualities; so that, though analysis of them increases our understanding, it does not lead us to the discovery of any higher grade of reality. The coherence, which the system seeks to preserve, is the discovery that the process, or concrescence, of any one actual entity involves the other actual entities among its components. In this way the obvious solidarity of the world receives its explanation.

In all philosophic theory there is an ultimate which is actual in virtue of its accidents. It is only then capable of characterization through its accidental embodiments, and apart from these accidents is devoid of [11] actuality. In the philosophy of organism this ultimate is termed 'creativity'; and God is its primordial, non-temporal accident.* In monistic philosophies, Spinoza's or absolute idealism, this ultimate is God, who is also equivalently termed 'The Absolute.' In such monistic schemes, the ultimate is illegitimately allowed a final, 'eminent' reality, beyond that ascribed to any of its accidents. In this general position the philosophy of organism seems to approximate more to some strains of Indian, or Chinese, thought, than to western Asiatic, or European, thought. One side makes process ultimate; the other side makes fact ultimate.

SECTION III†

In its turn every philosophy will suffer a deposition. But the bundle of philosophic systems expresses a variety of general truths about the universe, awaiting coordination and assignment of their various spheres of validity. Such progress in coordination is provided by the advance of philosophy; and in this sense philosophy has advanced from Plato onwards. According to this account of the achievement of rationalism, the chief error in philosophy is overstatement. The aim at generalization is sound, but the estimate of success is exaggerated. There are two main forms of such overstatement. One form is what I have termed,† elsewhere,[2] the 'fallacy of misplaced concreteness.' This fallacy consists in neglecting the degree of abstraction involved when an actual entity is considered merely

[2] Cf. *Science and the Modern World,* Ch. III.

so far as it exemplifies certain categories of thought. There are aspects of actualities which are simply ignored so long as we restrict thought to these categories. Thus the success of a philosophy is to be measured by its comparative avoidance of this fallacy, when thought is restricted within its categories.

The other form of overstatement consists in a false estimate of logical procedure in respect to certainty, and in respect to premises. Philosophy has been haunted by the unfortunate notion that its method is dogmatically to indicate premises which are severally clear, distinct, and [12] certain; and to erect upon those premises a deductive system of thought.

But the accurate expression of the final generalities is the goal of discussion and not its origin. Philosophy has been misled by the example of mathematics; and even in mathematics the statement of the ultimate logical principles is beset with difficulties, as yet insuperable.[3] The verification of a rationalistic scheme is to be sought in its general success, and not in the peculiar certainty, or initial clarity, of its first principles. In this connection the misuse of the *ex absurdo* argument has to be noted; much philosophical reasoning is vitiated by it. The only logical conclusion to be drawn, when a contradiction issues from a train of reasoning, is that at least one of the premises involved in the inference is false. It is rashly assumed without further question that the peccant premise can at once be located. In mathematics this assumption is often justified, and philosophers have been thereby misled. But in the absence of a well-defined categoreal scheme of entities, issuing in a satisfactory metaphysical system, every premise in a philosophical argument is under suspicion.

Philosophy will not regain its proper status until the gradual elaboration of categoreal schemes, definitely stated at each stage of progress, is recognized as its proper objective. There may be rival schemes, inconsistent among themselves; each with its own merits and its own failures. It will then be the purpose of research to conciliate the differences. Metaphysical categories are not dogmatic statements of the obvious; they are tentative formulations of the ultimate generalities.

If we consider any scheme of philosophic categories as one complex assertion, and apply to it the logician's alternative, true or false, the answer must be that the scheme is false. The same answer must be given to a like ques- [13] tion respecting the existing formulated principles of any science.

The scheme is true with unformulated qualifications, exceptions, limitations, and new interpretations in terms of more general notions. We do not yet know how to recast the scheme into a logical truth. But the scheme is a matrix from which true propositions applicable to particular circumstances can be derived. We can at present only trust our trained instincts

---

[3] Cf. *Principia Mathematica*, by Bertrand Russell and A. N. Whitehead, Vol. I, Introduction and Introduction to the Second Edition. These introductory discussions are practically due to Russell, and in the second edition wholly so.

as to the discrimination of the circumstances in respect to which the scheme is valid.

The use of such a matrix is to argue from it boldly and with rigid logic. The scheme should therefore be stated with the utmost precision and definiteness, to allow of such argumentation. The conclusion of the argument should then be confronted with circumstances to which it should apply.

The primary advantage thus gained is that experience is not interrogated with the benumbing repression of common sense. The observation acquires an enhanced penetration by reason of the expectation evoked by the conclusion of the argument. The outcome from this procedure takes one of three forms: (i) the conclusion may agree with the observed facts; (ii) the conclusion may exhibit general agreement, with disagreement in detail; (iii) the conclusion may be in complete disagreement with† the facts.

In the first case, the facts are known with more adequacy and the applicability of the system to the world has been elucidated. In the second case, criticisms of the observation of the facts and of the details of the scheme are both required. The history of thought shows that false interpretations of observed facts enter into the records of their observation. Thus both theory, and received notions as to fact, are in doubt. In the third case, a fundamental reorganization of theory is required either by way of limiting it to some special province, or by way of entire abandonment of its main categories of thought.

[14] After the initial basis of a rational life, with a civilized language, has been laid, all productive thought has proceeded either by the poetic insight of artists, or by the imaginative elaboration of schemes of thought capable of utilization as logical premises. In some measure or other, progress is always a transcendence of what is obvious.

Rationalism never shakes off its status of an experimental adventure. The combined influences of mathematics and religion, which have so greatly contributed to the rise of philosophy, have also had the unfortunate effect of yoking it with static dogmatism. Rationalism is an adventure in the clarification of thought, progressive and never final. But it is an adventure in which even partial success has importance.

SECTION IV

The field of a special science is confined to one genus of facts, in the sense that no statements are made respecting facts which lie outside that genus. The very circumstance that a science has naturally arisen concerning a set of facts secures that facts of that type have definite relations among themselves which are very obvious to all mankind. The common obviousness of things arises when their explicit apprehension carries immediate importance for purposes of survival, or of enjoyment—that is to say, for purposes of 'being' and of 'well-being.' Elements in human experience, singled out in this way, are those elements concerning which language is copious and, within its limits, precise. The special sciences, therefore, deal with topics which lie open to easy inspection and are readily expressed by words.

The study of philosophy is a voyage towards the larger generalities. For this reason in the infancy of science, when the main stress lay in the discovery of the most general ideas usefully applicable to the subject-matter in question, philosophy was not sharply distinguished from science. To this day, a new science with any substantial novelty in its notions is considered to be in some way [15] peculiarly philosophical. In their later stages, apart from occasional disturbances, most sciences accept without question the general notions in terms of which they develop. The main stress is laid on the adjustment and the direct verification of more special statements. In such periods scientists repudiate philosophy; Newton, justly satisfied with his physical principles, disclaimed metaphysics.

The fate of Newtonian physics warns us that there is a development in scientific first principles, and that their original forms can only be saved by interpretations of meaning and limitations of their field of application—interpretations and limitations unsuspected during the first period of successful employment. One chapter in the history of culture is concerned with the growth of generalities. In such a chapter it is seen that the older generalities, like the older hills, are worn down and diminished in height, surpassed by younger rivals.

Thus one aim of philosophy is to challenge the half-truths constituting the scientific first principles. The systematization of knowledge cannot be conducted in watertight compartments. All general truths condition each other; and the limits of their application cannot be adequately defined apart from their correlation by yet wider generalities. The criticism of principles must chiefly take the form of determining the proper meanings to be assigned to the fundamental notions of the various sciences, when these notions are considered in respect to their status relatively to each other. The determination of this status requires a generality transcending any special subject-matter.

If we may trust the Pythagorean tradition, the rise of European philosophy was largely promoted by the development of mathematics into a science of abstract generality. But in its subsequent development the method of philosophy has also been vitiated by the example of mathematics. The primary method of mathematics is deduction; the primary method of philosophy is descrip- [16] tive generalization. Under the influence of mathematics, deduction has been foisted onto philosophy as its standard method, instead of taking its true place as an essential auxiliary mode of verification whereby to test the scope of generalities. This misapprehension of philosophic method has veiled the very considerable success of philosophy in providing generic notions which add lucidity to our apprehension of the facts of experience. The depositions of Plato, Aristotle,

Thomas Aquinas, Descartes, Spinoza, Leibniz,† Locke, Berkeley, Hume, Kant, Hegel, merely mean that ideas which these men introduced into the philosophic tradition must be construed with limitations, adaptations, and inversions, either unknown to them, or even explicitly repudiated by them. A new idea introduces a new alternative; and we are not less indebted to a thinker when we adopt the alternative which he discarded. Philosophy never reverts to its old position after the shock of a great philosopher.

SECTION V

Every science must devise its own instruments. The tool required for philosophy is language. Thus philosophy redesigns language in the same way that, in a physical science, pre-existing appliances are redesigned. It is exactly at this point that the appeal to facts is a difficult operation. This appeal is not solely to the expression of the facts in current verbal statements. The adequacy of such sentences is the main question at issue. It is true that the general agreement of mankind as to experienced facts is best expressed in language. But the language of literature breaks down precisely at the task of expressing in explicit form the larger generalities— the very generalities which metaphysics seeks to express.

The point is that every proposition refers to a universe exhibiting some general systematic metaphysical character. Apart from this background, the separate entities which go to form the proposition, and the proposition as a whole, are without determinate character. Nothing [17] has been defined, because every definite entity requires a systematic universe to supply its requisite status. Thus every proposition proposing a fact* must, in its complete analysis, propose the general character of the universe required for that fact. There are no self-sustained facts, floating in nonentity. This doctrine, of the impossibility of tearing a proposition from its systematic context in the actual world, is a direct consequence of the fourth and the twentieth of the fundamental categoreal explanations which we shall be engaged in expanding and illustrating. A proposition can embody partial truth because it only demands a certain type of systematic environment, which is presupposed in its meaning. It does not refer to the universe in all its detail.

One practical aim of metaphysics is the accurate analysis of propositions; not merely of metaphysical propositions, but of quite ordinary propositions such as 'There is beef for dinner today,' and 'Socrates is mortal.' The one genus of facts which constitutes the field of some special science requires some common metaphysical presupposition respecting the universe. It is merely credulous to accept verbal phrases as adequate statements of propositions. The distinction between verbal phrases and complete propositions is one of the reasons why the logicians' rigid alternative, 'true or false,' is so largely irrelevant for the pursuit of knowledge.

The excessive trust in linguistic phrases has been the well-known reason vitiating so much of the philosophy and physics among the Greeks and among the mediaeval thinkers who continued the Greek traditions. For example John Stuart Mill writes:

> They [the Greeks] ‡ had great difficulty in distinguishing between things which their language confounded, or in putting mentally together things which it distinguished,‡ and could hardly combine the objects in nature into any classes but those which were made for them by the popular phrases of their own country; or at least could not help fancying those classes to be natural, and all others arbitrary and artificial. Ac- [18] cordingly, scientific investigation among the Greek schools of speculation and their followers in the Middle Ages, was little more than a mere sifting and analysing of the notions attached to common language. They thought that by determining the meaning of words they could become acquainted with facts.[4]

Mill then proceeds to quote from Whewell [5] a paragraph illustrating the same weakness of Greek thought.

But neither Mill, nor Whewell, tracks this difficulty about language down to its sources. They both presuppose that language does enunciate well-defined propositions. This is quite untrue. Language is thoroughly indeterminate, by reason of the fact that every occurrence presupposes some systematic type of environment.

For example, the word 'Socrates,' referring to the philosopher, in one sentence may stand for an entity presupposing a more closely defined background than the word 'Socrates,' with the same reference, in another sentence. The word 'mortal' affords an analogous possibility. A precise language must await a completed metaphysical knowledge.

The technical language of philosophy represents attempts of various schools of thought to obtain explicit expression of general ideas presupposed by the facts of experience. It follows that any novelty in metaphysical doctrines exhibits some measure of disagreement with statements of the facts to be found in current philosophical literature. The extent of disagreement measures the extent of metaphysical divergence. It is, therefore, no valid criticism on one metaphysical school to point out that its doctrines do not follow from the verbal expression of the facts accepted by another school. The whole contention is that the doctrines in question supply a closer approach to fully expressed propositions.

The truth itself is nothing else than how the composite natures of the organic actualities of the world obtain ade- [19] quate representation in the divine nature. Such representations compose the 'consequent nature' of God, which evolves in its relationship to the evolving world without dero-

---

[4] ‡*Logic*, Book V, Ch. III.
[5] Cf. Whewell's *History of the Inductive Sciences*.

gation to the eternal completion of its primordial conceptual nature. In this way the 'ontological principle' is maintained—since there can be no determinate truth, correlating impartially the partial experiences of many actual entities, apart from one actual entity to which it can be referred. The reaction of the temporal world on the nature of God is considered subsequently in Part V: it is there termed 'the consequent nature of God.'

Whatever is found in 'practice' must lie within the scope of the metaphysical description. When the description fails to include the 'practice,' the metaphysics is inadequate and requires revision. There can be no appeal to practice to supplement metaphysics, so long as we remain contented with our metaphysical doctrines. Metaphysics is nothing but the description of the generalities which apply to all the details of practice.

No metaphysical system can hope entirely to satisfy these pragmatic tests. At the best such a system will remain only an approximation to the general truths which are sought. In particular, there are no precisely stated axiomatic certainties from which to start. There is not even the language in which to frame them. The only possible procedure is to start from verbal expressions which, when taken by themselves with the current meaning of their words, are ill-defined and ambiguous. These are not premises to be immediately reasoned from apart from elucidation by further discussion; they are endeavours to state general principles which will be exemplified in the subsequent description of the facts of experience. This subsequent elaboration should elucidate the meanings to be assigned to the words and phrases employed. Such meanings are incapable of accurate apprehension apart from a correspondingly accurate apprehension of the metaphysical background which the [20] universe provides for them. But no language can be anything but elliptical, requiring a leap of the imagination to understand its meaning in its relevance to immediate experience. The position of metaphysics in the development of culture cannot be understood without remembering that no verbal statement is the adequate expression of a proposition.

An old established metaphysical system gains a false air of adequate precision from the fact that its words and phrases have passed into current literature. Thus propositions expressed in its language are more easily correlated to our flitting intuitions into metaphysical truth. When we trust these verbal statements and argue as though they adequately analysed meaning, we are led into difficulties which take the shape of negations of what in practice is presupposed. But when they are proposed as first principles they assume an unmerited air of sober obviousness. Their defect is that the true propositions which they do express lose their fundamental character when subjected to adequate expression. For example consider the type of propositions such as 'The grass is green,' and 'The whale is big.' This subject-predicate form of statement seems so simple, leading straight to a metaphysical first principle; and yet in these examples it conceals such complex, diverse meanings.

SECTION VI

It has been an objection to speculative philosophy that it is over-ambitious. Rationalism, it is admitted, is the method by which advance is made within the limits of particular sciences. It is, however, held that this limited success must not encourage attempts to frame ambitious schemes expressive of the general nature of things.

One alleged justification of this criticism is ill-success: European thought is represented as littered with metaphysical systems, abandoned and unreconciled.

Such an assertion tacitly fastens upon philosophy the old dogmatic test. The same criterion would fasten ill- [21] success upon science. We no more retain the physics of the seventeenth century than we do the Cartesian philosophy of that century. Yet within limits, both systems express important truths. Also we are beginning to understand the wider categories which define their limits of correct application. Of course, in that century, dogmatic views held sway; so that the validity both of the physical notions, and of the Cartesian notions, was misconceived. Mankind never quite knows what it is after. When we survey the history of thought, and likewise the history of practice, we find that one idea after another is tried out, its limitations defined, and its core of truth elicited. In application to the instinct for the intellectual adventures demanded by particular epochs, there is much truth in Augustine's rhetorical phrase, *Securus judicat orbis terrarum*. At the very least, men do what they can in the way of systematization, and in the event achieve something. The proper test is not that of finality, but of progress.

But the main objection, dating from the sixteenth century and receiving final expression from Francis Bacon, is the uselessness of philosophic speculation. The position taken by this objection is that we ought to describe detailed matter of fact, and elicit the laws with a generality strictly limited to the systematization of these described details. General interpretation, it is held, has no bearing upon this procedure; and thus any system of general interpretation, be it true or false, remains intrinsically barren. Unfortunately for this objection, there are no brute, self-contained matters of fact, capable of being understood apart from interpretation as an element in a system. Whenever we attempt to express the matter of immediate experience, we find that its understanding leads us beyond itself, to its contemporaries, to its past, to its future, and to the universals in terms of which its definiteness is exhibited. But such universals, by their very character of universality, embody the potentiality of other facts with variant types of definiteness. Thus [22] the understanding of the immediate brute fact requires its metaphysical interpretation as an item in a world with some systematic relation to it. When thought comes upon the scene, it finds the interpretations as matters of practice. Philosophy does not initiate interpretations. Its search for a rationalistic scheme is the search for more adequate criticism, and for more adequate justification, of the interpretations which we perforce employ. Our habitual experience is a complex of failure and success in the enterprise of interpretation. If we desire a record of uninterpreted experience, we must ask a stone to record its autobiography. Every scientific memoir in its record of the 'facts' is shot through and through with interpretation. The methodology of rational interpretation is the product of the fitful vagueness of consciousness. Elements which shine with immediate distinctness, in some circumstances, retire into penumbral shadow in other circumstances, and into black darkness on other occasions. And yet all occasions proclaim themselves as actualities within the flux of a solid world, demanding a unity of interpretation.

Philosophy is the self-correction by consciousness of its own initial excess of subjectivity. Each actual occasion contributes to the circumstances of its origin additional formative elements deepening its own peculiar individuality. Consciousness is only the last and greatest of such elements *naturalism* by which the selective character of the individual obscures the external totality from which it originates and which it embodies. An actual individual, of such higher grade, has truck with the totality of things by reason of its sheer actuality; but it has attained its individual depth of being by a selective emphasis limited to its own purposes. The task of philosophy is to recover the totality obscured by the selection. It replaces in rational experience what has been submerged in the higher sensitive experience and has been sunk yet deeper by the initial operations of consciousness itself. The selectiveness of individual experience is moral so far as it con-[23] forms to the balance of importance disclosed in the rational vision; and conversely the conversion of the intellectual insight into an emotional force corrects the sensitive experience in the direction of morality. The correction is in proportion to the rationality of the insight.

Morality of outlook is inseparably conjoined with generality of outlook. The antithesis between the general good and the individual interest can be abolished only when the individual is such that its interest is the general good, thus exemplifying the loss of the minor intensities in order to find them again with finer composition in a wider sweep of interest.

Philosophy frees itself from the taint of ineffectiveness by its close relations with religion and with science, natural and sociological. It attains its chief importance by fusing the two, namely, religion and science, into one rational scheme of thought. Religion should connect the rational generality of philosophy with the emotions and purposes springing out of existence in a particular society, in a particular epoch, and conditioned by particular antecedents. Religion is the translation of general ideas into particular thoughts, particular emotions, and particular purposes; it is directed to the end of stretching individual interest beyond its self-defeating particularity. Philosophy finds religion, and modifies it; and conversely religion is among the data of experience which philosophy must weave into its own scheme. Religion is an ultimate craving to infuse into the insistent particularity of emotion that non-temporal generality which primarily belongs to conceptual thought alone. In the higher organisms the differences of tempo between the mere emotions and the conceptual experiences produce a life-tedium, unless this supreme fusion has been effected. The two sides of the organism require a reconciliation in which emotional experiences illustrate a conceptual justification, and conceptual experiences find an emotional illustration.

[24] This demand for an intellectual justification of brute experience has also been the motive power in the advance of European science. In this sense scientific interest is only a variant form of religious interest. Any survey of the scientific devotion to 'truth,' as an ideal, will confirm this statement. There is, however, a grave divergence between science and religion in respect to the phases of individual experience with which they are concerned. Religion is centered upon the harmony of rational thought with the sensitive reaction to the percepta from which experience originates. Science is concerned with the harmony of rational thought with the percepta themselves. When science deals with emotions, the emotions in question are percepta and not immediate passions—other people's emotion and not our own; at least our own in recollection, and not in immediacy. Religion deals with the formation of the experiencing subject; whereas science deals with the objects, which are the data forming the primary phase in this experience. The subject originates from, and amid, given conditions; science conciliates thought with this primary matter of fact; and religion conciliates the thought involved in the process with the sensitive reaction involved in that same process. The process is nothing else than the experiencing subject itself. In this explanation it is presumed that an experiencing subject is one occasion of sensitive reaction to an actual world. Science finds religious experiences among its percepta; and religion finds scientific concepts among the conceptual experiences to be fused with particular sensitive reactions.

The conclusion of this discussion is, first, the assertion of the old doctrine that breadth of thought reacting with intensity of sensitive experience stands out as an ultimate claim of existence; secondly, the assertion that empirically the development of self-justifying thoughts has been achieved by the complex process of generalizing† from particular topics, of imaginatively schematizing the generalizations, and finally by renewed comparison [25] of the imagined scheme with the direct experience to which it should apply.

There is no justification for checking generalization at any particular stage. Each phase of generalization exhibits its own peculiar simplicities which stand out just at that stage, and at no other stage. There are simplicities connected with the motion of a bar of steel which are obscured if we refuse to abstract from the individual molecules; and there are certain simplicities concerning the behaviour of men which are obscured if we refuse to abstract from the individual peculiarities of particular specimens. In the same way, there are certain general truths, about the actual things in the common world of activity, which will be obscured when attention is confined to some particular detailed mode of considering them. These general truths, involved in the meaning of every particular notion respecting the actions of things, are the subject-matter‡ for speculative philosophy.

Philosophy destroys its usefulness when it indulges in brilliant feats of explaining away. It is then trespassing with the wrong equipment upon the field of particular sciences. Its ultimate appeal is to the general consciousness of what in practice we experience. Whatever thread of presupposition characterizes social expression throughout the various epochs of rational society† must find its place in philosophic theory. Speculative boldness must be balanced by complete humility before logic, and before fact. It is a disease of philosophy when it is neither bold nor humble, but merely a reflection of the temperamental presuppositions of exceptional personalities.

Analogously, we do not trust any recasting of scientific theory depending upon a single performance of an aberrant experiment, unrepeated. The ultimate test is always widespread, recurrent experience; and the more general the rationalistic scheme, the more important is this final appeal.

The useful function of philosophy is to promote the [26] most general systematization of civilized thought. There is a constant reaction between specialism and common sense. It is the part of the special sciences to modify common sense. Philosophy is the welding of imagination and common sense into a restraint upon specialists, and also into an enlargement of their imaginations. By providing the generic notions philosophy should make it easier to conceive the infinite variety of specific instances which rest unrealized in the womb of nature.

CHAPTER II

THE CATEGOREAL SCHEME ‡

SECTION I

[27] THIS chapter contains an anticipatory sketch of the primary notions which constitute the philosophy of organism. The whole of the subsequent discussion in these lectures has the purpose of rendering this summary intelligible, and of showing that it embodies generic notions inevitably presupposed in our reflective experience—presupposed, but rarely expressed in explicit distinction. Four notions may be singled out from this summary, by reason of the fact that they involve some divergence from antecedent philosophical thought. These notions are, that of an 'actual entity,' that of a 'prehension,' that of a 'nexus,' and that of the 'ontological principle.' Philosophical thought has made for itself difficulties by dealing exclusively in very abstract notions, such as those of mere awareness, mere private sensation, mere emotion, mere purpose, mere appearance, mere causation. These are the ghosts of the old 'faculties,' banished from psychology, but still haunting metaphysics. There can be no 'mere' togetherness of such abstractions. The result is that philosophical discussion is enmeshed in the fallacy of 'misplaced concreteness.' [1] In the three notions—actual entity, prehension, nexus—an endeavour has been made to base philosophical thought upon the most concrete elements in our experience.

'Actual entities'—also termed 'actual occasions'—are the final real things of which the world is made up. There is no going behind actual entities to find anything [28] more real. They differ among themselves: God is an actual entity, and so is the most trivial puff of existence in far-off empty space. But, though there are gradations of importance, and diversities of function, yet in the principles which actuality exemplifies all are on the same level. The final facts are, all alike, actual entities; and these actual entities are drops of experience, complex and interdependent.

In its recurrence to the notion of a plurality of actual entities the philosophy of organism is through and through Cartesian.† The 'ontological principle' broadens and extends a general principle laid down by John Locke in his *Essay* (Bk. II, Ch. XXIII, Sect. 7),† when he asserts that *"power"* is *"a great part of our complex ideas of substances."*† The notion

---

[1] Cf. my *Science and the Modern World*, Ch. III.

of 'substance' is transformed into that of 'actual entity'; and the notion of 'power' is transformed into the principle that the reasons for things are always to be found in the composite nature of definite actual entities— in the nature of God for reasons of the highest absoluteness, and in the nature of definite temporal actual entities for reasons which refer to a particular environment. The ontological principle can be summarized as: no actual entity, then no reason.

Each actual entity is analysable in an indefinite number of ways. In some modes of analysis the component elements are more abstract than in other modes of analysis. The analysis of an actual entity into 'prehensions' is that mode of analysis which exhibits the most concrete elements in the nature of actual entities. This mode of analysis will be termed the 'division' of the actual entity in question. Each actual entity is 'divisible' in an indefinite number of ways, and each way of 'division' yields its definite quota of prehensions. A prehension reproduces in itself the general characteristics of an actual entity: it is referent to an external world, and in this sense will be said to have a 'vector character'; it involves emotion, and purpose, and valuation, and causation. In fact, any characteristic of an actual entity is reproduced [29] in a prehension. It might have been a complete actuality; but, by reason of a certain incomplete partiality, a prehension is only a subordinate element in an actual entity. A reference to the complete actuality is required to give the reason why such a prehension is what it is in respect to its subjective form. This subjective form is determined by the subjective aim at further integration, so as to obtain the 'satisfaction' of the completed subject. In other words, final causation and atomism are interconnected philosophical principles.

With the purpose of obtaining a one-substance cosmology, 'prehensions' are a generalization from Descartes' mental 'cogitations,' and from Locke's 'ideas,' to express the most concrete mode of analysis applicable to every grade of individual actuality. Descartes and Locke maintained a two-substance ontology—Descartes explicitly, Locke by implication. Descartes, the mathematical physicist, emphasized his account of corporeal substance; and Locke, the physician and the sociologist, confined himself to an account of mental substance. The philosophy of organism, in its scheme for one type of actual entities, adopts the view that Locke's account of mental substance embodies, in a very special form, a more penetrating philosophic description than does Descartes' account of corporeal substance. Nevertheless, Descartes' account must find its place in the philosophic scheme. On the whole, this is the moral to be drawn from the *Monadology*‡ of Leibniz. His monads are best conceived as generalizations of contemporary notions of mentality. The contemporary notions of physical bodies only enter into his philosophy subordinately and derivatively. The philosophy of organism endeavours to hold the balance more evenly. But it does start with a generalization of Locke's account of mental operations.

Actual entities involve each other by reason of their prehensions of each other. There are thus real individual facts of the togetherness of actual entities, which are real, individual, and particular, in the same sense in [30] which actual entities and the prehensions are real, individual, and particular. Any such particular fact of togetherness among actual entities is called a 'nexus' (plural form is written 'nexūs'). The ultimate facts of immediate actual experience are actual entities, prehensions, and nexūs. All else is, for our experience, derivative abstraction.

The explanatory purpose of philosophy is often misunderstood. Its business is to explain the emergence of the more abstract things from the more concrete things. It is a complete mistake to ask how concrete particular fact can be built up out of universals. The answer is, 'In no way.' The true philosophic question [2] is, How can concrete fact exhibit entities abstract from itself and yet participated in by its own nature?

In other words, philosophy is explanatory of abstraction, and not of concreteness. It is by reason of their instinctive grasp of this ultimate truth that, in spite of much association with arbitrary fancifulness and atavistic mysticism, types of Platonic philosophy retain their abiding appeal; they seek the forms in the facts. Each fact is more than its forms, and each form 'participates' throughout the world of facts. The definiteness of fact is due to its forms; but the individual fact is a creature, and creativity is the ultimate behind all forms, inexplicable by forms, and conditioned by its creatures.

SECTION II

The Categories

    I. The Category of the Ultimate.
   II. Categories of Existence.
  III. Categories of Explanation.
  IV. Categoreal Obligations.

It is the purpose of the discussion in these lectures to make clear the meaning of these categories, their appli- [31] cability, and their adequacy. The course of the discussion will disclose how very far they are from satisfying this ideal.

Every entity should be a specific instance of one category of existence, every explanation should be a specific instance of categories of explanation, and every obligation should be a specific instance of categoreal obliga-

---

[2] In this connection I may refer to the second chapter of my book *The Principle of Relativity*, Cambridge University Press,† 1922.

tions. The Category‡ of the Ultimate expresses the general principle presupposed in the three more special categories.

The Category of the Ultimate

Δ   'Creativity,' 'many,' 'one' are the ultimate notions involved in the meaning of the synonymous terms 'thing,' 'being,' 'entity.' These three notions complete the Category of the Ultimate and are presupposed in all the more special categories.

The term 'one' does not stand for 'the integral number *one*,' which is a complex special notion. It stands for the general idea underlying alike the indefinite article '*a* or *an*,' and the definite article '*the*,' and the demonstratives '*this* or *that*,' and the relatives '*which* or *what* or *how*.' It stands for the singularity of an entity. The term 'many' presupposes the term 'one,' and the term 'one' presupposes the term 'many.' The term 'many' conveys the notion of 'disjunctive diversity'; this notion is an essential* element in the concept of 'being.' There are many 'beings' in disjunctive diversity.

'Creativity' is the universal of universals characterizing ultimate matter of fact. It is that ultimate principle by which the many, which are the* universe disjunctively, become the one actual occasion, which is the universe conjunctively. It lies in the nature of things that the many enter into complex unity.

'Creativity' is the principle of *novelty*. An actual occasion is a novel entity diverse from any entity in the 'many' which it unifies. Thus 'creativity' introduces novelty into the content of the many, which are the [32] universe disjunctively. The 'creative advance' is the application of this ultimate principle of creativity to each novel situation which it originates.

'Together' is a generic term covering the various special ways in which various sorts of entities are 'together' in any one actual occasion. Thus 'together' presupposes the notions 'creativity,' 'many,' 'one,' 'identity' and 'diversity.' The ultimate metaphysical principle is the advance from disjunction to conjunction, creating a novel entity other than the entities given in disjunction. The novel entity is at once the togetherness of the 'many' which it finds, and also it is one among the disjunctive 'many' which it leaves; it is a novel entity, disjunctively among the many entities which it synthesizes. The many become one, and are increased by one. In their natures, entities are disjunctively 'many' in process of passage into conjunctive unity. This Category of the Ultimate replaces Aristotle's category of 'primary substance.'

Thus the 'production of novel togetherness' is the ultimate notion embodied in the term 'concrescence.' These ultimate notions of 'production of novelty' and of 'concrete togetherness' are inexplicable either in terms of higher universals or in terms of the components participating in the concrescence. The analysis of the components abstracts from the concrescence. The sole appeal is to intuition.

The Categories of Existence

There are eight Categories of Existence:

(i) Actual Entities (also termed Actual Occasions), *or* Final Realities, *or* Rēs Verae.

(ii) Prehensions, *or* Concrete Facts of Relatedness.

(iii) Nexūs (plural of Nexus), *or* Public Matters of Fact.

(iv) Subjective Forms, *or* Private Matters of Fact.

(v) Eternal Objects, *or* Pure Potentials for the Specific Determination of Fact, *or* Forms of Definiteness.

(vi) Propositions, *or* Matters of Fact in Potential [33] Determination, *or* Impure Potentials for the Specific Determination of Matters of Fact, *or* Theories.

(vii) Multiplicities, *or* Pure Disjunctions of Diverse Entities.

(viii) Contrasts, *or* Modes of Synthesis of Entities in one Prehension, *or* Patterned Entities.‡

Among these eight categories of existence, actual entities and eternal objects stand out with a certain extreme finality. The other types of existence have a certain intermediate character. The eighth category includes an indefinite progression of categories, as we proceed from 'contrasts' to 'contrasts of contrasts,' and on indefinitely to higher grades of contrasts.

The Categories of Explanation

There are twenty-seven Categories of Explanation:

(i) That the actual world is a process, and that the process is the becoming of actual entities. Thus actual entities are creatures; they are also termed 'actual occasions.'

(ii) That in the becoming of an actual entity, the *potential* unity of many entities in disjunctive diversity‡—actual and non-actual—acquires the *real* unity of the one actual entity; so that the actual entity is the real concrescence of many potentials.

(iii) That in the becoming of an actual entity, novel prehensions, nexūs, subjective forms, propositions, multiplicities, and contrasts, also become; but there are no novel eternal objects.

(iv) That the potentiality for being an element in a real concrescence* of many entities into one actuality† is the one general metaphysical character attaching to all entities, actual and non-actual; and that every item in its universe is involved in each concrescence. In other words, it belongs to the nature of a 'being' that it is a potential for every 'becoming.' This is the 'principle of relativity.'

(v) That no two actual entities originate from an iden- [34] tical universe; though the difference between the two universes only consists in some actual entities, included in one and not in the other, and in the subordinate entities which each actual entity introduces into the world. The eternal objects are the same for all actual entities. The nexus of actual entities in the universe correlate to a concrescence† is termed 'the actual world' correlate to that concrescence.

(vi) That each entity in the universe of a given concrescence *can*, so far as its own nature is concerned, be implicated in that concrescence in one or other of many modes; but *in fact* it is implicated only in *one* mode: that the particular mode of implication is only rendered fully determinate by that concrescence, though it is conditioned by the correlate universe. This indetermination, rendered determinate in the real concrescence, is the meaning of 'potentiality.' It is a *conditioned* indetermination, and is therefore called a '*real* potentiality.'

(vii) That an eternal object can be described only in terms of its potentiality for 'ingression' into the becoming of actual entities; and that its analysis only discloses other eternal objects. It is a pure potential. The term 'ingression' refers to the particular mode in which the potentiality of an eternal object is realized in a particular actual entity, contributing to the definiteness of that actual entity.

(viii) That two descriptions are required for an actual entity: (a) one which is analytical of its potentiality for 'objectification' in the becoming of other actual entities, and (b) another which is analytical of the process which constitutes its own becoming.

The term 'objectification' refers to the particular mode in which the potentiality of one actual entity is realized in another actual entity.

(ix) That *how* an actual entity *becomes* constitutes *what* that actual entity *is*;‡ so that the two descriptions of an actual entity are not independent. Its 'being' is [35] constituted by its 'becoming.' This is the 'principle of process.'

(x) That the first analysis of an actual entity, into its most concrete elements, discloses it to be a concrescence of prehensions, which have originated in its process of becoming. All further analysis is an analysis of prehensions. Analysis in terms of prehensions is termed 'division.'

(xi) That every prehension consists of three factors: (a) the 'subject' which is prehending, namely, the actual entity in which that prehension is a concrete element; (b) the 'datum' which is prehended; (c) the 'subjective form' which is *how* that subject prehends that datum.

Prehensions of actual entities—i.e., prehensions whose data involve actual entities—are termed 'physical prehensions'; and prehensions of eternal objects are termed 'conceptual prehensions.' Consciousness is not necessarily involved in the subjective forms of either type of prehension.

(xii) That there are two species of prehensions: (a) 'positive prehensions' which are termed 'feelings,' and (b) 'negative prehensions' which are said to 'eliminate from feeling.' Negative prehensions also have subjective forms. A negative prehension holds its datum as inoperative in the progressive concrescence of prehensions constituting the unity of the subject.

(xiii) That there are many species of subjective forms, such as emotions, valuations, purposes, adversions, aversions, consciousness, etc.

(xiv) That a nexus is a set of actual entities in the unity of the related-ness constituted by their prehensions of each other, or—what is the same thing conversely expressed—constituted by their objectifications in each other.

(xv) That a proposition is the unity of certain actual entities in their potentiality for forming a nexus, with its potential relatedness partially defined by certain eternal objects which have the unity of one complex eternal [36] object. The actual entities involved are termed the 'logical sub-jects,' the complex eternal object is the 'predicate.'

(xvi) That a multiplicity consists of many entities, and its unity is con-stituted by the fact that all its constituent entities severally satisfy at least one condition which no other entity satisfies.

Every statement about a particular multiplicity can be expressed as a statement referent either (a) to *all* its members severally, or (b) to an indefinite *some* of its members severally, or (c) as a denial of one of these statements. Any statement, incapable of being expressed in this form, is not a statement about a multiplicity, though it may be a statement about an entity closely allied to some multiplicity, i.e., systematically allied to each member of some multiplicity.

(xvii) That whatever is a datum for a feeling has a unity *as felt*. Thus the many components of a complex datum have a unity: this unity is a 'contrast' of entities. In a sense this means that there are an endless num-ber of categories of existence, since the synthesis of entities into a contrast in general produces a new existential type. For example, a proposition is, in a sense, a 'contrast.' For the practical purposes of 'human understand-ing,' it is sufficient to consider a few basic types of existence, and to lump the more derivative types together under the heading of 'contrasts.' The most important of such 'contrasts' is the 'affirmation-negation' contrast in which a proposition and a nexus obtain synthesis in one datum, the members of the nexus being the 'logical subjects' of the proposition.

(xviii) That every condition to which the process of becoming conforms in any particular instance† has its reason *either* in the character of some actual entity in the actual world of that concrescence, *or* in the character of the subject which is in process of concrescence. This category of ex-planation is termed the 'ontological principle.' It could also be termed the 'principle of efficient, [37] and final, causation.' This ontological principle means that actual entities are the only *reasons*; so that to search for a *reason* is to search for one or more actual entities. It follows that any condition to be satisfied by one actual entity in its process expresses a fact either about the 'real internal constitutions' of some other actual entities, or about the 'subjective aim' conditioning that process.

The phrase 'real internal constitution' is to be found in Locke's *Essay Concerning Human Understanding* (III, III, 15): "And thus the real internal (but generally in substances unknown) constitution of things, whereon their discoverable qualities depend, may be called their 'essence.'" Also the terms 'prehension' and 'feeling' are to be compared with the various significations of Locke's term 'idea.' But they are adopted as more general and more neutral terms than 'idea' as used by Locke, who seems to restrict them to *conscious mentality*. Also the ordinary logical account of 'propositions' expresses only a restricted aspect of their rôle in the universe, namely, when they are the data of feelings whose subjective forms are those of judgments. It is an essential doctrine in the philosophy of organism that the primary function of a proposition is to be relevant as a lure for feeling. For example, some propositions are the data of feelings with subjective forms such as to constitute those feelings to be the enjoyment of a joke. Other propositions are felt with feelings whose subjective forms are horror, disgust, or indignation. The 'subjective aim,' which controls the becoming of a subject, is that subject feeling a proposition with the subjective form of purpose to realize it in that process of self-creation.

(xix) That the fundamental types of entities are actual entities, and eternal objects; and that the other types of entities only express how all entities of the two fundamental types are in community with each other, in the actual world.

[38] (xx) That to 'function' means to contribute determination to the actual entities in the nexus of some actual world. Thus the determinateness and self-identity of one entity cannot be abstracted from the community of the diverse functionings of all entities. 'Determination' is analysable into 'definiteness' and 'position,' where 'definiteness't is the illustration of select eternal objects, and 'position' is relative status in a nexus of actual entities.

(xxi) An entity is actual, when it has significance for itself. By this it is meant that an actual entity functions in respect to its own determination. Thus an actual entity combines self-identity with self-diversity.

(xxii) That an actual entity by functioning in respect to itself plays diverse rôles in self-formation without losing its self-identity. It is self-creative; and in its process of creation transforms its diversity of rôles into one coherent rôle. Thus 'becoming' is the transformation of incoherence into coherence, and in each particular instance ceases with this attainment.

(xxiii) That this self-functioning is the real internal constitution of an actual entity. It is the 'immediacy' of the actual entity. An actual entity is called the 'subject' of its own immediacy.

(xxiv) The functioning of one actual entity in the self-creation of another actual entity is the 'objectification' of the former for the latter actual entity. The functioning of an eternal object in the self-creation of an actual entity is the 'ingression' of the eternal object in the actual entity.

(xxv) The final phase in the process of concrescence, constituting an actual entity, is one complex, fully determinate feeling. This final phase is termed the 'satisfaction.' It is fully determinate (a) as to its genesis, (b) as to its objective character for the transcendent creativity, and (c) as to its prehension—positive or negative—of every item in its universe.

(xxvi) Each element in the genetic process of an actual [39] entity has one self-consistent function, however complex, in the final satisfaction.

(xxvii) In a process of concrescence, there is a succession of phases in which new prehensions arise by integration of prehensions in antecedent phases. In these integrations 'feelings' contribute their 'subjective forms' and their 'data' to the formation of novel integral prehensions; but 'negative prehensions' contribute only their 'subjective forms.' The process continues till all prehensions are components in the one determinate integral satisfaction.

SECTION III

There are nine Categoreal Obligations:

(i) *The Category of Subjective Unity.* The many feelings which belong to an incomplete phase in the process of an actual entity, though unintegrated by reason of the incompleteness of the phase, are compatible for integration by reason of the unity of their subject.

(ii) *The Category of Objective Identity.* There can be no duplication of any element in the objective datum of the 'satisfaction' of an actual entity, so far as concerns the function of that element in the 'satisfaction.'

Here, as always, the term 'satisfaction' means the one complex fully determinate feeling which is the completed phase in the process. This category expresses that each element has one self-consistent function, however complex. Logic is the general analysis of self-consistency.

(iii) *The Category of Objective Diversity.* There can be no 'coalescence' of diverse elements in the objective datum of an actual entity, so far as concerns the functions of those elements in that satisfaction.

'Coalescence' here means the notion of diverse elements exercising an absolute identity of function, devoid of the contrasts inherent in their diversities.

(iv) *The Category of Conceptual Valuation.* From each physical feeling there is the derivation of a purely [40] conceptual feeling whose datum is the eternal object determinant of the definiteness of the actual entity, or of the nexus, physically felt.

*(v) *The Category of Conceptual Reversion.* There is secondary origination of conceptual feelings with data which are partially identical with, and partially diverse from, the eternal objects forming the data in the first phase of the mental pole. The diversity is a relevant diversity determined by the subjective aim.

Note that category (iv) concerns conceptual reproduction of physical feeling, and category (v) concerns conceptual diversity from physical feeling.

(vi) *The Category of Transmutation.* When (in accordance with category [iv], or with categories [iv] and [v])† one and the same conceptual feeling is derived impartially by a prehending subject from its analogous simple† physical feelings of various actual entities in its actual world, then, in a subsequent phase of integration of these simple physical feelings together with the derivate conceptual feeling, the prehending subject may transmute the *datum* of this conceptual feeling into a characteristic of some *nexus* containing those prehended actual entities among its members, or of some part of that nexus. In this way the nexus (or its part), thus characterized, is the objective datum of a feeling entertained by this prehending subject.

It is evident that the complete datum of the transmuted feeling is a contrast, namely, 'the nexus, as one, in contrast with the eternal object.' This type of contrast is one of the meanings of the notion 'qualification of physical substance by quality.'

This category is the way in which the philosophy of organism, which is an atomic theory of actuality, meets a perplexity which is inherent in all monadic cosmologies. Leibniz in his *Monadology* meets the same difficulty by a theory of 'confused' perception. But he fails to make clear how 'confusion' originates.

(vii) *The Category of Subjective Harmony.* The val- [41] uations of conceptual feelings are mutually determined by the adaptation of those feelings to be contrasted elements congruent with the subjective aim.

Category (i) and category (vii) jointly express a pre-established harmony in the process of concrescence of any one subject. Category (i) has to do with data felt, and category (vii) with the subjective forms of the conceptual feelings. This pre-established harmony is an outcome of the fact that no prehension can be considered in abstraction from its subject, although it originates in the process creative of its subject.

(viii) *The Category of Subjective Intensity.* The subjective aim, whereby there is origination of conceptual feeling, is at‡ intensity of feeling (α) in the immediate subject, and (β) in the *relevant* future.

This double aim—at the *immediate* present and the *relevant* future—is less divided than appears on the surface. For the determination of the *relevant* future, and the *anticipatory* feeling respecting provision for its grade of intensity, are elements affecting the immediate complex of feeling. The greater part of morality hinges on the determination of relevance in the future. The relevant future consists of those elements in the anticipated future which are felt with effective intensity by the present subject by reason of the real potentiality for them to be derived from itself.

(ix) *The Category of Freedom and Determination.* The concrescence of each individual actual entity is internally determined and is externally free.

This category can be condensed into the formula, that in each concrescence whatever is determinable is determined, but that there is always a remainder for the decision of the subject-superject of that concrescence. This subject-superject is the universe in that synthesis, and beyond it there is nonentity. This final decision is the reaction of the unity of the whole to its own internal determination. This reaction is the final modification of emotion, appreciation, and purpose. But the decision [42] of the whole arises out of the determination of the parts, so as to be strictly relevant to it.

SECTION IV

The whole of thet discussion in the subsequent parts either leads up to these categories (of the four types) or is explanatory of them, or is considering our experience of the world in the light of these categories. But a few preliminary notes may be useful.

It follows from the fourth category of explanation that the notion of 'complete abstraction' is self-contradictory. For you cannot abstract the universe from any entity, actual or non-actual, so as to consider that entity in complete isolation. Whenever we think of some entity, we are asking, What is it fit for here? In a sense, every entity pervades the whole world; for this question has a definite answer for each entity in respect to any actual entity or any nexus of actual entities.

It follows from the first category of explanation that 'becoming' is a creative advance into novelty. It is for this reason that the meaning of the phrase 'the actual world' is relative to the becoming of a definite actual entity which is both novel and actual, relatively to that meaning, and to no other meaning of that phrase. Thus, conversely, each actual entity corresponds to a meaning of 'the actual world' peculiar to itself. This point is dealt with more generally in categories of explanation (iii) and (v). An actual world is a nexus; and the actual world of one actual entity sinks to the level of a subordinate nexus in actual worlds beyond that actual entity.

The first, the fourth, the eighteenth, and twenty-seventh categories state different aspects of one and the same general metaphysical truth. The first category states the doctrine in a general way: that every ultimate actuality embodies in its own essence what Alexander [43] terms 'a principle of unrest,' namely, its becoming. The fourth category applies this doctrine to the very notion of an 'entity.' It asserts that the notion of an 'entity' means 'an element contributory to the process of becoming.' We have in this category the utmost generalization of the notion of 'relativity.' The eighteenth category asserts that the obligations imposed on the becoming of any particular actual entity arise from the constitutions of other actual entities.

The four categories of explanation, (x) to (xiii), constitute the repudia-

---

[3] Cf. "Artistic Creation and Cosmic Creation," *Proc. Brit. Acad.*, 1927, Vol. XIII.

tion of the notion of vacuous actuality, which haunts realistic philosophy. The term 'vacuous actuality' here means the notion of a *res vera* devoid of subjective immediacy. This repudiation is fundamental for the organic philosophy (cf. Part II, Ch. VII, 'The Subjectivist Principle'). The notion of 'vacuous actuality' is very closely allied to the notion of the 'inherence of quality in substance.' Both notions—in their misapplication as fundamental metaphysical categories—find their chief support in a misunderstanding of the true analysis of 'presentational immediacy' (cf. Part II, Ch. II, Sects. I and V).

It is fundamental to the metaphysical doctrine of the philosophy of organism, that the notion of an actual entity as the unchanging subject of change is completely abandoned. An actual entity is at once the subject experiencing and the superject of its experiences. It is subject-superject, and neither half of this description can for a moment be lost sight of. The term 'subject' will be mostly employed when the actual entity is considered in respect to its own real internal constitution. But 'subject' is always to be construed as an abbreviation of 'subject-superject.'*

The ancient doctrine that 'no one crosses the same river twice' is extended. No thinker thinks twice; and, to put the matter more generally, no subject experiences twice. This is what Locke ought to have meant by his doctrine of time as a 'perpetual perishing.'

[44] This repudiation directly contradicts Kant's 'First Analogy of Experience' in either of its ways of phrasing (1st or 2nd† edition). In the philosophy of organism it is not 'substance' which is permanent, but 'form.' Forms suffer changing relations; actual entities 'perpetually perish' subjectively, but are immortal objectively. Actuality in perishing acquires objectivity, while it loses subjective immediacy. It loses the final causation which is its internal principle of unrest, and it acquires efficient causation whereby it is a ground of obligation characterizing the creativity.

Actual occasions in their 'formal' constitutions are devoid of all indetermination. Potentiality has passed into realization. They are complete and determinate matter of fact, devoid of all indecision. They form the ground of obligation. But eternal objects, and propositions, and some more complex sorts of contrasts, involve in their own natures indecision. They are, like all entities, potentials for the process of becoming. Their ingression expresses the *definiteness* of the actuality in question. But their own natures do not in themselves disclose in what actual entities this potentiality of ingression is realized. Thus they involve indetermination in a sense more complete than do the former set.

A multiplicity merely enters into process through its individual members. The only statements to be made about a multiplicity express how its individual members enter into the process of the actual world. Any entity which enters into process in this way belongs to the multiplicity, and no other entities do belong to it. It can be treated as a unity for this purpose, and this purpose only. For example, each of the six kinds of entities just mentioned is a multiplicity† (i.e., not the individual entities of the kinds, but the collective kinds of the entities). A multiplicity has solely a disjunctive relationship to the actual world. The 'universe' comprising the absolutely initial data for an actual entity is a multiplicity. The treatment of a multiplicity as though it [45] had the unity belonging to an entity of any one of the other six kinds produces logical errors. Whenever the word 'entity' is used, it is to be assumed, unless otherwise stated, that it refers to an entity of one of the six kinds, and *not* to a multiplicity.

There is no emergent evolution concerned with a multiplicity, so that every statement about a multiplicity is a disjunctive statement about its individual members. Entities of any of the first six kinds, and generic contrasts, will be called 'proper entities.'

In its development the subsequent discussion of the philosophy of organism is governed by the belief that the subject-predicate form of proposition is concerned with high abstractions, except in its application to subjective forms. This sort of abstraction, apart from this exception, is rarely relevant to metaphysical description. The dominance of Aristotelian logic from the late classical period onwards has imposed on metaphysical thought the categories naturally derivative from its phraseology. This dominance of his logic does not seem to have been characteristic of Aristotle's own metaphysical speculations. The divergencies, such as they are, in these lectures from other philosophical doctrines mostly depend upon the fact that many philosophers, who in their explicit statements criticize the Aristotelian notion of 'substance,' yet implicitly throughout their discussions presuppose that the 'subject-predicate' form of proposition embodies the finally adequate mode of statement about the actual world. The evil produced by the Aristotelian 'primary substance' is exactly this habit of metaphysical emphasis upon the 'subject-predicate' form of proposition.

CHAPTER III
SOME DERIVATIVE NOTIONS

SECTION I

[46] THE primordial created fact is the unconditioned conceptual valuation of the entire multiplicity of eternal objects. This is the 'primordial nature' of God. By reason of this complete valuation, the objectification of God in each derivate actual entity results in a graduation of the relevance of eternal objects to the concrescent phases of that derivate occasion. There will be additional ground of relevance for select eternal objects by reason of their ingression into derivate actual entities belonging to the actual world of the concrescent occasion in question. But whether or no this be the case, there is always the definite relevance derived from God. Apart from God, eternal objects unrealized in the actual world would be relatively non-existent for the concrescence in question. For effective relevance requires agency of comparison, and agency belongs exclusively to actual occasions.** This divine ordering is itself matter of fact, thereby conditioning creativity. Thus possibility which transcends realized temporal matter of fact has a real relevance to the creative advance. God is the primordial creature; but the description of his nature is not exhausted by this conceptual side of it. His 'consequent nature' results from his physical prehensions of the derivative actual entities (cf. Part V).

'Creativity' is another rendering of the Aristotelian 'matter,' and of the modern 'neutral stuff.' But it is divested of the notion of passive receptivity, either of 'form,' or of external relations; it is the pure notion of the activity conditioned by the objective immortality of [47] the actual world— a world which is never the same twice, though always with the stable element of divine ordering. Creativity is without a character of its own in exactly the same sense in which the Aristotelian 'matter' is without a character of its own. It is that ultimate notion of the highest generality at * the base of actuality. It cannot be characterized, because all characters are more special than itself. But creativity is always found under conditions, and described as conditioned. The non-temporal act of all-inclusive unfettered valuation is at once a creature of creativity and a condition for creativity. It shares this double character with all creatures. By reason of its character as a creature, always in concrescence and never in the past, it receives a reaction from the world; this reaction is its consequent nature. It is here termed 'God'; because the contemplation of our natures, as enjoying real feelings derived from the timeless source of all order, acquires that 'subjective form' of refreshment and companionship at which religions aim.

This function of creatures, that they constitute the shifting character of creativity, is here termed the 'objective immortality' of actual entities. Thus God has objective immortality in respect to his primordial nature and his consequent nature. The objective immortality of his consequent nature is considered later (cf. Part V); we are now concerned with his primordial nature.

God's immanence in the world in respect to his primordial nature is an urge towards the future based upon an appetite in the present. Appetition is at once the conceptual valuation of an immediate physical feeling combined with the urge towards realization of the datum conceptually prehended. For example,† 'thirst' is an immediate physical feeling integrated with the conceptual prehension of its quenching.

Appetition [1] is immediate matter of fact including in itself a principle of unrest, involving realization of what [48] is not and may be. The immediate occasion thereby conditions creativity so as to procure, in the future, physical realization of its mental pole, according to the various valuations inherent in its various conceptual prehensions. All physical experience is accompanied by an appetite for, or against, its continuance: an example is the appetition of self-preservation. But the origination of the novel conceptual prehension has, more especially, to be accounted for. Thirst is an appetite towards a difference—towards something relevant, something largely identical, but something with a definite novelty. This is an example at a low level which shows the germ of a free imagination.

In what sense can unrealized abstract form be relevant? What is its basis of relevance? 'Relevance' must express some real fact of togetherness among forms. The ontological principle can be expressed as: All real togetherness is togetherness in the formal constitution of an actuality. So if there be a relevance of what in the temporal world is unrealized, the relevance must express a fact of togetherness in the formal constitution of a non-temporal actuality. But by the principle of relativity there can only be one non-derivative actuality, unbounded by its prehensions of an actual world. Such a primordial superject of creativity achieves, in its unity of satisfaction, the complete conceptual valuation of all eternal objects. This is the ultimate, basic adjustment of the togetherness of eternal objects on which creative order depends. It is the conceptual adjustment of all appetites in the form of aversions and adversions. It constitutes the meaning of relevance. Its status as an actual efficient fact is recognized by terming it the 'primordial nature of God.'

The word 'appetition' illustrates a danger which lurks in technical terms. This same danger is also illustrated in the psychology derived from Freud.

[1] Cf. Leibniz's *Monadology*.

The mental poles of actualities contribute various grades of complex feelings to the actualities including them as factors. The [49] basic operations of mentality are 'conceptual prehensions.' These are the only operations of 'pure' mentality. All other mental operations are 'impure,' in the sense that they involve integrations of conceptual prehensions with the physical prehensions of the physical pole. Since 'impurity' in prehension refers to the prehension arising out of the integration of 'pure' physical prehensions with 'pure' mental prehensions, it follows that an 'impure't mental prehension is also an 'impure' physical prehension and conversely. Thus the term 'impure' applied to a prehension has a perfectly definite meaning; and does not require the terms 'mental' or 'physical,' except for the direction of attention in the discussion concerned.

The technical term 'conceptual prehension' is entirely neutral, devoid of all suggestiveness. But such terms present great difficulties to the understanding, by reason of the fact that they suggest no particular exemplifications. Accordingly, we seek equivalent terms which have about them the suggestiveness of familiar fact. We have chosen the term 'appetition,' which suggests exemplifications in our own experience, also in lower forms of life such as insects and vegetables. But even in human experience 'appetition' suggests a degrading notion of this basic activity in its more intense operations. We are closely concerned with what Bergson calls 'intuition'—with some differences however. Bergson's 'intuition't is an 'impure' operation; it is an integral feeling derived from the synthesis of the conceptual prehension with the physical prehension from which it has been derived according to the 'Category of Conceptual Reproduction' (Categoreal Obligation† IV). It seems that Bergson's term 'intuition' has the same meaning as 'physical purpose' in Part III of these lectures. Also Bergson's 'intuition' seems to abstract from the subjective form of emotion and purpose. This subjective form is an essential element in the notion of 'conceptual prehension,' as indeed in that of any prehension. It is an essential element in 'physical purpose' (cf. Part III). If we con- [50] sider these 'pure' mental operations in their most intense operations, we should choose the term 'vision.' A conceptual prehension is a direct vision of some possibility of good or of† evil—of some possibility as to how actualities *may* be *definite*. There is no reference to particular actualities, or to any particular actual world. The phrase 'of good or of evil' has been added to include a reference to the subjective form; the mere word 'vision' abstracts from this factor in a conceptual prehension. If we say that God's primordial nature is a completeness of 'appetition,'† we give due weight to the subjective form—at a cost. If we say that God's primordial nature is 'intuition,' we suggest mentality which is 'impure' by reason of synthesis with physical prehension. If we say that God's primordial nature is 'vision,' we suggest a maimed view of the subjective form, divesting it of yearning after concrete fact—no particular facts, but after *some* actuality. There is deficiency in God's primordial nature which the term 'vision' obscures.

One advantage of the term 'vision' is that it connects this doctrine of God more closely with philosophical tradition. 'Envisagement' is perhaps a safer term than 'vision.' To sum up: God's 'primordial nature' is abstracted from his commerce with 'particulars,' and is therefore devoid of those 'impure' intellectual cogitations which involve propositions (cf. Part III). It is God in abstraction, alone with himself. As such it is a mere factor in God, deficient in actuality.

SECTION II

The notions of 'social order' and of 'personal order' cannot be omitted from this preliminary sketch. A 'society,' in the sense in which that term is here used, is a nexus with social order; and an 'enduring object,' or 'enduring creature,' is a society whose social order has taken the special form of 'personal order.'

A nexus enjoys 'social order' where (i) there is a common element of form illustrated in the definiteness [51] of each of its included actual entities, and (ii) this common element of form arises in each member of the nexus by reason of the conditions imposed upon it by its prehensions of some other members of the nexus, and (iii) these prehensions impose that condition of reproduction by reason of their inclusion of positive feelings of that* common form. Such a nexus is called a 'society,' and the common form is the 'defining characteristic' of the society. The notion† of 'defining characteristic' is allied to the Aristotelian notion of† 'substantial form.'

The common element of form is simply a complex eternal object exemplified in each member of the nexus. But the social order of the nexus is not the mere fact of this common form exhibited by all its members. The reproduction of the common form throughout the nexus is due to the genetic relations of the members of the nexus among each other, and to the additional fact that genetic relations include feelings of the common form. Thus the defining characteristic is inherited throughout the nexus, each member deriving it from those other members of the nexus which are antecedent to its own concrescence.

A nexus enjoys 'personal order' when (α) it is a 'society,' and (β) when the genetic relatedness of its members orders these members 'serially.'

By this 'serial ordering' arising from the genetic relatedness, it is meant that any member of the nexus—excluding the first and the last, if there be such—constitutes a 'cut' in the nexus, so that (a) this member inherits from all members on one side of the cut, and from no members on the other side of the cut, and (b) if A and B are two members of the nexus and B inherits from A, then the side of B's‡ cut, inheriting from B, forms part of the side of A's cut, inheriting from A, and the side of A's cut from which A inherits forms part of the side of B's cut from which B inherits. Thus the nexus forms a single line of inheritance of its defining characteristic. Such a nexus is called an 'enduring object.' It might have been

termed a 'person,' in the legal sense [52] of that term. But unfortunately
'person' suggests the notion of consciousness, so that its use would lead to
misunderstanding. The nexus 'sustains a character,' and this is one of the
meanings of the Latin word *persona*. But an 'enduring object,' *qua* 'person,' does more than sustain a character. For this sustenance arises out of
the special genetic relations among the members of the nexus. An ordinary
physical object, which has temporal endurance, is a society. In the ideally
simple case, it has personal order and is an 'enduring object.' A society may
(or may not) be analysable into many strands of 'enduring objects.' This
will be the case for most ordinary physical objects. These enduring objects
and 'societies,' analysable into strands of enduring objects, are the permanent entities which enjoy adventures of change throughout time and
space. For example, they form the subject-matter of the science of dynamics. Actual entities perish, but do not change; they are what they are.
A nexus which (i) enjoys social order, and (ii) is analysable into strands
of enduring objects may be termed a 'corpuscular society.' A society may
be more or less corpuscular, according to the relative importance of the
defining characteristics of the various enduring objects compared to that
of the defining characteristic of the whole corpuscular nexus.

SECTION III

There is a prevalent misconception that 'becoming' involves the notion
of a unique seriality for its advance into novelty. This is the classic notion
of 'time,' which philosophy took over from common sense. Mankind made
an unfortunate generalization from its experience of enduring objects. Recently physical science has abandoned this notion. Accordingly we should
now purge cosmology of a point of view which it ought never to have
adopted as an ultimate metaphysical principle. In these lectures the term
'creative advance' is not to be construed in the sense of a uniquely serial
advance.

[53] Finally, the extensive continuity of the physical universe has usually
been construed to mean that there is a continuity of becoming. But if we
admit that 'something becomes,' it is easy, by employing Zeno's method, to
prove that there can be no continuity of becoming.[2] There is a becoming
of continuity, but no continuity of becoming. The actual occasions are the
creatures which become, and they constitute a continuously extensive
world. In other words, extensiveness becomes, but 'becoming' is not itself
extensive.

Thus the ultimate metaphysical truth is atomism. The creatures are
atomic. In the present cosmic epoch there is a creation of continuity. Perhaps such creation is an ultimate metaphysical truth holding of all cosmic

[2] Cf. Part II, Ch. II, Sect. II; and also my *Science and the Modern World*,
Ch. VII, for a discussion of this argument.

epochs; but this does not* seem to be a necessary conclusion. The more likely opinion is that extensive continuity is a special condition arising from the society of creatures which constitute our immediate epoch. But atomism does not exclude complexity† and universal relativity. Each atom is a system of all things.

The proper balance between atomism and continuity is of importance to physical science. For example, the doctrine, here explained, conciliates Newton's corpuscular theory of light with the wave theory. For both a corpuscle, and an advancing element of a† wave front, are merely a permanent form propagated from atomic creature to atomic creature. A corpuscle is in fact an 'enduring object.' The notion of an 'enduring object' is, however, capable of more or less completeness of realization. Thus, in different stages of its career, a wave of light may be more or less corpuscular. A train of such waves at all stages of its career involves social order; but in the earlier stages this social order takes the more special form of loosely related strands of personal order. This dominant personal order gradually vanishes as the time advances. Its defining characteristics become less and [54] less important, as their various features peter out. The waves then become a nexus with important social order, but with no strands of personal order. Thus the train of waves starts as a corpuscular society, and ends as a society which is not corpuscular.

SECTION IV

Finally, in the cosmological scheme here outlined one implicit assumption of the philosophical tradition is repudiated. The assumption is that the basic elements of experience are to be described in terms of one, or all, of the three ingredients, consciousness, thought, sense-perception. The last term is used in the sense of 'conscious perception in the mode of presentational immediacy.' Also in practice sense-perception is narrowed down to visual perception. According to the philosophy of organism these three components are unessential elements in experience, either physical or mental. Any instance of experience is dipolar, whether that instance be God or an actual occasion of the world. The origination of God is from the mental pole, the origination of an actual occasion is from the physical pole; but in either case these elements, consciousness, thought, sense-perception, belong to the derivative 'impure' phases of the concrescence, if in any effective sense they enter at all.

This repudiation is the reason why, in relation to the topic under discussion, the status of presentational immediacy is a recurrent theme throughout the subsequent Parts† of these lectures.

PART II
DISCUSSIONS AND APPLICATIONS

CHAPTER I
FACT AND FORM

SECTION I

[62] ALL human discourse which bases its claim to consideration on the truth of its statements must appeal to the facts. In none of its branches can philosophy claim immunity to this rule. But in the case of philosophy the difficulty arises that the record of the facts is in part dispersed vaguely through the various linguistic expressions of civilized language and of literature, and is in part expressed more precisely under the influence of schemes of thought prevalent in the traditions of science and philosophy.

In this second part of these lectures, the scheme of [63] thought which is the basis of the philosophy of organism is confronted with various interpretations of the facts widely accepted in thet European tradition, literary, philosophic, and scientific. So far as concerns philosophy only a selected group can be explicitly mentioned. There is no point in endeavouring to force the interpretations of divergent philosophers into a vague agreement. What is important is that the scheme of interpretation here adopted can claim for each of its main positions the express authority of one, or the other, of some supreme master of thought—Plato, Aristotle, Descartes, Locke, Hume, Kant. But ultimately nothing rests on authority; the final court of appeal is intrinsic reasonableness.

The safest general characterization of the European philosophical tradition is that it consists of a series of footnotes to Plato. I do not mean the systematic scheme of thought which scholars have doubtfully extracted from his writings. I allude to the wealth of general ideas scattered through them. His personal endowments, his wide opportunities for experience at a great period of civilization, his inheritance of an intellectual tradition not yet stiffened by excessive systematization, have made his writingst an inexhaustible mine of suggestion. Thus in one sense by stating my belief that the train of thought in these lectures is Platonic, I am doing no more than expressing the hope that it falls within the European tradition. But I do mean more: I mean that if we had to render Plato's general point of view with the least changes made necessary by the intervening two thousand years of human experience in social organization, in aesthetic attainments, in science, and in religion, we should have to set about the construction of a philosophy of organism. In such a philosophy the actualities constituting the process of the world are conceived as exemplifying the ingression (or 'participation') of other things which constitute the potentialities of definiteness for any actual existence. The things which are temporal arise by their participation in the things which are eternal. The [64] two sets are mediated by a thing which combines the actuality of what is temporal with the timelessness of what is potential. This final entity is the divine element in the world, by which the barren inefficient disjunction of abstract potentialities obtains primordially the efficient conjunction of ideal realization. This ideal realization of potentialities in a primordial actual entity constitutes the metaphysical stability whereby the actual process exemplifies general principles of metaphysics, and attains the ends proper to specific types of emergent order. By reason of the actuality of this primordial valuation of pure potentials, each eternal object has a definite, effective relevance to each concrescent process. Apart from such orderings,** there would be a complete disjunction of eternal objects unrealized in the temporal world. Novelty would be meaningless, and inconceivable. We are here extending and rigidly applying Hume's principle, that ideas of reflection are derived from actual facts.

By this recognition of the divine element the general Aristotelian principle is maintained that, apart from things that are actual, there is nothing —nothing either in fact or in efficacy. This is the true general principle which also underlies Descartes' dictum: "For this reason, when we perceive any attribute, we therefore conclude that some existing thing or substance to which it may be attributed, is necessarily present." [1] And again: "for every clear and distinct conception (*perceptio*) is without doubt something, and hence cannot derive its origin from what is nought, . . ." [2] This general principle will be termed the 'ontological principle.' It is the principle that everything is positively somewhere in actuality, and in potency everywhere. In one of its applications this principle issues in the doctrine of 'conceptualism.' Thus [65] the search for a reason is always the search for an actual fact which is the vehicle of the reason. The ontological principle, as here defined, constitutes the first step in the description of the universe as a solidarity [3] of many actual entities. Each actual entity is conceived as an act of experience arising out of data. It is a process of 'feeling' the many data, so as to absorb them into the unity of one individual 'satisfaction.' Here 'feeling' is the term used for the basic generic operation of passing from the objectivity of the data to the subjectivity of the actual entity in question. Feelings are variously specialized

---

[1] *Principles of Philosophy*, Part I, 52; translation by Haldane and Ross. All quotations from Descartes are from this translation.*

[2] *Meditation IV*, towards the end.

[3] The word 'solidarity' has been borrowed from Professor Wildon Carr's *Presidential Address* to the Aristotelian Society, Session 1917–1918. The address— "The Interaction of Body and Mind"—develops the fundamental principle suggested by this word.

operations, effecting a transition into subjectivity. They replace the 'neutral stuff' of certain realistic philosophers. An actual entity is a process, and is not describable in terms of the morphology of a 'stuff.' This use of the term 'feeling' has a close analogy to Alexander's [4] use of the term 'enjoyment'; and has also some kinship with Bergson's use of the term 'intuition.' A near analogy is Locke's use of the term 'idea,' including 'ideas of particular things' (cf. his *Essay*, III, III, 2, 6, and 7). But the word 'feeling,' as used in these lectures, is even more reminiscent of Descartes. For example: "Let it be so; still it is at least quite certain that it seems to me that I see light, that I hear noise and that I feel heat. That cannot be false; properly speaking it is what is in me called feeling (*sentire*); and used in this precise sense that is no other thing than thinking." [5]

In Cartesian language, the essence of an actual entity consists solely in the fact that it is a prehending thing (i.e., a substance whose whole essence or nature is to prehend).[6] A 'feeling' belongs to the positive species [66] of 'prehensions.' There are two species of prehensions, the 'positive species' and the 'negative species.' An actual entity has a perfectly definite bond with each item in the universe. This determinate bond is its prehension of that item. A negative prehension is the definite exclusion of that item from positive contribution to the subject's own real internal constitution. This doctrine involves the position that a negative prehension expresses a bond. A positive prehension is the definite inclusion of that item into positive contribution to the subject's own real internal constitution. This positive inclusion is called its 'feeling' of that item. Other entities are required to express *how* any one item is felt. All actual entities in the actual world, relatively to a given actual entity as 'subject,' are necessarily 'felt' by that subject, though in general vaguely. An actual entity as felt is said to be 'objectified' for that subject. Only a selection of eternal objects are 'felt' by a given subject, and these eternal objects are then said to have 'ingression' in that subject. But those eternal objects which are not felt are not therefore negligible. For each negative prehension has its own subjective form, however trivial and faint. It adds to the emotional complex, though not to the objective data. The emotional complex is the subjective form of the final 'satisfaction.' The importance of negative prehensions arises from the fact, that (i) actual entities form a system, in the sense of entering into each other's constitutions, (ii) that by the ontological principle every entity is felt by some actual entity, (iii) that, as a consequence of (i) and (ii), every entity in the actual world of a concrescent actuality has some gradation of real relevance to that concrescence, (iv) that, in consequence of (iii), the negative prehension of an entity is a

---

[4] Cf. his *Space, Time and Deity, passim.*
[5] *Meditation II*, Haldane and Ross translation.
[6] For the analogue to this sentence cf. *Meditation VI*; substitute '*Ens prehendens*' fort '*Ens cogitans.*'

positive fact with its emotional subjective form,† (v) there is a mutual sensitivity of the subjective forms of prehensions, so that they are not indifferent to each other, (vi) the concrescence issues in one concrete feeling, the satisfaction.

SECTION II

[67] That we fail to find in experience any elements intrinsically incapable of exhibition as examples of general theory† is the hope of rationalism. This hope is not a metaphysical premise. It is the faith which forms the motive for the pursuit of all sciences alike, including metaphysics.

In so far as metaphysics enables us to apprehend the rationality of things, the claim is justified. It is always open to us, having regard to the imperfections of all metaphysical systems, to lose hope at the exact point where we find ourselves. The preservation of such faith must depend on an ultimate moral intuition into the nature of intellectual action—that it should embody the adventure of hope. Such an intuition marks the point where metaphysics—and indeed every science—gains assurance from religion and passes over into religion. But in itself the faith does not embody a premise from which the theory starts; it is an ideal which is seeking satisfaction. In so far as we believe that doctrine, we are rationalists.

There must, however, be limits to the claim that all the elements in the universe are explicable by 'theory.' For 'theory' itself requires that there be 'given' elements so as to form the material for theorizing. Plato himself recognizes this limitation: I quote from Professor A. E. Taylor's summary of the *Timaeus*:

> In the real world there is always, over and above "law," a factor of the "simply given" or "brute fact," not accounted for and to be accepted simply as given. It is the business of science never to acquiesce in the merely given, to seek to "explain" it as the consequence, in virtue of rational law, of some simpler initial "given." But, however far science may carry this procedure, it is always forced to retain *some* element of brute fact, the merely given, in its account of things. It is the presence in nature of this element of the given, this surd or irrational as it has [68] sometimes been called, which Timaeus appears to be personifying in his language about Necessity.[7]

So far as the interpretation of Plato is concerned, I rely upon the authority of Professor Taylor. But, apart from this historical question, a clear understanding of the 'given' elements in the world is essential for any form of Platonic realism.

For rationalistic thought, the notion of 'givenness' carries with it a reference beyond the mere data in question. It refers to a 'decision' whereby what is 'given' is separated off from what for that occasion is 'not

---

[7] *Plato, The Man and His Work*, Lincoln MacVeagh, New York, 1927.*

given.' This element of 'givenness' in things implies some activity procuring limitation. The word 'decision' does not here imply conscious judgment, though in some 'decisions' consciousness will be a factor. The word is used in its root sense of a 'cutting off.' The ontological principle declares that every decision is referable to one or more actual entities, because in separation from actual entities there is nothing, merely nonentity—'The rest is silence.'

The ontological principle asserts the relativity of decision; whereby every decision expresses the relation of the actual thing, *for which* a decision is made, to an actual thing *by which* that decision is made. But 'decision' cannot be construed as a casual adjunct of an actual entity. It constitutes the very meaning of actuality. An actual entity arises from decisions *for* it, and by its very existence provides decisions *for* other actual entities which supersede it. Thus the ontological principle is the first stage in constituting a theory embracing the notions of 'actual entity,' 'givenness,' and 'process.' Just as 'potentiality for process' is the meaning of the more general term 'entity,' or 'thing'; so 'decision' is the additional meaning imported by the word 'actual' into the phrase 'actual entity.' 'Actuality' is the decision amid 'potentiality.' It represents stubborn fact which cannot be evaded. The real internal constitution of an actual [69] entity progressively constitutes a decision conditioning the creativity which transcends that actuality. The Castle Rock at Edinburgh exists from moment to moment, and from century to century, by reason of the decision** effected by its own historic route of antecedent occasions. And if, in some vast upheaval of nature, it were shattered into fragments, that convulsion would still be conditioned by the fact that it was the destruction of *that* rock. The point to be emphasized is the insistent particularity of things experienced and of the act of experiencing. Bradley's doctrine [8]—Wolf-eating-Lamb as a universal qualifying the absolute—is a travesty of the evidence. *That* wolf eat* *that* lamb at *that* spot at *that* time: the wolf knew it; the lamb knew it; and the carrion birds knew it. Explicitly in the verbal sentence, or implicitly in the understanding of the subject entertaining it, every expression of a proposition includes demonstrative elements. In fact each word, and each symbolic phrase, is such an element, exciting the conscious prehension of some entity belonging to one of the categories of existence.

SECTION III

Conversely, where there is no decision involving exclusion, there is no givenness. For example, the total multiplicity of Platonic forms is not 'given.' But in respect of each actual entity, there is givenness of such forms. The determinate definiteness of each actuality is an expression of a selection from these forms. It grades them in a diversity of relevance. This

[8] Cf. *Logic*, Bk. I, Ch. II, Sect. 42.

ordering of relevance starts from those forms which are, in the fullest sense, exemplified, and passes through grades of relevance down to those forms which in some faint sense are proximately relevant by reason of contrast with actual fact. This whole gamut of relevance is 'given,' and must be referred to the decision of actuality.

The term 'Platonic form' has here been used as the [70] briefest way of indicating the entities in question. But these lectures are not an exegesis of Plato's writings; the entities in question are not necessarily restricted to those which he would recognize as 'forms.' Also the term 'idea' has a subjective suggestion in modern philosophy, which is very misleading for my present purposes; and in any case it has been used in many senses and has become ambiguous. The term 'essence,' as used by the Critical Realists, also suggests their use of it, which diverges from what I intend. Accordingly, by way of employing a term devoid of misleading suggestions, I use the phrase 'eternal object' for what in the preceding paragraph of this section I have termed a 'Platonic form.' Any entity whose conceptual recognition does not involve a necessary reference to any definite actual entities of the temporal world is called an 'eternal object.'

In this definition the 'conceptual recognition' must of course be an operation constituting a real feeling belonging to some actual entity. The point is that the actual subject which is merely conceiving the eternal object is not thereby in direct relationship to some other actual entity, apart from any other peculiarity in the composition of that conceiving subject. This doctrine applies also to the† primordial nature of God, which is his complete envisagement of eternal objects; he‡ is not thereby directly related to the given course of history. The given course of history presupposes his primordial nature, but his primordial nature does not presuppose it.

An eternal object is always a potentiality for actual entities; but in itself, as conceptually felt, it is neutral as to the fact of its physical ingression in any particular actual entity of the temporal world. 'Potentiality' is the correlative of 'givenness.' The meaning of 'givenness' is that what *is* 'given' *might not have been 'given'; and that what *is not* 'given' *might have been* 'given.'

Further, in the complete particular 'givenness' for an actual entity there is an element of exclusiveness. The [71] various primary data and the concrescent feelings do not form a mere multiplicity. Their synthesis in the final unity of one actual entity is another fact of 'givenness.' The actual entity terminates its becoming in one complex feeling involving a completely determinate bond with every item in the universe, the bond being either a* positive or a negative prehension. This termination is the 'satisfaction' of the actual entity. Thus the addition of another component alters this *synthetic* 'givenness.' Any additional component is therefore contrary to this integral 'givenness' of the original. This principle may be illustrated by our visual perception of a picture. The pattern of colours is 'given' for us.

But an extra patch of red does not constitute a mere addition; it alters the whole balance. Thus in an actual entity the balanced unity of the total 'givenness' excludes anything that is not given.

This is the doctrine of the emergent unity of the superject. An actual entity is to be conceived both as a subject presiding over its own immediacy of becoming, and a superject which is the atomic creature exercising its function of objective immortality. It has become a 'being'; and it belongs to the nature of every 'being' that it is a potential for every 'becoming.'

This doctrine, that the final 'satisfaction' of an actual entity is intolerant of any addition, expresses the fact that every actual entity—since it is what it is—is finally its own reason for what it omits. In the real internal constitution of an actual entity there is always some element which is contrary to an omitted element. Here 'contrary' means the impossibility of joint entry in the same sense. In other words, indetermination has evaporated from 'satisfaction,' so that there is a complete determination of 'feeling,' or of 'negation of feeling,' respecting the universe. This evaporation of indetermination is merely another way of considering the process whereby the actual entity arises from its data. Thus, in another sense, each actual entity includes the uni- [72] verse, by reason of its determinate attitude towards every element in the universe.

Thus the process of becoming is dipolar, (i) by reason of its qualification by the determinateness of the actual world, and (ii) by its conceptual prehensions of the indeterminateness of eternal objects. The process is constituted by the influx of eternal objects into a novel determinateness of feeling which absorbs the actual world into a novel actuality.

The 'formal' constitution of an actual entity is a process of transition from indetermination towards terminal determination. But the indetermination is referent to determinate data. The 'objective' constitution of an* actual entity is its terminal determination, considered as a complex of component determinates by reason of which the actual entity is a datum for the creative advance. The actual entity on its physical side is composed of its determinate feelings of its actual world, and on its mental side is originated by its conceptual appetitions.

Returning to the correlation of 'givenness' and 'potentiality,' we see that 'givenness' refers to 'potentiality,' and 'potentiality' to 'givenness'; also we see that the completion of 'givenness' in actual fact converts the 'not-given' for that fact into 'impossibility' for *that* fact. The individuality of an actual entity involves an exclusive limitation. This element of 'exclusive limitation' is the definiteness essential for the synthetic unity of an actual entity. This synthetic unity forbids the notion of *mere* addition to the included elements.

It is evident that 'givenness' and 'potentiality' are both meaningless apart from a multiplicity of potential entities. These potentialities are the 'eternal objects.' Apart from 'potentiality' and 'givenness,' there can be no nexus of actual things in process of supersession by novel actual things. The alternative is a static monistic universe, without unrealized potentialities; since 'potentiality' is then a meaningless term.

[73] The scope of the ontological principle is not exhausted by the corollary that 'decision' must be referable to an actual entity. Everything must be somewhere; and here 'somewhere' means 'some actual entity.' Accordingly the general potentiality of the universe must be somewhere; since it retains its proximate relevance to actual entities for which it is unrealized. This 'proximate relevance' reappears in subsequent concrescence as final causation regulative of the emergence of novelty. This 'somewhere' is the non-temporal actual entity. Thus 'proximate relevance' means 'relevance as in the primordial mind of God.'†

It is a contradiction in terms to assume that some explanatory fact can float into the actual world out of nonentity. Nonentity is nothingness. Every explanatory fact refers to the decision and to the efficacy‡ of an actual thing. The notion of 'subsistence' is merely the notion of how eternal objects can be components of the primordial nature of God. This is a question for subsequent discussion (cf. Part V). But eternal objects, as in God's primordial nature, constitute the Platonic world of ideas.

There is not, however, one entity which is merely the *class* of all eternal objects. For if we conceive any class of eternal objects, there are additional eternal objects which presuppose that class but do not belong to it. For this reason, at the beginning of this section, the phrase 'the multiplicity of Platonic forms' was used, instead of the more natural phrase 'the† class of Platonic forms.' A multiplicity is a type of complex thing which has the unity derivative from some qualification which participates in each of its components severally; but a multiplicity has no unity derivative *merely* from its various components.

SECTION IV

The doctrine just stated—that every explanatory fact refers to the decision and to the efficacy of an actual [74] thing—requires discussion in reference to the ninth Categoreal Obligation. This category states that 'The concrescence of each individual actual entity is internally determined and is externally free.'

The peculiarity of the course of history illustrates the joint relevance of the 'ontological principle' and of this categoreal obligation. The evolution of history can be rationalized by the consideration of the determination of successors by antecedents. But, on the other hand, the evolution of history is incapable of rationalization because it exhibits a selected flux of participating forms. No reason, internal to history, can be assigned why that flux of forms, rather than another flux, should have been illustrated. It is true that any flux must exhibit the character of internal determination. So much follows from the ontological principle. But every instance of internal determination assumes *that* flux up to *that* point. There is no reason why there could be no alternative flux exhibiting that principle of internal determination. The actual flux presents itself with the character of being merely 'given.' It does not disclose any peculiar character of 'perfection.' On the contrary, the imperfection of the world is the theme of every religion which offers a way of escape, and of every sceptic who deplores the prevailing superstition. The Leibnizian theory of the 'best of possible worlds' is an audacious fudge produced in order to save the face of a Creator constructed by contemporary, and antecedent, theologians. Further, in the case of those actualities whose immediate experience is most completely open to us, namely, human beings, the final decision of the immediate subject-superject, constituting the ultimate modification of subjective aim, is the foundation of our experience of responsibility, of approbation or of disapprobation, of self-approval or of self-reproach, of freedom, of emphasis. This element in experience is too large to be put aside merely as misconstruction. It governs the whole tone of human life. It can be illustrated‡ by striking [75] instances from fact or from fiction. But these instances are only conspicuous illustrations of human experience during each hour and each minute. The ultimate freedom of things, lying beyond all determinations, was whispered by Galileo—*E pur si muove*—freedom for the inquisitors to think wrongly, for Galileo to think rightly, and for the world to move in despite of Galileo and inquisitors.

The doctrine of the philosophy of organism is that, however far the sphere of efficient causation be pushed in the determination of components of a concrescence—its data, its emotions, its appreciations, its purposes, its phases of subjective aim—beyond the determination of these components there always remains the final reaction of the self-creative unity of the universe. This final reaction completes the self-creative act by putting the decisive stamp of creative emphasis upon the determinations of efficient cause. Each occasion exhibits its measure of creative emphasis in proportion to its measure of subjective intensity. The absolute standard of such intensity is that of the primordial nature of God, which is neither great nor small because it arises out of no actual world. It has within it no components which are standards of comparison. But in the temporal world for occasions of relatively slight experient intensity, their decisions of creative emphasis are individually negligible compared to the determined components which they receive and transmit. But the final accumulation of all such decisions—the decision of God's nature and the decisions of all occasions—constitutes that special element in the flux of forms in history, which is 'given' and incapable of rationalization beyond the fact that within it every component which is determinable is internally determined.

The doctrine is, that each concrescence is to be referred to a definite free initiation and a definite free conclusion. The initial fact is macrocosmic, in the sense of having equal relevance to all occasions; the final fact is micro-

[76] cosmic, in the sense of being peculiar to that occasion. Neither fact is capable of rationalization, in the sense of tracing the antecedents which determine it. The initial fact is the primordial appetition, and the final fact is the decision of emphasis, finally creative of the 'satisfaction.'

SECTION V

The antithetical terms 'universals' and 'particulars' are the usual words employed to denote respectively entities which nearly, though not quite,[9] correspond to the entities here termed 'eternal objects,' and 'actual entities.' These terms, 'universals' and 'particulars,' both in the suggestiveness of the two words and in their current philosophical use, are somewhat misleading. The ontological principle, and the wider doctrine of universal relativity, on which the present metaphysical discussion is founded, blur the sharp distinction between what is universal and what is particular. The notion of a universal is of that which can enter into the description of many particulars; whereas the notion of a particular is that it is described by universals, and does not itself enter into the description of any other particular. According to the doctrine of relativity which is the basis of the metaphysical system of the present lectures, both these notions involve a misconception. An actual entity cannot be described, even inadequately, by universals; because other actual entities do enter into the description of any one actual entity. Thus every so-called 'universal' is particular in the sense of being just what it is, diverse from everything else; and every so-called 'particular' is universal in the sense of entering into the constitutions of other actual entities. The contrary opinion led to the collapse of Descartes' many substances into Spinoza's one substance; to Leibniz's windowless monads with their pre-established harmony; to the sceptical reduction of Hume's philosophy—a reduction first effected by Hume himself, [77] and reissued with the most beautiful exposition by Santayana in his *Scepticism and Animal Faith.*

The point is that the current view of universals and particulars inevitably leads to the epistemological position stated by Descartes:

From this I should conclude that I knew the wax by means of vision and not simply by the intuition of the mind; unless by chance I remember that, when looking from a window and saying I see men who pass in the street, I really do not see them, but infer that what I see is men, just as I say that I see wax. And yet what do I see from the window but hats and coats which may cover automatic machines? Yet I judge these to be men. And similarly solely by the faculty of judgment [*judicandi*] which rests in my mind, I comprehend that which I believed I saw with my eyes.[10]

[9] For example, prehensions and subjective forms are also 'particulars.'
[10] *Meditation II.*

In this passage it is assumed [11] that Descartes—the Ego in question—is a particular, characterized only by universals. Thus his impressions—to use Hume's word—are characterizations by universals. Thus there is no perception of a particular actual entity. He arrives at the belief in the actual entity by 'the faculty of judgment.' But on this theory he has absolutely no analogy upon which to found any such inference with the faintest shred of probability. Hume, accepting Descartes' account of perception (in this passage), which also belongs to Locke in some sections of his *Essay*, easily draws the sceptical conclusion. Santayana irrefutably exposes the full extent to which this scepticism must be carried. The philosophy of organism recurs to Descartes' alternative theory of '*realitas objectiva*,' and endeavours to interpret it in terms of a consistent ontology. Descartes endeavoured to combine the two theories; but his unquestioned acceptance of the subject-predicate dogma forced him [78] into a representative theory of perception, involving a '*judicium*' validated by our assurance of the power and the goodness of God. The philosophy of organism in its account of prehension takes its stand upon the Cartesian terms '*realitas objectiva*,' '*inspectio*,' and '*intuitio*.' The two latter terms are transformed into the notion of a 'positive prehension,' and into operations described in the various categories of physical and conceptual origination. A recurrence to the notion of 'God' is still necessary to mediate between physical and conceptual prehensions, but not in the crude form of giving a limited letter of credit to a '*judicium*.'

Hume, in effect, agrees that 'mind' is a process of concrescence arising from primary data. In his account, these data are 'impressions of sensation'; and in such impressions no elements other than universals are discoverable. For the philosophy of organism, the primary data are always actual entities absorbed into feeling in virtue of certain universals shared alike by the objectified actuality and the experient subject (cf. Part III). Descartes takes an intermediate position. He explains perception in Humian terms, but adds an apprehension of particular actual entities in virtue of an '*inspectio*' and a '*judicium*' effected by the mind (*Meditations* II and III).† Here he is paving the way for Kant, and for the degradation of the world into 'mere appearance.'

All modern philosophy hinges round the difficulty of describing the world in terms of subject and predicate, substance and quality, particular and universal. The result always does violence to that immediate experience which we express in our actions, our hopes, our sympathies, our purposes, and which we enjoy in spite of our lack of phrases for its verbal

---

[11] Perhaps inconsistently with what Descartes says elsewhere: in other passages the mental activity involved seems to be *analysis* which discovers '*realitas objectiva*' as a component element of the idea in question. There is thus '*inspectio*' rather than '*judicium*.'

analysis. We find ourselves in a buzzing [12] world, amid a democracy of fellow creatures; whereas, under some disguise or other, orthodox philosophy can only introduce us to solitary substances, each enjoying an illusory experience: "O Bottom, thou [79] art changed! what do I see on thee?"* The endeavour to interpret experience in accordance with the overpowering deliverance of common sense† must bring us back to some restatement of Platonic realism, modified so as to avoid the pitfalls which the philosophical investigations of the seventeenth and eighteenth centuries have disclosed.

The true point of divergence is the false notion suggested by the contrast between the natural meanings of the words 'particular' and 'universal.' The 'particular' is thus conceived as being just its individual self with no necessary relevance to any other particular. It answers to Descartes' definition of substance: "And when we conceive of substance, we merely conceive an existent thing which requires nothing but itself in order to exist." [13] This definition is a true derivative from Aristotle's definition: A primary substance is "neither asserted of a subject nor present in a subject." [14] We must add the title phrase of Descartes' *The Second Meditation*: "Of the Nature of the Human Mind; and that it is more easily known than the Body," together with his two statements: ". . . thought constitutes the nature of thinking substance," and "everything that we find in mind is but so many diverse forms of thinking." [15] This sequence of quotations exemplifies the set of presuppositions which led to Locke's empiricism and to Kant's critical philosophy—the two dominant influences from which modern thought is derived. This is the side of seventeenth-century philosophy which is here discarded.

The principle of universal relativity directly traverses Aristotle's dictum, 'A substance† is not present in a subject.' On the contrary, according to this principle an actual entity *is* present in other actual entities. In fact if we allow for degrees of relevance, and for negligible relevance, we must say that every actual entity is present in every other actual entity. The philosophy of organism [80] is mainly devoted to the task of making clear the notion of 'being present in another entity.' This phrase is here borrowed from Aristotle: it is not a fortunate phrase, and in subsequent discussion it will be replaced by the term 'objectification.' The Aristotelian phrase suggests the crude notion that one actual entity is added to another *simpliciter*. This is not what is meant. One rôle of the eternal objects is that they are those elements which express how any one actual entity is constituted by its synthesis of other actual entities, and how that actual entity develops from the primary dative phase into its own individual actual

---

[12] This epithet is, of course, borrowed from William James.
[13] *Principles of Philosophy*, Part I, 51.*
[14] *Aristotle* by W. D. Ross, Ch. II.
[15] *Principles of Philosophy*, Part I, 53.

existence, involving its individual enjoyments and appetitions. An actual entity is concrete because it is such a particular concrescence of the universe.

SECTION VI

A short examination of Locke's *Essay Concerning†* *Human Understanding* will throw light on the presuppositions from which the philosophy of organism originates. These citations from Locke are valuable as clear statements of the obvious deliverances of common sense, expressed with their natural limitations. They cannot be bettered in their character of presentations of facts which have to be accepted by any satisfactory system of philosophy.

The first point to notice is that in some of his statements Locke comes very near to the explicit formulation of an organic philosophy of the type being developed here. It was only his failure to notice that his problem required a more drastic revision of traditional categories than that which he actually effected, that led to a vagueness of statement, and the intrusion of inconsistent elements. It was this conservative, other side of Locke which led to his sceptical overthrow by Hume. In his turn, Hume (despite his explicit repudiation in his *Treatise*, Part I, Sect. VI) was a thorough conservative, and in his explanation of mentality and its content never moved away from the subject-predicate habits of thought [81] which had been impressed on the European mind by the overemphasis on Aristotle's logic during the long mediaeval period. In reference to this twist of mind, probably Aristotle was not an Aristotelian. But Hume's sceptical reduction of knowledge entirely depends (for its arguments) on the tacit presupposition of the mind as subject and of its contents as predicates—a presupposition which explicitly he repudiates.

The merit of Locke's *Essay Concerning†* *Human Understanding* is its adequacy, and not its consistency. He gives the most dispassionate descriptions of those various elements in experience which common sense never lets slip. Unfortunately he is hampered by inappropriate metaphysical categories which he never criticized. He should have widened the title of his book into 'An Essay Concerning† Experience.' His true topic is the analysis of the types of experience enjoyed by an actual entity. But this complete experience is nothing other than what the actual entity is in itself, for itself. I will adopt the pre-Kantian phraseology, and say that the experience enjoyed by an actual entity is that entity *formaliter*. By this I mean that the entity, when considered 'formally,' is being described in respect to those forms of its constitution whereby it is that individual entity with its own measure of absolute self-realization. Its 'ideas of things' are *what* other things are for it. In the phraseology of these lectures, they are its 'feelings.' The actual entity is composite and analysable; and its 'ideas' express how, and in what sense, other things are components in its own constitution. Thus the form of its constitution is to be found by an analysis of the Lockian ideas. Locke talks of 'understanding' and 'perception.' He should have started with a more general neutral term to express the synthetic concrescence whereby the many things of the universe become the one actual entity. Accordingly I have adopted the term 'prehension,' to express the activity whereby an actual entity effects its own concretion of other things.

[82] The 'prehension' of one actual entity by another actual entity is the complete transaction, analysable into the objectification of the former entity as one of the data for the latter, and into the fully clothed feeling whereby the datum is absorbed into the subjective satisfaction—'clothed' with the various elements of its 'subjective form.' But this definition can be stated more generally so as to include the case of the prehension of an eternal object by an actual entity; namely, The 'positive prehension' of an entity by an actual entity is the complete transaction analysable into the ingression, or objectification, of that entity as a datum for feeling, and into the feeling whereby this datum is absorbed into the subjective satisfaction. I also discard Locke's term 'idea.' Instead of that term, the other things, in their limited rôles as elements for the actual entity in question, are called 'objects' for that thing. There are four main types of objects, namely, 'eternal objects,' 'propositions,' 'objectified' actual entities and nexūs. These 'eternal objects' are Locke's ideas as explained in his *Essay* (II, I, 1),† where he writes:

> *Idea is the object of thinking.*—Every man being conscious to himself
> that he thinks, and that which his mind is applied about, whilst think-
> ing, being the ideas that are there, it is past doubt that men have in
> their mind several ideas, such as are† those expressed by the words,
> "whiteness, hardness, sweetness, thinking, motion, man, elephant, army,
> drunkenness," and others.

But later† (III, III, 2), when discussing general terms (and subconsciously, earlier in his discussion of 'substance' in II, XXIII), he adds parenthetically another type of ideas which are practically what I term 'objectified actual entities' and 'nexūs.' He calls them 'ideas of particular things'; and he explains why, in general, such ideas cannot have their separate names. The reason is simple and undeniable: there are too many actual entities. He writes: "But it is beyond the power of human capacity to frame and retain distinct ideas of all the particular things we meet with: every bird and beast men saw, [83] every tree and plant that affected the senses, could not find a place in the most capacious understanding." The context shows that it is not the impossibility of an 'idea' of any particular thing which is the seat of the difficulty; it is solely their number. This notion of a direct 'idea' (or 'feeling') of an actual entity is a presupposition of all common sense; Santayana ascribes it to 'animal faith.' But it accords very ill with the sensationalist theory of knowledge which can be derived

from other parts of Locke's writings. Both Locke and Descartes wrestle
with exactly the same difficulty.

The principle that I am adopting is that consciousness presupposes experience, and not experience consciousness. It is a special element in the
subjective forms of some feelings. Thus an actual entity may, or may not,
be conscious of some part of its experience. Its experience is its complete
formal constitution, including its consciousness, if any. Thus, in Locke's
phraseology, its 'ideas of particular things' are those other things exercising
their function as felt components of its constitution. Locke would only term
them 'ideas' when these objectifications belong to that region of experience
lit up by consciousness. In Section 4† of the same chapter, he definitely
makes all knowledge to be "founded in particular things." He writes:
". . . yet a distinct name for every particular thing would not be of any
great use for the improvement of knowledge: which, *though founded in
particular things*,[16] enlarges itself by general views; to which things reduced
into sorts† under general names, are properly subservient." Thus for Locke,
in this passage, there are not first the qualities and then the conjectural
particular things; but conversely. Also he illustrates his meaning of a 'particular thing' by a 'leaf,' a 'crow,' a 'sheep,' a 'grain of sand.' So he is not
thinking of a particular patch of colour, or other sense-datum.[17] For example, [84] in Section 7 of the same chapter, in reference to children he
writes: "The ideas of the nurse and the mother are well framed in their
minds; and, like pictures of them there, represent only those individuals."
This doctrine of Locke's must be compared with Descartes' doctrine of
'*realitas objectiva*.' Locke inherited the dualistic separation of mind from
body. If he had started with the one fundamental notion of an actual entity, the complex of ideas disclosed in consciousness would have at once
turned into the complex constitution of the actual entity disclosed in its
own consciousness, so far as it *is* conscious—fitfully, partially, or not at all.
Locke definitely states how ideas become general. In Section 6 of the
chapter he writes: ". . . and ideas become general by separating from
them the circumstances of time, and place, and any other ideas that may
determine them to this or that particular existence." Thus for Locke the
abstract idea is preceded by the 'idea of a particular existent'; "[children]
frame an idea which they find those many particulars do partake in." This
statement of Locke's should be compared with the Category of Conceptual Valuation, which is the fourth categoreal obligation.

Locke discusses the constitution of actual things under the term 'real
essences.' He writes (Section 15,† same chapter): "And thus the real in-

---

[16] My italics.

[17] As he is in I, II, 15, where he writes, "The senses at first let in particular
ideas, and furnish the yet empty cabinet; . . ." Note the distinction between
'particular ideas' and 'ideas of particular things.'

ternal (but generally in substances unknown) constitution of things, whereon their discoverable qualities depend, may be called their 'essence.' " The point is that Locke entirely endorses the doctrine that an actual entity arises out of a complex constitution involving other entities, though,† by his unfortunate use of such terms as 'cabinet,' he puts less emphasis on the notion of 'process' than does Hume.

Locke has in fact stated in his work one main problem for the philosophy of organism. He discovers that the mind is a unity arising out of the active prehension of ideas into one concrete thing. Unfortunately, he presupposes both the Cartesian dualism whereby minds are one kind of particulars, and natural entities are another kind [85] of particulars, and also the subject-predicate dogma. He is thus, in company with Descartes, driven to a theory of representative perception. For example, in one of the quotations already cited,† he writes: "and, like pictures of them there, *represent* only those individuals." This doctrine obviously creates an insoluble problem for epistemology, only to be solved either by some sturdy make-believe of 'animal faith,' with Santayana, or by some doctrine of illusoriness†— some doctrine of mere appearance, inconsistent if taken as real—with Bradley. Anyhow 'representative perception' can never, within its own metaphysical doctrines, produce the title deeds to guarantee the validity of the representation of fact by idea.

Locke and the philosophers of his epoch—the seventeenth and eighteenth centuries—are misled by one fundamental misconception. It is the assumption, unconscious and uncriticized, that logical simplicity can be identified with priority in the process constituting an experient occasion. Locke founded the first two books of his *Essay* on this presupposition, with the† exception of his early sections on 'substance,' which are quoted immediately below. In the third and fourth books of the *Essay* he abandons this presupposition, again unconsciously as it seems.

This identification of priority in logic with priority in practice has vitiated thought and procedure from the first discovery of mathematics and logic by the Greeks. For example, some of the worst defects in educational procedure have been due to it. Locke's nearest approach to the philosophy of organism, and—from the point of view of that doctrine—his main oversight, are best exemplified by the first section of his chapter, 'Of our Complex Ideas of Substances' (II, XXIII, 1). He writes:

> The mind, being, as I have declared, furnished with a great number of the simple ideas conveyed in by the senses, as they are found in exterior things, or by reflection on its own operations, takes notice, also, that a certain number of these simple ideas go constantly together; [86] which being presumed to belong to one thing, and words being suited to common apprehensions, and made use of for quick dispatch, are called, so united in one subject, by one name; which, by inadvertency, we are apt afterward to talk of and consider as one simple idea, which indeed is a complication of many ideas together: because,

as I have said, not imagining how these simple ideas can subsist by themselves, we accustom ourselves to suppose some *substratum* wherein they do subsist, and from which they do result; which therefore we call "substance."

In this section, Locke's first statement, which is the basis of the remainder of the section, is exactly the primary assumption of the philosophy of organism: "The mind, being . . . furnished with a great number of the simple ideas conveyed in by the senses, *as they are found in exterior things, . . .*" Here the last phrase, 'as they are found in exterior things,' asserted what later I shall call the *vector* character of the primary feelings. The universals involved obtain that status by reason of the fact that '*they are found in exterior things.*' This is Locke's assertion and it is the assertion of the philosophy of organism. It can also be conceived as a development of Descartes' doctrine of '*realitas objectiva.*' The universals are the only elements in the data describable by concepts, because concepts are merely the analytic functioning of universals. But the 'exterior things,' although they are not expressible by concepts in respect to their individual particularity, are no less data for feeling; so that the concrescent actuality arises from feeling their status of individual particularity; and thus that particularity is included as an element from which feelings originate, and which they concern.

The sentence later proceeds with, "a certain number of these simple ideas go constantly together." This can only mean that in the immediate perception 'a certain number of these simple ideas' are found together in an exterior thing, and that the recollection of antecedent moments of experience discloses that the same fact, of [87] togetherness in an exterior thing, holds for the same set of simple ideas. Again, the philosophy of organism agrees that this description is true for moments of immediate experience. But Locke, owing to the fact that he veils his second premise under the phrase 'go constantly together,' omits to consider the question whether the 'exterior things' of the successive moments are to be identified.

The answer of the philosophy of organism is that, in the sense in which Locke is here speaking, the exterior things of successive moments are not to be identified with each other. Each exterior thing is either one actual entity, or (more frequently) is a nexus of actual entities with immediacies mutually contemporary. For the sake of simplicity we will speak only of the simpler case where the 'exterior thing' means one actual entity at the moment in question. But what Locke is explicitly concerned with is the notion of the self-identity of the one enduring physical body which lasts for years, or for seconds, or for ages. He is considering the current philosophical notion of an individualized particular substance (in the Aristotelian sense) which undergoes adventures of change, retaining its substantial form amid transition of† accidents. Throughout his *Essay,* he in effect retains this notion while rightly insisting on its vagueness and obscurity. The philosophy of organism agrees with Locke and Hume, that the non-in-

[?]

dividualized substantial form is nothing else than the collection of universals—or, more accurately, the one complex universal—common to the succession of 'exterior things' at successive moments respectively. In other words, an 'exterior thing' is either one 'actual entity,' or is a 'society' with a 'defining characteristic.' For the organic philosophy, these 'exterior things' (in the former sense) are the final concrete actualities. The individualized substance (of Locke) must be construed to be the historic route constituted by some society of fundamental 'exterior things,' stretching from the first 'thing' to the last 'thing.'

[88] But Locke, throughout his *Essay,* rightly insists that the chief ingredient in the notion of 'substance' is the notion of 'power.' The philosophy of organism holds that,† in order to understand 'power,' we must have a correct notion of how each individual actual entity contributes to the datum *from which* its successors arise and *to which* they must conform. The reason why the doctrine of power is peculiarly relevant to the enduring things, which the philosophy of Locke's day conceived as individualized substances, is that any likeness between the successive occasions of a‡ historic route procures a corresponding identity between their contributions to the datum of any subsequent actual entity; and it therefore secures a corresponding intensification in the imposition of conformity. The principle is the same as that which holds for the more sporadic occasions in empty space; but the uniformity along the historic route increases the degree of conformity which that route exacts from the future. In particular each historic route of like occasions tends to prolong itself, by reason of the weight of uniform inheritance derivable from its members. The philosophy of organism abolishes the detached mind. Mental activity is one of the modes of feeling belonging to all actual entities in some degree, but only amounting to conscious intellectuality in some actual entities. This higher grade of mental activity is the intellectual self-analysis of the entity in an earlier stage of incompletion, effected by intellectual feelings produced in a later stage of concrescence.[18]

The perceptive constitution of the actual entity presents the problem, How can the other actual entities, each with its own formal existence, also enter objectively into the perceptive constitution of the actual entity in question? This is the problem of the solidarity of the universe. The classical doctrines of universals and particulars, of subject and predicate, of individual substances not present in other individual substances, of [89] the externality of relations, alike render this problem incapable of solution. The answer given by the organic philosophy is the doctrine of prehensions, involved in concrescent integrations, and terminating in a definite, complex unity of feeling. To be actual must mean that all actual things are alike objects, enjoying objective immortality in fashioning creative actions; and that all actual things are subjects, each prehending the universe from which

---

[18] Cf. Part III, Ch. V.

it arises. The creative action is the universe always becoming one in a particular unity of self-experience, and thereby adding to the multiplicity which is the universe as many. This insistent concrescence into unity is the outcome of the ultimate self-identity of each entity. No entity—be it 'universal' or 'particular'—can play disjoined rôles. Self-identity requires that every entity have one conjoined, self-consistent function, whatever be the complexity of that function.

SECTION VII

There is another side of Locke, which is his doctrine of 'power.' This doctrine is a better illustration of his admirable adequacy than of his consistency; there is no escape from Hume's demonstration that no such doctrine is compatible with a purely sensationalist philosophy. The establishment of such a philosophy, though derivative from Locke, was not his explicit purpose. Every philosophical school in the course of its history requires two presiding philosophers. One of them under the influence of the main doctrines of the school should survey experience with some adequacy, but inconsistently. The other philosopher should reduce the doctrines of the school to a rigid consistency; he will thereby effect a *reductio ad absurdum*. No school of thought has performed its full service to philosophy until these men have appeared. In this way the school of sensationalist empiricism derives its importance from Locke and Hume.

Locke introduces his doctrine of 'power' as follows (II, XXI, 1-3†):

This idea how got.—The mind being [90] every day informed, by the senses, of the alteration of those simple ideas it observes in things without, and taking notice how one comes to an end and ceases to be, and another begins to exist which was not before; reflecting also on what passes within itself, and observing a constant change of its ideas, sometimes by the impression of outward objects on the senses, and sometimes by the determination of its own choice; and concluding, from what it has so constantly observed to have been, that the like changes will for the future be made in the same things† by like agents, and by the like ways; considers in one thing the possibility of having any of its simple ideas changed, and in another the possibility of making that change; and so comes by that idea which we call "power." Thus we say, fire has a power to melt gold; . . . and gold has a power to be melted: . . . In which and the† like cases, the power we consider is in reference to the change of perceivable ideas: for we cannot observe any alteration to be made in, or operation upon, any thing, but by the observable change of its sensible ideas; nor conceive any alteration to be made, but by conceiving a change of some of its ideas. . . .* Power thus considered is twofold; viz. as able to make, or able to receive, any change: the one may be called "active," and the other "passive," power. . . .* I confess power includes in it some kind of relation,—a relation to action or change; as, indeed, which of our ideas, of what kind soever, when attentively considered, does not? For our ideas of extension, duration, and number, do they not all contain in them a secret relation of the parts? Figure and motion have something relative in them much more visibly. And sensible qualities, as colours and smells, etc., what are they but the powers of different bodies in relation to our perception? . . . Our idea therefore of power, I think, may well have a place amongst other simple ideas, and be considered as one of them, being one of those that make a principal ingredient in our complex ideas of substances, as we shall hereafter have occasion to observe.

[91] In this important passage, Locke enunciates the main doctrines of the philosophy of organism, namely: the principle of relativity; the relational character of eternal objects, whereby they constitute the forms of the objectifications of actual entities for each other; the composite character of an actual entity (i.e., a substance); the notion of 'power' as making a principal ingredient in that of actual entity (substance). In this latter notion, Locke adumbrates both the ontological principle, and also the principle that the 'power' of one actual entity on the other is simply how the former is objectified in the constitution of the other. Thus the problem of perception and the problem of power are one and the same, at least so far as perception is reduced to mere prehension of actual entities. Perception, in the sense of consciousness of such prehension, requires the additional factor of the conceptual prehension of eternal objects, and a process of integration of the two factors (cf. Part III).

Locke's doctrine of 'power' is reproduced in the philosophy of organism by the doctrine of the two types of objectification, namely, (α) 'causal objectification,' and (β) 'presentational objectification.'

In 'causal objectification' what is felt *subjectively* by the objectified actual entity is transmitted *objectively* to the concrescent actualities which supersede it. In Locke's phraseology the objectified actual entity is then exerting 'power.' In this type of objectification the eternal objects, relational between object and subject, express the formal constitution of the objectified actual entity.

In 'presentational objectification' the relational eternal objects fall into two sets, one set contributed by the 'extensive' perspective of the perceived from the position of the perceiver, and the other set by the antecedent concrescent phases of the perceiver. What is ordinarily termed 'perception' is consciousness of presentational objectification. But according to the philosophy of organism there can be consciousness of both types of objectification. There can be such consciousness of both [92] types because, according to this philosophy, the knowable is the complete nature of the knower, at least such phases of it as are antecedent to that operation of knowing.

Locke misses one essential doctrine, namely, that the doctrine of internal relations makes it impossible to attribute 'change' to any actual entity. Every actual entity is what it is, and is with its definite status in the universe, determined by its internal relations to other actual entities. 'Change' is the description of the adventures of eternal objects in the evolving universe of actual things.

The doctrine of internal relations introduces another consideration which cannot be overlooked without error. Locke considers the 'real essence' and the 'nominal essence' of things. But on the theory of the general relativity of actual things between each other, and of the internality of these relations, there are two distinct notions hidden under the term 'real essence,' both of importance. Locke writes (III, III, 15):

Essence may be taken for the being of any thing, whereby it is what it is. And thus the real internal (but generally in substances unknown) constitution of things, whereon their discoverable qualities depend, may be called their "essence." . . . It is true, there is ordinarily supposed a real constitution of the sorts of things: and it is past doubt there must be some real constitution, on which any collection of simple ideas co-existing must depend. But it being evident that things are ranked under names into sorts or species only as they agree to certain abstract ideas to which we have annexed those† names, the essence of each genus or sort comes to be nothing but that abstract idea, which the general or "sortal" (if I may have leave so to call it from "sort," as I do "general" from *genus*) name stands for. And this† we shall find to be that which the word "essence" imparts in its most† familiar use. These two sorts of essences, I suppose, may not unfitly be termed, the one the "real," the other the "nominal," essence.

[93] The fundamental notion of the philosophy of organism is expressed in Locke's phrase, "it is past doubt there must be some real constitution, on which any collection of simple ideas co-existing must depend." Locke makes it plain (cf. II, II, 1) that by a 'simple idea' he means the ingression in the actual entity (illustrated by 'a piece of wax,' 'a piece of ice,' 'a rose') of some abstract quality which is not complex (illustrated by 'softness,' 'warmth,' 'whiteness'). For Locke such simple ideas, *coexisting*† in an actual entity, require a *real* constitution for that entity. Now in the philosophy of organism, passing beyond Locke's explicit statement, the notion of a real constitution is taken to mean that the eternal objects function by introducing the multiplicity of actual entities as constitutive of the actual entity in question. Thus the constitution is 'real' because it assigns its status in the real world to the actual entity. In other words the actual entity, in virtue of being *what* it is, is also *where* it is. It is somewhere because it is some actual thing with its correlated actual world. This is the direct denial of the Cartesian doctrine, ". . . an existent thing which requires nothing but itself in order to exist." It is also inconsistent with Aristotle's phrase, "neither asserted of a subject nor present in a subject."

I am certainly not maintaining that Locke grasped explicitly the implications of his words as thus developed for the philosophy of organism. But it is a short step from a careless phrase to a flash of insight; nor is it unbelievable that Locke saw further into metaphysical problems than some of his followers. But abandoning the question of what Locke had in his own mind, the 'organic doctrine' demands a 'real essence' in the sense of a complete analysis of the relations, and inter-relations of the actual entities which are formative of the actual entity in question, and an 'abstract essence' in which the specified actual entities are replaced by the notions of unspecified entities in *such* a combination; this is the notion of an unspecified actual entity. Thus the real [94] essence involves real objectifications of specified actual entities; the abstract essence is a complex eternal object. There is nothing self-contradictory in the thought of many actual entities with the same abstract essence; but there can only be one actual entity with the same real essence. For the real essence indicates 'where' the entity is, that is to say, its status in the real world; the abstract essence omits the particularity of the status.

The philosophy of organism in its appeal to the facts can thus support itself by an appeal to the insight of John Locke, who in British philosophy is the analogue to Plato, in the epoch of his life, in personal endowments, in width of experience, and in dispassionate statement of conflicting intuitions.

This doctrine of organism is the attempt to describe the world as a process of generation of individual actual entities, each with its own absolute self-attainment. This concrete finality of the individual is nothing else than a decision referent beyond itself. The 'perpetual perishing' (cf. Locke, II, XIV, 1†) of individual absoluteness is thus foredoomed. But the 'perishing' of absoluteness is the attainment of 'objective immortality.' This last conception expresses the further element in the doctrine of organism—that the process of generation is to be described in terms of actual entities.

CHAPTER II
THE EXTENSIVE CONTINUUM

SECTION I

[95] WE must first consider the perceptive mode in which there is clear, distinct consciousness of the 'extensive' relations of the world. These relations include the 'extensiveness' of space and the 'extensiveness' of time. Undoubtedly, this clarity, at least in regard to space, is obtained only in ordinary perception through the senses. This mode of perception is here termed 'presentational immediacy.' In this 'mode' the contemporary world is consciously prehended as a continuum of extensive relations.

It cannot be too clearly understood that some chief notions of European thought were framed under the influence of a misapprehension, only partially corrected by the scientific progress of the last century. This mistake consists in the confusion of mere potentiality with actuality. Continuity concerns what is potential; whereas actuality is incurably atomic.

This misapprehension is promoted by the neglect of the principle that, so far as physical† relations are concerned, contemporary events happen in *causal* independence of each other.[1] This principle will have to be explained later, in connection with an examination of process and of time. It receives an exemplification in the character of our perception of the world of contemporary actual entities. That contemporary world is objectified [96] for us as '*realitas objectiva*,' illustrating bare extension with its various parts discriminated by differences of sense-data.† These qualities, such as colours, sounds, bodily feelings, tastes, smells, together with the perspectives introduced by extensive relationships, are the relational eternal objects whereby the contemporary actual entities are elements in our constitution. This is the type of objectification which (in Sect. VII of the previous chapter) has been termed 'presentational objectification.'

In this way, by reason of the principle of contemporary independence, the contemporary world is objectified for us under the aspect of passive potentiality. The very sense-data by which its parts are differentiated are supplied by antecedent states of our own bodies, and so is their distribution in contemporary space. Our direct perception of the contemporary world is thus reduced to extension, defining (i) our own geometrical perspectives, and (ii) possibilities of mutual perspectives for other contemporary entities

---

[1] This principle lies on the surface of the fundamental Einsteinian formula for the physical continuum.

inter se, and (iii) possibilities of division. These possibilities of division constitute the external world a continuum. For a continuum is divisible; so
far as the contemporary world is divided by actual entities, it is not a continuum, but is atomic. Thus the contemporary world is perceived with its
potentiality for extensive division, and not in its actual atomic division.

The contemporary world as perceived by the senses is the datum for
contemporary actuality, and is therefore continuous—divisible but not
divided. The contemporary world is in fact divided and atomic, being a
multiplicity of definite actual entities. These contemporary actual entities
are divided from each other, and are not themselves divisible into other
contemporary actual entities. This antithesis will have to be discussed later
(cf. Part IV). But it is necessary to adumbrate it here.

This limitation of the way in which the contemporary actual entities are
relevant to the 'formal' existence of the subject in question is the first
example of the general [97] principle, that objectification relegates into irrelevance, or into a subordinate relevance, the full constitution of the objectified entity. Some real component in the objectified entity assumes the
rôle of being how that particular entity is a datum in the experience of the
subject. In this case, the objectified contemporaries are only directly relevant to the subject in their character of arising from a datum which is an
extensive continuum. They do, in fact, atomize this continuum; but the
aboriginal potentiality, which they include and realize, is what they contribute as the relevant factor in their objectifications. They thus exhibit the
community of contemporary actualities as a common world with mathematical relations—where the term 'mathematical' is used in the sense in
which it would have been understood by Plato, Euclid, and Descartes,
before the modern discovery of the true definition of pure mathematics.

The bare mathematical potentialities of the extensive continuum require an additional content in order to assume the rôle of real objects for
the subject. This content is supplied by the eternal objects† termed sense-
data. These objects are 'given' for the experience of the subject. Their
givenness does not arise from the 'decision' of the contemporary entities
which are thus objectified. It arises from the functioning of the antecedent
physical body of the subject; and this functioning can in its turn be analysed as representing the influence of the more remote past, a past common alike to the subject and to its contemporary actual entities. Thus
these sense-data are eternal objects playing a complex relational rôle;
they connect the actual entities of the past with the actual entities of the
contemporary world, and thereby effect objectifications of the contemporary things and of the past things. For instance, we see the contemporary
chair, but we see it *with* our eyes; and we touch the contemporary chair,
but we touch it *with* our hands. Thus colours objectify the chair in one
way, and objectify the eyes in another way, as elements in the experience
of the subject. [98] Also touch objectifies the chair in one way, and ob-

jectifies the hands in another way, as elements in the experience of the subject. But the eyes and the hands are in the past (the almost immediate past) and the chair is in the present. The chair, thus objectified, is the objectification of a contemporary nexus of actual entities in its unity as one nexus. This nexus is illustrated as to its constitution by the spatial region, with its perspective relations. This region is, in fact, atomized by the members of the nexus. By the operation of the Category of Transmutation (cf. Parts III and IV), in the objectification an abstraction is made from the multiplicity of members and from all components of their formal constitutions, except the occupation of this region. This prehension, in the particular example considered, will be termed the prehension of a 'chair-image.' Also the intervention of the past is not confined to antecedent eyes and hands. There is a more remote past throughout nature external to the body. The direct relevance of this remote past, relevant by reason of its direct objectification in the immediate subject, is practically negligible, so far as concerns prehensions of a strictly physical type.

But external nature has an indirect relevance by the transmission through it of analogous prehensions. In this way there are in it various historical routes of intermediate objectifications. Such relevant historical routes lead up to various parts of the animal body, and transmit into it prehensions which form the physical influence of the external environment on the animal body. But this external environment which is in the past of the concrescent subject is also, with negligible exceptions, in the past of the nexus which is the objectified chair-image. If there be a 'real chair,' there will be another historical route of objectifications from nexus to nexus in this environment. The members of each nexus will be mutually contemporaries. Also the historical route will lead up to the nexus which is the chair-image. The complete nexus, composed of this historical route and the [99] chair-image, will form a 'corpuscular' society. This society is the 'real chair.'

The prehensions of the concrescent subject and the formal constitutions of the members of the contemporary nexus which is the chair-image are thus conditioned by the properties of the same environment in the past. The animal body is so constructed that, with rough accuracy and in normal conditions, important emphasis is thus laid upon those regions in the contemporary world which are particularly relevant for the future existence of the enduring object of which the immediate percipient is one occasion.

A reference to the Category of Transmutation will show that perception of contemporary 'images' in the mode of 'presentational immediacy' is an 'impure' prehension. The subsidiary 'pure' physical prehensions are the components which provide some definite information as to the physical world; the subsidiary 'pure' mental prehensions are the components by reason of which the theory of 'secondary qualities' was introduced into the theory of perception. The account here given traces back these secondary qualities to their root in physical prehensions expressed by the '*withness* of the body.'

If the familiar correlations between physical paths and the life-histories of a chair and of the animal body are not satisfied, we are apt to say that our perceptions are delusive. The word 'delusive' is all very well as a technical term; but it must not be misconstrued to mean that what we *have* directly perceived, we have *not* directly perceived. Our direct perception, via our senses, of an immediate extensive shape, in a certain geometrical perspective to ourselves, and in certain general geometrical relations to the contemporary world, remains an ultimate fact. Our inferences are at fault. In Cartesian phraseology, it is a final '*inspectio*' (also termed '*intuitio*') which, when purged of all '*judicium*'—i.e., of 'inference'—is final for belief. This whole question of 'delusive' perception must be considered later (cf. Part III, Chs. III to V) in more [100] detail. We can, however, see at once that there are grades of 'delusiveness.' There is the non-delusive case, when we see a chair-image and there *is* a chair. There is the partially delusive case when we have been looking in a mirror; in this case, the chair-image we see is not the culmination of the corpuscular society of entities which we call the real chair. Finally, we may have been taking drugs, so that the chair-image we see has no familiar counterpart in any historical route of a corpuscular society. Also there are other delusive grades where the lapse of time is the main element. These cases are illustrated by our perceptions of the heavenly bodies. In delusive cases we are apt, in a confusing way, to say that the societies of entities which we did not see but correctly inferred are the things that we 'really' saw.

The conclusion of this discussion is that the ingression of the eternal objects termed 'sense-data'† into the experience of a subject cannot be construed as the simple objectification of the actual entity to which, in ordinary speech, we ascribe that sense-datum as a quality. The ingression involves a complex relationship, whereby the sense-datum emerges as the 'given' eternal object by which some past entities are objectified (for example, colour seen *with* the eyes and bad temper inherited *from* the viscera) and whereby the sense-datum also enters into the objectification of a society of actual entities in the contemporary world. Thus a sense-datum has ingression into experience by reason of its forming the *what* of a very complex multiple integration of prehensions within that occasion. For example, the ingression of a visual sense-datum involves the causal objectification of various antecedent bodily organs and the presentational objectification of the shape seen, this shape being a nexus of contemporary actual entities. In this account of the ingression of sense-data, the animal body is nothing more than the most intimately relevant part of the antecedent settled world. To sum up this account: When we perceive a contemporary extended shape which we term a 'chair,' the sense- [101] data involved are not necessarily elements in the 'real internal constitution' of this chair-image: they are elements—in some way of feeling—in the 'real internal constitutions' of those antecedent organs of the human body *with* which we perceive the 'chair.' The *direct* recognition of such antecedent actual entities, *with* which we perceive contemporaries, is hindered and, apart from exceptional circumstances, rendered impossible by the spatial and temporal vagueness which infect such data. Later (cf. Part III, Chs. III to V) the whole question of this perception of a nexus vaguely, that is to say, without distinction of the actual entities composing it, is discussed in terms of the theory of prehensions, and in relation to the Category of Transmutation.

SECTION II

This account of 'presentational immediacy' presupposes two metaphysical assumptions:

(i) That the actual world, in so far as it is a community of entities which are settled, actual, and already become, conditions and limits the potentiality for creativeness beyond itself. This 'given' world provides determinate data in the form of those objectifications of themselves which the characters of its actual entities can provide. This is a limitation laid upon the general potentiality provided by eternal objects, considered merely in respect to the generality of their natures. Thus, relatively to any actual entity, there is a 'given' world of settled actual entities and a 'real' potentiality, which is the datum for creativeness beyond that standpoint. This datum, which is the primary phase in the process constituting an actual entity, is nothing else than the actual world itself in its character of a possibility for the process of being felt. This exemplifies the metaphysical principle that every 'being' is a potential for a 'becoming.' The actual world is the 'objective content' of each new creation.

Thus we have always to consider two meanings of [102] potentiality: (a) the 'general' potentiality, which is the bundle of possibilities, mutually consistent or alternative, provided by the multiplicity of eternal objects, and (b) the 'real' potentiality, which is conditioned by the data provided by the actual world. General potentiality is absolute, and real potentiality is relative to some actual entity, taken as a standpoint whereby the actual world is defined. It must be remembered that the phrase 'actual world' is like 'yesterday' and 'tomorrow,' in that it alters its meaning according to standpoint. The actual world must always mean the community of all actual entities, including the primordial actual entity called 'God' and the temporal actual entities.

Curiously enough, even at this early stage of metaphysical discussion, the influence of the 'relativity theory' of modern physics is important. According to the classical 'uniquely serial' view of time, two contemporary actual entities define the same actual world. According to the modern view no two actual entities define the same actual world. Actual entities are called 'contemporary' when neither belongs to the 'given' actual world defined by the other.

The differences between the actual worlds of a pair of contemporary entities, which are in a certain sense 'neighbours,' are negligible for most human purposes. Thus the difference between the 'classical' and the 'relativity' view of time only rarely has any important relevance. I shall always adopt the relativity view; for one reason, because it seems better to accord with the general philosophical doctrine of relativity which is presupposed in the philosophy of organism; and for another reason, because with rare exceptions the classical doctrine can be looked on as a special case of the relativity doctrine—a case which does not seem to accord with experimental evidence. In other words, the classical view seems to limit a general philosophical doctrine; it is the larger assumption; and its consequences, taken in conjunction with other scientific principles, seem to be false.

[103] (ii) The second metaphysical assumption is that the real potentialities relative to all standpoints are coordinated as diverse determinations of one extensive continuum. This extensive continuum is one relational complex in which all potential objectifications find their niche. It underlies the whole world, past, present, and future. Considered in its full generality, apart from the additional conditions proper only to the cosmic epoch of electrons, protons, molecules, and star-systems, the properties of this continuum are very few and do not include the relationships of metrical geometry. An extensive continuum is a complex of entities united by the various allied relationships of whole to part, and of overlapping so as to possess common parts, and of contact, and of other relationships derived from these primary relationships. The notion of a 'continuum' involves both the property of indefinite divisibility and the property of unbounded extension. There are always entities beyond entities, because nonentity is no boundary. This extensive continuum expresses the solidarity of all possible standpoints throughout the whole process of the world. It is not a fact prior to the world; it is the first determination of order—that is, of real potentiality—arising out of the general character of the world. In its full generality beyond the present epoch, it does not involve shapes, dimensions, or measurability; these are additional determinations of real potentiality arising from our cosmic epoch.

This extensive continuum is 'real,' because it expresses a fact derived from the actual world and concerning the contemporary actual world. All actual entities are related according to the determinations of this continuum; and all possible actual entities in the future must exemplify these determinations in their relations with the already actual world. The reality of the future is bound up with the reality of this continuum. It is the reality of what is potential, in its character of a real component of what is actual. Such a real component must be interpreted in [104] terms of the relatedness of prehensions. This task will be undertaken in Chapter V of Part IV of these lectures.

Actual entities atomize the extensive continuum. This continuum is in itself merely the potentiality for division; an actual entity effects this division. The objectification of the contemporary world merely expresses that world in terms of its potentiality for subdivision and in terms of the mutual perspectives which any such subdivision will bring into real effectiveness. These are the primary governing data for any actual entity; for they express how all actual entities are in the solidarity of one world. With the becoming of any actual entity what was previously potential in the space-time continuum is now the primary real phase in something actual. For each process of concrescence a regional standpoint in the world, defining a limited potentiality for objectifications, has been adopted. In the mere extensive continuum there is no principle to determine what regional quanta shall be atomized, so as to form the real perspective standpoint for the primary data constituting the basic phase in the concrescence of an actual entity. The factors in the actual world whereby this determination is effected will be discussed at a later stage of this investigation. They constitute the initial phase of the 'subjective aim.' This initial phase is a direct derivate from God's primordial nature. In this function, as in every other, God is the organ of novelty, aiming at intensification.

In the mere continuum there are contrary potentialities; in the actual world there are definite atomic actualities determining one coherent system of real divisions throughout the region of actuality. Every actual entity in its relationship to other actual entities is in this sense somewhere in the continuum, and arises out of the data provided by this standpoint. But in another sense it is everywhere throughout the continuum; for its constitution includes the objectifications of the actual world and thereby includes the continuum; also the [105] potential objectifications of itself contribute to the real potentialities whose solidarity the continuum expresses. Thus the continuum is present in each actual entity, and each actual entity pervades the continuum.

This conclusion can be stated otherwise. Extension, apart from its spatialization and temporalization, is that general scheme of relationships providing the capacity that many objects can be welded into the real unity of one experience. Thus, an act of experience has an objective scheme of extensive order by reason of the double fact that its own perspective standpoint has extensive content, and that the other actual entities are objectified with the retention of their extensive relationships. These extensive relationships are more fundamental than their more special spatial and temporal relationships. Extension is the most general scheme of real potentiality, providing the background for all other organic relations. The potential scheme does not determine its own atomization by actual entities. It is divisible; but its real division by actual entities depends upon more particular characteristics of the actual entities constituting the antecedent environment. In respect to time, this atomization takes the special form [2] of the 'epochal theory of time.' In respect to space, it means that every actual entity in the temporal world is to be credited with a spatial volume for its perspective standpoint. These conclusions are required by the consideration [3] of Zeno's arguments, in connection with the presumption that an actual entity is an act of experience. The authority of William James can be quoted in support of this conclusion. He writes: "Either your experience is of no content, of no change, or it is of a perceptible amount of content or change. Your acquaintance with reality grows literally by buds or drops of perception. Intellectually and on reflection you can divide these into components, but as immediately given, [106] they come totally or not at all." [4] James also refers to Zeno. In substance I agree with his argument from Zeno; though I do not think that he allows sufficiently for those elements in Zeno's paradoxes which are the product of inadequate mathematical knowledge. But I agree that a valid argument remains after the removal of the invalid parts.

The argument, so far as it is valid, elicits a contradiction from the two premises: (i) that in a becoming something (*res vera*) becomes, and (ii) that every act of becoming is divisible into earlier and later sections which are themselves acts of becoming. Consider, for example, an act of becoming during one second. The act is divisible into two acts, one during the earlier half of the second, the other during the later half of the second. Thus that which becomes during the whole second presupposes that which becomes during the first half-second. Analogously, that which becomes during the first half-second presupposes that which becomes during the first quarter-second, and so on indefinitely. Thus if we consider the process of becoming up to the beginning of the second in question, and ask what then becomes, no answer can be given. For, whatever creature we indicate presupposes an earlier creature which became after the beginning of the second and antecedently to the indicated‡ creature. Therefore there is nothing which becomes, so as to effect a transition into the second in question.

The difficulty is not evaded by assuming that something becomes at each non-extensive instant of time. For at the beginning of the second of time there is no next instant at which something can become.

Zeno in his 'Arrow in Its Flight' seems to have had an obscure grasp of this argument. But the introduction of motion brings in irrelevant details. The true difficulty is to understand how the arrow survives the lapse of

---

[2] Cf. my *Science and the Modern World*, Ch. VII.
[3] Cf. *loc. cit.*; and Part IV of the present work.
[4] *Some Problems of Philosophy*, Ch X; my attention was drawn to this passage by its quotation in *Religion in the† Philosophy of William James*, by Professor J. S. Bixler.

time. [107] Unfortunately Descartes' treatment of 'endurance' is very superficial, and subsequent philosophers have followed his example.

In his 'Achilles and the Tortoise' Zeno produces an invalid argument depending on ignorance of the theory of infinite convergent numerical series. Eliminating the irrelevant details of the race and of motion—details which have endeared the paradox to the literature of all ages—consider the first half-second as one act of becoming, the next quarter-second as another such act, the next eighth-second as yet another, and so on indefinitely. Zeno then illegitimately assumes this infinite series of acts of becoming can never be exhausted. But there is no need to assume that an infinite series of acts of becoming, with a first act, and each act with an immediate successor,† is inexhaustible in the process of becoming. Simple arithmetic assures us that the series just indicated will be exhausted in the period of one second. The way is then open for the intervention of a new act of becoming which lies beyond the whole series. Thus this paradox of Zeno is based upon a mathematical fallacy.

The modification of the 'Arrow' paradox, stated above, brings out the principle that every act of becoming must have an immediate successor, if we admit that something becomes. For otherwise we cannot point out what creature becomes as we enter upon the second in question. But we cannot, in the absence of some additional premise, infer that every act of becoming must have had an immediate predecessor.

The conclusion is that in every act of becoming there is the becoming of something with temporal extension; but that the act itself is not extensive, in the sense that it is divisible into earlier and later acts of becoming which correspond to the extensive divisibility of what has become.

In this section, the doctrine is enunciated that the creature is extensive, but that its act of becoming is not extensive. This topic is resumed in Part IV. How- [108] ever, some anticipation of Parts III and IV is now required.

The *res vera,* in its character of concrete satisfaction, is divisible into prehensions which concern its first temporal half and into prehensions which concern its second temporal half. This divisibility is what constitutes its extensiveness. But this concern with a temporal and spatial sub-region means that the datum of the prehension in question is the actual world, objectified with the perspective due to that sub-region. A prehension, however, acquires subjective form, and this subjective form is only rendered fully determinate by integration with conceptual prehensions belonging to the mental pole of the *res vera.* The concrescence is dominated by a subjective aim which essentially concerns the creature as a final superject. This subjective aim is this subject itself determining its own self-creation as one creature. Thus the subjective aim does not share in this divisibility. If we confine attention to prehensions concerned with the earlier half, their subjective forms have arisen from nothing. For the subjective aim which belongs to the whole is now excluded. Thus the evolution of subjective form could not be referred to any actuality. The ontological principle has been violated. Something has floated into the world from nowhere.

The summary statement of this discussion is, that the mental pole determines the subjective forms and that this pole is inseparable from the total *res vera*.

SECTION III

The discussion of the previous sections has merely given a modern shape to the oldest of European philosophic doctrines. But as a doctrine of common sense, it is older still—as old as consciousness itself. The most general notions underlying the words 'space' and 'time' are those which this discussion has aimed at expressing in their true connection with the actual world. The alternative doctrine, which is the Newtonian cosmology, emphasized the [109] 'receptacle' theory of space-time, and minimized the factor of potentiality. Thus bits of space and time were conceived as being as actual as anything else, and as being 'occupied' by other actualities which were the bits of matter. This is the Newtonian 'absolute' theory of space-time, which philosophers have never accepted, though at times some have acquiesced. Newton's famous *Scholium* [5] to his first eight definitions in his *Principia* expresses this point of view with entire clearness:

Hitherto I have laid down the definitions of such words as are less known, and explained the sense in which I would have them to be understood in the following discourse. I do not define time, space, place, and motion, as being well known to all. Only I must observe, that the vulgar conceive those quantities under no other notions but from the relation they bear to sensible objects. And thence arise certain prejudices, for the removing of which, it will be convenient to distinguish them into absolute and relative, true and apparent, mathematical and common.

I. Absolute, true, and mathematical time, of itself, and from its own nature, flows equably without regard to anything external, and by another name is called duration: relative, apparent, and common time, is some sensible and external (whether accurate or unequable) measure of duration by thet means of motion, which is commonly used instead of true time; such as an hour, a day, a month, a year.

II. Absolute space, in its own nature, and without regard to anything external, remains always similar and immovable. Relative space is some movable dimension or measure of the absolute spaces; which our senses determine by its position to bodies, and which is vulgarly taken for immovable space; . . . Absolute and relative space are the same in figure and magnitude; but they do not remain always numerically the same. . . .

IV. . . . As the order of the parts of time is [110] immutable, so also is the order of the parts of space. Suppose those parts to be

[5] Andrew Motte's translation; new edition revised, London, 1803.

moved out of their places, and they will be moved (if the expression may be allowed) out of themselves. For times and spaces are, as it were, the places as well of themselves as of all other things. All things are placed in time as to order of succession; and in space as to order of‡ situation. It is from their essence or nature that they are places; and that the primary places of things should be movable, is absurd. These are, therefore, the absolute places; and translations out of those places are the only absolute motions. . . . Now no other places are immovable but those that, from infinity to infinity, do all retain the same given positions one to another; and upon this account must ever remain unmoved; and do thereby constitute, what I call, immovable space. The causes by which true and relative motions are distinguished, one from the other, are the forces impressed upon bodies to generate motion. True motion is neither generated nor altered, but by some force impressed upon the body moved: but relative motion may be generated or altered without any force impressed upon the body. For it is sufficient only to impress some force on other bodies with which the former is compared, that by their giving way, that relation may be changed, in which the relative rest or motion of this other body did consist. . . . The effects which distinguish absolute from relative motion are, the forces of receding from the axis of circular motion. For there are no such forces in a circular motion purely relative, but, in a true and absolute circular motion, they are greater or less, according to the quantity of motion. . . . Wherefore relative quantities are not the quantities themselves, whose names they bear, but those sensible measures of them (either accurate or inaccurate) which are commonly used instead of the measured quantities themselves. . . .

I have quoted at such length from Newton's *Scholium* because this document constitutes the clearest, most definite, and most influential statement among the cos- [111] mological speculations of mankind, speculations of a type which first assume scientific importance with the Pythagorean school preceding and inspiring Plato. Newton is presupposing four types of entities which he does not discriminate in respect to their actuality: for him minds are actual things, bodies are actual things, absolute durations of time are actual things, and absolute places are actual things. He does not use the word 'actual'; but he is speaking of matter of fact, and he puts them all on the same level in that respect. The result is to land him in a clearly expressed but complex and arbitrary scheme of relationships between spaces *inter se*; between durations *inter se*; and between minds, bodies, times and places, for the conjunction of them all into the solidarity of the one universe. For the purposes of science it was an extraordinarily clarifying statement, that is to say, for all the purposes of science within the next two hundred years, and for most of its purposes since that period. But, as a fundamental statement, it lies completely open to sceptical attack; and also, as Newton himself admits, diverges from common sense—"the vulgar conceive those quantities under no other notions but from the relation they bear to sensible objects." Kant only saved it by reducing it to the description of a construct by means of which 'pure intuition' introduces an order for chaotic data; and for the schools of transcendentalists derived from Kant this construct has remained in the inferior position of a derivative from the proper ultimate substantial reality. For them it is an element in 'appearance'; and appearance is to be distinguished from reality. The philosophy of organism is an attempt, with the minimum of critical adjustment, to return to the conceptions of 'the vulgar.'† In the first place, the discussion must fasten on the notion of a 'sensible object,' to quote Newton's phrase. We may expand Newton's phrase, and state that the common sense of mankind conceives that all its notions ultimately refer to actual entities, or as Newton terms them, 'sensible objects.' Newton, basing himself upon [112] current physical notions, conceived 'sensible objects' to be the material bodies to which the science of dynamics applies. He was then left with the antithesis between 'sensible objects' and empty space. Newton, indeed, as a private opinion, conjectured that there is a material medium pervading space. But he also held that there *might* not be such a medium. For him the notion 'empty space'—that is, mere spatiality—had sense, conceived as an independent actual existence 'from infinity to infinity.' In this he differed from Descartes. Modern physics sides with Descartes. It has introduced the notion of the 'physical field.' Also the latest speculations tend to remove the sharp distinction between the 'occupied' portions of the field and the 'unoccupied' portion. Further, in these lectures (cf. Ch. III of Part II), a distinction is introduced, not explicitly in the mind either of 'the vulgar' or of Newton. This distinction is that between (i) an actual entity, (ii) an enduring object, (iii) a corpuscular society, (iv) a non-corpuscular society, (v) a non-social nexus. A non-social nexus is what answers to the notion of 'chaos.' The extensive continuum is that general relational element in experience whereby the actual entities experienced, and that unit experience itself, are united in the solidarity of one common world. The actual entities atomize it, and thereby make real what was antecedently merely potential. The atomization of the extensive continuum is also its temporalization; that is to say, it is the process of the becoming of actuality into what in itself is merely potential. The systematic scheme, in its completeness embracing the actual past and the potential future, is prehended in the positive experience of each actual entity. In this sense, it is Kant's 'form of intuition'; but it is derived from the actual world *qua datum*, and thus is not 'pure' in Kant's sense of that term. It is not productive of the ordered world, but derivative from it. The prehension of this scheme is one more example that actual fact includes in its own constitution [113] real potentiality which is referent beyond itself. The former example is 'appetition.'

SECTION IV

Newton in his description of space and time has confused what is 'real' potentiality with what is actual fact. He has thereby been led to diverge from the judgment of 'the vulgar' who "conceive those quantities under no other notions but from the relation they bear to sensible objects."† The philosophy of organism starts by agreeing with 'the vulgar' except that the term 'sensible object' is replaced by 'actual entity'; so as to free our notions from participation in an epistemological† theory as to sense-perception. When we further consider how to adjust Newton's other descriptions to the organic theory, the surprising fact emerges that we must identify the atomized quantum of extension correlative to an actual entity, with Newton's absolute place and absolute duration. Newton's proof that motion does not apply to absolute place, which in its nature is immovable, also holds. Thus an actual entity never moves: it is where it is and what it is. In order to emphasize this characteristic by a phrase connecting the notion of 'actual entity' more closely with our ordinary habits of thought, I will also use the term 'actual occasion' in the place of the term 'actual entity.' Thus the actual world is built up of actual occasions; and by the ontological principle whatever things there are in any sense of 'existence,' are derived by abstraction from actual occasions. I shall use the term 'event' in the more general sense of a nexus of actual occasions, inter-related in some determinate fashion in one extensive quantum. An actual occasion is the limiting type of an event with only one member.

It is quite obvious that meanings have to be found for the notions of 'motion' and of 'moving bodies.' For the present, this enquiry must be postponed to a later chapter [114] (cf. Part IV and also Ch. III of this Part). It is sufficient to say that a molecule in the sense of a moving body, with a history of local change, is not an actual occasion; it must therefore be some kind of nexus of actual occasions. In this sense it is an event, but not an actual occasion. The fundamental meaning of the notion of 'change' is 'the difference between actual occasions comprised in some determinate event.'

A further elucidation of the status of the extensive continuum in the organic philosophy is obtained by comparison with Descartes' doctrine of material bodies. It is at once evident that the organic theory is much closer to Descartes' views than to Newton's. On this topic Spinoza is practically a logical systematization of Descartes, purging him of inconsistencies. But this attainment of logical coherence is obtained by emphasizing just those elements in Descartes which the philosophy of organism rejects. In this respect, Spinoza performs the same office for Descartes that Hume does for Locke. The philosophy of organism may be conceived as a recurrence to Descartes and to Locke, in respect to just those elements in their philosophies which are usually rejected by reason of their inconsistency with the elements which their successors developed. Thus the philosophy of organism is pluralistic in contrast with Spinoza's monism; and is a doctrine of experience prehending actualities, in contrast with Hume's sensationalist phenomenalism.

First let us recur to Descartes at the stage of thought antecedent to his disastrous classification of substances into two species, bodily substance and mental substance. At the beginning of *Meditation I*, he writes:

> For example, there is the fact that I am here, seated by the fire, attired in a dressing gown, having this paper in my hands and other similar matters. And how could I deny that these hands and this body are mine, were it not perhaps that I compare myself to certain persons, devoid of sense. . . . But they are mad, and I should not [115] be any thet less insane were I to follow examples so extravagant.
>
>   At the same time I must remember that I am a man, and that consequently I am in the habit of sleeping, and in my dreams representing to myself the same things or sometimes even less probable things, than do those who are insane in their waking moments. . . . At the same time we must at least confess that the things which are represented to us in sleep are like painted representations which can only have been formed as the counterparts of something real and true [*ad similitudinem rerum verarum*], and that in this way those general things at least, i.e. eyes, a head, hands, and a whole body, are not imaginary things, but things really existent. . . . And for the same reason, although these general things, to wit, [a body],[6] eyes, a head, hands, and such like, may be imaginary, we are bound at the same time to confess that there are at least some other objects yet more simple and more universal, which are real and true [*vera esse*]; and of these just in the same way as with certain real colours, all these images of things which dwell in our thoughts, whether true and real or false and fantastic, are formed.
>
>   To such a class of things pertains corporeal nature in general, and its extension, the figure of extended things, their quantity or magnitude and number, as also the place in which they are, the time which measures their duration, and so on. . . .

In *Meditation II*, after a slight recapitulation, he continues, speaking of God:

> Then without doubt I exist also if he deceives me, and let him deceive me as much as he will, he can never cause me to be nothing so long as I think that I am something. So that after having reflected well and carefully examined all things, we must come to the definite conclusion that this proposition: I am, I exist, is necessarily true each time that I pronounce it, or that I mentally conceive it.

[116] At the end of the quotation from *Meditation I*, Descartes uses the

---

[6] Haldane and Ross enclose in square brackets phrases appearing in the French version, and not in the Latin. I have compared with the Latin.

phrase *res vera* in the same sense as that in which I have used the term 'actual.' It means 'existence' in the fullest sense of that term, beyond which there is no other. Descartes, indeed, would ascribe to God 'existence' in a generically different sense. In the philosophy of organism, as here developed, God's existence is not generically different from that of other actual entities, except that he is 'primordial' in a sense to be gradually explained.

Descartes does not explicitly frame the definition of actuality in terms of the ontological principle, as given in Section IV‡ of this chapter, that actual occasions form the ground from which all other types of existence are derivative and abstracted; but he practically formulates an equivalent in subject-predicate phraseology, when he writes: "For this reason, when we perceive any attribute, we therefore conclude that some existing thing or substance to which it may be attributed, is necessarily present." [7] For Descartes the word 'substance' is the equivalent of my phrase 'actual occasion.' I refrain from the term 'substance,' for one reason because it suggests the subject-predicate notion; and for another reason because Descartes and Locke permit their substances to undergo adventures of changing qualifications, and thereby create difficulties.

In the quotation from the second *Meditation:* "I am, I exist, is necessarily true each time that I pronounce it, or that I mentally conceive it,"† Descartes adopts the position that an act of experience is the primary type of actual occasion. But in his subsequent developments he assumes that his mental substances endure change. Here he goes beyond his argument. For each time he pronounces 'I am, I exist,' the actual occasion, which is the ego, is different; and the 'he' which is common to the two egos is an eternal object or, alternatively, the nexus of successive occasions. Also in the quotation from the first [117] *Meditation* he begins by appealing to an act of experience—"I am here, seated by the fire. . . ." He then associates this act of experience with his body—"these hands and body are mine." He then finally appeals for some final notion of actual entities in the remarkable sentence: "And for the same reason, although these general things, to wit, [a body], eyes, a head, hands, and such like, may be imaginary, we are bound at the same time to confess that there are at least some other objects yet more simple and more universal, which are real and true; and of these . . . all these images of things which dwell in our thoughts, whether true and real or false and fantastic, are formed."

Notice the peculiarly intimate association with immediate experience which Descartes claims for his body, an association beyond the mere sense-perception of the contemporary world—"these hands and feet are mine." In the philosophy of organism this immediate association is the recognition of them as distinguishable data whose formal constitutions are immediately felt in the origination of experience. In this function the

---

[7] *Principles of Philosophy*, Part I, 52.

animal body does not differ in principle from the rest of the past actual world; but it does differ in an intimacy of association by reason of which its spatial and temporal connections obtain some definition in the experience of the subject. What is vague for the rest of the world has obtained some additional measure of distinctness for the bodily organs. But, in principle, it would be equally true to say, 'The actual world is mine.'

Descartes also asserts that "objects yet more simple and more universal, which are real and true" are what the "images of things which dwell† in our thoughts"† are formed of. This does not seem to accord with his theory of perception, of a later date, stated in his *Principles*, Part IV, 196, 197, 198. In the later theory the emphasis is on the *judicium*, in the sense of 'inference,' and not in the sense of *inspectio* of *realitas objectiva*. But it does accord with the organic theory, that the objectifications of other actual occasions form the given data from which an actual occa-[118] sion originates. He has also brought the body into its immediate association with the act of experience. Descartes, with Newton, assumes that the extensive continuum is actual in the full sense of being an actual entity. But he refrains from the additional material bodies which Newton provides. Also in his efforts to guard his representative 'ideas' from the fatal gap between mental symbol and actuality symbolized, he practically, in some sentences, expresses the doctrine of objectification here put forward. Thus:

> Hence the idea of the sun will be the sun itself existing in the mind, not indeed formally, as it exists in the sky, but objectively, i.e. in the way in which objects are wont to exist in the mind; and this mode of being is truly much less perfect than that in which things exist outside the mind, but it is not on that account mere nothing, as I have already said.[8]

Both Descartes and Locke, in order to close the gap between idea representing and 'actual entity represented,' require this doctrine of 'the sun itself existing in the mind.' But though, as in this passage, they at times casually state it in order to push aside the epistemological difficulty, they neither of them live up to these admissions. They relapse into the tacit presupposition of the mind with its private ideas which are in fact qualities without intelligible connection with the entities represented.

But if we take the doctrine of objectification seriously, the extensive continuum at once becomes the primary factor in objectification. It provides the general scheme of extensive perspective which is exhibited in all the mutual objectifications by which actual entities prehend each other. Thus in itself, the extensive continuum is a scheme of real potentiality which must find exemplification† in the mutual prehension of all actual entities. It also finds exemplification in each actual entity considered

---

[8] *Reply to Objections I*: I have already quoted this passage in my *Science and the† Modern World*, note to Ch. IV.

'formally.' In this sense, actual entities are extensive, [119] since they arise out of a potentiality for division, which in actual fact is not divided (cf. Part IV). It is for this reason, as stated above, that the phrase 'actual occasion' is used in the place of 'actual entity.'

Descartes' doctrine of the physical world as exhibiting an extensive plenum of actual entities is practically the same as the 'organic' doctrine. But Descartes' bodies have to move, and this presupposition introduces new obscurities. It is exactly at this point that Newton provides a clear conception in comparison with that of Descartes. In the 'organic' doctrine, motion is not attributable to an actual occasion.

In the 'organic' theory, (i) there is only one type of temporal actual entity; (ii) each such actual entity is extensive; (iii) from the standpoint of any one actual entity, the 'given' actual world is a nexus of actual entities, transforming the potentiality of the extensive scheme into a plenum of actual occasions; (iv) in this plenum, motion cannot be significantly attributed to any actual occasion; (v) the plenum is continuous in respect to the potentiality from which it arises, but each actual entity is atomic; (vi) the term 'actual occasion' is used synonymously† with 'actual entity'; but chiefly when its character of extensiveness has some direct relevance to the discussion, either extensiveness in the form of temporal extensiveness, that is to say 'duration,' or extensiveness in the form of spatial extension, or in the more complete signification of spatio-temporal extensiveness.

SECTION V

The baseless metaphysical doctrine of 'undifferentiated endurance' is a subordinate derivative from the misapprehension of the proper character of the extensive scheme.

In our perception of the contemporary world via presentational immediacy, nexūs of actual entities are objectified for the percipient under the perspective of their characters of extensive continuity. In the perception of a contemporary stone, for example, the separate indi- [120] viduality of each actual entity in the nexus constituting the stone is merged into the unity of the extensive plenum, which for Descartes and for common sense, is the stone. The complete objectification is effected by the generic extensive perspective of the stone, specialized into the specific perspective of some sense-datum, such as some definite colour, for example. Thus the immediate percept assumes the character of the quiet undifferentiated endurance of the material stone, perceived by means of its quality of colour. This basic notion dominates language, and haunts both science and philosophy. Further, by an unfortunate application of the excellent maxim, that our conjectural explanation should always proceed by the utilization of a *vera causa*, whenever science or philosophy has ventured to extrapolate beyond the limits of the immediate deliverance of direct perception, a satisfactory explanation has always complied with the condition that substances with undifferentiated endurance of essential attributes be produced, and that activity be explained as the occasional modification of their accidental qualities and relations. Thus the imaginations of men are dominated by the quiet extensive stone with its relationships of positions, and its quality of colour—relationships and qualities which occasionally change. The stone, thus interpreted, guarantees the *vera causa*, and conjectural explanations in science and philosophy follow its model.

Thus in framing cosmological theory, the notion of continuous stuff with permanent attributes, enduring without differentiation, and retaining its self-identity through any stretch of time however small or large, has been fundamental. The stuff undergoes change in respect to accidental qualities and relations; but it is numerically self-identical in its character of one actual entity throughout its accidental adventures. The admission of this fundamental metaphysical concept has wrecked the various systems of pluralistic realism.

This metaphysical concept has formed the basis of scientific materialism. For example, when the activities [*121*] associated with so-called empty space required scientific formulation, the scientists of the nineteenth century produced the materialistic ether as the ultimate substratum whose accidental adventures constituted these activities.

But the interpretation of the stone, on which the whole concept is based, has proved to be entirely mistaken. In the first place, from the seventeenth century onwards the notion of the simple inherence of the colour in the stone has had to be given up. This introduces the further difficulty that it is the colour which is extended and only inferentially the stone, since now we have had to separate the colour from the stone. Secondly, the molecular theory has robbed the stone of its continuity, of its unity, and of its passiveness. The stone is now conceived as a society of separate molecules in violent agitation. But the metaphysical concepts, which had their origin in a mistake about the stone, were now applied to the individual molecules. Each atom was still a stuff which retained its self-identity and its essential attributes in any portion of time—however short, and however long—provided that it did not perish. The notion of the undifferentiated endurance of substances with essential attributes and with accidental adventures† was still applied. This is the root doctrine of materialism: the substance, thus conceived, is the ultimate actual entity.

But this materialistic concept has proved to be as mistaken for the atom as it was for the stone. The atom is only explicable as a society with activities involving rhythms with their definite periods. Again the concept shifted its application: protons and electrons were conceived as materialistic electric charges whose activities could be construed as locomotive adventures. We are now approaching the limits of any reasonable certainty in our scientific knowledge; but again there is evidence that the concept may be mistaken. The mysterious quanta of energy have made their appearance, derived, as it would seem, from the recesses of protons, or of electrons. Still worse for the concept, these quanta seem to dissolve [*122*] into the vibrations of light. Also the material of the stars seems to be wasting itself in the production of the vibrations.

Further, the quanta of energy are associated by a simple law with the periodic rhythms which we detect in the molecules. Thus the quanta are, themselves, in their own nature, somehow vibratory; but they emanate from the protons and electrons. Thus there is every reason to believe that rhythmic periods cannot be dissociated from the protonic and electronic entities.

The same concept has been applied in other connections where it even more obviously fails. It is said that 'men are rational.' This is palpably false: they are only intermittently rational—merely liable to rationality. Again the phrase 'Socrates is mortal' is only another way of saying that 'perhaps he will die.' The intellect of Socrates is intermittent: he occasionally sleeps and he can be drugged or stunned.

The simple notion of an enduring substance sustaining persistent qualities, either essentially or accidentally, expresses a useful abstract for many purposes of life. But whenever we try to use it as a fundamental statement of the nature of things, it proves itself mistaken. It arose from a mistake and has never succeeded in any of its applications. But it has had one success: it has entrenched itself in language, in Aristotelian logic, and in metaphysics. For its employment in language and in logic, there is—as stated above—a sound pragmatic defence. But in metaphysics the concept is sheer error. This error does not consist in the employment of the word 'substance'; but in the employment of the notion of an actual entity which is characterized by essential qualities, and remains numerically one amidst the changes of accidental relations and of accidental qualities. The contrary doctrine is that an actual entity never changes, and that it is the outcome of whatever can be ascribed to it in the way of quality or relationship. There then remain two alternatives for philosophy: (i) a monistic universe [123] with the illusion of change; and (ii) a pluralistic universe in which 'change' means the diversities among the actual entities which belong to some one society of a definite type.

SECTION VI

We can now, in a preliminary way, summarize some of the agreements and disagreements between the philosophy of organism and the seventeenth-century founders of the modern philosophic and scientific traditions.

It is the basis of any realistic philosophy, that in perception there is a disclosure of objectified data, which are known as having a community with the immediate experience for which they are data. This 'community' is a community of common activity involving mutual implication. This premise is asserted as a primary fact, implicitly assumed in every detail of our organization of life. It is implicitly asserted by Locke in his statement (II, XXIII, 7, heading), "*Power, a great part of our complex ideas of* substances."† The philosophy of organism extends the Cartesian subjectivism by affirming the 'ontological principle' and by construing it as the definition of 'actuality.' This amounts to the assumption that each actual entity is a locus for the universe. Accordingly Descartes' other statement, that every attribute requires a substance,† is merely a special, limited example of this more general principle.

Newton, in his treatment of space, transforms potentiality into actual fact, that is to say, into a creature, instead of a datum for creatures. According to the philosophy of organism, the extensive space-time continuum is the fundamental aspect of the limitation laid upon abstract potentiality by the actual world. A more complete rendering of this limited, 'real' potentiality is the 'physical field.' A new creation has to arise from the actual world as much as from pure potentiality: it arises from the total universe and not solely from its mere abstract elements. It also adds to that universe. Thus [124] every actual entity springs from *that* universe which there *is for it.* Causation is nothing else than one outcome of the principle that every actual entity has to house *its* actual world.

According to Newton, a portion of space cannot move. We have to ask how this truth, obvious from Newton's point of view, takes shape in the organic theory. Instead of a region of space, we should consider a bit of the physical field. This bit, expressing one way in which the actual world involves the potentiality for a new creation, acquires the unity of an actual entity. The physical field is, in this way, atomized with definite divisions: it becomes a 'nexus'† of actualities. Such a quantum (i.e., each actual division) of the extensive continuum is the primary phase of a creature. This quantum is constituted by its totality of relationships and cannot move. Also the creature cannot have any external adventures, but only the internal adventure of becoming. Its birth is its end.

This is a theory of monads; but it differs from Leibniz's in that his monads change. In the organic theory, they merely *become.* Each monadic creature is a mode of the process of 'feeling' the world, of housing the world in one unit of complex feeling, in every way determinate. Such a unit is an 'actual occasion'; it is the ultimate creature derivative from the creative process.

The term 'event' is used in a more general sense. An event is a nexus of actual occasions inter-related in some determinate fashion in some extensive quantum: it is either a nexus in its formal completeness, or it is an objectified nexus. One actual occasion is a limiting type of event. The most general sense of the meaning of change is 'the differences between actual occasions in one event.' For example, a molecule is a historic route of actual occasions; and such a route is an 'event.' Now the motion of the molecule is nothing else than the differences between the successive occasions of its life-history in respect to the extensive quanta from which they arise; [125] and the changes in the molecule are the consequential differences in the actual occasions.

The organic doctrine is closer to Descartes than to Newton. Also it is close to Spinoza; but Spinoza bases his philosophy upon the monistic substance, of which the actual occasions are inferior modes. The philosophy of organism inverts this point of view.

As to the direct knowledge of the actual world as a datum for the immediacy of feeling, we first refer to Descartes in *Meditation I*, "These hands and this body are *mine*"; also to Hume in his many assertions of the type, we see *with our eyes*. Such statements witness to direct knowledge of the antecedent functioning of the body in sense-perception. Both agree— though Hume more explicitly—that sense-perception of the contemporary world is accompanied by perception of the 'withness' of the body. It is this withness that makes the body the starting point for our knowledge of the circumambient world. We find here our direct knowledge of 'causal efficacy.' Hume and Descartes in their theory of direct perceptive knowledge dropped out this withness of the body; and thus confined perception to presentational immediacy. Santayana, in his doctrine of 'animal faith,' practically agrees with Hume and Descartes as to this withness of the actual world, including the body. Santayana also excludes our knowledge of it from givenness. Descartes calls it a certain kind of 'understanding'; Santayana calls it 'animal faith' provoked by 'shock'; and Hume calls it 'practice.'

But we must—to avoid 'solipsism of the present moment'—include in direct perception something more than presentational immediacy. For the organic theory, the most primitive perception is 'feeling the body as functioning.' This is a feeling of the world in the past; it is the inheritance of the world as a complex of feeling; namely, it is the feeling of derived feelings. The later, sophisticated perception is 'feeling the contemporary world.' Even this presentational immediacy begins with [126] sense-presentation of the contemporary body. The body, however, is only a peculiarly intimate bit of the world. Just as Descartes said, 'this body is mine'; so he should have said, 'this actual world is mine.' My process of 'being myself' is my origination from my possession of the world.

It is obvious that there arise the questions of comparative relevance and of comparative vagueness, which constitute the perspective of the world. For example, the body is that portion of the world where, in causal perception, there is some distinct separation of regions. There is not, in causal perception, this distinctness for the past world external to the body. We eke out our knowledge by 'symbolic transference' from causal perception to sense-presentation, and vice versa.

Those realists, who base themselves upon the notion of substance, do not get away from the notion of actual entities which move and change. From the point of view of the philosophy of organism, there is great merit in Newton's immovable receptacles. But for Newton they are eternal. Locke's notion of time hits the mark better: time is 'perpetually perishing.' In the organic philosophy an actual entity has 'perished' when it is complete. The pragmatic use of the actual entity, constituting its static life, lies in the future. The creature perishes *and* is immortal. The actual entities beyond it can say, 'It is mine.' But the possession imposes conformation.

This conception of an actual entity in the fluent world is little more than an expansion of a sentence in the *Timaeus*: [9] "But that which is conceived by opinion with the help of sensation and without reason, is always in a† process of becoming and perishing and never really is." Bergson, in his protest against "spatialization," is only echoing Plato's phrase 'and never really is.'

---

[9] 28A;† Jowett's translation. Professor A. E. Taylor in his *Commentary On Plato's Timaeus* renders the word δόξα by 'belief' or 'judgment' in the place of Jowett's word 'opinion.' Taylor's translation brings out the Platonic influence in Descartes' *Meditations*, namely Plato's δόξα is the Cartesian *judicium*.

CHAPTER III

THE ORDER OF NATURE

SECTION I

[127] IN this, and in the next chapter, among modern philosophers we are chiefly concerned with Hume and with Kant, and among ancient philosophers with the *Timaeus* of Plato. These chapters are concerned with the allied problems of 'order in the universe,' of 'induction,' and of 'general truths.' The present chapter is wholly concerned with the topic of 'order.' For the organic doctrine the problem of order assumes primary importance. No actual entity can rise beyond what the actual world as a datum from its standpoint—*its* actual world—allows it to be. Each such entity arises from a primary phase of the concrescence of objectifications which are in some respects settled: the basis of its experience is 'given.' Now the correlative of 'order' is 'disorder.' There can be no peculiar meaning in the notion of 'order' unless this contrast holds. Apart from it, 'order' must be a synonym for 'givenness.' But 'order' means more than 'givenness,' though it presupposes 'givenness';† 'disorder' is also 'given.' Each actual entity requires a totality of 'givenness,' and each totality of 'givenness' attains its measure of 'order.'

Four grounds of 'order' at once emerge:

(i) That 'order' in the actual world is differentiated from mere 'givenness' by introduction of adaptation for the attainment of an end.

(ii) That this end is concerned with the gradations of intensity in the satisfactions of actual entities (members of the nexus) in whose formal constitutions the nexus [128] (i.e., antecedent members of the nexus) in question is objectified.

(iii) That the heightening of intensity arises from order such that the multiplicity of components in the nexus can enter explicit feeling as *contrasts,* and are not dismissed into negative prehensions as *incompatibilities.*

(iv) That 'intensity' in the *formal constitution* of a subject-superject involves 'appetition' in its *objective* functioning as superject.

'Order' is a mere generic term: there can only be some definite specific 'order,' not merely 'order' in the vague. Thus every definite total phase of 'givenness' involves a reference to that specific 'order' which is its dominant ideal, and involves the specific 'disorder' due to its inclusion of 'given' components which exclude the attainment of the full ideal. The attainment is partial, and thus there is 'disorder'; but there is some attainment, and thus there is some 'order.' There is not just one ideal 'order' which all actual entities should attain and fail to attain. In each case there is an ideal peculiar to each particular actual entity, and arising from the dominant components in its phase of 'givenness.' This notion of 'dominance' will have to be discussed later in connection with the notion of the systematic character of a 'cosmic epoch' and of the subordinate systematic characters of 'societies' included in a cosmic epoch. The notion of one ideal arises from the disastrous overmoralization of thought under the influence of fanaticism, or pedantry. The notion of a dominant ideal peculiar to each actual entity is Platonic.

It is notable that no biological science has been able to express itself apart from phraseology which is meaningless unless it refers to ideals proper to the organism in question. This aspect of the universe impressed itself on that great biologist and philosopher, Aristotle. His philosophy led to a wild overstressing of the notion of 'final causes'† during the Christian middle ages; and thence, by a reaction, to the correlative overstressing of [129] the notion of 'efficient causes' during the modern scientific period. One task of a sound metaphysics is to exhibit final and efficient causes in their proper relation to each other. The necessity and the difficulty of this task are stressed by Hume in his *Dialogues Concerning Natural Religion*.

Thus the notion of 'order' is bound up with the notion of an actual entity as involving an attainment which is a specific satisfaction. This satisfaction is the attainment of something individual to the entity in question. It cannot be construed as a component contributing to its own concrescence; it is the ultimate fact, individual to the entity. The notion of 'satisfaction' is the notion of the 'entity as concrete' abstracted from the 'process of concrescence'; it is the outcome separated from the process, thereby losing the actuality of the atomic entity, which is both process and outcome. 'Satisfaction' provides the individual element in the composition of the actual entity—that element which has led to the definition of substance as 'requiring nothing but itself in order to exist.' But the 'satisfaction' is the 'superject' rather than the 'substance' or the 'subject.' It closes up the entity; and yet is the superject adding its character to the creativity whereby there is a becoming of entities superseding the one in question. The 'formal' reality of the actuality in question belongs to its process of concrescence and not to its 'satisfaction.' This is the sense in which the philosophy of organism interprets Plato's phrase 'and never really is'; for the superject can only be interpreted in terms of its 'objective immortality.'

'Satisfaction' is a generic term: there are specific differences between the 'satisfactions' of different entities, including gradations of intensity. These specific differences can only be expressed by the analysis of the components in the concrescence out of which the actual entity arises. The intensity of satisfaction is promoted by the 'order' in the phases from which concrescence arises and through which it passes; it is enfeebled by the [130] 'disorder.' The components in the concrescence are thus 'values' contributory to the 'satisfaction.' The concrescence is thus the building up of a determinate 'satisfaction,' which constitutes the completion of the actual togetherness of the discrete components. The process of concrescence terminates with the attainment of a fully *determinate* 'satisfaction'; and the creativity thereby passes over into the 'given' primary phase for the concrescence of other actual entities. This transcendence is thereby established when there is attainment of *determinate* 'satisfaction' completing the antecedent entity. Completion is the perishing of immediacy: 'It never really is.'†

No actual entity can be conscious of its own satisfaction; for such knowledge would be a component in the process, and would thereby alter the satisfaction. In respect to the entity in question the satisfaction can only be considered as a creative determination, by which the objectifications of the entity beyond itself are settled. In other words, the 'satisfaction' of an entity can only be discussed in terms of the usefulness of that entity. It is a qualification of creativity. The tone of feeling embodied in this satisfaction passes into the world beyond, by reason of these objectifications. The world is self-creative; and the actual entity as self-creating creature passes into its immortal function of part-creator of the transcendent world. In its self-creation the actual entity is guided by its ideal of itself as individual satisfaction and as transcendent creator. The enjoyment of this ideal is the 'subjective aim,' by reason of which the actual entity is a determinate process.

This subjective aim is not primarily intellectual; it is the lure for feeling. This lure for feeling is the germ of mind. Here I am using the term 'mind' to mean the complex of mental operations involved in the constitution of an actual entity. Mental operations do not necessarily involve consciousness. The concrescence, absorb- [131] ing the derived data into immediate privacy, consists in mating the data with ways of feeling provocative of the private synthesis. These subjective ways of feeling are not merely receptive of the data as alien facts; they clothe the dry bones with the flesh of a real being, emotional, purposive, appreciative. The miracle of creation is described in the vision of the prophet Ezekiel: "So I prophesied as he commanded me, and the breath came into them, and they lived, and stood up upon their feet, an exceeding great army." [1]

The breath of feeling which creates a new individual fact has an origination not wholly traceable to the mere data. It conforms to the data, in that it feels the data. But the *how* of feeling, though it is germane to the data, is not fully determined by the data. The relevant feeling is not settled, as to its inclusions or exclusions of 'subjective form,' by the data about which the feeling is concerned. The concrescent process is the elimination of these indeterminations of subjective forms. The quality of feeling has to be definite in respect to the eternal objects with which feeling clothes itself

[1] Ezekiel, xxxvii:10.†

in its self-definition. It is a mode of ingression of eternal objects into the
actual occasion. But this self-definition is analysable into two phases. First,
the conceptual ingression of the eternal objects in the double rôle of being
germane to the data and of being potentials for physical feeling. This is
the ingression of an eternal object in the rôle of a conceptual lure for feeling. The second phase is the admission of the lure into the reality of feeling,
or its rejection from this reality. The *relevance* of an eternal object in its
rôle of lure is a fact inherent in the data. In this sense the eternal object
is a constituent of the 'objective lure.' But the admission into, or rejection
from, reality of conceptual feeling is the originative decision of the actual
occasion. In this sense an actual occasion is *causa sui*. The subjective forms
of the prehen- [132] sions in one phase of concrescence control the specific
integrations of prehensions in later phases of that concrescence.

An example of the lure for feeling is given by Hume himself. In the first
section of his *Treatise** he lays down the proposition, *"That all our simple
ideas in their first appearance, are derived from simple impressions, which
are correspondent to them, and which they exactly represent."* It must be
remembered that in the organic philosophy the 'data of objectifications' are
the nearest analogue to Hume's 'simple impressions.' Thus, modifying
Hume's principle, the only lure to conceptual feeling is an exact conformation to the qualities realized in the objectified actualities. But Hume
(*loc. cit.*) notes an exception which carries with it the exact principle
which has just been laid down, namely, the principle of relevant potentials,
unrealized in the datum and yet constituent of an 'objective lure' by
proximity to the datum. The point is that 'order' in the actual world introduces a derivative 'order' among eternal objects. Hume writes:

There is, however, one contradictory phenomenon, which may prove,
that it is not absolutely impossible for ideas to go before their correspondent impressions. I believe it will readily be allowed, that the several distinct ideas of colours, which enter by the eyes, or† those of
sounds, which are conveyed by the hearing, are really different from
each other, though, at the same time, resembling. Now, if this be true
of different colours, it must be no less so of the different shades of the
same colour, that each of them produces a distinct idea, independent of
the rest. . . . Suppose, therefore, a person to have enjoyed his sight for
thirty years, and to have become perfectly well acquainted with colours
of all kinds, excepting one particular shade of blue, for instance, which
it never hast been his fortune to meet with. Let all the different shades
of that colour, except that single one, be placed before him, descending
gradually from the deepest to the [133] lightest; it is plain, that he
will perceive a blank, where that shade is wanting, and will be sensible
that there is a greater distance in that place, betwixt† the contiguous
colours, than in any other. Now I ask, whether it is possible for him,
from his own imagination, to supply this deficiency, and† raise up to
himself the idea of that particular shade, though it had never been

conveyed to him by his senses? I believe there are few but will be of opinion that he can; and this may serve as a proof, that the simple ideas are not always derived from the correspondent impressions; though the instance† is so particular and singular, that it is scarce worth our observing, and does not merit that, for it alone, we should alter our general maxim.

This passage requires no comment, except for its final clause. Hume puts the 'instance' aside as being 'particular and singular'; it is exactly this estimate which is challenged by the philosophy of organism. The analysis of concrescence, here adopted, conceives that there is an origination of conceptual feeling, admitting or rejecting whatever is apt for feeling by reason of its germaneness to the basic data. The gradation of eternal objects in respect to this germaneness is the 'objective lure' for feeling; the concrescent process admits a selection from this 'objective lure' into subjective efficiency. This is the subjective 'ideal of itself' which guides the process. Also the basic data are constituted by the actual world which 'belongs to' that instance of concrescent process. Feelings are 'vectors'; for they feel what is *there* and transform it into what is *here*.

The term 'potential difference' is an old one in physical science; and recently it has been introduced in physiology with a meaning diverse from, though generically allied to, its older meaning in physics. The ultimate fact in the constitution of an actual entity which suggests this term is the objective lure for feeling. In the comparison of two actual entities, the contrast be- [134] tween their objective lures is their 'potential difference'; and all other uses of this phrase are abstractions derivative from this ultimate meaning.

The 'objectifications' of the actual entities in the actual world, relative to a definite actual entity, constitute the efficient causes out of which *that* actual entity arises; the 'subjective aim' at 'satisfaction' constitutes the final cause, or lure, whereby there is determinate concrescence; and that attained 'satisfaction' remains as an element in the content of creative purpose. There is, in this way, transcendence of the creativity; and this transcendence effects determinate objectifications for the renewal of the process in the concrescence of actualities beyond that satisfied superject.

Thus an actual entity has a threefold† character: (i) it has the character 'given' for it by the past; (ii) it has the subjective character aimed at in its process of concrescence; (iii) it has the superjective character, which is the pragmatic value of its specific satisfaction qualifying the transcendent creativity.

In the case of the primordial actual entity, which is God, there is no past. Thus the ideal realization of conceptual feeling takes the precedence. God differs from other actual entities in the fact that Hume's principle, of the derivate character of conceptual feelings, does not hold for him. There is still, however, the same threefold character: (i) The 'primordial nature' of God is the concrescence of a† unity of conceptual feelings, including among their data all eternal objects. The concrescence is directed by the subjective aim, that the subjective forms of the feelings shall be such as to constitute the eternal objects into relevant lures of feeling* severally appropriate for all realizable basic conditions. (ii) The 'consequent nature' of God is the physical prehension by God of the actualities of the evolving universe. His‡ primordial nature directs such perspectives of objectification that each novel actuality in the temporal world contributes such elements as it can to a realization in God [135] free from inhibitions of intensity by reason of discordance. (iii) The 'superjective nature'† of God is the character of the pragmatic value of his specific satisfaction qualifying the transcendent creativity in the various temporal instances.

This is the conception of God, according to which he is considered as the outcome of creativity, as the foundation of order, and as the goad‡ towards novelty. 'Order' and 'novelty' are but the instruments of his subjective aim which is the intensification of 'formal immediacy.' It is to be noted that every actual entity, including God, is something individual for its own sake; and thereby transcends the rest of actuality. And also it is to be noted that every actual entity, including God, is a creature transcended by the creativity which it qualifies. A temporal occasion in respect to the second element of its character, and God in respect to the first element of his character satisfy Spinoza's definition of substance, that it is *causa sui*. To be *causa sui* means that the process of concrescence is its own reason for the decision in respect to the qualitative clothing of feelings. It is finally responsible for the decision by which any lure for feeling is admitted to efficiency. The freedom inherent in the universe is constituted by this element of self-causation.

In the subsequent discussion, 'actual entity' will be taken to mean a conditioned actual entity of the temporal world, unless God is expressly included in the discussion. The term 'actual occasion' will always exclude God from its scope.

The philosophy of organism is the inversion of Kant's philosophy. *The Critique of Pure Reason* describes the process by which subjective data pass into the appearance of an objective world. The philosophy of organism seeks to describe how objective data pass into subjective satisfaction, and how order in the objective data provides intensity in the subjective satisfaction. For Kant, the world emerges from the subject; for the philosophy of [136] organism, the subject emerges from the world—a 'superject' rather than a 'subject.' The word 'object' thus means an entity which is a potentiality for being a component in feeling; and the word 'subject' means the entity constituted by the process of feeling, and including this process. The feeler is the unity emergent from its own feelings; and feelings are the details of the process intermediary between this unity and its many data. The data are the potentials for feeling; that is to say, they are objects. The process is the elimination of indeterminateness of feeling from the unity of one subjective experience. The degree of order in the datum is measured by the degree of richness in the objective lure. The 'intensity' achieved belongs to the subjective form of the satisfaction.

SECTION II

It has been explained in the previous section that the notion of 'order' is primarily applicable to the objectified data for individual actual entities. It has been necessary to give a sketch of some categories applying to an actual entity in order to show how this can be the case. But there is a derivative sense of the term 'order,' which is more usually in our minds when we use that word. We speak of the 'order of nature,' meaning thereby the order reigning in that limited portion of the universe,[2] or even of the surface of the earth, which has come under our observation. We also speak of a man of orderly life, or of disorderly life. In any of these senses, the term 'order' evidently applies to the relations among themselves enjoyed by many actual entities which thereby form a society. The term 'society' will always be restricted to mean a nexus of actual entities which are 'ordered' among themselves in the sense to be explained in this section.[3] [137] The point of a 'society,' as the term is here used, is that it is self-sustaining; in other words, that it is its own reason. Thus a society is more than a set of entities to which the same class-name applies: that is to say, it involves more than a merely mathematical conception of 'order.' To constitute a society, the class-name has got to apply to each member, by reason of genetic derivation from other members of that same society. The members of the society are alike because, by reason of their common character, they impose on other members of the society the conditions which lead to that likeness.

This likeness[4] consists in the fact that (i) a certain element of 'form' is a contributory component to the individual satisfaction of each member of the society; and that (ii) the contribution by the element to the objectification of any one member of the society for prehension by other members promotes its analogous reproduction in the satisfactions of those other members. Thus a set of entities is a society (i) in virtue of a 'defining characteristic' shared by its members, and (ii) in virtue of the presence of the defining characteristic being due to the environment provided by the society itself.

For example, the life of** man is a historic route of actual occasions which in a marked degree—to be discussed more fully later—inherit from each other. That set of occasions, dating from his first acquirement of the

---

[2] Cf. *The Fitness of the Environment*, New York, Macmillan, 1913, *The Order of Nature*, Harvard Univ. Press, 1917, and *Blood*, Harvard Univ. Press, 1928, Ch. 1, all† by Professor L. J. Henderson. These works are fundamental for any discussion of this subject.

[3] Also cf.† Part I, Ch. III, Sect. II.

[4] Cf. Part I, Ch. III, Sect. II.

Greek language and including all those occasions up to his loss of any adequate knowledge of that language, constitutes a society in reference to knowledge of the Greek language. Such knowledge is a common character-istic inherited from occasion to occasion along the historic route. This example has purposely been chosen for its reference to a somewhat trivial element of order, viz. knowledge of the Greek language; a more important character of order would have been that complex character in virtue of which a man is considered to be the same enduring person from birth to death. Also in this in- [138] stance the members of the society are arranged in a serial order by their genetic relations. Such a society is said [5] to possess 'personal order.'

Thus a society is, for each of its members, an environment with some element of order in it, persisting by reason of the genetic relations between its own members. Such an element of order is the order prevalent in the society.

But there is no society in isolation. Every society must be considered with its background of a wider environment of actual entities, which also contribute their objectifications to which the members of the society must conform. Thus the given contributions of the environment must at least be permissive of the self-sustenance of the society. Also, in proportion to its importance, this background must contribute those general characters which the more special character of the society presupposes for its mem-bers. But this means that the environment, together with the society in question, must form a larger society in respect to some more general characters than those defining the society from which we started. Thus we arrive at the principle that every society requires a social background, of which it is itself a part. In reference to any given society the world of actual entities is to be conceived as forming a background in layers of social order, the defining characteristics becoming wider and more general as we widen the background. Of course, the remote actualities of the background have their own specific characteristics of various types of social order. But such specific characteristics have become irrelevant for the society in question by reason of the inhibitions and attenuations introduced by discordance, that is to say, by disorder.

The metaphysical characteristics of an actual entity—in the proper gen-eral sense of 'metaphysics'—should be those which apply to all actual en-tities. It may be doubted whether such metaphysical concepts have ever [139] been formulated in their strict purity—even taking into account the most general principles of logic and of mathematics. We have to con-fine ourselves to societies sufficiently wide, and yet such that their defining characteristics cannot safely be ascribed to all actual entities which have been or may be.

The causal laws which dominate a social environment are the product

[5] Cf. Part I, Ch. III, Sect. II.

of the defining characteristic of that society. But the society is only efficient through its individual members. Thus in a society, the members can only exist by reason of the laws which dominate the society, and the laws only come into being by reason of the analogous characters of the members of the society.

But there is not any perfect attainment of an ideal order whereby the indefinite endurance of a society is secured. A society arises from disorder, where 'disorder' is defined by reference to the ideal for that society; the favourable background of a larger environment either itself decays, or ceases to favour the persistence of the society after some stage of growth: the society then ceases to reproduce its members, and finally after a stage of decay passes out of existence. Thus a system of 'laws' determining reproduction in some portion of the universe gradually rises into dominance; it has its stage of endurance, and passes out of existence with the decay of the society from which it emanates.

The arbitrary, as it were 'given,' elements in the laws of nature warn us that we are in a special cosmic epoch. Here the phrase 'cosmic epoch' is used to mean that widest society of actual entities whose immediate relevance to ourselves is traceable. This epoch is characterized by electronic and protonic actual entities, and by yet more ultimate actual entities which can be dimly discerned in the quanta of energy. Maxwell's equations of the electromagnetic field hold sway by reason of the throngs of electrons and of protons. Also each electron is a society of electronic occasions, and each proton is a soci- [140] ety of protonic occasions. These occasions are the reasons for the electromagnetic laws; but their capacity for reproduction, whereby each electron and each proton has a long life, and whereby new electrons and new protons come into being, is itself due to these same laws. But there is disorder in the sense that the laws are not perfectly obeyed, and that the reproduction is mingled with instances of failure. There is accordingly a gradual transition to new types of order, supervening upon a gradual rise into dominance on the part of the present natural laws.

But the arbitrary factors in the order of nature are not confined to the electromagnetic laws. There are the four dimensions of the spatio-temporal continuum, the geometrical axioms, even the mere dimensional character of the continuum—apart from the particular number of dimensions—and the fact of measurability. In later chapters (cf. Part IV) it will be evident that all these properties are additional to the more basic fact of extensiveness; also, that even extensiveness allows of grades of specialization, arbitrarily one way or another, antecedently to the introduction of any of these additional notions. By this discovery the logical and mathematical investigations of the last two centuries are very relevant to philosophy. For the cosmological theories of Descartes, Newton, Locke, Hume, and Kant were framed in ignorance of that fact. Indeed, in the *Timaeus* Plato seems to be more aware of it than any of his successors, in the sense that he frames statements whose meaning is elucidated by its explicit recognition. These 'given' factors in geometry point to the wider society of which the electronic cosmic epoch constitutes a fragment.

A society does not in any sense create the complex of eternal objects which constitutes its defining characteristic. It only elicits that complex into importance for its members, and secures the reproduction of its membership. In speaking of a society—unless the context ex- [141] pressly requires another interpretation—'membership' will always refer to the actual occasions, and not to subordinate enduring objects composed of actual occasions such as the life of an electron or of a man. These latter societies are the strands of 'personal' order which enter into many societies; generally speaking, whenever we are concerned with occupied space, we are dealing with this restricted type of corpuscular societies; and whenever we are thinking of the physical field in empty space, we are dealing with societies of the wider type. It seems as if the careers of waves of light illustrate the transition from the more restricted type to the wider type.

Thus our cosmic epoch is to be conceived primarily as a society of electromagnetic occasions, including electronic and protonic occasions, and only occasionally—for the sake of brevity in statement—as a society of electrons and protons. There is the same distinction between thinking of an army either as a class of men, or as a class of regiments.

SECTION III

Thus the physical relations, the geometrical relations of measurement, the dimensional relations, and the various grades of extensive relations, involved in the physical and geometrical theory of nature, are derivative from a series of societies of increasing width of prevalence, the more special societies being included in the wider societies. This situation constitutes the physical and geometrical order of nature. Beyond these societies there is disorder, where 'disorder' is a relative term expressing the lack of importance possessed by the defining characteristics of the societies in question beyond their own bounds. When those societies decay, it will not mean that their defining characteristics cease to exist; but that they lapse into unimportance for the actual entities in question. The term 'disorder' refers to a society only partially influential in impressing its characteristics in the [142] form of prevalent laws. This doctrine, that order is a social product, appears in modern science as the statistical theory of the laws of nature, and in the emphasis on genetic relation.

But there may evidently be a state in which there are no prevalent societies securing any congruent unity of effect. This is a state of chaotic disorder; it is disorder approaching an absolute sense of that term. In such an ideal state, what is 'given' for any actual entity is the outcome of thwarting, contrary decisions from the settled world. Chaotic disorder means lack of dominant definition of compatible contrasts in the satisfactions attained, and consequent enfeeblement of intensity. It means the lapse towards slighter actuality. It is a natural figure of speech, but only a figure of speech, to conceive a slighter actuality as being an approach towards nonentity. But you cannot approach nothing; for there is nothing to approach. It is an approach towards the futility of being a faint compromise between contrary reasons. The dominance of societies, harmoniously requiring each other, is the essential condition for depth of satisfaction.

The *Timaeus* of Plato, and the *Scholium* of Newton—the latter already in large part quoted—are the two statements of cosmological theory which have had the chief influence on Western thought. To the modern reader, the *Timaeus*, considered as a statement of scientific details, is in comparison with the *Scholium* simply foolish. But what it lacks in superficial detail, it makes up for by its philosophic depth. If it be read as an allegory, it conveys profound truth; whereas the *Scholium* is an immensely able statement of details which, although abstract and inadequate as a philosophy, can within certain limits be thoroughly trusted for the deduction of truths at the same level of abstraction as itself. The penalty of its philosophical deficiency is that the *Scholium* conveys no hint of the limits of its own application. The practical effect is that the readers, and almost certainly Newton himself, so construe its meaning as to fall into [143] what I have elsewhere [6] termed the 'fallacy of misplaced concreteness.' It is the office of metaphysics to determine the limits of the applicability of such abstract notions.

The *Scholium* betrays its abstractness by affording no hint of that aspect of self-production, of generation, of φύσις, of *natura naturans,* which is so prominent in nature. For the *Scholium*, nature is merely, and completely, *there*, externally designed and obedient. The full sweep of the modern doctrine of evolution would have confused the Newton of the *Scholium*, but would have enlightened the Plato of the *Timaeus*. So far as Newton is concerned, we have his own word for this statement. In a letter to Bentley, he writes: "When I wrote my treatise about our system, I had an eye upon such principles as might work with considering men for the belief of a Deity; . . ." [7] The concept in Newton's mind is that of a fully articulated system requiring a definite supernatural origin with that articulation. This is the form of the cosmological argument, now generally abandoned as invalid; because our notion of causation concerns the relations of states of things within the actual world, and can only be illegitimately extended to a transcendent derivation. The notion of God, which will be discussed later (cf. Part V), is that of an actual entity immanent in the actual world, but transcending any finite cosmic epoch—a being at once actual, eternal, immanent, and transcendent. The transcendence of

---

[6] Cf. *Science and the Modern World*, Ch. III.

[7] This quotation is taken from Jebb's *Life of Bentley*, Ch. II. The *Life* is published in the English Men of Letters series.

God is not peculiar to him. Every actual entity, in virtue of its novelty, transcends its universe, God included.

In the *Scholium*, space and time, with all their current mathematical properties, are ready-made for the material masses; the material masses are ready-made for the 'forces' which constitute their action and reaction; and space, and time, and material masses, and forces, are [144] alike ready-made for the initial motions which the Deity impresses throughout the universe. It is not possible to extract from the *Scholium*—construed with misplaced concreteness—either a theism, or an atheism, or an epistemology, which can survive a comparison with the facts. This is the inescapable conclusion to be inferred from Hume's *Dialogues Concerning Natural Religion*. Biology is also reduced to a mystery; and finally physics itself has now reached a stage of experimental knowledge inexplicable in terms of the categories of the *Scholium*.

In the *Timaeus*, there are many phrases and statements which find their final lucid expression in the *Scholium*. While noting this concurrence of the two great cosmological documents guiding Western thought, it cannot be too clearly understood that, within its limits of abstraction, what the *Scholium* says is true, and that it is expressed with the lucidity of genius. Thus any cosmological document which cannot be read as an interpretation of the *Scholium* is worthless. But there is another side to the *Timaeus* which finds no analogy in the *Scholium*. In general terms, this side of the *Timaeus* may be termed its metaphysical character, that is to say, its endeavour to connect the *behaviour* of things with the *formal nature* of things. The behaviour apart from the things is abstract, and so are the things apart from their behaviour. Newton—wisely, for his purposes—made this abstraction which the *Timaeus* endeavours to avoid.

In the first place, the *Timaeus* connects behaviour with the ultimate molecular characters of the actual entities. Plato conceives the notion of definite societies of actual molecular entities, each society with its defining characteristics. He does not conceive this assemblage of societies as *causa sui*. But he does conceive it as the work of subordinate deities, who are the animating principles of those departments of nature. In Greek thought, either poetic or philosophic, the separation between the φύσις and such deities had not that absolute character which it has for us who have inherited the Semitic Jehovah.

[145] Newton could have accepted a molecular theory as easily as Plato, but there is this difference between them: Newton would have been surprised at the modern quantum theory and at the dissolution of quanta into vibrations; Plato would have expected it. While we note the many things said by Plato in the *Timaeus* which are now foolishness, we must also give him credit for that aspect of his teaching in which he was two thousand years ahead of his time. Plato accounted for the sharp-cut differences between kinds of natural things, by assuming an approximation of the mole-

cules of the fundamental kinds respectively to the mathematical forms of the regular solids. He also assumed that certain qualitative contrasts in occurrences, such as that between musical notes, depended on the participation of these occurrences in some of the simpler ratios between integral numbers. He thus obtained a reason why there should be an approximation to sharp-cut differences between kinds of molecules, and why there should be sharp-cut relations of harmony standing out amid dissonance. Thus 'contrast'—as the opposite of incompatibility—depends on a certain simplicity of circumstance; but the higher contrasts depend on the assemblage of a multiplicity of lower contrasts, this assemblage again exhibiting higher types of simplicity.

It is well to remember that the modern quantum theory,‡ with its surprises in dealing with the atom, is only the latest instance of a well-marked character of nature, which in each particular instance is only explained by some *ad hoc* dogmatic assumption. The theory of biological evolution would not in itself lead us to expect the sharply distinguished genera and species which we find in nature. There might be an occasional bunching of individuals round certain typical forms; but there is no explanation of the almost complete absence of intermediate forms. Again Newton's *Scholium* gives no hint of the ninety-two possibilities for atoms, or of the limited number of ways in which atoms can be combined so as to form molecules. Physicists are now explaining these [146] chemical facts by means of conceptions which Plato would have welcomed.

There is another point in which the organic philosophy only repeats Plato. In the *Timaeus* the origin of the present cosmic epoch is traced back to an aboriginal disorder, chaotic according to our ideals. This is the evolutionary doctrine of the philosophy of organism. Plato's notion has puzzled critics who are obsessed with the Semitic [8] theory of a wholly transcendent God creating out of nothing an accidental universe. Newton held the Semitic theory. The *Scholium* made no provision for the evolution of matter—very naturally, since the topic lay outside its scope. The result has been that the non-evolution of matter has been a tacit presupposition throughout modern thought. Until the last few years the sole alternatives were: either the material universe, with its present type of order, is eternal; or else it came into being, and will pass out of being, according to the fiat of Jehovah. Thus, on all sides, Plato's allegory of the evolution of a new type of order based on new types of dominant societies became a daydream, puzzling to commentators.

Milton, curiously enough, in his *Paradise Lost* wavers between the *Timaeus* and the Semitic doctrine. This is only another instance of the intermixture of classical and Hebrew notions on which his charm of

[8] The book of Genesis is too primitive to bear upon this point.

thought depends. In the description of Satan's journey across Chaos, Satan discovers

> The secrets of the hoary deep, a dark
> Illimitable ocean, without bound,
> Without dimension, where length, breadth and highth,
> And time and place are lost; where eldest Night †
> And Chaos, ancestors of Nature, hold
> Eternal anarchy amidst the noise
> Of endless wars, and by confusion stand.[9]

Milton is here performing for Plato the same poetic service that Lucretius performed for Democritus—with [147] less justification, since Plato was quite capable of being his own poet. Also the fact of Satan's journey helped to evolve order; for he left a permanent track, useful for the devils and the damned.

The appeal to Plato in this section has been an appeal to the facts against the modes of expression prevalent in the last few centuries. These recent modes of expression are partly the outcome of a mixture of theology and philosophy, and are partly due to the Newtonian physics, no longer accepted as a fundamental statement. But language and thought have been framed according to that mould; and it is necessary to remind ourselves that this is not the way in which the world has been described by some of the greatest intellects. Both for Plato and for Aristotle the process of the actual world has been conceived as a real incoming of forms into real potentiality, issuing into that real togetherness which is an actual thing. Also, for the *Timaeus*, the creation of the world is the incoming of a type of order establishing a cosmic epoch. It is not the beginning of matter of fact, but the incoming of a certain type of social order.

SECTION IV

The remainder of this chapter will be devoted to a discussion—largely conjectural—of the hierarchy of societies composing our present epoch. In this way, the preceding discussion of 'order' may be elucidated. It is to be carefully noted that we are now deserting metaphysical generality. We shall be considering the more special possibilities of explanation consistent with our general cosmological doctrine, but not necessitated by it.

The physical world is bound together by a general type of relatedness which constitutes it into an extensive continuum. When we analyse the properties of this continuum we discover that they fall into two classes, of which one—the more special—presupposes the other—the more general.[10] The more general type of properties [148] expresses the mere fact of 'extensive connection,' of 'whole and part,' of various types of 'geometrical

[9] *Paradise Lost*, Bk. II.
[10] Cf. Part IV for a detailed discussion.

elements' derivable by 'extensive abstraction'; but excluding the introduction of more special properties by which straight lines are definable [11] and measurability thereby introduced.

In these general properties of extensive connection, we discern the defining characteristic of a vast nexus extending far beyond our immediate cosmic epoch. It contains in itself other epochs, with more particular characteristics incompatible with each other. Then from the standpoint of our present epoch, the fundamental society in so far as it transcends our own epoch seems a vast confusion mitigated by the few, faint elements of order contained in its own defining characteristic of 'extensive connection.' We cannot discriminate its other epochs of vigorous order, and we merely conceive it as harbouring the faint flush of the dawn of order in our own epoch. This ultimate, vast society constitutes the whole environment within which our epoch is set, so far as systematic characteristics are discernible by us in our present stage of development. In the future the growth of theory may endow our successors with keener powers of discernment.

Our logical analysis, in company with immediate intuition (*inspectio*), enables us to discern a more special society within the society of pure extension. This is the 'geometrical' society. In this society [12] those specialized relationships hold, in virtue of which straight lines are defined. Systematic geometry is illustrated in such a geometrical society; and metrical relationships can be defined in terms of the analogies of function within the scheme of any one systematic geometry. These 'analogies of function' are what is meant by the notion of 'congruence.' This notion is nonsense apart from a systematic geometry. The inclusion of *extensive quantity* [149] among fundamental categoreal notions is a complete mistake. This notion is definable in terms of each systematic geometry finding its application in a geometrical society. It is to be noticed that a systematic geometry is determined by the definition of straight lines applicable to the society in question. Contrary to the general opinion, this definition is possible in independence of the notion of 'measurement.' It cannot however be proved that in the same geometrical society there may not be competing families of loci with equal claims to the status of being a complete family of straight lines.

Given a family of straight lines, expressing a system of relatedness in a 'geometric' society, the notion of 'congruence' and thence of 'measurement' is now determinable in a systematic way throughout the society. But again in this case there certainly are competing systems of measurement. Hence in connection with *each* family of straight lines—allowing there be more than one such family—there are alternative systems [13] of *metrical* geom-

---

[11] Cf. Part IV, Chs.† III, IV, V.

[12] Cf. Part IV, especially Chs. III, IV, V.

[13] The existence of alternative systems was demonstrated by Cayley in his "Sixth Memoir on Quantics" in *Transactions of the Royal Society*, 1859.†

etry, no one system being more fundamental than the other. Our present cosmic epoch is formed by an 'electromagnetic' society, which is a more special society contained within the geometric society. In this society yet more special defining characteristics obtain. These characteristics presuppose those of the two wider societies within which the 'electromagnetic' society is contained. But in the 'electromagnetic' society the ambiguity as to the relative importance of competing families of straight lines (if there be such competing families), and the ambiguity as to the relative importance of competing definitions of congruence, are determined in favour of one family and one [14] congruence-definition. This determination is effected by an additional set of physical relationships throughout the society. But this set has lost [150] its merely systematic character because it constitutes our neighbourhood. These relationships involve components expressive of certain individual diversities, and identities between the occasions which are the members of the nexus. But these diversities and identities are correlated according to a systematic law expressible in terms of the systematic measurements derived from the geometric nexus. We here arrive at the notion of physical quantities which vary from individual to individual; this is the notion of the systematization of individual differences, the notion of 'Law.'

It is the ideal of mathematical physicists to formulate this systematic law in its complete generality for our epoch. It is sufficient for our purposes to indicate the presumed character of this law by naming the members of the society 'electromagnetic occasions.' Thus our present epoch is dominated by a society of electromagnetic occasions. In so far as this dominance approaches completeness, the systematic law which physics seeks is absolutely dominant. In so far as the dominance is incomplete, the obedience is a statistical fact with its corresponding lapses.

The electromagnetic society exhibits the physical electromagnetic field which is the topic of physical science. The members of this nexus are the electromagnetic occasions.

But in its turn, this electromagnetic society would provide no adequate order for the production of individual occasions realizing peculiar 'intensities' of experience unless it were pervaded by more special societies, vehicles of such order. The physical world exhibits a bewildering complexity of such societies, favouring each other, competing with each other.

The most general examples of such societies are the regular trains of waves, individual electrons, protons, individual molecules, societies of molecules such as inorganic bodies, living cells, and societies of cells such as vegetable and animal bodies.

---

[14] The transformations into an indefinite variety of coordinates, to which the 'tensor theory' refers, all presuppose one congruence-definition.† The invariance of the Einsteinian 'ds' expresses this fact.

SECTION V

[151] It is obvious that the simple classification (cf. Part I, Ch. III, Sect. II) of societies into 'enduring objects,' 'corpuscular societies,' and 'non-corpuscular societies' requires amplification. The notion of a society which includes subordinate societies and nexūs with a definite pattern of structural inter-relations† must be introduced. Such societies will be termed 'structured.'

A structured society as a whole provides a favourable environment for the subordinate societies which it harbours within itself. Also the whole society must be set in a wider environment permissive of its continuance. Some of the component groups of occasions in a structured society can be termed 'subordinate societies.' But other such groups must be given the wider designation of 'subordinate nexūs.' The distinction arises because in some instances a group of occasions, such as, for example, a particular enduring entity, could have retained the dominant features of its defining characteristic in the general environment, apart from the structured society. It would have lost some features; in other words, the analogous sort of enduring entity in the general environment is, in its mode of definiteness, not quite identical with the enduring entity within the structured environment. But, abstracting such additional details from the generalized defining characteristic, the enduring object with that generalized characteristic may be conceived as independent of the structured society within which it finds itself.† For example, we speak of a molecule within a living cell, because its general molecular features are independent of the environment of the cell. Thus a molecule is a subordinate society in the structured society which we call the 'living cell.'

But there may be other nexūs included in a structured society which, excepting the general systematic characteristics of the external environment, present no features capable of genetically sustaining themselves apart from [152] the special environment provided by that structured society. It is misleading, therefore, to term such a nexus a 'society' when it is being considered in abstraction from the whole structured society. In such an abstraction it can be assigned no 'social' features. Recurring to the example of a living cell, it will be argued that the occasions composing the 'empty' space within the cell exhibit special features which analogous occasions outside the cell are devoid of. Thus the nexus, which is the empty space within a living cell, is called a 'subordinate nexus,' but not a 'subordinate society.'

Molecules are structured societies, and so in all probability are separate electrons and protons. Crystals are structured societies. But gases are not structured societies in any important sense of that term; although their individual molecules are structured societies.

It must be remembered that each individual occasion within a special form of society includes features which do not occur in analogous occasions in the external environment. The first stage of systematic investigation must always be the identification of analogies between occasions within the society and occasions without it. The second stage is constituted by the more subtle procedure of noting the differences between behaviour within and without the society, differences† of behaviour exhibited by occasions which also have close analogies to each other. The history of science is marked by the vehement, dogmatic denial of such differences, until they are found out.

An obvious instance of such distinction of behaviour is afforded by the notion of the deformation of the shape of an electron according to variations in its physical situation.

A 'structured society' may be more or less 'complex' in respect to the multiplicity of its associated sub-societies and sub-nexūs and to the intricacy of their structural pattern.

A structured society which is highly complex can be [153] correspondingly favourable to intensity of satisfaction for certain sets of its component members. This intensity arises by reason of the ordered complexity of the contrasts which the society stages for these components.†

The structural relations gather intensity from this intensity in the individual experiences. Thus the growth of a complex structured society exemplifies the general purpose pervading nature. The mere complexity of givenness which procures incompatibilities has been superseded by the complexity of order which procures contrasts.

SECTION VI

The doctrine that every society requires a wider social environment leads to the distinction that a society may be more or less 'stabilized' in reference to certain sorts of changes in that environment. A society is 'stabilized' in reference to a species of change when it can persist through an environment whose relevant parts exhibit that sort of change. If the society would cease to persist through an environment with that sort of heterogeneity, then the society is in that respect 'unstable.' A complex society which is stable provided that the environment exhibits certain features† is said to be 'specialized' in respect to those features. The notion of 'specialization' seems to include both that of 'complexity' and that of strictly conditioned 'stability.'

An unspecialized society can survive through important changes in its environment. This means that it can take on different functions in respect to its relationship to a changing environment. In general the defining characteristic of such a society will not include any particular determination of structural pattern. By reason of this flexibility of structural pattern, the society can adopt that special pattern adapted to the circumstances of the moment. Thus an unspecialized society is apt to be deficient in structural pattern, when viewed as a whole.

[154] Thus in general an unspecialized society does not secure conditions favourable for intensity of satisfaction among its members, whereas† a structured society with a high grade of complexity will in general be deficient in survival value. In other words, such societies will in general be 'specialized' in the sense of requiring a very special sort of environment.

Thus the problem† for Nature is the production of societies which are 'structured' with a high 'complexity,' and which are at the same time 'unspecialized.' In this way, intensity is mated with survival.

SECTION VII

There are two ways in which structured societies have solved this problem. Both ways depend on that enhancement of the mental pole, which is a factor in intensity of experience. One way is by eliciting a massive average objectification of a nexus, while eliminating the detailed diversities of the various members of the nexus in question. This method, in fact, employs the device of blocking out unwelcome detail. It depends on the fundamental truth that objectification is abstraction. It utilizes this abstraction inherent in objectification so as to dismiss the thwarting elements of a nexus into negative prehensions. At the same time the complex intensity in the structured society is supported by the massive objectifications of the many environmental nexūs, each in its unity as *one* nexus, and not in its multiplicity as *many* actual occasions.

This mode of solution requires the intervention of mentality operating in accordance with the Category of Transmutation (i.e., Categoreal Obligation VI). It ignores diversity of detail by overwhelming the nexus by means of some congenial uniformity which pervades it. The environment may then change indefinitely so far as concerns the ignored details—so long as they can be ignored.

The close association of all physical bodies, organic and [155] inorganic alike, with 'presented loci' definable [15] by straight lines, suggests that this development of mentality is characteristic of the actual occasions which make up the structured societies which we know as 'material bodies.' This close association is evidenced by the importance of 'acceleration' in the science of dynamics.† For 'acceleration' is nothing else than a mode of estimating the shift from one family of 'presented loci' to another such family (cf. Part IV).

Such mentality represents the first grade of ascent beyond the mere reproductive stage which employs nothing more than the Category of Conceptual Reproduction (i.e., Categoreal Obligation IV). There is some initiative of conceptual integration, but no originality in conceptual prehension. This initiative belongs to the Category of Transmutation, and the excluded originality belongs to the Category of Reversion.

[15] Cf. Ch. IV of this Part† and also Part IV.

These material bodies belong to the lowest grade of structured societies which are obvious to our gross apprehensions. They comprise societies of various types of complexity—crystals, rocks, planets, and suns. Such bodies are easily the most long-lived of the structured societies known to us, capable of being traced through their individual life-histories.

The second way of solving the problem is by an initiative in conceptual prehensions, i.e., in appetition. The purpose of this initiative is to receive the novel elements of the environment into explicit feelings with such subjective forms as conciliate them with the complex experiences proper to members of the structured society. Thus in each concrescent occasion its subjective aim originates novelty to match the novelty of the environment.

In the case of the higher organisms, this conceptual initiative amounts to *thinking* about the diverse experiences; in the case of lower organisms,† this conceptual initiative merely amounts to thoughtless adjustment of aesthetic emphasis in obedience to an ideal of harmony. [156] In either case the creative determination which transcends the occasion in question has been deflected by an impulse original to that occasion. This deflection in general originates a self-preservative reaction throughout the whole society. It may be unfortunate or inadequate; and in the case of persistent failure we are in the province of pathology.

This second mode of solution also presupposes the former mode. Thus the Categories of Conceptual Reversion and of Transmutation are both called into play.

Structured societies in which the second mode of solution has importance are termed 'living.' It is obvious that a structured society may have more or less 'life,' and that there is no absolute gap between 'living' and 'non-living' societies. For certain purposes, whatever 'life' there is in a society may be important; and for other purposes, unimportant.

A structured society in which the second mode is unimportant, and the first mode is important will be termed 'inorganic.'

In accordance with this doctrine of 'life,' the primary meaning of 'life' is the origination of conceptual novelty—novelty of appetition. Such origination can only occur in accordance with the Category of Reversion. Thus a society is only to be termed 'living' in a derivative sense. A 'living society' is one which includes some 'living occasions.' Thus a society may be more or less 'living,' according to the prevalence in it of living occasions. Also an occasion may be more or less living according to the relative importance of the novel factors in its final satisfaction.

Thus the two ways in which dominant members of structured societies secure stability amid environmental novelties are (i) elimination of diversities of detail, and (ii) origination of novelties of conceptual reaction. As the result, there is withdrawal or addition of those details of emphasis whereby the subjective aim directs the [157] integration of prehensions in the concrescent phases of dominant members.

SECTION VIII

There is yet another factor in 'living' societies which requires more detached analysis. A structured society consists in the patterned intertwining of various nexūs with markedly diverse defining characteristics. Some of these nexūs are of lower types than others, and some will be of markedly higher types. There will be the 'subservient' nexūs and the 'regnant' nexūs within the same structured society. This structured society will provide the immediate environment which sustains each of its sub-societies, subservient and regnant alike. In a living society only some of its nexūs will be such that the mental poles of all their members have any *original* reactions. These will be its 'entirely living' nexūs, and in practice a society is only called 'living' when such nexūs are regnant. Thus a living society involves nexūs which are 'inorganic,' and nexūs which are inorganic do not need the protection of the whole 'living' society for their survival in a changing external‡ environment. Such nexūs are societies. But 'entirely living' nexūs do require such protection, if they are to survive. According to this conjectural theory, an 'entirely living' nexus is not a 'society.' This is the theory of the animal body, including a unicellular body as a particular instance. A complex inorganic system of interaction is built up for the protection of the 'entirely living' nexūs, and the originative actions of the living elements are protective of the whole system. On the other hand, the reactions† of the whole system provide the intimate environment required by the 'entirely living' nexūs. We do not know of any living society devoid of its subservient apparatus of inorganic societies.

'Physical Physiology' deals with the subservient inorganic apparatus; and 'Psychological Physiology' seeks to deal with 'entirely living' nexūs, partly in abstraction [158] from the inorganic apparatus, and partly in respect to their response to the inorganic apparatus, and partly in regard to their response to each other. Physical Physiology has, in the last century, established itself as a unified science; Psychological Physiology is still in the process of incubation.

It must be remembered that an integral living society, as we know it, not only includes the subservient inorganic apparatus, but also includes many living nexūs,† at least one for each 'cell.'

SECTION IX

It will throw light upon the cosmology of the philosophy of organism to conjecture some fundamental principles of Psychological Physiology as suggested by that cosmology and by the preceding conjectures concerning the 'societies' of our epoch. These principles are not necessitated by this cosmology; but they seem to be the simplest principles which are both consonant with that cosmology, and also fit the facts.

In the first instance, consider a single living cell. Such a cell includes subservient inorganic societies, such as molecules and electrons. Thus, the cell is an 'animal body'; and we must presuppose the 'physical physiology' proper to this instance. But what of the individual living occasions?

The first question to be asked is as to whether the living occasions, in abstraction from the inorganic occasions of the animal body, form a corpuscular sub-society, so that each living occasion is a member of an enduring entity with its personal order. In particular we may ask whether this corpuscular society reduces to the extreme instance of such a society, namely, to one enduring entity with its one personal order.†

The evidence before us is of course extremely slight; but so far as it goes, it suggests a negative answer to both these questions. A cell gives no evidence whatever of a single unified mentality, guided in each of its occa-
[159] sions by inheritance from its own past. The problem to be solved is that of a certain originality in the response of a cell to external stimulus. The theory of an enduring entity with its inherited mentality gives us a reason why this mentality should be swayed by its own past. We ask for something original at the moment, and we are provided with a reason for limiting originality. Life is a bid for freedom: an enduring entity binds any one of its occasions to the line of its ancestry. The doctrine of the enduring soul with its permanent characteristics is exactly the irrelevant answer to the problem which life presents. That problem is, How can there be originality? And the answer explains how the soul need be no more original than a stone.

The theory of a corpuscular society, made up of many enduring entities, fits the evidence no better. The same objections apply. The root fact is that 'endurance' is a device whereby an occasion is peculiarly bound by a single line of physical ancestry, while 'life' means novelty, introduced in accordance with the Category of Conceptual Reversion. There are the same objections to *many* traditions as there are to *one* tradition. What has to be explained is originality of response to stimulus. This amounts to the doctrine that an organism is 'alive' when in some measure its reactions are inexplicable by *any* tradition of pure physical inheritance.

Explanation by 'tradition' is merely another phraseology for explanation by 'efficient cause.' We require explanation by 'final cause.' Thus a single occasion is alive when the subjective aim which determines its process of concrescence has introduced a novelty of definiteness not to be found in the inherited data of its primary phase. The novelty is introduced conceptually and disturbs the inherited 'responsive' adjustment of subjective forms. It alters the 'values,' in the artist's sense of that term.

It follows from these considerations that in abstraction from its animal body an 'entirely living' nexus is not [160] properly a society at all, since 'life' cannot be a defining characteristic. It is the name for originality, and not for tradition. The mere response to stimulus is characteristic of all societies whether inorganic or alive. Action and reaction are bound together. The characteristic of life is reaction adapted to the capture of intensity, under a large variety of circumstances. But the reaction is dictated by the present and not by the past. It is the clutch at vivid immediacy.

SECTION X

Another characteristic of a living society is that it requires food. In a museum the crystals are kept under glass cases; in zoological gardens the animals are fed. Having regard to the universality of reactions with environment, the distinction is not quite absolute. It cannot, however, be ignored. The crystals are not agencies requiring the destruction of elaborate societies derived from the environment; a living society is such an agency. The societies which it destroys are its food. This food is destroyed by dissolving it into somewhat simpler social elements. It has been robbed of something. Thus, all societies require interplay with their environment; and in the case of living societies this interplay takes the form of robbery. The living society may, or may not, be a higher type of organism than the food which it disintegrates. But whether or no it be for the general good, life is robbery. It is at this point that with life morals become acute. The robber requires justification.

The primordial appetitions which jointly constitute God's purpose are seeking intensity, and not preservation. Because they are primordial, there is nothing to preserve. He, in his primordial nature, is unmoved by love for this particular, or that particular; for in this foundational process of creativity, there are no preconstituted particulars. In the foundations of his being, God is indifferent alike to preservation and to novelty. [161] He cares not whether an immediate occasion be old or new, so far as concerns derivation from its ancestry. His aim [16] for it is depth of satisfaction as an intermediate step towards the fulfilment of his own being. His tenderness is directed towards each actual occasion, as it arises.

Thus God's purpose in the creative advance is the evocation of intensities. The evocation of societies is purely subsidiary to this absolute end. The characteristic of a living society is that a complex structure of inorganic societies is woven together for the production of a non-social nexus characterized by the intense physical experiences of its members. But such an experience is derivate from the complex order of the material animal body, and not from the simple 'personal order' of past occasions with analogous experience. There is intense experience without the shackle of reiteration from the past. This is the condition for spontaneity of conceptual reaction. The conclusion to be drawn from this argument is that life is a characteristic of 'empty space' and not of space 'occupied' by any corpuscular society. In a nexus of living occasions, there is a certain social deficiency. Life lurks in the interstices of each living cell, and in the in-

[16] Cf. Part V.

terstices of the brain. In the history of a living society, its more vivid manifestations wander to whatever quarter is receiving from the animal body an enormous variety of physical experience. This experience, if treated inorganically, must be reduced to compatibility by the normal adjustments of mere responsive reception. This means the dismissal of incompatible elements into negative prehensions.

The complexity of the animal body is so ordered that in the critical portions of its interstices the varied datum of physical experience is complex, and on the edge of a compatibility beyond that to be achieved by mere inorganic treatment. A novel conceptual prehension disturbs [162] the subjective forms of the initial responsive phase. Some negative prehensions are thus avoided, and higher contrasts are introduced into experience.

So far as the functioning of the animal body is concerned, the total result is that the transmission of physical influence, through the empty space within it, has not been entirely in conformity with the physical laws holding for inorganic societies. The molecules within an animal body exhibit certain peculiarities of behaviour not to be detected outside an animal body. In fact, living societies illustrate the doctrine that the laws of nature develop together with societies which constitute an epoch. There are statistical expressions of the prevalent types of interaction. In a living cell, the statistical balance has been disturbed.

The connection of 'food' with 'life' is now evident. The highly complex inorganic societies required for the structure of a cell, or other living body, lose their stability amid the diversity of the environment. But, in the physical field of empty space produced by the originality of living occasions, chemical dissociations and associations take place which would not otherwise occur. The structure is breaking down and being repaired. The food is that supply of highly complex societies from the outside which, under the influence of life, will enter into the necessary associations to repair the waste. Thus life acts as though it were a catalytic agent.

The short summary of this account of a living cell is as follows: (i) an extremely complex and delicately poised chemical structure; (ii) for the occasions in the interstitial† 'empty' space a complex objective datum derived from this complex structure; (iii) under normal 'responsive' treatment, devoid of originality, the complex detail reduced to physical simplicity by negative prehensions; (iv) this detail preserved for positive feeling by the emotional and purposive readjustments produced by originality of conceptual feeling (appetition); (v) the physical distortion of the field, leading to instability of [163] the structure; (vi) the structure accepting repair by food from the environment.

SECTION XI

The complexity of nature is inexhaustible. So far we have argued that the nature of life is not to be sought by its identification with some society of occasions, which are living in virtue of the defining characteristic of that society. An 'entirely living' nexus is, in respect to its life, not social. Each member of the nexus derives the necessities of its being from its prehensions of its complex social environment; by itself the nexus lacks the genetic power which belongs to 'societies.' But a living nexus, though non-social in virtue of its 'life,' may support a thread of personal order along some historical route of its members. Such an enduring entity is a 'living person.' It is not of the essence of life to be a living person. Indeed a living person requires that its immediate environment be a living, non-social nexus.

The defining characteristic of a living person is some definite type of hybrid prehensions transmitted from occasion to occasion of its existence. The term 'hybrid' is defined more particularly in Part III. It is sufficient to state here that a 'hybrid' prehension is the prehension by one subject of a conceptual prehension, or of an 'impure' prehension, belonging to the mentality of another subject. By this transmission the mental originality of the living occasions receives a character and a depth. In this way originality is both 'canalized'—to use Bergson's word—and intensified. Its range is widened within limits. Apart from canalization, depth of originality would spell disaster for the animal body. With it, personal mentality can be evolved, so as to combine its individual originality with the safety of the material organism on which it depends. Thus life turns back into society: it binds originality within bounds, and gains the massiveness due to reiterated character.

In the case of single cells, of vegetation, and of the [164] lower forms of animal life, we have no ground for conjecturing living personality. But in the case of the higher animals there is central direction, which suggests that in their case each animal body harbours a living person, or living persons. Our own self-consciousness is direct awareness of ourselves as such persons.[17] There are limits to such unified control, which indicate dissociation of personality, multiple personalities in successive alternations, and even multiple personalities in joint possession. This last case belongs to the pathology of religion, and in primitive times has been interpreted as demoniac possession. Thus, though life in its essence is the gain of intensity through freedom, yet it can also submit to canalization and so gain the massiveness of order. But it is not necessary merely to presuppose the drastic case of personal order. We may conjecture, though without much evidence, that even in the lowest form of life the entirely living nexus is canalized into some faint form of mutual conformity. Such conformity amounts to social order depending on hybrid prehensions of originalities in the mental poles of the antecedent members of the nexus. The survival power, arising from adaptation and regeneration, is thus explained. Thus life is a passage from physical order to pure mental originality, and from

[17] This account of a living personality requires completion by reference to its objectification in the consequent nature of God. Cf. Part V, Ch. II.

pure mental originality to canalized mental originality. It must also be noted that the pure mental originality works by the canalization of relevance arising from the primordial nature of God. Thus an originality in the temporal world is conditioned, though not determined, by an initial subjective aim supplied by the ground of all order and of all originality.

Finally, we have to consider the type of structured‡ society which gives rise to the traditional body-mind problem. For example, human mentality is partly the outcome of the human body, partly the single directive [165] agency of the body, partly a system of cogitations which have a certain irrelevance to the physical relationships of the body. The Cartesian philosophy is based upon the seeming fact—the plain fact—of one body and one mind, which are two substances in causal‡ association. For the philosophy of organism the problem is transformed.

Each actuality is essentially bipolar, physical and mental, and the physical inheritance is essentially accompanied by a conceptual reaction partly conformed to it, and partly introductory of a‡ relevant novel contrast, but always introducing emphasis, valuation, and purpose. The integration of the physical and mental side into a unity of experience is a self-formation which is a process of concrescence, and which by the principle of objective immortality characterizes the creativity which transcends it. So though mentality is non-spatial, mentality is always a reaction from, and integration with, physical experience which is spatial. It is obvious that we must not demand another mentality presiding over these other actualities (a kind of Uncle Sam, over and above all the U.S. citizens). All the life in the body is the life of the individual cells. There are thus millions upon millions of centres of life in each animal body. So what needs to be explained is not dissociation of personality but unifying control, by reason of which we not only have unified behaviour, which can be observed by others, but also consciousness of a unified experience.

A good many actions do not seem to be due to the unifying control, e.g., with proper stimulants a heart can be made to go on beating after it has been taken out of the body. There are centres of reaction and control which cannot be identified with the centre of experience. This is still more so with insects. For example, worms and jellyfish seem to be merely harmonized cells, very little centralized; when cut in two, their parts go on performing their functions independently. Through a series of animals we can trace a progressive rise into a [166] centrality of control. Insects have some central control; even in man, many of the body's actions are done with some independence, but with an organ of central control of very high-grade character in the brain.

The state of things, according to the philosophy of organism, is very different from the Scholastic view of St. Thomas Aquinas, of the mind as informing the body. The living body is a coordination of high-grade actual occasions; but in a living body of a low type the occasions are much nearer to a democracy. In a living body of a high type there are grades of occasions so coordinated by their paths of inheritance through the body, that a peculiar richness of inheritance is enjoyed by various occasions in some parts of the body. Finally, the brain is coordinated so that a peculiar richness of inheritance is enjoyed now by this and now by that part; and thus there is produced the presiding personality at that moment in the body. Owing to the delicate organization of the body, there is a returned influence, an inheritance of character derived from the presiding occasion and modifying the subsequent occasions through the rest of the body.

We must remember the extreme generality of the notion of an enduring object—a genetic character inherited through a historic route of actual occasions. Some kinds of enduring objects form material bodies, others do not. But just as the difference between living and non-living occasions is not sharp, but more or less, so the distinction between an enduring object which is an atomic material body and one which is not† is again more or less. Thus the question as to whether to call an enduring object a transition of matter or of character is very much a verbal question as to where you draw the line between the various properties (cf. the way in which the distinction between matter and radiant energy has now vanished).

Thus in an animal body the presiding occasion, if there be one, is the final node, or intersection, of a complex [167] structure of many enduring objects. Such a structure pervades the human body. The harmonized relations of the parts of the body constitute this wealth of inheritance into a harmony of contrasts, issuing into intensity of experience. The inhibitions of opposites have been adjusted into the contrasts of opposites. The human mind is thus conscious of its bodily† inheritance. There is also an enduring object formed by the inheritance from presiding occasion to presiding occasion. This endurance of the mind is only one more example of the general principle on which the body is constructed. This route of presiding occasions probably wanders from part to part of the brain, dissociated from the physical material atoms. But central personal dominance is only partial, and in pathological cases is apt to vanish.

CHAPTER IV
ORGANISMS AND ENVIRONMENT

SECTION I

[168] So far the discussion has chiefly concentrated upon the discrimination of the modes of functioning which in germ, or in mere capacity, are represented in the constitution of each actual entity. The presumption that there is only one genus of actual entities constitutes an ideal of cosmological theory to which the philosophy of organism endeavours to conform. The description of the generic character of an actual entity should include God, as well as the lowliest actual occasion, though there is a specific difference between the nature of God and that of any occasion.

Also the differences between actual occasions, arising from the characters of their data, and from the narrowness and widths of their feelings, and from the comparative importance of various stages, enable a classification to be made whereby these occasions are gathered into various types. From the metaphysical standpoint these types are not to be sharply discriminated; as a matter of empirical observation, the occasions do seem to fall into fairly distinct classes.

The character of an actual entity is finally governed by its datum; whatever be the freedom of feeling arising in the concrescence, there can be no transgression of the limitations of capacity inherent in the datum. The datum both limits and supplies. It follows from this doctrine that the character of an organism depends on that of its environment. But the character of an environment is the sum of the characters of the various societies of actual entities which jointly constitute that envi- [169] ronment; although it is pure assumption that every environment is completely overrun by societies of entities. Spread through the environment there may be many entities which cannot be assigned to any society of entities. The societies in an environment will constitute its orderly element, and the non-social actual entities will constitute its element of chaos. There is no reason, so far as our knowledge is concerned, to conceive the actual world as purely orderly, or as purely chaotic.

Apart from the reiteration gained from its societies, an environment does not provide the massiveness of emphasis capable of dismissing its contrary elements into negative prehensions. Any ideal of depth of satisfaction, arising from the combination of narrowness and width, can only be achieved through adequate order. In proportion to the chaos there is triviality. There are different types of order; and it is not true that in proportion to the orderliness there is depth. There are various types of order, and some of them provide more trivial satisfaction than do others. Thus, if there is to be progress beyond limited ideals, the course of history by way of escape must venture along the borders of chaos in its substitution of higher for lower types of order.

The immanence of God gives reason for the belief that pure chaos is intrinsically impossible. At the other end of the scale, the immensity of the world negatives the belief that any state of order can be so established that beyond it there can be no progress. This belief in a final order, popular in religious and philosophic thought, seems to be due to the prevalent fallacy that all types of seriality necessarily involve terminal instances. It follows that Tennyson's phrase,

no Divine satisfaction?

> . . . one† far-off divine event
> To which the whole creation moves,

presents a fallacious conception of the universe.

An actual entity must be classified in respect to its [170] 'satisfaction,' and this arises out of its datum by the operations constituting its 'process.' Satisfactions can be classified by reference to 'triviality,' 'vagueness,' 'narrowness,' 'width.' Triviality and vagueness are characteristics in the satisfaction which have their origins respectively in opposed characteristics in the datum. Triviality arises from lack of coordination in the factors of the datum, so that no feeling arising from one factor is reinforced by any feeling arising from another factor. In other words, the specific constitution of the actual entity in question is not such as to elicit depth of feeling from contrasts thus presented. Incompatibility has predominated over contrast. Then the process can involve no coordinating intensification either from a reinforced narrowness, or from enhancement of relevance due to the higher contrasts derived from harmonized width. Triviality is due to the wrong sort of width; that is to say, it is due to width without any reinforced narrowness in its higher categories. Harmony is this combination of width and narrowness. Some narrow concentration on a limited set of effects is essential for depth; but the difference arises in the levels of the categories of contrast involved. A high category involves unplumbed potentiality for the realization of depth in its lower components. Thus 'triviality' arises from excess of incompatible differentiation.

On the other hand, 'vagueness' is due to excess of identification. In the datum the objectifications of various actual entities are replicas with faint coordinations of perspective contrast. Under these conditions the contrasts between the various objectifications are faint, and there is deficiency in supplementary feeling discriminating the objects from each other. There can thus be intensive narrowness in the prehension of the whole nexus, by reason of the common character,† combined with vagueness, which is the irrelevance of the differences between the definite actual entities of the nexus. The objectified entities reinforce each other by their likeness. But there [171] is lack of differentiation among the component objectifications owing to the deficiency in relevant contrasts.

In this way a group of actual entities contributes to the satisfaction as one extensive whole. It is divisible, but the actual divisions, and their sporadic differences of character, have sunk into comparative irrelevance beside the one character belonging to the whole and any of its parts.

By reason of vagueness, many count as one, and are subject to indefinite possibilities of division into such multifold unities. When there is such vague prehension, the differences between the actual entities so prehended are faint chaotic factors in the environment, and have thereby been relegated to irrelevance. Thus vagueness is an essential condition for the narrowness which is one condition for depth of relevance. It enables a background to contribute its relevant quota, and it enables a social group in the foreground to gain concentrated relevance for its community of character. The right chaos, and the right vagueness, are jointly required for any effective harmony. They produce the massive simplicity which has been expressed by the term 'narrowness.' Thus chaos is not to be identified with evil; for harmony requires the due coordination of chaos, vagueness, narrowness, and width.

According to this account, the background in which the environment is set must be discriminated into two layers. There is first the relevant background, providing a massive systematic uniformity. This background is the presupposed world to which all ordinary propositions refer. Secondly, there is the more remote chaotic background which has merely an irrelevant triviality, so far as concerns direct objectification in the actual entity in question. This background represents those entities in the actual world with such perspective remoteness that there is even a chaos of diverse cosmic epochs. In the background there is triviality, vagueness, and massive uniformity; in the foreground discrimination and [172] contrasts, but always negative prehensions of irrelevant diversities.

SECTION II

Intensity is the reward of narrowness. The domination of the environment by a few social groups is the factor producing both the vagueness of discrimination between actual entities and the intensification of relevance of common characteristics. These are the two requisites for narrowness. The lower organisms have low-grade types of narrowness; the higher organisms have intensified contrasts in the higher categories. In describing the capacities, realized or unrealized, of an actual occasion, we have, with Locke, tacitly taken human experience as an example upon which to found the generalized description required for metaphysics. But when we turn to the lower organisms we have first to determine which among such capacities fade from realization into irrelevance, that is to say, by comparison with human experience which is our standard.

In any metaphysical scheme founded upon the Kantian or Hegelian traditions, experience is the product of operations which lie among the higher of the human modes of functioning. For such schemes, ordered experience is the result of schematization of modes of *thought*, concerning causation, substance, quality, quantity.

The process by which experiential unity is attained† is thereby conceived in the guise of modes of thought. The exception is to be found in Kant's preliminary sections on 'Transcendental Aesthetic,' by which he provides space and time. But Kant, following Hume, assumes the radical disconnection of impressions *qua data*; and therefore conceives his transcendental aesthetic‡ to be the mere description of a subjective process appropriating the data by orderliness of feeling.

The philosophy of organism aspires to construct a critique of pure feeling, in the philosophical position in [173] which Kant put his *Critique of Pure Reason*. This should also supersede the remaining *Critiques* required in the Kantian philosophy. Thus in the organic philosophy Kant's 'Transcendental Aesthetic' becomes a distorted fragment of what should have been his main topic. The datum includes its own interconnections, and the first stage of the process of feeling is the reception into the *responsive conformity of feeling whereby the datum, which is mere potentiality, becomes the individualized basis for a complex unity of realization.

This conception, as found in the philosophy of organism, is practically identical with Locke's ways of thought in the latter half of his *Essay*. He speaks of the ideas in the perceived objects, and tacitly presupposes their identification with corresponding ideas in the perceiving mind. The ideas in the objects have been appropriated by the subjective functioning of the perceiving mind. This mode of phraseology can be construed as a casual carelessness of speech on the part of Locke, or a philosophic inconsistency. But apart from this inconsistency Locke's philosophy falls to pieces; as in fact was its fate in the hands of Hume.

There is, however, a fundamental misconception to be found in Locke, and in prevalent doctrines of perception. It concerns the answer to the question† as to the description of the primitive types of experience. Locke assumes that the utmost primitiveness is to be found in sense-perception. The seventeenth-century physics, with the complexities of primary and secondary qualities, should have warned philosophers that sense-perception was involved in complex modes of functioning. Primitive feeling is to be found at a lower level. The mistake was natural for mediaeval and Greek philosophers: for they had not modern physics before them as a plain warning. In sense-perception we have passed the Rubicon, dividing direct perception from the higher forms of mentality, which play with error and thus found intellectual empires.

[174] The more primitive types of experience are concerned with sense-reception, and not with sense-perception. This statement will require some

prolonged explanation. But the course of thought can be indicated by adopting Bergson's admirable phraseology, sense-reception is 'unspatialized,' and sense-perception is 'spatialized.' In sense-reception the sensa are the definiteness of emotion: they are emotional forms transmitted from occasion to occasion. Finally in some occasion of adequate complexity, the Category of Transmutation endows them with the new function of characterizing nexūs.

SECTION III

In the first place, those eternal objects which will be classified under the name 'sensa' constitute the lowest category of eternal objects. Such eternal objects do not express a manner of relatedness between other eternal objects. They are not contrasts, or patterns. Sensa are necessary as components in any actual entity, relevant in the realization of the higher grades. But a sensum does not, for its own realization, require any eternal object of a lower grade, though it does involve the potentiality of pattern and does gain access of intensity from some realization of status in some realized pattern. Thus a sensum requires, as a rescue from its shallowness of zero width, some selective relevance of wider complex eternal objects which include it as a component; but it does not involve the relevance of any eternal objects which it presupposes. Thus, in one sense, a sensum is simple; for its realization does not involve the concurrent realization of certain definite eternal objects, which are its definite simple components. But, in another sense, each sensum is complex; for it cannot be dissociated from its potentiality for ingression into *any* actual entity, and from† its potentiality of contrasts and of patterned relationships with other eternal objects. Thus each sensum shares the characteristic common to all eternal objects, that it introduces the notion of the logi- [175] cal variable, in both forms, the unselective 'any' and the selective 'some.'

It is possible that this definition of 'sensa' excludes some cases of contrast which are ordinarily termed 'sensa' and that it includes some emotional qualities which are ordinarily excluded. Its convenience consists in the fact that it is founded on a metaphysical principle, and not on an empirical investigation of the physiology of the human body.

Narrowness in the lowest category achieves such intensity as belongs to such experience, but fails by reason of deficiency of width. Contrast elicits depth, and only shallow experience is possible when there is a lack of patterned contrast. Hume notices the comparative failure of the higher faculty of imagination in respect to mere sensa. He exaggerates this comparative failure into a dogma of absolute inhibition to imagine a novel sensum; whereas the evidence which he himself adduces, of the imagination of a new shade of colour to fill a gap in a graduated scale of shades, shows† that a contrast between given shades can be imaginatively extended so as to generate the imagination of the missing shade. But Hume's example also shows that imagination finds its easiest freedom among the higher categories of eternal objects.

A pattern is in a sense simple: a pattern is the 'manner' of a complex contrast abstracted from the specific eternal objects which constitute the 'matter' of the contrast. But the pattern refers unselectively to any eternal objects with the potentiality of being elements in the 'matter' of some contrast in that 'manner.'

A pattern and a sensum are thus both simple in the sense that neither involves other specified eternal objects in its own realization. The *manner* of a pattern is the individual essence of the pattern. But no individual essence is realizable apart from some of its potentialities of relationship, that is, apart from its relational essence. But a pattern lacks simplicity in another sense, in which [176] a sensum retains simplicity. The realization of a pattern necessarily involves the concurrent realization of a group of eternal objects capable of contrast in that pattern. The realization of the pattern is through the realization of this contrast. The realization might have occurred by means of another contrast in the same pattern; but some complex contrast in that pattern is required. But the realization of a sensum in its ideal shallowness of intensity, with zero width, does not require any other eternal object, other than its intrinsic apparatus of individual and relational essence; it can remain just itself, with its unrealized potentialities for patterned contrasts. An actual entity with this absolute narrowness has an ideal faintness of satisfaction, differing from the ideal zero of chaos, but equally impossible. For realization means ingression in an actual entity, and this involves the synthesis of all ingredients with data derived from a complex universe. Realization is ideally distinguishable from the ingression of contrasts, but not in fact.

The simplest grade of actual occasions must be conceived as experiencing a few sensa, with the minimum of patterned contrast. The sensa are then experienced emotionally, and constitute the specific feelings whose intensities sum up into the unity of satisfaction. In such occasions the process is deficient in its highest phases; the process is the slave to the datum. There is the individualizing phase of conformal feeling, but the originative phases of supplementary and conceptual feelings† are negligible.

SECTION IV

According to this account, the experience of the simplest grade of actual entity is to be conceived as the unoriginative response to the datum with its simple content of sensa. The datum is simple, because it presents the objectified experiences of the past under the guise of simplicity. Occasions A, B, and C enter into the experience of occasion M as themselves experiencing [177] sensa s_1 and s_2 unified by some faint contrast between s_1 and s_2. Occasion M responsively feels sensa s_1 and s_2 as its own sensations. There is thus a transmission of sensation emotion from A, B, and C to M. If M had the wit of self-analysis, M would know that it felt its own sensa, by reason of a transfer from A, B, and C to itself. Thus the (unconscious) direct perception of A, B, and C is merely the causal efficacy of A, B, and C as elements in the constitution of M. Such direct perception will suffer from vagueness; for if A, B, and C tell the same tale with minor variation of intensity, the discrimination of A, and B, and C from each other will be irrelevant. There may thus remain a sense of the causal efficacy of actual presences, whose exact relationships in the external world are shrouded. Thus the experience of M is to be conceived as a quantitative emotion arising from the contribution of sensa from A, B, C and proportionately conformed to by M.

Generalizing from the language of physics, the experience of M is an intensity arising out of specific sensa, directed from A, B, C. There is in fact a directed influx from A, B, C of quantitative feeling, arising from specific forms of feeling. The experience has a vector character, a common measure of intensity, and specific forms of feelings conveying that intensity. If we substitute the term 'energy' for the concept of a quantitative emotional intensity, and the term 'form of energy' for the concept of 'specific form of feeling,' and remember that in physics 'vector' means definite transmission from elsewhere, we see that this metaphysical description of the simplest elements in the constitution of actual entities agrees absolutely with the general principles according to which the notions of modern physics are framed. The 'datum' in metaphysics is the basis of the vector-theory in physics; the quantitative satisfaction in metaphysics is the basis of the scalar localization of energy in physics; the 'sensa' in metaphysics are the basis of the diversity of specific forms under which energy clothes itself. Sci- [178] entific descriptions are, of course, entwined with the specific details of geometry and physical laws, which arise from the special order of the cosmic epoch in which we find ourselves. But the general principles of physics are exactly what we should expect as a specific exemplification of the metaphysics required by the philosophy of organism. It has been a defect in the modern philosophies that they throw no light whatever on any scientific principles. Science should investigate particular species, and metaphysics should investigate the generic notions under which those specific principles should fall. Yet, modern realisms have had nothing to say about scientific principles; and modern idealisms have merely contributed the unhelpful suggestion that the phenomenal world is one of the inferior avocations of the Absolute.

The direct perception whereby the datum in the immediate subject is inherited from the past can thus, under an abstraction, be conceived as the transference of throbs of emotional energy, clothed in the specific forms provided by sensa. Since the vagueness in the experient† subject will veil the separate objectifications wherein there are individual contributions to the total satisfaction, the emotional energy in the final satisfaction wears the aspect of a total intensity capable of all gradations of ideal variation. But in its origin it represents the totality arising from the contributions of separate objects to that form of energy. Thus, having regard to its origin, a real atomic structure of each form of energy is discernible, so much from each objectified actual occasion; and only a finite number of actual occasions will be relevant.

This direct perception, characterized by mere subjective responsiveness and by lack of origination in the higher phases, exhibits the constitution of an actual entity under the guise of receptivity. In the language of causation, it describes the efficient causation operative in the actual world. In the language of epistemology, as framed by Locke, it describes how the ideas of particular [179] existents are absorbed into the subjectivity of the percipient and are the datum for its experience of the external world. In the language of science, it describes how the quantitative intensity of localized energy bears in itself the vector marks of its origin, and the specialities of its specific forms; it also gives a reason for the atomic quanta to be discerned in the building up of a quantity of energy. In this way, the philosophy of organism—as it should—appeals to the facts.

SECTION V

The current accounts of perception are the stronghold of modern metaphysical difficulties. They have their origin in the same misunderstanding which led to the incubus of the substance-quality categories. The Greeks looked at a stone, and perceived that it was grey. The Greeks were ignorant of modern physics; but modern philosophers discuss perception in terms of categories derived from the Greeks.

The Greeks started from perception in its most elaborate and sophisticated form, namely, visual perception. In visual perception, crude perception is most completely made over by the originative phases in experience, phases which especially prominent in human experience. If we wish to disentangle the two earlier prehensive phases—the receptive phases, namely, the datum and the subjective response—from the more advanced originative phases, we must consider what is common to all modes of perception, amid the bewildering variety of originative amplification.

On this topic I am content to appeal to Hume. He writes: "But my senses convey to me only the impressions of coloured points, disposed in a certain manner. If *the eye is sensible* of any thing† further, I desire it may be pointed out to me." [1] And again: "It is universally allowed by the writers on optics, that *the eye* at all times sees an equal number of physical points, and that a man [180] on the top of a mountain has no larger an image presented to his senses, than when he is cooped up in the narrowest court or chamber." [2]

In each of these quotations Hume explicitly asserts that the *eye* sees.

[1] *Treatise*, Bk. I,‡ Part II, Sect. III. Italics not his.
[2] *Treatise*, Bk. I, Part III, Sect. IX.*

The conventional comment on such a passage is that Hume, for the sake of intelligibility, is using common forms of expression; that he is only really speaking of impressions on the mind; and that in the dim future, some learned scholar will gain reputation by emending 'eye' into 'ego.' The reason for citing the passages is to enforce the thesis that the form of speech is literary and intelligible because it expresses the ultimate truth of animal perception. The ultimate momentary 'ego' has as its datum the 'eye as experiencing such-and-sucht sights.' In the second quotation, the reference to the number of physical points is a reference to the excited area on the retina. Thus the 'eye as experiencing such-and-such sights' is passed on as a datum, from the cells of the retina, throught the train of actual entities forming the relevant nerves, up to the brain. Any direct relation of eye to brain is entirely overshadowed by this intensity of indirect transmission. Of course this statement is merely a pale abstraction from the physiological theory of vision. But the physiological account does not pretend to be anything more than indirect inductive knowledge. The point here to be noticed is the immediate literary obviousness of 'the eye as experiencing such-and-such sights.' This is the very reason why Hume uses the expression in spite of his own philosophy. The conclusion, which the philosophy of organism draws, is that in human experience the fundamental fact of perception is the inclusion, in the datum, of the objectification of an antecedent part of the human body with such-and-such experiences. Hume agrees with this conclusiont sufficiently well so as to argue from it, when it suits his purpose. He writes:

> I would fain ask those philosophers, who found so much of their reasonings on the distinction [181] of substance and accident, and imagine we have clear ideas of each, whether the idea of *substance* be derived from the impressions of sensation or reflection? If it be conveyed to ust by our senses, I ask, which of them, and after what manner? If it be perceived by the eyes, it must be a colour; if by the ears, a sound; if by the palate, a taste; and so of the other senses.[3]

We can prolong Hume's list: the feeling *of* the stone is *in the hand*; the feeling *of* the food is the ache *in the stomach*; the compassionate yearning is *in the bowels*, according to biblical writers; the feeling of well-being is in the viscera *passim*; ill temper is the emotional tone derivative from the disordered liver.

In this list, Hume's and its prolongation, for some cases—as in sight, for example—the supplementary phase in the ultimate subject overbalances in importance the datum inherited from the eye. In other cases, as in touch, the datum of 'the feeling in the hand' maintains its importance, however much the intensity, or even the character, of the feeling may be due to supplementation in the ultimate subject: this instance should be contrasted with that of sight. In the instance of the ache the stomach, as

---

[3] *Treatise*, Bk. I, Part I, Sect. VI.

datum, is of chief importance, and the food though obscurely felt is secondary—at least, until the intellectual analysis of the situation due to the doctor, professional or amateur. In the instances of compassion, well-being, and ill temper, the supplementary feelings in the ultimate subject predominate, though there are obscure references to the bodily organs as inherited data.

This survey supports the view that the predominant basis of perception is perception of the various bodily organs, as passing on their experiences by channels of transmission and of enhancement. It is the accepted doctrine in physical science that a living body is to be interpreted according to what is known of other sections of the physical universe. This is a sound axiom; but it [182] is double-edged. For it carries with it the converse deduction that other sections of the universe are to be interpreted in accordance with what we know of the human body.

It is also a sound rule that all interpretation should be based upon a *vera causa*. Now the original reliance upon 'the grey stone' has been shown by modern physics to be due to a misapprehension of a complex situation; but we have direct knowledge of the relationship of our central intelligence to our bodily feelings. According to this interpretation, the human body is to be conceived as a complex 'amplifier'—to use the language of the technology of electromagnetism. The various actual entities, which compose the body, are so coordinated that the experiences of any part of the body are transmitted to one or more central occasions to be inherited with enhancements accruing upon the way, or finally added by reason of the final integration. The enduring personality is the historic route of living occasions which are severally dominant in the body at successive instants. The human body is thus achieving on a scale of concentrated efficiency a type of social organization, which with every gradation of efficiency constitutes the orderliness whereby a cosmic epoch shelters in itself intensity of satisfaction.

The crude aboriginal character of direct perception is inheritance. What is inherited is feeling-tone with evidence of its origin: in other words, vector feeling-tone. In the higher grades of perception vague feeling-tone differentiates itself into various types of sensa—those of touch, sight, smell, etc.—each transmuted into a definite prehension of tonal contemporary nexūs† by the final percipient.

SECTION VI

In principle, the animal body is only the more highly organized and immediate part of the general environment for its dominant actual occasion, which is the ultimate [183] percipient. But the transition from without to within the body marks the passage from lower to higher grades of actual occasions. The higher the grade, the more vigorous and the more original is the enhancement from the supplementary phase. Pure receptivity and transmission give† place to the trigger-action of life whereby there is release of energy in novel forms. Thus the transmitted datum acquires sensa enhanced in relevance or even changed in character by the passage from the low-grade external world into the intimacy of the human body. The datum transmitted from the stone becomes the touch-feeling in the hand, but it preserves the vector character† of its origin from the stone. The touch-feeling in the hand with this vector origin from the stone is transmitted to the percipient in the brain. Thus the final perception is the perception of the stone through the touch in the hand. In this perception the stone is vague and faintly relevant in comparison with the hand. But, however dim, it is there.

In the transmission of inheritance from A to B, to C, to D, A is objectified by the eternal object S as a datum for B; where S is a sensum or a complex pattern of sensa. Then B is objectified for C. But the datum for B is thereby capable of some relevance for C, namely, A as objectified for B becomes reobjectified for C; and so on to D, and throughout the line of objectifications. Then for the ultimate subject M the datum includes A as thus transmitted, B as thus transmitted, and so on. The final objectifications for M are effected by a set $S,$† of eternal objects which is a modification of the original group S. The modification consists partly in relegation of elements into comparative irrelevance, partly in enhancement of relevance for other elements, partly in supplementation by eliciting into important relevance some eternal objects not in the original S. Generally there will be vagueness in the distinction between A, and B, and C, and D, etc., in their function as components in the datum for M. Some of the line, A and C for instance, may stand out [184] with distinctness by reason of some peculiar feat of original supplementation which retains its undimmed importance in subsequent transmission. Other members of the chain may sink into oblivion. For example, in touch there is a reference to the stone in contact with the hand, and a reference to the hand; but in normal, healthy, bodily operations the chain of occasions along the arm sinks into the background, almost into complete oblivion. Thus M, which has some analytic consciousness of its datum, is conscious of the feeling in its hand as the hand touches the stone. According to this account, perception in its primary form is consciousness of the causal efficacy of the external world by reason of which the percipient is a concrescence from a definitely constituted datum. The vector character of the datum is this causal efficacy.

Thus perception, in this primary sense, is perception of the settled world in the past as constituted by its feeling-tones, and as efficacious by reason of those feeling-tones. Perception, in this sense of the term, will be called 'perception in the mode of causal efficacy.' Memory is an example of perception in this mode. For memory is perception relating to the data from some historic route of ultimate percipient subjects M_1, M_2, M_3, etc., leading up to M which is the memorizing percipient.

SECTION VII

It is evident that 'perception in the mode of causal efficacy' is not that sort of perception which has received chief attention in the philosophical tradition. Philosophers have disdained the information about the universe obtained through their visceral feelings, and have concentrated on visual feelings.

What we ordinarily term our visual perceptions are the result of the later stages in the concrescence of the percipient occasion. When we register in consciousness our visual perception of a grey stone, something more than bare sight is meant. The 'stone' has a reference [185] to its past, when it could have been used as a‡ missile if small enough, or as a seat if large enough. A 'stone' has certainly a history, and probably a future. It is one of the elements in the actual world which has got to be referred to as an actual reason and not as an abstract potentiality. But we all know that the mere sight involved, in the perception of the grey stone, is the sight of a grey shape contemporaneous with the percipient, and with certain spatial relations to the percipient, more or less vaguely defined. Thus the mere sight is confined to the illustration of the geometrical perspective relatedness, of a certain contemporary spatial region, to the percipient, the illustration being effected by the mediation of 'grey.' The sensum 'grey' rescues that region from its vague confusion with other regions.

Perception which merely, by means of a sensum, rescues from vagueness a contemporary spatial region, in respect to its spatial shape and its spatial perspective from the percipient, will be called 'perception in the mode of presentational immediacy.'

Perception in this mode has already been considered in Part II, Chapter II. A more elaborate discussion of it can now be undertaken.[4] The definition, which has just been given, extends beyond the particular case of sight. The unravelling of the complex interplay between the two modes of perception—causal efficacy and presentational immediacy—‡is one main problem of the theory of perception.[5] The ordinary philosophical discussion of perception is almost wholly concerned with this interplay, and ignores the two pure modes which are essential for its proper explanation. The interplay between the two modes will be termed 'symbolic reference.'

[186] Such symbolic reference is so habitual in human experience that great care is required to distinguish the two modes. In order to find ob-

---

[4] Also cf.‡ subsequent discussions in Parts III and IV.

[5] Cf. my Barbour-Page lectures, *Symbolism, Its Meaning and Effect*, delivered at the University of Virginia, April, 1927 (New York: Macmillan, 1927; Cambridge University Press, 1928).‡ Another discussion of this question is there undertaken, with other illustrations. Cf. also Professor Norman Kemp Smith's *Prolegomena to an Idealist Theory of Knowledge*, Macmillan, 1924.

vious examples of the pure mode of causal efficacy we must have recourse to the viscera and to memory; and to find examples of the pure mode of presentational immediacy we must have recourse to so-called 'delusive' perceptions. For example, the image of a grey stone as seen in a mirror illustrates the space behind the mirror; the visual delusions arising from some delirium, or some imaginative excitement, illustrate surrounding spatial regions; analogously for the double-vision due to maladjustment of the eyes; the sight at night, of the stars and nebulae and Milky Way, illustrates vague regions of the contemporary sky; the feelings in amputated limbs illustrate spaces beyond the actual body; a bodily pain, referred to some part not the cause of the disorder, illustrates the painful region though not the pain-giving region. All these are perfectly good examples of the pure mode of presentational immediacy.

The epithet 'delusive,' which fits many, if not all, of these examples of presentational immediacy, is evidence that the mediating eternal object is not to be ascribed to the donation of the perceived region. It must have acquired its ingression in this mode from one of the originative phases of the percipient occasion. To this extent, the philosophy of organism is in agreement with the seventeenth-century doctrine of primary and secondary qualities, the mediating eternal object being, in this mode of ingression, a secondary quality. But in the philosophy of organism the doctrine does not have the consequences which follow in the earlier philosophies.

The account of perception in the pure mode of presentational immediacy, which has just been given, agrees absolutely with Descartes' doctrine of perception in general, so far as can be judged from his arguments which presuppose perception, and putting aside a few detached [187] passages wherein he comes near to the doctrine of 'objectification' and near to Locke's second doctrine of 'ideas determined to particular existents.' Anyhow, his conclusion immediately follows that, in perception, thus described, all that is perceived is that the object has extension and is implicated in a complex of extensive relatedness with the animal body of the percipient. Part of the difficulties of Cartesian philosophy, and of any philosophy which accepts this account as a complete account of perception, is to explain how we know more than this meagre fact about the world although our only avenue of direct knowledge limits us to this barren residium. Also, if this be all that we perceive about the physical world, we have no basis for ascribing the origination of the mediating sensa to any functioning of the human body. We are thus driven to the Cartesian duality of substances, bodies and minds. Perception is to be ascribed to mental functioning in respect to the barren extensive universe. We have already done violence to our immediate conviction by thus thrusting the human body out of the story; for, as Hume himself declares, we know that we see *by our eyes*, and taste *by our palates*. But when we have gone so far, it is inevitable to take a further step, and to discard our other conviction that we are perceiving a world of actual things within which we find ourselves. For a barren, extensive world is not really what we mean. We thus reduce perceptions to consciousness of impressions on the mind, consisting of sensa with 'manners' of relatedness. We then come to Hume, and to Kant. Kant's philosophy is an endeavour to retrieve some meaning for the two convictions which we have successively discarded. We have noted that Locke wavers in his account of perception, so that in the earlier portion of his *Essay* he agrees with Hume, and in the later portion with the philosophy of organism. We have also noted that Hume is inconsistent to the extent of arguing from a conviction which is discarded in his philosophy.

SECTION VIII

[188] Presentational immediacy illustrates the contemporary world in respect to its potentiality for extensive subdivision into atomic actualities and in respect to the scheme of perspective relationships which thereby eventuates. But it gives no information as to the actual atomization of this contemporary 'real potentiality.' By its limitations it exemplifies the doctrine, already stated above, that the contemporary world happens independently of the actual occasion with which it is contemporary. This is in fact the definition of contemporaneousness (cf. Part II, Ch. II, Sect. I); namely, that actual occasions, A and B, are mutually contemporary, when A does not contribute to the datum for B, and B does not contribute to the datum for A, except that both A and B are atomic regions in the potential scheme of spatio-temporal extensiveness which is a datum for both A and B.

Hume's polemic respecting causation is, in fact, one prolonged, convincing argument that pure presentational immediacy does not disclose any causal influence, either whereby one actual entity is constitutive of the percipient actual entity, or whereby one perceived actual entity is constitutive of another perceived actual entity. The conclusion is that, in so far as concerns their disclosure by presentational immediacy, actual entities in the contemporary universe are causally independent of each other.

The two pure modes of perception in this way disclose a variety of loci defined by reference to the percipient occasion M. For example, there are the actual occasions of the settled world which provide the datum for M; these lie in M's causal past. Again, there are the potential occasions for which M decides its own potentialities of contribution to their data; these lie in M's causal future. There are also those actual occasions which lie neither in M's causal past, nor in M's causal future. Such actual occasions are called M's 'contemporaries.' These [189] three loci are defined solely by reference to the pure mode of causal efficacy.

We now turn to the pure mode of presentational immediacy. One great difference from the previous way‡ of obtaining loci at once comes into view. In considering the causal mode, the past and the future were defined positively, and the contemporaries of M were defined negatively as lying neither in M's past nor in M's future. In dealing with presentational immediacy the opposite way must be taken. For presentational immediacy gives positive information only about the immediate present as defined by itself. Presentational immediacy illustrates, by means of sensa, potential subdivisions within a cross-section of the world, which is in this way objectified for M. This cross-section is M's immediate present. What is in this way illustrated is the potentiality for subdivision into actual atomic occasions; we can also recognize potentialities for subdivision of regions whose subdivisions remain unillustrated by any contrast of sensa. There are well-known limitations to such direct perceptions of unillustrated potentiality, a perception outrunning the real illustration of division by contrasted sensa. Such limitations constitute the *minima sensibilia*.

Hume's polemic respecting causation constitutes a proof that M's 'immediate present' lies within the locus of M's contemporaries. The presentation to M of this locus, forming its immediate present, contributes to M's datum two facts about the universe: one fact is that there is a 'unison of becoming,' constituting a positive relation of all the occasions in this community to any one of them. The members of this community share in a common immediacy; they are in 'unison' as to their becoming: that is to say, any pair of occasions in the locus are contemporaries. The other fact is the subjective illustration of the potential extensive subdivision with complete vagueness respecting the actual atomization. For example, the stone, which in the immediate [190] present is a group of many actual occasions, is illustrated as one grey spatial region. But, to go back to the former fact, the many actual entities of the present stone and the percipient are connected together in the 'unison of immediate becoming.' This community of concrescent occasions, forming M's immediate present, thus establishes a principle of common relatedness, a principle realized as an element in M's datum. This is the principle of mutual relatedness in the 'unison of becoming.' But this mutual relatedness is independent of the illustration by those sensa† through which presentational immediacy for M is effected. Also the illustration by these sensa has unequal relevance for M, throughout the locus. In its spatially remote parts it becomes vaguer and vaguer, fainter and fainter; and yet the principle of 'unison of becoming' still holds, in despite of the fading importance of the sensa. We thus find that the locus—namely, M's immediate present—is determined by the condition of 'mutual unison' independently of variations of relevant importance in M's illustrative sensa, and extends to their utmost bounds of faintness, and is equally determinate beyond such bounds. We thus gain the conception of a locus in which any two atomic actualities are in 'concrescent unison,' and which is particularized by the fact that M belongs to it, and so do all actual occasions belonging to extensive regions which lie in M's immediate present as illustrated by importantly relevant sensa. This complete region is the prolongation of M's immediate present beyond M's direct perception, the prolongation being effected by the principle of 'concrescent unison.'

A complete region, satisfying the principle of 'concrescent unison,' will be called a 'duration.' A duration is a cross-section of the universe; it is the immediate present condition of the world at some epoch, according to the old 'classical' theory of time—a theory never doubted until within the last few years. It will have been seen that the philosophy of organism accepts and defines this [191] notion. Some measure of acceptance is imposed upon metaphysics. If the notion be wholly rejected no appeal to universal obviousness of conviction can have any weight; since there can be no stronger instance of this force of obviousness.

The 'classical' theory of time tacitly assumed that a duration included the directly perceived immediate present of each one of its members. The converse proposition certainly follows from the account given above, that the immediate present of each actual occasion lies in a duration. An actual occasion will be said [6] to be 'cogredient† with' or 'stationary in' the duration including its directly perceived immediate present. The actual occasion is included in its own immediate present; so that each actual occasion through its percipience in the pure mode of presentational immediacy—if such percipience has important relevance—defines one duration in which it is included. The percipient occasion is 'stationary' in this duration.

But the classical theory also assumed the converse of this statement. It assumed that any actual occasion only lies in one duration; so that if N lies in the duration including M's immediate present, then M lies in the duration including N's immediate present. The philosophy of organism, in agreement with recent physics, rejects this conversion; though it holds that such rejection is based on scientific examination of our cosmic epoch, and not on any more general metaphysical principle. According to the philosophy of organism, in the present cosmic epoch only one duration includes all M's immediate present; this one duration will be called M's 'presented duration.' But M itself lies in many durations; each duration including M also includes some portions of M's presented duration. In the case of human perception practically all the important portions are thus included; also in human experience the relationship to such dura- [192] tions is what we express by the notion of 'movement.'

To sum up this discussion. In respect to any one actual occasion M there are three distinct nexūs of occasions to be considered:

(i) The nexus of M's contemporaries, defined by the characteristic that M and any one of its contemporaries happen in causal independence of each other.

(ii) Durations including M;† any such duration is defined by the characteristic that any two of its members are contemporaries. (It follows that

[6] Cf. my *Principles of Natural Knowledge*, Ch. XI, and my *Concept of Nature*, Ch. V.

any member of such a duration is contemporary with M, and thence that such durations are all included in the locus (i). The characteristic property of a duration is termed 'unison of becoming.')

(iii) M's presented locus, which is the contemporary nexus perceived in the mode of presentational immediacy, with its regions defined by sensa. It is assumed, on the basis of direct intuition, that M's presented locus is closely related to some one duration including M. It is also assumed, as the outcome of modern physical theory, that there is more than one duration including M. The single duration which is so related to M's presented locus is termed 'M's presented duration.' But this connection is criticized in the following sections of this chapter. In Part IV, the connection of these 'presented' loci to regions defined by straight lines is considered in more detail; the notion of 'strain-loci'‡ is there introduced.

SECTION IX

Physical science has recently arrived at the stage in which the practical identification, made in the preceding section, between the 'presented locus' of an actual entity, and a locus in 'unison of becoming' with the actual entity must be qualified.

The two notions, 'presented locus' and 'unison of becoming,' are distinct. The identification merely rests on the obvious experience of daily life. In any recasting of [193] thought it is obligatory to include the identification as a practical approximation to the truth, sufficient for daily life. Subject to this limitation, there is no reason for rejecting any distinction between them which the evidence suggests.

In the first place, the presented locus is defined by some systematic relation to the human body—so far as we rely, as we must, upon human experience. A certain state of geometrical strain in the body, and a certain qualitative physiological excitement in the cells of the body, govern the whole process of presentational immediacy. In sense-perception the whole function of antecedent occurrences outside the body is merely to excite these strains and physiological excitements within the body. But any other means of production would do just as well, so long as the relevant states of the body are in fact produced. The perceptions are functions of the bodily states. The geometrical details of the projected sense-perception depend on the geometrical strains in the body, the qualitative sensa depend on the physiological excitements of the requisite cells in the body.

Thus the presented locus must be a locus with a systematic geometrical relation to the body. According to all the evidence, it is completely independent of the contemporary actualities which in fact make up the nexus of actualities in the locus. For example, we see a picture on the wall with direct vision. But if we turn our back to the wall, and gaze into a good mirror, we see the same sight as an image behind the mirror. Thus, given the proper physiological state of the body, the locus presented in sense-perception is independent of the details of the actual happenings which it includes. This is not to say† that sense-perception is irrelevant to the real world. It demonstrates to us the real extensive continuum in terms of ** which these contemporary happenings have their own experiences qualified. Its additional information in terms of the qualitative sensa has relevance in proportion to the relevance of the immediate bodily state to the imme- [194] diate happenings throughout the locus. Both are derived from a past which is practically common to them all. Thus there is always some relevance; the correct interpretation of this relevance is the art of utilizing the perceptive mode of presentational immediacy as a means for understanding the world as a medium.

But the question which is of interest for this discussion is how this systematic relevance, of body to presented locus, is definable. This is not a mere logical question. The problem is to point out that element in the nature of things constituting such a geometrical relevance of the body to the presented locus. If there be such an element, we can understand that a certain state of the body may lift it into an important factor of our experience.

The only possible elements capable of this extended *systematic* relevance beyond the body are straight lines and planes. Planes are definable in terms of straight lines, so that we can concentrate attention upon straight lines.

It is a dogma of science that straight lines are not definable in terms of mere notions of extension. Thus, in the expositions of recent physical theory, straight lines are defined in terms of the actual physical happenings. The disadvantage of this doctrine is that there is no method of characterizing the possibilities of physical events antecedently to their actual occurrence. It is easy to verify that in fact there is a tacit relevance to an underlying system, by reference to which the physical loci—including those called 'straight lines'—are defined. The question is how to define this underlying system in terms of 'pure' straight lines, determinable without reference to the casual** details of the happenings.

It will be shown later (cf. Part IV, Chs. III and IV) that this dogma of the indefinability of straight lines is mistaken. Thus the *systematic* relation of the body to the presented locus occasions no theoretical difficulty.

All measurement is effected by observations of sensa [195] with geometrical relations within this presented locus. Also all scientific observation of the unchanged character of things ultimately depends† upon the maintenance of directly observed geometrical analogies within such loci.

However far the testing of instruments is carried, finally all scientific interpretation is based upon the assumption of directly observed unchangeability of some instrument for seconds, for hours, for months, for years. When we test this assumption we can only use another instrument; and there† cannot be an infinite regress of instruments.

Thus ultimately all science depends upon direct observation of homology of status within a system. Also the observed system is the complex of geometrical relations within some presented locus.

In the second place, a locus of entities in 'unison of becoming' obviously depends on the particular actual entities. The question, as to how the extensive continuum is in fact atomized by the atomic actualities, is relevant to the determination of the locus. The factor of temporal endurance selected for any one actuality will depend upon its initial 'subjective aim.' The categoreal conditions which govern the 'subjective aim' are discussed later in Part III. They consist generally in satisfying some condition of a maximum, to be obtained by the transmission of inherited types of order. This is the foundation of the 'stationary' conditions in terms of which the ultimate formulations of physical science can be mathematically expressed.

Thus the loci of 'unison of becoming' are only determinable in terms of the actual happenings of the world. But the conditions which they satisfy are expressed in terms of measurements derived from the qualification of actualities by the systematic character of the extensive continuum.

The term 'duration' will be used for a locus of 'unison of becoming,' and the terms 'presented locus' and 'strain- [196] locus' for the systematic locus involved in presentational immediacy.[7]

The strain-loci provide the systematic geometry with its homology of relations throughout all its regions; the durations share in the deficiency of homology characteristic of the physical field which arises from the peculiarities of the actual events.

SECTION X

We can now sum up this discussion of organisms, order, societies,† nexūs.

The aim of the philosophy of organism is to express a coherent cosmology based upon the notions of 'system,' 'process,' 'creative advance into novelty,' '*res vera*' (in Descartes' sense), 'stubborn fact,' 'individual unity of experience,' 'feeling,' 'time as perpetual perishing,' 'endurance as re-creation,' 'purpose,' 'universals as forms of definiteness,' 'particulars—i.e., *rēs verae*—as ultimate agents of stubborn fact.'

Every one of these notions is explicitly formulated either by Descartes or by Locke. Also no one can be dropped without doing violence to common sense. But neither Descartes nor Locke weaves these notions into one coherent system of cosmology. In so far as either philosopher is systematic, he relies on alternative notions which in the end lead to Hume's extreme of sensationalism.

In the philosophy of organism it is held that the notion of 'organism' has two meanings, interconnected but intellectually separable, namely, the microscopic meaning and the macroscopic meaning.** The microscopic

---

[7] In *The Concept of Nature* these two loci were not discriminated, namely, durations and strain-loci.

meaning is concerned with the formal constitution of an actual occasion, considered as a process of realizing an individual unity of experience. The macroscopic meaning is concerned with the givenness of the actual world, considered as the stubborn fact which at once limits and provides [197] opportunity for the actual occasion. The canalization of the creative urge, exemplified in its massive reproduction of social nexūs, is for common sense the final illustration of the power of stubborn fact. Also in our experience, we essentially arise out of our bodies which are the stubborn facts of the immediate relevant past. We are also carried on by our immediate past of personal experience; we finish a sentence *because* we have begun it. The sentence may embody a new thought, never phrased before, or an old one rephrased with verbal novelty. There need be no well-worn association between the sounds of the earlier and the later words. But it remains remorselessly true, that we finish a sentence *because* we have begun it. We are governed by stubborn fact.

It is in respect to this 'stubborn fact' that the theories of modern philosophy are weakest. Philosophers have worried themselves about remote consequences, and the inductive formulations of science. They should confine attention to the rush of immediate transition. Their explanations would then be seen in their native absurdity.

CHAPTER V

LOCKE AND HUME

SECTION I

[198] A MORE detailed discussion of Descartes, Locke, and Hume—in this and in the succeeding chapter—may make plain how deeply the philosophy of organism is founded on seventeenth-century thought and how at certain critical points it diverges from that thought.

We shall understand better the discussion, if we start with some analysis of the presuppositions upon which Hume's philosophy rests. These presuppositions were not original to Hume, nor have they ceased with him. They were largely accepted by Kant and are widely prevalent in modern philosophy. The philosophy of organism can be best understood by conceiving it as accepting large portions of the expositions of Hume and Kant, with the exception of these presuppositions, and of inferences directly derived from them. Hume is a writer of unrivalled clearness; and, as far as possible, it will be well to allow him to express his ideas in his own words. He writes:

> We may observe, that it is universally allowed by philosophers, and is besides pretty obvious of itself, that nothing is ever really present with the mind but its perceptions or impressions and ideas, and that external objects become known to us only by those perceptions they occasion. To hate, to love, to think, to feel, to see; all this is nothing but to perceive.[1]

Again:

> All the perceptions of the human mind resolve themselves into two distinct kinds, which I shall call *impressions* and *ideas*. The difference betwixt these consists in [199] the degrees of force and liveliness, with which they strike upon the mind, and make their way into our thought or consciousness. Those perceptions which enter with most force and violence, we may name *impressions*; and, under this name, I comprehend all our sensations, passions, and emotions, as they make their first appearance in the soul. By *ideas*, I mean the faint images of these in thinking and reasoning; such as, for instance, are all the perceptions excited by the present discourse, excepting only those which arise from the sight and touch, and excepting the immediate pleasure or uneasiness it may occasion.[2]

[1] *Treatise*, Bk. I, Part II, Sect. VI.
[2] *Treatise*, Bk. I, Part I, Sect. I.

130

The exceptions made in the above quotation are, of course, due to the fact that the 'perceptions' arising in these excepted ways are 'impressions' and not 'ideas.' Hume immediately draws attention to the fact that he deserts Locke's wide use of the term 'idea,' and restores it to its more usual and narrow meaning. He divides both ideas and impressions into 'simple' and 'complex.' He then adds:

> . . . we shall here content ourselves with establishing one general proposition, *That all our simple ideas in their first appearance, are derived from simple impressions, which are correspondent to them, and which they exactly represent.*[3]

When Hume passes on to complex impressions and ideas, his admirable clearness partially deserts him. He fails to distinguish sufficiently between (i) the *'manner'* (or *'order'*) in which many simples constitute some one complex perception, i.e., impression or idea; and (ii) the *efficacious fact* by reason of which this complex perception arises; and (iii) the mere multiplicity of simples which constitute the complex perception in this definite *manner*. In this respect Hume's followers only differ from Hume by discarding some of that clarity which never wholly deserts him. Each one of these three notions is an essential element in his argument. He writes:

> [200] . . . we may conclude with certainty, that the idea of extension is nothing but a copy of these coloured† points, and of the manner of their appearance.[4]

Also he writes:

> Were ideas entirely loose and unconnected, chance† alone would join them; and it is impossible the same simple ideas should† fall regularly into complex ones (as they commonly do), without some bond of union among them, some associating quality, by which one idea naturally introduces another. This uniting principle among ideas is not to be considered as an inseparable connection; for that has been already [5] excluded from the imagination: nor yet are we to conclude, that without it the mind cannot join two ideas; for nothing is more free than that faculty: but we are only to regard it as a gentle force, which commonly prevails, and is the cause why, among other things, languages so nearly correspond to each other; Nature, in a manner, pointing out to every one those simple ideas, which are most proper to be united into a complex one.[6]

As a final quotation, to illustrate Hume's employment of the third notion, we have:

> The idea of a substance as well as that of a mode, is *nothing but a collection* of simple ideas, that are united by the imagination, and have a particular name assigned them, . . . But the difference betwixt these

[3] *Treatise*, Bk. I, Part I, Sect. I.

[4] *Treatise*, Bk. I, Part II, Sect. III.

[5] Cf. Hume's previous section.

[6] *Treatise*, Bk. I, Part I, Sect. IV.

ideas consists in this, that the particular qualities, which form a† substance, are commonly referred to an unknown *something* [italics
Hume's], in which they are supposed to inhere; or granting this fiction
should not take place, are at least supposed to be closely and inseparably connected by the relations of contiguity and causation.
The effect of this is, that whatever new simple quality we discover to
have the *same connection* with the rest, we immediately comprehend
it among them, even though it did not enter into the first conception
of the substance. . . . The *principle of union* being regarded as the
chief part of the complex [201] idea, gives entrance to whatever quality afterwards occurs, and·is equally comprehended by it, as are the
others, which first presented themselves. . . .[7]

In this last quotation, the phrase 'principle of union' is ambiguous as
between 'manner' and 'efficacious' reason. In either sense, it is inconsistent
with the phrase 'nothing but a collection,' which at the beginning of the
quotation settles so simply the notion of 'substance.'

Returning to the first of this sequence of three quotations, we note that
any particular 'manner' of composition must itself be a simple idea, or impression. For otherwise we require yet another 'manner' of composition
for the original manner, and so on indefinitely. Thus there is either a
vicious infinity or a final simple idea. But Hume admits that there are
novel compound ideas which are not copies of compound impressions.
Thus he should also admit that there is a novel simple idea conveying the
novel 'manner,' which is not a copy of an impression. He has also himself
drawn attention to another exception in respect to missing shades of
colour in a graduated colour scheme. This exception cannot be restricted
to colour, and must be extended to sound, and smell, and to all gradua-
tions of sensations. Thus Hume's proposition, that simple ideas are all
copies of simple impressions, is subject to such considerable qualifications
that it cannot be taken for an ultimate philosophical principle, at least
not when enunciated in Hume's unguarded fashion. Hume himself, in
the passage (Part I, Sect. IV) quoted above for its relevance to his doctrine of the association of ideas, says, ". . . for nothing is more free than
that faculty [i.e., the imagination]." But he limits its freedom to the
production of novel complex ideas, disregarding the exceptional case of
missing shades. This question of imaginative freedom is obviously treated
very superficially by Hume. Imagination is never very free: it does not
seem to be limited to complex ideas, as asserted by [202] him; but such
freedom as it has in fact seems to establish the principle of the possibility
of diverse actual entities with diverse grades of imaginative freedom,
some more, some less, than the instances in question.

In this discussion of Hume's doctrine of imaginative freedom, two
other points have been left aside. One such point is the difference be-

---

[7] *Treatise*, Bk. I, Part I, Sect. VI. Italics not in edition quoted, except where
noted.*

tween various grades of generic abstraction, for example, scarlet, red, colour, sense-datum, manner of connectedness of diverse sense-data. The other point is the contrast between 'simplicity' and 'complexity.' We may doubt whether 'simplicity' is ever more than a relative term, having regard to some definite procedure of analysis. I hold this to be the case; and by reason of this opinion find yet another reason for discarding Hume's doctrine which would debar imagination from the free conceptual production of any type of eternal objects, such as Hume calls 'simple.' But there is no such fact as absolute freedom; every actual entity possesses only such freedom† as is inherent in the primary phase 'given' by its standpoint of relativity to its actual universe. Freedom, givenness, potentiality, are notions which presuppose each other and limit each other.

SECTION II

Hume, at the end of this passage on the connectedness of ideas, places the sentence ". . . Nature, in a manner, pointing out to every one those simple ideas, which are most *proper* to be *united* into a complex one." *
Hume's philosophy is occupied with the double search, first, for manners of unity, whereby many simples become one complex impression; and secondly, for a standard of propriety by which to criticize the production of ideas.

Hume can find only one standard of propriety, and that is, *repetition*. Repetition is capable of more or less: the more often impressions are repeated, the more proper it is that ideas should copy them. Fortunately, and without any reason so far as Hume can discover, complex [203] impressions, often repeated, are also often copied by their corresponding complex ideas.

Also the frequency of ideas following upon the frequency of their correlate impressions is also attended by an expectation of the repetition of the impression. Hume also believes, without any reason he can assign, that this expectation is pragmatically justified. It is this pragmatic justification, without metaphysical reason, which constitutes the propriety attaching to 'repetition.' This is the analysis of the course of thought involved in Hume's doctrine of the association of ideas in its relation to causation, and in Hume's final appeal to practice.

It is a great mistake to attribute to Hume any disbelief in the importance of the notion of 'cause and effect.' Throughout the *Treatise* he steadily affirms its fundamental importance; and finally, when he cannot fit it into his metaphysics, he appeals beyond his metaphysics to an ultimate justification outside any rational systematization. This ultimate justification is 'practice.'

Hume writes:

As our senses show us in *one* instance two bodies, or motions, or qualities, in certain relations of succession and contiguity, so our *memory* presents us only with a *multitude* of instances wherein we always find like bodies, motions, or qualities, in like relations. From the mere *repetition* of any past impression, even to infinity, there never will arise any *new original idea,* such as that of a *necessary connection;* and the *number* of impressions has in this case no more effect than if we confined ourselves to *one only.* But though this reasoning seems just and obvious, yet, as it would be folly to despair too soon, we shall continue the thread of our discourse; and having found, that after the discovery of the *constant conjunction* of any objects, we *always* draw an inference from one object to another, we shall now examine the nature of that inference, and of the transition from the impression to the idea. Perhaps it will appear in the end, that the necessary connection depends on the inference, instead of the inference's depending on [204] the necessary connection. . . . The only connection or relation of objects, which can lead us *beyond* the immediate impressions of our memory and senses, is that of *cause and effect;* and that because it is the only one, on which we can found a just inference from one object to another. The idea of cause and effect is derived from *experience* [italics Hume's], which informs us, that such particular objects, in all past instances, have been constantly conjoined with each other: and as an object similar to one of these is supposed to be immediately present in its impression, we thence *presume* on the existence of one similar to its usual attendant. According to this account of things, which is, I think, in every point unquestionable, probability is founded on the presumption of a resemblance betwixt those objects of which we have had experience, and those of which we have had none; and, therefore, it is *impossible* † this *presumption* can arise from *probability.*[8]

Hume's difficulty with 'cause and effect' is that it lies "beyond the immediate impressions of our memory and senses."† In other words, this *manner* of connection is not given in any impression. Thus the whole basis of the idea, its propriety, is to be traced to the repetition of impressions. At this point of his argument, Hume seems to have overlooked the difficulty that 'repetition' stands with regard to 'impressions' in exactly the same position as does 'cause and effect.' Hume has confused a 'repetition of impressions' with an 'impression of repetitions of impressions.' In Hume's own words on another topic (Part II, Sect. V):

For whence should it be derived? Does it arise from an impression of sensation or of reflection? Point it out distinctly to us, that we may know its nature and qualities. But if you cannot point out *any such impression* [Hume's italics], you may be certain you are mistaken, when you imagine you have *any such idea.**

Hume's answer to this criticism would, of course, be [205] that he admits 'memory.' But the question is what is consistent with Hume's own

---

[8] *Treatise,* Bk. I, Part III, Sect. VI. Italics not in *Treatise.*

doctrine. This is Hume's doctrine of memory (Part III, Sect. V): "Since therefore the memory is known, neither by the order of its *complex* ideas, nor † the nature of its *simple* ones; it follows, that the difference betwixt it and the imagination lies in its superior force and vivacity." But (in Part I, Sect. I) he writes: "By *ideas* I mean the faint images of these [i.e., impressions] in thinking and reasoning," and later on he expands 'faint' into "degree of force and vivacity." [9] Thus, purely differing in 'force and vivacity,' we have the order: impressions, memories, ideas.

This doctrine is very unplausible; and, to speak bluntly, is in contradiction to plain fact. But, even worse, it omits the vital character of memory, namely, that it is *memory*. In fact the whole notion of *repetition* is lost in the 'force and vivacity' doctrine. What Hume does explain is that with a number of different perceptions immediately concurrent, he sorts them out into three different classes according to force and vivacity. But the repetition character, which he ascribes to simple ideas, and which is the whole point of memory, finds no place in his explanation. Nor can it do so, without an entire recasting of his fundamental philosophic notions.

SECTION III

Hume's argument has become circular. In the beginning of his *Treatise*, he lays down the 'general proposition': "*That all our simple ideas in their first appearance, are derived from simple impressions, . . .*" He proves this by an empirical survey. But the proposition itself employs—covertly, so far as language is concerned—the notion of 'repetition,' which itself is not an 'impression.' Again, later he finds 'necessary connection': he discards [206] this because he can find no corresponding impression. But the original proposition was only founded on an empirical survey; so the argument for dismissal is purely circular. Further, if Hume had only attended to his own excellent Part II, Section VI, "Of the Idea of Existence, and of external Existence,"† he would have remembered that whatever we do think of, thereby in some sense 'exists.' Thus, having the idea of 'necessary connection,' the only question is as to its exemplification in the connectedness of our 'impressions.' He muddles the importance of an idea with the fact of our entertainment of the idea. We cannot even be wrong in thinking that we think of 'necessary connection,' unless we *are* thinking of 'necessary connection.' Of course, we may be very wrong in believing that the notion is important.

The reasons for this examination of Hume, including the prolonged quotations, are (i) that Hume states with great clearness important aspects of our experience; (ii) that the defects in his statements are emi-

[9] This doctrine of 'force and vivacity' is withdrawn in the last sentence* of Hume's Appendix to the *Treatise*. But the argument in the *Treatise* is substantially built upon it. In the light of the retraction the whole 'sensationalist' doctrine requires reconsideration. The withdrawal cannot be treated as a minor adjustment.

nently natural defects which emerge with great clearness, owing to the excellence of his presentation; and (iii) that Hume differs from the great majority of his followers chiefly by the way in which he faces up to the problems raised by his own philosophy.

The first point to notice is that Hume's philosophy is pervaded by the notion of 'repetition,' and that memory is a particular example of this character of experience, that in some sense there is entwined in its fundamental nature the fact that it is repeating something. Tear 'repetition' out of 'experience,' and there is nothing left. On the other hand, 'immediacy,' or 'first-handedness,' is another element in experience. Feeling overwhelms repetition; and there remains the immediate, first-handed fact, which is the actual world in an immediate complex unity of feeling.

There is another contrasted pair of elements in experience, clustering round the notion of time, namely, 'endurance' and 'change.' Descartes, who emphasizes the notion [207] of 'substance,' also emphasizes 'change.' Hume, who minimizes the notion of 'substance,' similarly emphasizes 'change.' He writes:

> Now as time is composed of parts that are not coexistent, an unchangeable object, since it produces none but coexistent impressions, produces none that can give us the idea of time; and, consequently, that idea must be derived from a succession of changeable objects, and time in its first appearance can never be severed from such a succession.[10]

Whereas Descartes writes:

> . . . for this [i.e., 'the nature of time or of the duration of things'] is of such a kind that its parts do not depend one upon the other, and never co-exist; and from the fact that we now are, it does not follow that we shall be a moment afterwards, if some cause—the same that first produced us—does not continue so to produce us; that is to say, to conserve us.

And again:

> We shall likewise have a very different understanding of *duration*, *order* and *number*, if, in place of mingling with the idea that we have of them what properly speaking pertains to the conception of substance, we merely consider that the duration of each thing is a mode under which we shall consider this thing in so far as it continues to exist; . . .[11]

We have certainly to make room in our philosophy for the two contrasted notions, one that every actual entity endures, and the other that every morning is a new fact with its measure of change.

These various aspects can be summed up in the statement that *experience* involves a *becoming*, that *becoming* means that *something be-*

[10] *Treatise*, Bk. I, Part II, Sect. III.
[11] *Principles*, Part I, 21, and 55.

comes, and that *what becomes* involves *repetition* transformed into *novel immediacy.*

This statement directly traverses one main presupposition which Descartes and Hume agree in stating explicitly. This presupposition is that of the individual independence of successive temporal occasions. For [208] example, Descartes, in the passage cited above, writes: "[The nature of time is such]† that its parts do not depend one upon the other, . . ." Also Hume's impressions are self-contained, and he can find no temporal relationship other than mere serial order. This statement about Hume requires qualifying so far as concerns the connection between 'impressions' and 'ideas.' There is a relation of 'derivation' of 'ideas' from 'impressions' which he is always citing and never discussing. So far as it is to be taken seriously—for he never refers it to a correlate 'impression'—it constitutes an exception to the individual independence of successive 'perceptions.' This presupposition of individual independence is what I have elsewhere [12] called, the 'fallacy of simple location.' The notion of 'simple location' is inconsistent with any admission of 'repetition'; Hume's difficulties arise from the fact that he starts with simple locations and ends with repetition. In the organic philosophy the notion of repetition is fundamental. The doctrine of objectification is an endeavour† to express how what is settled in actuality is repeated under limitations, so as to be 'given' for immediacy. Later, in discussing 'time,' this doctrine will be termed the doctrine of 'objective immortality.'

SECTION IV

The doctrine of the individual independence of real facts is derived from the notion that the subject-predicate form of statement conveys a truth which is metaphysically ultimate. According to this view, an individual substance with its predicates constitutes the ultimate type of actuality. If there be one individual, the philosophy is monistic; if there be many individuals, the philosophy is pluralistic. With this metaphysical presupposition, the relations between individual substances constitute metaphysical nuisances: there is no place for them. Accordingly—in defiance of the most obvious deliverance of our intuitive 'prejudices'—every [209] respectable philosophy of the subject-predicate type is monistic.

The exclusive dominance of the substance-quality metaphysics was enormously promoted by the logical bias of the mediaeval period. It was retarded by the study of Plato and of Aristotle. These authors included the strains of thought which issued in this doctrine, but included them inconsistently mingled with other notions. The substance-quality metaphysics triumphed with exclusive dominance in Descartes' doctrines. Unfortunately he did not realize that his notion of the *'res vera'* did not entail the same disjunction of ultimate facts as that entailed by the Aris-

[12] Cf. *Science and the Modern World,* Ch. III.

totelian notion of 'primary substance.' Locke led a revolt from this dominance, but inconsistently. For him and also for Hume, in the background and tacitly presupposed in all explanations, there remained the mind with its perceptions. The perceptions, for Hume, are what the mind knows about itself; and tacitly the knowable facts are always treated as qualities of a subject—the subject being the mind. His final criticism of the notion of the 'mind' does not alter the plain fact that the whole of the previous discussion has included this presupposition. Hume's final criticism only exposes the metaphysical superficiality of his preceding exposition.

In the philosophy of organism a subject-predicate proposition is considered as expressing a high abstraction.

The metaphysical superiority of Locke over Hume is exhibited in his wide use of the term 'idea,' which Locke himself introduced and Hume abandoned. Its use marks the fact that his tacit subject-predicate bias is slight in its warping effect. He first (I, I, 8*) explains: ". . . I have used it [i.e., idea] to express whatever is meant by phantasm, notion, species, or whatever it is which the mind can be employed about in thinking; . . ." But later (III, III, 6†), without any explicit notice of the widening of use, he writes: ". . . and ideas *become* [13] [210] *general* by separating from them the circumstances of time, and place, and any other ideas that may *determine them to this or that particular existence.*" Here, for Locke, the operations of the mind originate from ideas 'determined' to particular existents. This is a fundamental principle with Locke; it is a casual concession to the habits of language with Hume; and it is a fundamental principle with the philosophy of organism. In an earlier section (II, XXIII, 1) Locke expresses more vaguely the same doctrine, though in this context he immediately waters it down into an unexplained notion of 'going constantly together': "The mind, being, . . . furnished with a great number of the simple ideas conveyed in by the senses, as they are found *in exterior things,* . . . takes notice, also, that a certain number of these simple ideas *go constantly together.*"

But Locke wavers in his use of this principle of some sort of perception of 'particular existents'; and Hume seeks consistency by abandoning it; while the philosophy of organism seeks to reconstruct Locke by abandoning those parts of his philosophy which are inconsistent with this principle. But the principle itself is to be found plainly stated by Locke.

Hume has only impressions of 'sensation' and of 'reflection.' He writes: "The first kind arises in the soul originally, from unknown causes." [14] Note the tacit presupposition of 'the soul' as subject, and 'impression of sensation' as predicate. Also note the dismissal of any intrinsic relevance to a particular existent, which is an existent in the same sense as the 'soul' is an existent; whereas Locke illustrates his meaning by referring (cf. III,

[13] Italics mine.*
[14] *Treatise*, Bk. I, Part I, Sect. II.

III, 7) to a 'child'—corresponding to 'the soul' in Hume's phrase—and to its 'nurse' *of whom* the child has its 'idea.'

Hume is certainly inconsistent, because he cannot entirely disregard common sense. But his inconsistencies are violent, and his main argument negates Locke's use. [211] As an example of his glaring inconsistency of phraseology, note:

As to those *impressions,* which arise from the *senses,* their ultimate cause is, in my opinion, perfectly inexplicable by human reason, and it will always be impossible to decide with certainty, whether they arrive immediately from the object, or are produced by the creative power of the mind, or are derived from the Author of our being.[15]

Here he inconsistently speaks of *the object,* whereas he has nothing on hand in his philosophy which justifies the demonstrative word '*the.*' In the second reference '*the object*' has emerged into daylight. He writes: "There is no object which implies the existence of any other, if we consider these objects in themselves, and never look beyond the ideas which we form of them." This quotation exhibits an ingenious confusion whereby Hume makes the best of two metaphysical worlds, the world with Locke's principle, and his own world which is without Locke's principle.

But Locke's principle amounts to this: That there are many actual existents, and that in some sense one actual existent repeats itself in another actual existent, so that in the analysis of the latter existent a component 'determined to' the former existent is discoverable. The philosophy of organism expresses this principle by its doctrines of 'prehension' and of 'objectification.' Locke always supposes that consciousness is consciousness of the ideas in the conscious mind. But he never separates the 'ideas' from the 'consciousness.' The philosophy of organism makes this separation, and thereby relegates consciousness to a subordinate metaphysical position; and gives to Locke's *Essay* a metaphysical interpretation which was not in Locke's mind. This separation asserts Kant's principle: "Gedanken ohne Inhalt sind leer, Anschauungen ohne Begriffe sind blind." [16] But Kant's principle is here applied in exactly the converse way to Kant's own use of it. Kant is obsessed with the mentality [212] of 'intuition,' and hence† with its necessary involution in consciousness. His‡ suppressed premise is 'Intuitions are never blind.'

SECTION V

In one important respect Hume's philosophical conceptions show a marked superiority over those of Locke. In the *Essay Concerning Human Understanding,* the emphasis is laid upon the morphological structure of 'human understanding.' The logical relationships of various sorts of 'ideas' are examined. Now, whether in physics, biology, or elsewhere, morphology,

15 *Treatise,* Bk. I, Part III, Sect. V; cf. also Sect. VI.†
16 *Critique of Pure Reason,* 'Transcendental Logic,' Introduction, Sect. I.†

in the sense of the analysis of logical relationships, constitutes the first stage of knowledge. It is the basis of the new 'mathematical' method which Descartes introduced. Morphology deals in analytical propositions, as they are termed by Kant. For example, Locke writes: "The common names of substances, as well as other general terms, stand for sorts: which [17] *is nothing else but* the being made signs of such complex ideas, wherein several particular substances do or might agree, by virtue of which they are capable of being comprehended in one common conception, and be signified by one name." And again: "*Our abstract ideas are to us the measures of species.*" And again: "Nor let any one say, that the power of propagation in animals by the mixture of male and female, and in plants by seeds, keeps the supposed real species distinct and entire." [18] In technical language, Locke had no use for genetic evolution.

On the other hand, Hume's train of thought unwittingly emphasizes 'process.' His very scepticism is nothing but the discovery that there is something in the world which cannot be expressed in analytic propositions. Hume discovered that "We murder to dissect." He did not say this, because he belonged to the mid-eighteenth century; and so left the remark to Wordsworth. But, in [213] effect, Hume discovered that an actual entity is at once a process, and is atomic; so that in no sense is it the sum of its parts. Hume proclaimed the bankruptcy of morphology.

Hume's account of the process discoverable in 'the soul' is as follows: first, impressions of sensation, of unknown origin; then, ideas of such impressions, 'derived from' the impressions; then, impressions of reflection 'derived from' the antecedent ideas; and then, ideas of impressions of reflection. Somewhere in this process, there is to be found repetition of impressions, and thence by 'habit'—by which we may suppose that a particular mode of 'derivation' is meant—by habit, a repetition of the correlate ideas; and thence expectancy of the repetition of the correlate impressions. This expectancy would be an 'impression of reflection.' It is difficult to understand why Hume exempts 'habit' from the same criticism as that applied to the notion of 'cause.' We have no 'impression' of 'habit,' just as we have no 'impression' of 'cause.' Cause, repetition, habit are all in the same boat.

Somewhat inconsistently, Hume never allows impressions of sensation to be derived from the correlate ideas; though, as the difference between them only consists in 'force and vivacity,' the reason for this refusal cannot be found in‡ his philosophy. The truth is that Hume retained an obstinate belief in an external world which his principles forbade him to confess in his philosophical constructions. He reserved that belief for his daily life, and for his historical and sociological writings, and for his *Dialogues Concerning Natural Religion.*

The merit of Hume's account is that the process described is within

[17] Italics mine.
[18] III, VI, 1, 22, 23.

'the soul.' In the philosophy of organism 'the soul' as it appears in Hume, and 'the mind' as it appears in Locke and Hume, are replaced by the phrases 'the actual entity,' and 'the actual occasion,' these phrases being synonymous.

Two defects, found equally in Locke and in Hume, are, first, the confusion between a Lockian 'idea' and [214] consciousness of such an idea; and, secondly, the assigned relations between 'ideas' of sensation and 'ideas' of reflection.† In Hume's language, this latter point is concerned with the relations between 'impressions of sensation' and 'impressions of reflection.' Hume and Locke, with the overintellectualist bias prevalent among philosophers, assume that emotional feelings are necessarily derivative from sensations. This is conspicuously not the case; the correlation between such feelings and sensations is on the whole a secondary effect. Emotions conspicuously brush aside sensations and fasten upon the 'particular' objects to which—in Locke's phrase—certain 'ideas' are '*determined.*' The confinement of our prehension of other actual entities to the mediation of private sensations is pure myth. The converse doctrine is nearer the truth: the more primitive mode of objectification is via emotional tone, and only in exceptional organisms does objectification, via sensation, supervene with any effectiveness. In their doctrine on this point, Locke and Hume were probably only repeating the mediaeval tradition, and they have passed on the tradition to their successors. None the less, the doctrine is founded upon no necessity of thought, and lacks empirical confirmation. If we consider the matter physiologically, the emotional tone depends mainly on the condition of the viscera which are peculiarly ineffective in generating sensations. Thus the whole notion of prehension should be inverted. We prehend other actual entities more primitively by direct mediation of emotional tone, and only secondarily and waveringly by direct mediation of sense. The two modes fuse with important effects upon our perceptive knowledge. This topic must be reserved (cf. Parts III and IV) for further discussion; but it is fundamental in the philosophy of organism. One difficulty in appealing to modern psychology, for the purpose of a preliminary survey of the nature of experience, is that so much of that science is based upon the presupposition of the sensationalist mythology. Thus the sim- [215] pler, more naïve surveys of Locke and Hume are philosophically the more useful.

Later, in Part III, a 'prehension' will be analysed into 'prehending subject,' 'object prehended,' and 'subjective form.' The philosophy of organism follows Locke in admitting particular 'exterior things' into the category of 'object prehended.' It also follows Hume in his admission at the end of his Appendix to the *Treatise*: "Had I said, that two ideas of the same object can only be different by their different *feeling*, I should have been nearer the truth." What Hume here calls 'feeling' is expanded in the philosophy of organism into the doctrine of 'subjective form.' But there is another ineradicable difference between some prehensions, namely, their diversity of prehending subjects, when the two prehensions are in that respect diverse. The subsequent uses of the term 'feeling' are in the sense of the 'positive' type of prehensions, and *not* in the sense in which Hume uses it in the above quotation.

The approximation of the philosophy of organism to Santayana's doctrine of 'animal faith' is effected by this doctrine of objectification by the mediation of 'feeling.'

Santayana would deny that 'animal faith' has in it any element of givenness. This denial is presumably made in deference to the sensationalist doctrine, that all knowledge of the external world arises by the mediation of private sensations. If we allow the term 'animal faith' to describe a kind of perception which has been neglected by the philosophic tradition, then practically the whole of Santayana's discussion [19] is in accord with the organic philosophy.

The divergence from, and the analogy to, Santayana's doctrine can be understood by quoting two sentences:

I propose therefore to use the word existence . . . to designate not data of intuition but facts or events believed to occur in nature. These facts or events will include, first, intuitions themselves, or instances of con- [216] sciousness, like pains and pleasures and all remembered experiences and mental discourse; and second, physical things and events, having a transcendent relation to the data of intuition which, in belief, may be used as signs for them; . . .*

It may be remarked in passing that this quotation illustrates Santayana's admirable clarity of thought, a characteristic which he shares with the men of genius of the seventeenth and eighteenth centuries. Now the exact point where Santayana differs from the organic philosophy is† his implicit assumption that 'intuitions themselves' cannot be among the 'data of intuition,' that is to say, the data of other intuitions. This possibility is what Santayana denies and the organic philosophy asserts. In this respect Santayana is voicing the position which, implicitly or explicitly, pervades modern philosophy. He is only distinguished by his clarity of thought. If Santayana's position be granted, there is a phenomenal veil, a primitive credulity associated with action and valuation, and a mysterious symbolism from the veil to the realities behind the veil. The only difference between such philosophers lies in their reading of the symbolism, some read more and some less. There can be no decision between them, since there are no rational principles which penetrate from the veil to the dark background of reality.

The organic philosophy denies this doctrine because, first, it is contrary to naïve experience; secondly, 'memory' is a very special instance of an antecedent act of experience becoming a datum of intuition for another act of experience; thirdly, the rejected doctrine is derived from the mis-

[19] Cf. his *Scepticism and Animal Faith.*

conception of Locke, already noted previously (cf. Part II, Ch. I, Sect. VI), that logical simplicity can be identified with priority in the concrescent process. Locke, in his first two books,† attempts to build up experience from the basic elements of simple 'ideas' of sensation. These simple ideas are practically Santayana's 'intuitions of essences.' Santayana explicitly [217] repudiates the misconception, but in so doing he knocks away one of the supports of his doctrine. A fourth reason for the rejection of the doctrine is that the way is thereby opened for a rational scheme of cosmology in which a final reality is identified with acts of experience.

CHAPTER VI
FROM DESCARTES TO KANT

SECTION I

[218] A COMPARISON of thet different ways in which Descartes and Locke respectively conceived the scope of their investigations at once discloses the very important shift which Locke introduced into the tradition of philosophic thought. Descartes asked the fundamental metaphysical question, What is it to be an actual entity? He found three kinds of actual entities, namely, cogitating minds, extended bodies, and God. His word for an actual entity was 'substance.' The fundamental proposition, whereby the analysis of actuality could be achieved, took the form of predicating a quality of the substance in question. A quality was either an accident or an essential attribute. In the Cartesian philosophy there was room for three distinct kinds of change: one was the change of accidents of an enduring substance; another was the origination of an individual substance; and the third was the cessation of the existence of an enduring substance. Any individual belonging to either of the first two kinds of substances did not require any other individual of either of these kinds in order to exist. But it did require the concurrence of God. Thus the essential attributes of a mind were its dependence on God and its cogitations; and the essential attributes of a body were its dependence on God and its extension. Descartes does not apply the term 'attribute' to the 'dependence on God'; but it is an essential element in his philosophy. It is quite obvious that the accidental relationships between diverse individual substances form a great difficulty for Descartes. If they are to be included in his scheme of the actual [219] world, they must be qualities of a substance. Thus a relationship is the correlation of a pair of qualities,† one belonging exclusively to one individual, and the other exclusively to the other individual. The correlaton itself must be referred to God as one of his accidental qualities. This is exactly Descartes' procedure in his theory of representative ideas. In this theory, the perceived individual has one quality; the perceiving individual has another† quality which is the 'idea' representing this quality; God is aware of the correlation; and the perceiver's knowledge of God guarantees for him the veracity of his idea. It is unnecessary to criticize this very artificial account of what common sense believes to be our direct knowledge of other actual entities. But it is the only account consistent with the metaphysical materials provided by Descartes, combined with his assumption of a multiplicity of actual entities. In this assumption of a

multiplicity of actual entities the philosophy of organism follows Descartes. It is, however,† obvious that there are only two ways out of Descartes' difficulties; one way is to have recourse to some form of monism; the other way is to reconstruct Descartes' metaphysical machinery.

But Descartes asserts one principle which is the basis of all philosophy: he holds that the whole pyramid of knowledge is based upon the immediate operation of knowing which is either an essential (for Descartes), or a contributory, element in the composition of an immediate actual entity. This is also a first principle for the philosophy of organism. But Descartes allowed the subject-predicate form of proposition, and the philosophical tradition derived from it, to dictate his subsequent metaphysical development. For his philosophy, 'actuality' meant 'to be a substance with inhering qualities.' For the philosophy of organism, the percipient occasion is its own standard of actuality. If in its knowledge other actual entities appear, it can only be because they conform to its standard of actuality. There can only be [220] evidence of a world of actual entities, if the immediate actual entity discloses them as essential to its own composition. Descartes' notion of an unessential experience of the external world is entirely alien to the organic philosophy. This is the root point of divergence; and is the reason why the organic philosophy has to abandon any approach to the substance-quality notion of actuality. The organic philosophy interprets experience as meaning the 'self-enjoyment of being one among many, and of being one arising out of the composition of many.' Descartes interprets experience as meaning the 'self-enjoyment, by an individual substance, of its qualification by ideas.' †

SECTION II

Locke explicitly discards metaphysics. His enquiry has a limited scope:

This therefore being my purpose, to inquire into the original, certainty, and extent of human knowledge, together with the grounds and degrees of belief, opinion, and assent, I shall not at present meddle with the physical consideration of the mind, or trouble myself to examine wherein its essence consists, . . . It shall suffice to my present purpose, to consider the discerning faculties of a man as they are employed about the objects which they have to do with; . . .[1]

The enduring importance of Locke's work comes from the candour, clarity, and adequacy with which he stated the evidence, uninfluenced by the bias of metaphysical theory. He explained, in the sense of stating plainly, and not in the more usual sense of 'explaining away.' By an ironic development in the history of thought, Locke's successors, who arrogated to themselves the title of 'empiricists,' have been chiefly employed in explaining away the obvious facts of experience in obedience to the a priori doctrine of sensationalism, inherited from the mediaeval philosophy which

---

[1] *Essay*, I, I, 2.

they despised. Locke's *Essay* is the invaluable storehouse for those who wish to [221] confront their metaphysical constructions by a recourse to the facts.

Hume clipped his explanation by this a priori theory, which he states explicitly in the first quotation made from his *Treatise* in the previous chapter. It cannot be too often repeated:

> We may observe, that it is universally allowed by philosophers, and is besides pretty obvious of itself, that nothing is ever really present with the mind but its perceptions† or impressions and ideas, and that external objects become known to us only by those perceptions they occasion. To hate, to love, to think, to feel, to see; all this is nothing but to perceive.

Hume, in agreement with what 'is universally allowed by philosophers,' interprets this statement in a sensationalist sense. In accordance with this sense, an impression is nothing else than a particular instance of the mind's awareness of a universal, which may either be simple, or may be a manner of union of many simple universals. For Hume, hating, loving, thinking, feeling, are nothing but perceptions derivate from these fundamental impressions. This is the a priori sensationalist dogma, which bounds all Hume's discoveries in the realm of experience. It is probable that this dogma was in Locke's mind throughout the earlier portion of his *Essay*. But Locke was not seeking consistency with any a priori dogma. He also finds in experience 'ideas' with characteristics which 'determine them to this or that particular existent.' Such inconsistency with their dogma shocks empiricists, who refuse to admit experience, naked and unashamed, devoid of their a priori figleaf. Locke is merely stating what, in practice, nobody doubts. But Locke would have agreed with Hume in refusing to admit that 'ideas of reflection' may be directly 'determined to some particular existent,' without the intervention of 'ideas of sensation.' In this respect, Locke was a sensationalist, and the philosophy of organism is not sensationalist. But Locke's avoidance of metaphysics only led him up to a stage of thought for which meta- [222] physics is essential to clarity. The questions as to the status of a 'particular existent,' and of an 'idea determined to a particular existent,' demand metaphysical discussion. Locke is never tired of disparaging the notion of 'substance'; but he gives no hint of alternative categories which he would employ to analyse† the notions of an 'actual entity' and of 'reality.' But his *Essay*, however, does contain a line of thought which can be developed into a metaphysic. In the first place, he distinctly holds that ideas of particular existents—for example, the child's idea of its mother—constitute the fundamental data which the mental functioning welds into a unity by a determinate process of absorption, including comparison, emphasis, and abstraction. He also holds that 'powers' are to be ascribed to particular existents whereby the constitutions of other particulars are conditioned. Correlatively, he holds that the constitutions of particular existents must be described so as to exhibit their 'capacities' for being conditioned by such 'powers' in other particulars. He also holds that all qualities have in some sense a relational element in them. Perhaps, though Locke does not say so, this notion of the relational element in qualities is illustrated in the following passage: "Besides, there is scarce any particular thing existing, which, in some of its simple ideas, does not communicate with a greater, and in others with a less, number of particular beings: . . ." [2] Locke here expresses the notion of an identity between two simple ideas in the form of a 'communication' between the particular existents which possess that common quality. This passage also illustrates Locke's habit of employing the term 'idea'† in a sense other than particular content of an act of awareness. Finally, Locke's notion of the passage of time is that something is 'perpetually perishing.' If he had grasped the notion that the actual entity 'perishes' in the passage of time, so that no actual entity changes, he would have arrived [223] at the point of view of the philosophy of organism. What he does say, is "perpetually perishing parts of succession." [3] Here, as elsewhere, Locke's neglect of ultimate questions revenges itself upon him. Nothing can make the various parts of his *Essay* mutually consistent. He never revises the substance-quality categories which remain presupposed throughout his *Essay*. In the first two books of the *Essay*, he professes to lay the foundations of his doctrine of ideas. These books are implicitly dominated by the notion of the ideas as mere qualifications of the substrate mind. In the third book of the *Essay* he is apparently passing on to the application of his established doctrine of ideas to the subordinate question of the function of language. But he tacitly introduces a new doctrine of ideas, which is difficult to conciliate with the sensationalist doctrine of the preceding books. Hume concentrates upon the doctrine of Locke's earlier books; the philosophy of organism concentrates upon that of the later books in the *Essay*. If Locke's *Essay* is to be interpreted as a consistent scheme of thought, undoubtedly Hume is right; but such an interpretation offers violence to Locke's contribution to philosophy.

SECTION III

In the philosophy of organism it is assumed that an actual entity is composite. 'Actuality' is the fundamental exemplification of composition; all other meanings of 'composition' are referent to this root-meaning. But 'actuality' is a general term, which merely indicates this ultimate type of composite unity: there are many composite unities to which this general term applies. There is no general fact of composition, not expressible in terms of the composite constitutions of the individual occasions. Every proposition is entertained in the constitution of some one actual entity, or severally in the constitutions of many actual entities. This is only [224]

[2] *Essay*, III, IX, 14.
[3] II, XIV, 1.

another rendering of the 'ontological principle.' It follows from the ontological principle, thus interpreted, that the notion of a 'common world' must find its exemplification in the constitution of each actual entity, taken by itself for analysis. For an actual entity cannot be a member of a 'common world,' except in the sense that the 'common world' is a constituent of its own constitution. It follows that every item of the universe, including all the other actual entities, is a constituent† in the constitution of any one actual entity. This conclusion has already been employed under the title of the 'principle of relativity.' This principle of relativity is the axiom by which the ontological principle is rescued from issuing in an extreme monism. Hume adumbrates this principle in his notion of 'repetition.'

Some principle is now required to rescue actual entities from being undifferentiated repetitions, each of the other, with mere numerical diversity. This requisite is supplied by the 'principle of intensive relevance.' The notion of intensive relevance is fundamental for the meaning of such concepts as 'alternative possibilities,' 'more or less,' 'important or negligible.' The principle asserts that any item of the universe, however preposterous as an abstract thought, or however remote as an actual entity, has its own gradation of relevance, as prehended, in the constitution of any one actual entity: it might have had more relevance; and it might have had less relevance, including the zero of relevance involved in the negative prehension; but in fact it has just *that* relevance whereby it finds its status in the constitution of *that* actual entity. It will be remembered that Hume finds it necessary to introduce the notion of variations in 'force and vivacity.' He is here making a particular application—and, as I believe, an unsuccessful application—of the general principle of intensive relevance.

There is interconnection between the degrees of relevance of different items in the same actual entity. This fact of interconnection is asserted in the 'principle of [225] compatibility and contrariety.' There are items which, in certain respective gradations of relevance, are contraries to each other; so that those items, with their respective intensities of relevance, cannot coexist in the constitution of one actual entity. If some group of items, with their variety of relevance, can coexist in one actual entity, then the group, as thus variously relevant, is a compatible group. The various specific essences of one genus, whereby an actual entity may belong to one or other of the species but cannot belong to more than one, illustrate the incompatibility between two groups of items. Also in so far as a specific essence is complex, the specific essence is necessarily composed of compatible items, if there has been any exemplification of that species. But 'feelings' are the entities which are primarily 'compatible' or 'incompatible.' All other usages of these terms are derivative.

The words 'real' and 'potential' are, in this exposition, taken in senses which are antithetical. In their primary senses, they qualify the 'eternal objects.' These eternal objects determine *how* the world of actual entities enters into the constitution of each one of its members via its feelings.

And they also express *how* the constitution of any one actual entity is analysable into phases, related as presupposed and presupposing. Eternal objects express *how* the predecessor-phase is absorbed into the successor-phase† without limitation of itself, but with additions necessary for the determination of an actual unity in the form of individual satisfaction. The *actual entities* enter into each others' constitutions under *limitations* imposed by incompatibilities [4] of feelings. Such incompatibilities relegate various elements in the constitutions of felt objects to the intensive zero, which is termed 'irrelevance.' The *preceding phases* enter into their successors with *additions* which eliminate the inde- [226] terminations. The *how* of the limitations, and the *how* of the additions, are alike the *realization* of eternal objects in the constitution of the actual entity in question. An eternal object in abstraction from any one particular actual entity is a potentiality for ingression into actual entities. In its ingression into any one actual entity, either as relevant or as irrelevant, it retains its potentiality of indefinite diversity of modes of ingression, a potential indetermination rendered determinate in this instance. The definite ingression into a particular actual entity is not to be conceived as the sheer evocation of that eternal object from 'not-being' into 'being'; it is the evocation of determination out of indetermination. Potentiality becomes reality; and yet retains its message of alternatives which the actual entity has avoided. In the constitution of an actual entity:—whatever component is red, might have been green; and whatever component is loved, might have been coldly esteemed. The term 'universal' is unfortunate in its application to eternal objects; for it seems to deny, and in fact it was meant to deny, that the actual entities also fall within the scope of the principle of relativity. If the term 'eternal objects' is disliked, the term 'potentials' would be suitable. The eternal objects are the pure potentials of the universe; and the actual entities differ from each other in their realization of potentials. Locke's term 'idea,' in his primary use of it in the first two books of the *Essay*, means the determinate ingression of an eternal object into the actual entity in question. But he also introduces the limitation† to conscious mentality, which is here abandoned.

Thus in the philosophy of organism, Locke's first use of the term 'idea' is covered by the doctrine of the 'ingression' of eternal objects into actual entities; and his second use of the same term is covered by the doctrine of the 'objectification' of actual entities. The two doctrines cannot be explained apart from each other: they constitute explanations of the two fundamental principles—[227] the ontological principle and the principle of relativity.

The four stages constitutive of an actual entity have been stated above in Part II, Chapter III, Section I. They can be named, datum, process,

---

[4] Dr. H. M. Sheffer has pointed out the fundamental logical importance of the notion of 'incompatibility'; cf. *Trans. Amer. Math. Soc.*,† Vol. XIV, pp. 481–488; and Introduction to Vol. I of *Principia Mathematica* (2nd edition).

satisfaction, decision. The two terminal stages have to do with 'becoming' in the sense of the transition from the settled actual world to the new actual entity relatively to which that settlement is defined. But such 'definition' must be found as an element in the actual entities concerned. The 'settlement' which an actual entity 'finds' is its datum. It is to be conceived as a limited perspective of the 'settled' world provided by the eternal objects concerned. This datum is 'decided' by the settled world. It is 'prehended' by the new superseding entity. The datum is the objective content of the experience. The decision, providing the datum, is a transference of self-limited appetition; the settled world provides the 'real potentiality' that its many actualities be felt compatibly; and the new concrescence starts from this datum. The perspective is provided by the elimination of incompatibilities. The final stage, the 'decision,' is how the actual entity, having attained its individual 'satisfaction,' thereby adds a determinate condition to the settlement for the future beyond itself. Thus the 'datum' is the 'decision received,' and the 'decision' is the 'decision transmitted.' Between these two decisions, received and transmitted, there lie the two stages, 'process' and 'satisfaction.' The datum is indeterminate as regards the final satisfaction. The 'process' is the addition of those elements of feeling whereby these indeterminations are dissolved into determinate linkages attaining the actual unity of an individual actual entity. The actual entity, in becoming itself, also solves the question as to *what* it is to be. Thus process is the stage in which the creative idea works towards the definition and attainment of a determinate individuality. Process is the growth and attainment of a final end. The progressive defini-
[228] tion of the final end is the efficacious condition for its attainment. The determinate unity of an actual entity is bound together by the final causation towards an ideal progressively defined by its progressive relation to the determinations and indeterminations of the datum. The ideal, itself felt, defines what 'self' shall arise from the datum; and the ideal is also an element in the self which thus arises.

According to this account, efficient causation expresses the transition from actual entity to actual entity; and final causation expresses the internal process whereby the actual entity becomes itself. There is the becoming of the datum, which is to be found in the past of the world; and there is the becoming of the immediate self from the datum. This latter becoming is the immediate actual process. An actual entity is at once the product of the efficient past, and is also, in Spinoza's phrase, *causa sui*. Every philosophy recognizes, in some form or other, this factor of self-causation, in what it takes to be ultimate actual fact. Spinoza's words have already been quoted. Descartes' argument, from the very fact of thinking, assumes that this freely determined operation is thereby constitutive of an occasion in the endurance of an actual entity. He writes (*Meditation II*): "I am, I exist, is necessarily true each time that I pronounce it, or that I mentally conceive it." Descartes in his own philosophy conceives the thinker as creating the occasional thought. The philosophy of organism inverts the order, and conceives the thought as a constituent operation in the creation of the occasional thinker. The thinker is the final end whereby there is the thought. In this inversion we have the final contrast between a philosophy of substance and a philosophy of organism. The operations of an organism are directed towards the organism as a 'superject,' and are not directed from the organism as a 'subject.' The operations are directed *from* antecedent organisms and *to* the immediate organism. They are 'vectors,' in that they convey the many [229] things into the constitution of the single superject. The creative process is rhythmic: it swings from the publicity of many things to the individual privacy; and it swings back from the private individual to the publicity of the objectified individual. The former swing is dominated by the final cause, which is the ideal; and the latter swing is dominated by the efficient cause,† which is actual.

SECTION IV

From the point of view of the philosophy of organism, the credit must be given to Hume that he emphasized the 'process' inherent in the fact of being a mind. His analysis of that process is faulty in its details. It was bound to be so; because, with Locke, he misconceived his problem to be the analysis of mental operations. He should have conceived it as the analysis of operations constituent of actual entities. He would then have found mental operations in their proper place. Kant followed Hume in this misconception; and was thus led to balance the world upon thought— oblivious to the scanty supply of thinking. But Hume, Kant, and the philosophy of organism agree that the task of the critical reason is the analysis of constructs; and 'construction' is 'process.' Hume's analysis of the construct which constitutes a mental occasion is: impressions of sensation, ideas of impressions of sensation, impressions of reflection, ideas of impressions of reflection. This analysis may be found obscurely in Locke. But Hume exhibits it as an orderly process; and then endeavours—and fails—to express in terms of it our ordinary beliefs, in which he shares.

For subsequent empiricists the pleasure of the dogma has overcome the metaphysical rule of evidence: that we must bow to those presumptions, which, in despite of criticism, we still employ for the regulation of our lives. Such presumptions are imperative in experience. Rationalism is the search for the coherence of such presumptions. Hume, in his series of ideas and of impressions,† derivates from impressions of sensation, implicitly allows [230] that the building-up of experience is a process of addition to original data. The philosophy of organism, in this respect, agrees with Hume. It disagrees with Hume as to the proper characterization of the primary data. In Hume's philosophy the primary impressions are characterized in terms of universals, e.g., in the first section of his *Treatise* he refers to the colour 'red' as an illustration. This is also the doctrine of the first two books of Locke's *Essay*. But in Locke's third book a different doctrine appears, and the primary data are explicitly said to be 'ideas of particular existents.' According to Locke's second doctrine, the ideas of universals are derived from these primary data by a process of comparison and analysis. The philosophy of organism agrees in principle with this second doctrine of Locke's. It is difficult, and trifling, to determine the exact extent of the agreement; because the expositions of Locke and Hume bring in the very derivative operations involving consciousness. The organic philosophy does not hold that the 'particular existents' are prehended apart from universals; on the contrary, it holds that they are prehended by the mediation of universals. In other words, each actuality is prehended by means of some element of its own definiteness. This is the doctrine of the 'objectification' of actual entities. Thus the primary stage in the concrescence of an actual entity is the way in which the antecedent universe enters into the constitution of the entity in question, so as to constitute the basis of its nascent individuality. A converse way of looking at this truth is that the relevance to other actual entities of its own status in the actual world† is the initial datum in the process of its concrescence. When it is desired to emphasize this interpretation of the datum, the phrase 'objective content' will be used synonymously with the term 'datum.' Of course, strictly speaking, the universals, to which Hume confines the datum, are also 'objects'; but the phrase 'objective content' is meant to emphasize the doctrine of 'objectification' of actual entities. If experi- [231] ence be not based upon an objective content, there can be no escape from a solipsist subjectivism. But Hume, and Locke in his main doctrine, fail to provide experience with any objective content. Kant, for† whom 'process' is mainly a process of thought, accepts Hume's doctrine as to the 'datum' and turns the 'apparent' objective content into the end of the construct. So far, Kant's 'apparent' objective content seems to take the place of the 'satisfaction' in the philosophy of organism. In this way there can be no real escape from the solipsist difficulty. But Kant in his appeal to 'practical reason' admits also the 'satisfaction' in a sense analogous to that in the philosophy of organism; and by an analysis of its complex character he arrives at ultimate actualities which, according to his account, cannot be discovered by any analysis of 'mere appearance.' This is a very complex doctrine, which has been reproduced in all philosophies derivative from Kant. The doctrine gives each actual entity two worlds, one world of mere appearance, and the other world compact of ultimate substantial fact. On this point, as to the absence of 'objective content' in the datum for experience, Santayana [5] seems to agree with Hume and Kant. But if his introduction of 'animal faith' is to be taken as a re-examination of the datum under the influence of the sceptical conclusion from Hume's doctrine, then

[5] Cf. *Scepticism and Animal Faith.*

he, as his second doctrine, is practically reasserting Locke's second doctrine. But if he is appealing to 'practice' away from the critical examination of our sources of information, he must be classed with Hume and Kant, although differing from them in every detail of procedure.

In view of the anti-rationalism of Hume's contented appeal to 'practice,' it is very difficult to understand—except as another example of anti-rationalism—the strong objection, entertained by Hume and by his 'empiricist' followers, to the anti-rationalistic basis of some forms of religious faith. This strain of anti-rationalism [232] which Locke and Hume explicitly introduced into philosophy marks the final triumph of the anti-rationalistic reaction against the rationalism of the Middle Ages. Rationalism is the belief that clarity can only be reached by pushing explanation to its utmost limits. Locke, who hoped to attain final clarity in his analysis of human understanding in divorce from metaphysics, was, so far, an anti-rationalist. But Hume, in so far as he is to be construed as remaining content with two uncoordinated sets of beliefs, one based on the critical examination of our sources of knowledge, and the other on the uncritical‡ examination of beliefs involved in 'practice,' reaches the high watermark of anti-rationalism in philosophy; for 'explanation' is the analysis of coordination.

SECTION V

The process whereby an actual entity, starting from its objective content, attains its individual satisfaction, will be more particularly analysed in Part III. The primary character of this process is that it is individual to the actual entity; it expresses how the datum, which involves the actual world, becomes a component in the one actual entity. There must therefore be no further reference to other actual entities; the elements available for the explanation are simply, the objective content, eternal objects, and the selective concrescence of feelings whereby an actual entity becomes itself. It must be remembered that the objective content is analysable into actual entities under limited perspectives provided by their own natures; these limited perspectives involve eternal objects in grades of relevance. If the 'process' were primarily a process of understanding, we should have to note that 'grades of relevance' are only other eternal objects in grades of relevance, and so on indefinitely. But we have not the sort of understandings which embrace such indefinite progressions. Accordingly there is here a vicious regress, if the process be essentially a process of understanding. But this is not the primary [233] description of it; the process is a process of 'feeling.' In feeling, what is felt is not necessarily analysed; in understanding, what is understood is analysed, in so far as it is understood. Understanding is a special form of feeling. Thus there is no vicious regress in feeling, by reason of the indefinite complexity of what is felt. Kant, in his

'Transcendental Aesthetic,'† emphasizes the doctrine that in intuition a complex datum is intuited as one.

Again the selection involved in the phrase 'selective concrescence' is not a selection among the components of the objective content; for, by hypothesis, the objective content is a datum. The compatibilities and incompatibilities which impose the perspective, transforming the actual world into the datum, are inherent in the nature of things. Thus the selection is a selection of relevant eternal objects whereby what is a datum from without is transformed into its complete determination as a fact within. The problem which† the concrescence solves is, how the many components of the objective content are to be unified in one felt content with its complex subjective form. This one felt content is the 'satisfaction,' whereby the actual entity is its particular individual self; to use Descartes' phrase, 'requiring nothing but itself in order to exist.' In the conception of the actual entity in its phase of satisfaction, the entity has attained its individual separation from other things; it has absorbed the datum, and it has not yet lost itself in the swing back to the 'decision' whereby its appetition becomes an element in the data of other entities superseding it. Time has stood still—if only it could.

Thus process is the admission of eternal objects in their new rôle of investing the datum with the individuality of the subject. The datum,* *qua*‡ mere datum, includes the many individualities of the actual world. The satisfaction includes these many individualities as subordinate contributors to the one individuality. The process admits or rejects† eternal objects which by their absorption into the subjective forms of the many feelings [234] effect this integration. The attainment of satisfaction relegates all eternal objects which are not 'felt' either as determinants of definiteness in the data,† or as determinants of definiteness in the subjective form of the satisfaction, into the status of contraries to the eternal objects which are thus felt. Thus all indeterminations respecting the potentialities of the universe are definitely solved so far as concerns the satisfaction of the subject in question.

The process can be analysed genetically into a series of subordinate phases which presuppose their antecedents. Neither the intermediate phases, nor the datum which is the primary phase of all, determine the final phase of determinate individualization. Thus an actual entity, on its *subjective side, is nothing else than what the universe is for it, including its own reactions. The reactions are the subjective forms of the feelings, elaborated into definiteness through stages of process. An actual entity achieves its own unity by its determinate feelings respecting every item of the datum. Every individual objectification in the datum has its perspective defined by its own eternal objects with their own relevance compatible with the relevance of other objectifications. Each such objectification, and each such complex of objectifications, in the datum is met with a correspondent feeling, with its determinate subjective form, until the many become one experience, the satisfaction. The philosophies of substance presuppose a subject which then encounters a datum, and then reacts to the datum. The philosophy of organism presupposes a datum which is met with feelings, and progressively attains the unity of a subject. But with this doctrine, 'superject' would be a better term than 'subject.' Locke's 'ideas of reflection' are the feelings, in so far as they have entered into consciousness.

It is by reference to feelings that the notion of 'immediacy' obtains its meaning. The mere objectification of actual entities by eternal objects lacks 'immediacy.' It is 'repetition'; and this is a contrary to 'immediacy.' [235] But 'process' is the rush of feelings whereby second-handedness attains subjective immediacy; in this way, subjective form overwhelms repetition, and transforms it into immediately felt satisfaction; objectivity is absorbed into subjectivity. It is useful to compare this analysis of the construction of an act of experience with Kant's. In the first place Kant's act of experience is essentially knowledge. Thus whatever is not knowledge is necessarily inchoate, and merely on its way to knowledge. In comparing Kant's procedure with that of the philosophy of organism, it must be remembered that an 'apparent' objective content is the end of Kant's process, and thus takes the place of 'satisfaction' in the process as analysed in the philosophy of organism. In Kant's phraseology at the beginning of the *Critique of Pure Reason*, this 'apparent' objective content is referred to as 'objects.' He also accepts Hume's sensationalist account of the datum. Kant places this sentence at the commencement of the *Critique*: "Objects therefore are given to us through our sensibility. Sensibility alone supplies us with intuitions. These intuitions become thought through the understanding, and hence arise conceptions." [6] This is expanded later in a form which makes Kant's adhesion to Hume's doctrine of the datum more explicit:

And here we see that the impressions of the senses give the first impulse to the whole faculty of knowledge with respect to them, and thus produce experience which consists of two very heterogeneous elements, namely, matter for knowledge, derived from the senses [*eine Materie† zur Erkenntniss aus den Sinnen*], and a certain form according to which it is arranged, derived from the internal source of pure intuition and pure thought, first brought into action by the former, and then producing concepts.[7]

Also:

Thoughts with- [236] out content are empty, intuitions without concepts are blind.[8]

[6] "Vermittelst der Sinnlichkeit also werden uns Gegenstände gegeben, und sie allein liefert uns Anschauungen;† durch den Verstand aber werden sie gedacht, und von ihm entspringen Begriffe." Translation in the text is Max Müller's.

[7] 'Transcendental Analytic,'† Ch. II, Sect. I (Max Müller).

[8] 'Transcendental Logic,' Introduction, Sect. I.*

In this last statement the philosophy of organism is in agreement with Kant; but for a different reason. It is agreed that the functioning of concepts is an essential factor in knowledge, so that 'intuitions without concepts are blind.' But for Kant, apart from concepts there is nothing to know; since objects related in a knowable world are the product of conceptual functioning whereby categoreal form is introduced into the sense-datum, which otherwise is intuited in the form of a mere spatio-temporal flux of sensations. Knowledge requires that this mere flux be particularized by conceptual functioning, whereby the flux is understood as a nexus of 'objects.' Thus for Kant the process whereby there is experience is a process from subjectivity to apparent objectivity. The philosophy of organism inverts this analysis, and explains the process as proceeding from objectivity to subjectivity, namely, from the objectivity, whereby the external world is a datum, to the subjectivity, whereby there is one individual experience. Thus, according to the philosophy of organism, in every act of experience there are objects for knowledge; but, apart from the inclusion of intellectual functioning in that act of experience, there is no knowledge.

We have now come to Kant, the great philosopher who first, fully and explicitly, introduced into philosophy the conception of an act of experience as a constructive functioning, transforming subjectivity into objectivity, or objectivity into subjectivity; the order is immaterial in comparison with the general idea. We find the first beginnings of the notion in Locke and in Hume. Indeed, in Locke, the process is conceived in its correct order, at least in the view of the philosophy of organism. But the whole notion is only vaguely and inadequately conceived. The full sweep of the notion is due to Kant. The second half of the modern period of philosophical thought is to be dated from Hume and Kant. In it the [237] development of cosmology has been hampered by the stress laid upon one, or other, of three misconceptions:

(i) The substance-quality doctrine of actuality.

(ii) The sensationalist doctrine of perception.

(iii) The Kantian doctrine of the objective world as a construct from subjective experience.

The combined influence of these allied errors has been to reduce philosophy to a negligible influence in the formation of contemporary modes of thought. Hume himself introduces the ominous appeal to 'practice'— not in criticism of his premises, but in supplement to his conclusions. Bradley, who repudiates Hume, finds the objective world in which we live, and move, and have our being, 'inconsistent if taken as real.' Neither side conciliates philosophical conceptions of a real world with the world of daily experience.

CHAPTER VII
THE SUBJECTIVIST PRINCIPLE

SECTION I

[238] It is impossible to scrutinize too carefully the character to be assigned to the datum in the act of experience. The whole philosophical system depends on it. Hume's doctrine of 'impressions of sensation' (*Treatise*, Book I, Part I, Sect. II) is twofold. I will call one part of his doctrine 'The Subjectivist Principle' and the other part 'The Sensationalist Principle.' It is usual to combine the two under the heading of the 'sensationalist doctrine'; but two principles are really involved, and many philosophers—Locke, for instance—are not equally consistent in their adhesion to both of them. The philosophy of organism denies both of these doctrines, in the form in which they are considered in this chapter, though it accepts a reformed subjectivist principle (cf. Sect. V† below and Part II, Ch. IX). Locke accepted the sensationalist principle, and was inconsistent in his statements respecting the subjectivist principle. With the exception of some lapses, he accepted the latter in the first two books of his *Essay*, and rejected it tacitly, but persistently, in the third and fourth books. Kant (in the *Critique of Pure Reason*) accepted the subjectivist principle, and rejected the sensationalist principle.

The sensationalist principle acquires dominating importance, if the subjectivist principle be accepted. Kant's realization of this importance constituted the basis of his contribution to philosophy. The history of modern philosophy is the story of attempts to evade the inflexible consequences of the subjectivist principle, explicitly or implicitly accepted. The great merit of Hume and of [239] Kant is the explicitness with which they faced the difficulty.

The subjectivist principle is, that the datum in the act of experience can be adequately analysed purely in terms of universals.

The sensationalist principle is, that the primary activity in the act of experience is the bare subjective entertainment of the datum, devoid of any subjective form of reception. This is the doctrine of *mere* sensation.

The subjectivist principle follows from three premises: (i) The acceptance of the 'substance-quality' concept as expressing the ultimate ontological principle. (ii) The acceptance of Aristotle's definition of a primary substance, as always a subject and never a predicate. (iii) The assumption that the experient subject is a primary substance. The first premise states that the final metaphysical fact is always to be expressed as

157

a quality inhering in a substance. The second premise divides qualities and primary substances into two mutually exclusive classes. The two premises together are the foundation of the traditional distinction between universals and particulars. The philosophy of organism denies the premises on which this distinction is founded. It admits two ultimate classes of entities, mutually exclusive. One class consists of 'actual entities,' which in the philosophical tradition are mis-described as 'particulars'; and the other class consists of forms of definiteness, here named 'eternal objects,' which in comparison with actual entities are mis-described as 'universals.' These mis-descriptions have already been considered (Part II, Ch. I, Sect. V).

Descartes held, with some flashes of inconsistency arising from the use of '*realitas objectiva*,' the subjectivist principle as to the datum. But he also held that this mitigation of the subjectivist‡ principle enabled the 'process' within experience to include a sound argument for the existence of God; and thence a sound argument for the general veridical character of those presumptions [240] as to the external world which somehow arise in the process.

According to the philosophy of organism, it is only by the introduction of covert inconsistencies into the subjectivist principle, as here stated, that there can be any escape from what Santayana calls, 'solipsism of the present moment.' Thus Descartes' mode of escape is either illusory, or its premises are incompletely stated. This covert introduction is always arising because common sense is inflexibly objectivist. We perceive other things which are in the world of actualities in the same sense as we are. Also our emotions are directed towards other things, including of course our bodily organs. These are our primary beliefs which philosophers proceed to dissect.

Now philosophy has always proceeded on the sound principle that its generalizations† must be based upon the primary elements in actual experience as starting-points. Greek philosophy had recourse to the common forms of language to suggest its generalizations. It found the typical statement, 'That stone is grey'; and it evolved the generalization that the actual world can be conceived as a collection of primary substances qualified by universal qualities. Of course, this was not the only generalization evolved: Greek philosophy was subtle and multiform, also it was not inflexibly consistent. But this general notion was always influencing thought, explicitly or implicitly.

A theory of knowledge was also needed. Again philosophy started on a sound principle, that all knowledge is grounded on perception. Perception was then analysed, and found to be the awareness that a universal quality is qualifying a particular substance. Thus perception is the catching of a universal quality in the act of qualifying a particular substance. It was then asked, how the perceiver perceives; and the answer is,† by his organs of sensation. Thus the universal qualities which qualify the perceived substances are, in respect to the [241] perceiver, his private sensations referred to particular substances other than himself. So far, the tradition of philosophy includes, among other elements, a factor of extreme objectivism in metaphysics, whereby the subject-predicate form of proposition is taken as expressing a fundamental metaphysical truth. Descartes modified traditional philosophy in two opposite ways. He increased the metaphysical emphasis on the substance-quality forms of thought. The actual things 'required nothing but themselves in order to exist,' and were to be thought of in terms of their qualities, some of them essential attributes, and others accidental modes. He also laid down the principle, that those substances which are the subjects enjoying conscious experiences† provide the primary data for philosophy, namely, themselves as in the enjoyment of such experience. This is the famous subjectivist bias which entered into modern philosophy through Descartes. In this doctrine Descartes undoubtedly made the greatest philosophical discovery since the age of Plato and Aristotle. For his doctrine directly traversed the notion that the proposition, 'This stone is grey,' expresses a primary form of known fact from which metaphysics can start its generalizations. If we are to go back to the subjective enjoyment of experience, the type of primary starting-point is 'my perception of this stone as grey.' Primitive men were not metaphysicians, nor were they interested in the expression of concrete experience. Their language merely expressed useful abstractions, such as 'greyness of the stone.' But like Columbus who never visited America, Descartes missed the full sweep of his own discovery, and he and his successors, Locke and Hume, continued to construe the functionings of the subjective enjoyment of experience according to the substance-quality categories. Yet if the enjoyment of experience be the constitutive subjective fact, these categories have lost all claim to any fundamental character in metaphysics. Hume—to proceed at once to the consistent exponent of the method— looked for a [242] universal quality to function as qualifying the mind, by way of explanation of its perceptive enjoyment. Now if we scan 'my perception of this stone as grey' in order to find a universal, the only available candidate is 'greyness.' Accordingly for Hume, 'greyness,' functioning as a sensation qualifying the mind, is a fundamental type of fact for metaphysical generalization. The result is Hume's simple impressions of sensation, which form the starting-point of his philosophy. But this is an entire muddle,† for the perceiving mind is not grey, and so grey is now made to perform a new rôle. From the original fact 'my perception of this stone as grey,' Hume extracts 'Awareness of sensation of greyness'; and puts it forward as the ultimate datum in this element of experience.

He has discarded the objective actuality of the stone-image in his search for a universal quality: this 'objective actuality' is Descartes' *realitas objectiva.*† Hume's search was undertaken in obedience to a metaphysical principle which had lost all claim to validity, if the Cartesian discovery be accepted. He is then content with 'sensation of greyness,' which is just as much a particular as the original stone-image. He is aware of *'this* sensation of greyness.' What he has done is to assert arbitrarily the 'subjectivist' and 'sensationalist' principles as applying to the datum for experience: the notion '*this* sensation of greyness' has no reference to any other actual entity. Hume thus applies to the experiencing subject Descartes' principle, that it requires no other actual entity in order to exist. The fact that finally Hume criticizes the Cartesian notion of mind† does not alter the other fact that his antecedent arguments presuppose that notion.

It is to be noticed that Hume can only analyse the sensation in terms of a† universal and of its realization in the prehending mind. For example, to take the first examples which in his *Treatise* he gives of such analysis, we find 'red,' 'scarlet,' 'orange,' 'sweet,' 'bitter.' Thus Hume describes 'impressions of sensation' in the exact terms in which the philosophy of organism describes con- [243] ceptual feelings. They are the particular feelings of universals, and are not feelings of other particular existents exemplifying universals. Hume admits this identification, and can find no distinction except in 'force and vivacity.' He writes: "The first circumstance that strikes my eye, is the great resemblance between our impressions and ideas in every particular except their degree of force and vivacity."*

In contrast to Hume, the philosophy of organism keeps 'this stone as grey' in the datum for the experience in question. It is, in fact, the 'objective datum' of a certain physical feeling, belonging to a derivative type in a late phase of a concrescence. But this doctrine fully accepts Descartes' discovery that subjective experiencing is the primary metaphysical situation which is presented to metaphysics for analysis. This doctrine is the 'reformed subjectivist principle,'† mentioned earlier in this chapter. Accordingly, the notion 'this stone as grey' is a derivative abstraction, necessary indeed as an element in the description of the fundamental experiential feeling, but delusive as a metaphysical starting-point. This derivative abstraction is called an 'objectification.'

The justification for this procedure is, first, common sense, and, secondly, the avoidance of the difficulties which have dogged the subjectivist and sensationalist principles of modern philosophy. Descartes' discovery on the side of subjectivism requires balancing by an 'objectivist' principle as to the datum for experience. Also, with the advent of Cartesian subjectivism, the substance-quality category has lost all claim to metaphysical primacy; and, with this deposition of substance-quality, we can reject the notion of individual substances, each with its private world of qualities and sensations.

SECTION II

In the philosophy of organism knowledge is relegated to the intermediate phase of process. Cognizance belongs to the genus of subjective forms which are admitted, or [244] not admitted, to the function of absorbing the objective content into the subjectivity of satisfaction. Its 'importance' is therefore no necessary element in the concrete actual entity. In the case of any one such entity, it may merely constitute an instance of what Locke terms 'a capacity.' If we are considering the society of successive actual occasions in the historic route forming the life of an enduring object, some of the earlier actual occasions may be without knowledge, and some of the later may possess knowledge. In such a case, the unknowing man has become knowing. There is nothing surprising in this conclusion; it happens daily for most of us, when we sleep at night and wake in the morning. Every actual entity has the capacity for knowledge, and there is graduation in the intensity of various items of knowledge; but, in general, knowledge seems to be negligible apart from a peculiar complexity in the constitution of some actual occasion.

We—as enduring objects with personal order—objectify the occasions of our own past with peculiar completeness in our immediate present. We find in those occasions, as known from our present standpoint, a surprising variation in the range and intensity of our realized knowledge. We sleep; we are half-awake; we are aware of our perceptions, but are devoid of generalities in thought; we are vividly absorbed within a small region of abstract thought while oblivious to the world around; we are attending to our emotions—some torrent of passion—to them and to nothing else; we are morbidly discursive in the width of our attention; and finally we sink back into temporary obliviousness, sleeping or stunned. Also we can remember factors experienced in our immediate past, which at the time we failed to notice. When we survey the chequered history of our own capacity for knowledge, does common sense allow us to believe that the operations of judgment, operations which require definition in terms of conscious apprehension, are those operations which are foundational in existence either as [245] an essential attribute for an actual entity, or as the final culmination whereby unity of experience is attained?†

The general case [1] of conscious perception is the negative perception, namely, 'perceiving this stone as not grey.' The 'grey' then has ingression in its full character of a conceptual novelty, illustrating an alternative. In the positive case, 'perceiving this stone as grey,' the grey has ingression in its character of a possible novelty, but in fact by its conformity emphasizing the dative grey, blindly felt. Consciousness is the feeling of negation: in the perception of 'the stone as grey,' such feeling is in barest germ; in the perception of 'the stone as not grey,' such feeling is in† full development. Thus the negative perception is the triumph of consciousness. It finally rises to the peak of free imagination, in which the conceptual novelties search through a universe in which they are not datively exemplified.

Consciousness is the subjective form involved in feeling the contrast between the 'theory' which *may* be erroneous and the fact which is 'given.' Thus consciousness involves the rise into importance of the contrast be-

[1] Cf. Part III, for the full account.

tween the eternal objects designated by the words 'any' and 'just that.' Conscious perception is, therefore, the most primitive form of judgment. The organic philosophy holds that consciousness only arises in a late derivative phase of complex integrations. If an actual occasion be such that phases of this sort are negligible in its concrescence, then in its experience there is no knowledge;† owing to the fact that consciousness is a subjective form belonging to the later phases, the prehensions which it directly irradiates are those of an 'impure' type. Consciousness only illuminates the more primitive types of prehension so far as these prehensions are still elements in the products of integration. Thus those elements of our experience which stand out clearly and distinctly in our consciousness are not its basic facts; they are the derivative modifications which arise in the process. For [246] example, consciousness only dimly illuminates the prehensions in the mode of causal efficacy, because these prehensions are primitive elements in our experience. But prehensions in the mode of presentational immediacy are among those prehensions which we enjoy with the most vivid consciousness. These prehensions are late derivatives in the concrescence of an experient subject. The consequences of the neglect of this law, that the late derivative elements are more clearly illuminated by consciousness than the primitive elements, have been fatal to the proper analysis of an experient occasion. In fact, most of the difficulties of philosophy are produced by it. Experience has been explained in a thoroughly topsy-turvy fashion, the wrong end first. In particular, emotional and purposeful experience have been made to follow upon Hume's impressions of sensation.

To sum up: (i) Consciousness is a subjective form arising in the higher phases of concrescence. (ii) Consciousness primarily illuminates the higher phase in which it arises, and only illuminates earlier phases derivatively, as they remain components in the higher phase. (iii) It follows that the order of dawning, clearly and distinctly, in consciousness is not the order of metaphysical priority.

SECTION III

The primitive form of physical experience is emotional—blind emotion—received as felt elsewhere in another occasion and conformally appropriated as a subjective passion. In the language appropriate to the higher stages of experience, the primitive element is *sympathy*, that is, feeling the feeling *in* another and feeling conformally *with* another. We are so used to considering the high abstraction, 'the stone as green,' that we have difficulty in eliciting into consciousness the notion of 'green' as the qualifying character of an emotion. Yet, the aesthetic feelings, whereby there is pictorial art, are nothing else than products of the contrasts [247] latent in a variety of colours qualifying emotion, contrasts which are made possible by their patterned relevance to each other. The separation of the emotional experience from the presentational intuition is a high abstraction of thought. Thus the primitive experience is emotional feeling,† felt in its relevance to a world beyond. The feeling is blind and the relevance is vague. Also feeling, and reference to an exterior world,† pass into appetition, which is the feeling of determinate relevance to a world about to be. In the phraseology of physics, this primitive experience is 'vector feeling,' that is to say, feeling from a beyond which is determinate and pointing to a beyond which is to be determined. But the feeling is subjectively rooted in the immediacy of the present occasion: it is what the occasion feels for itself, as derived from the past and as merging into the future. In this vector transmission of primitive feeling the primitive provision of width for contrast is secured by pulses of emotion, which in the coordinate division of occasions (cf. Part IV) appear as wave-lengths and vibrations. In any particular cosmic epoch, the order of nature has secured the necessary differentiation of function, so as to avoid incompatibilities, by shepherding the sensa characteristic of that epoch each into association with a definite pulse. Thus the transmission of each sensum is associated with its own wave-length. In physics, such transmission can be conceived as corpuscular or undulatory, according to the special importance of particular features in the instance considered. The higher phases of experience increase the dimension of width, and elicit contrasts of higher types. The clash of uncoordinated emotions in the lower categories is† avoided: the aspect of inhibition and of transitory satisfaction is diminished. Experience realizes itself as an element in what is everlasting (cf. Part V, Ch. II), and as embodying in itself the everlasting component of the universe. This gain does not necessarily involve consciousness. Also it involves enhanced subjective emphasis. The occasion [248] has become less of a detail and more of a totality, so far as its subjective experience is concerned. The feeling of this width, with its enhancement of permanence, takes the form of blind zest, which can become self-defeating by excess of subjective emphasis. The inhibitions of zest by lack of adequate width to combine the contraries inherent in the environment lead to the destruction of the type of order concerned. Every increase of sensitivity requires an evolution towards adaptation. It must be remembered, however, that emotion in human experience, or even in animal experience, is not bare emotion. It is emotion interpreted, integrated, and transformed into higher categories of feeling. But even so, the emotional appetitive elements in our conscious experience are those which most closely resemble the basic elements of all physical experience.

SECTION IV

The distinction between the various stages of concrescence consists in the diverse modes of ingression of the eternal objects involved. The immanent decision, whereby there is a supervening of stages in an actual entity, is always the determinant of a process of integration whereby completion is arrived at—at least, such 'formal' completion as is proper to a single actual entity. This determination originates with conceptual prehensions which enter into integration with the physical prehensions,† modifying both the data and the subjective forms.

The limitation whereby there is a perspective relegation of eternal objects to the background is the characteristic of decision. Transcendent decision includes God's decision. He is the actual entity in virtue of which the *entire* multiplicity of eternal objects obtains its graded relevance to each stage of concrescence. Apart from God, there could be no relevant novelty. Whatever arises in actual entities from God's decision, arises first conceptually, and is transmuted into the physical world (cf. Part III). In 'transcendent decision' there is transi- [249] tion from the past to the immediacy of the present; and in 'immanent decision' there is the process of acquisition of subjective form and the integration of feelings. In this process the creativity, universal throughout actuality, is characterized by the datum from the past; and it meets this dead datum—universalized into a character of creativity—by the vivifying novelty of subjective form selected from the multiplicity of pure potentiality. In the process, the old meets the new, and this meeting constitutes the satisfaction of an immediate particular individual.

Eternal objects in any one of their modes of subjective ingression are then functioning in the guise of subjective novelty meeting the objective datum from the past. This word 'feeling' is a mere technical term; but it has been chosen to suggest that functioning through which the concrescent actuality appropriates the datum so as to make it its own. There are three successive phases of feelings, namely, a phase of 'conformal'† feelings, one of 'conceptual' feelings, and one of 'comparative' feelings, including 'propositional' feelings in this last species. In the conformal feelings the *how* of feeling reproduces what is felt. Some conformation is necessary as a basis of vector transition, whereby the past is synthesized with the present. The one eternal object in its two-way function, as a determinant of the datum and as a determinant of the subjective form, is thus relational. In this sense the solidarity of the universe is based on the relational functioning of eternal objects. The two latter‡ phases can be put together as the 'supplemental' phase.

An eternal object when it has ingression through its function of objectifying the actual world, so as to present the datum for prehension, is functioning 'datively.' Hence, to sum up, there are four modes of functioning whereby an eternal object has ingression into the constitution of an actual entity: (i) as dative ingression, (ii) in conformal physical feeling, (iii) in conceptual feeling, (iv) in comparative feeling.

[250] But the addition of diverse eternal objects is not of the essence of 'supplementation': the essence consists in the adjustment of subjective importance by functioning of subjective origin. The graduated emotional

intensity of the subject is constituting itself by reference to the physical data, datively there and conformally felt. All references to 'attention' usually refer to such supplementation in which the addition of diverse eternal objects is at a minimum; whereas references to 'emotion' usually refer to such supplementation complicated by profuse addition of diverse eternal objects. Supplementary feeling is emotional and purposeful, because it is what is felt by mere reason of the subjective appropriation of the objective data. But it is of the essence of supplementary feeling that it does not challenge its initial phase of conformal feeling by any reference to incompatibility. The stages of the subjective ingression of eternal objects involve essential compatibility. The process exhibits an inevitable continuity of functioning. Each stage carries in itself the promise of its successor, and each succeeding stage carries in itself the antecedent out of which it arose. For example,† the complexity of the datum carries in itself the transition from the conformal feelings to supplementary feelings in which contrasts, latent in the datum, achieve real unity between the components. Thus components in the datum, which *qua* dative, are diverse, become united in specific realized contrast. As elements in the datum, the components are individually given, with the potentiality for a contrast, which in the supplementary stage is either included or excluded. The conformal stage merely transforms the objective content into subjective feelings. But the supplementary stage adds, or excludes, the realization of the contrasts by which the original datum passes into its emotional unity.

This account enables us to conceive the stage of consciousness as a prolongation of the stage of supplementation. The concrescence is an individualization of the whole universe. Every eternal object, whether relevant [251] or irrelevant to the datum, is still patient of its contrasts with the datum. The process by which such contrasts are admitted or rejected involves the stage of conceptual feeling; and consciousness is evidently only a further exhibition of this stage of supplementary feeling. Conceptual feelings do not necessarily involve consciousness. This point is elaborated in detail in Part III.

Again in this explanation, 'contrast' has appeared as the general case; while 'identification' is a sub-species arising when one and the same eternal object is contrasted in its two modes of functioning.

Thus the two latter stages of feeling are constituted by the realization of specific modes of diversity and identity, the realization also involving an adjustment of intensities of relevance. Mere diversity, and mere identity, are generic terms. Two components in the constitution of an actual entity are specifically diverse and specifically identical by reason of the definite potential contrast involved in the diversity of the implicated eternal objects, and by reason of the definite self-identity of each eternal object. The specific identity arising from the synthesis of diverse modes of functioning of one eternal object is the 'individual essence' of that eternal object. But the concrescence reaches the goal required by the Category of Objective

Unity, that in any subject one entity can only be felt once. Nothing can be duplicated. The many potentialities for one entity must be synthesized†‌ into one fact. Hence arise the incompatibilities productive of elimination.

Properly speaking, modes of functioning are compared, thereby evoking specific contrasts and specific identifications. The two latter stages of feeling are the stages of comparison; these stages involve comparisons, and comparisons of comparisons; and the admission, or exclusion, of an indefinite complexity of potentialities for comparison, in ascending grades.

The ultimate attainment is 'satisfaction.' This is the final characterization of the unity of feeling of the one [252] actual entity, the 'superject' which is familiarly termed the 'subject.' In a sense this satisfaction is two-dimensional. It has a dimension of narrowness, and a dimension of width. The dimension of narrowness refers to the intensities of individual emotions arising out of individual components in the datum. In this dimension, the higher levels of coordination are irrelevant. The dimension of width arises out of the higher levels of coordination, by which the intensities in the dimension of narrowness become subordinated to a coordination which depends upon the higher levels of comparison. The savouring of the complexity of the universe can enter into satisfaction only through the dimension of width. The emotional depths at the low levels have their limits: the function of width is to deepen the ocean of feeling, and to remove the diminutions of depth produced by the interference of diverse emotions uncoordinated at a higher level. In the place of the Hegelian hierarchy of categories of thought, the philosophy of organism finds a hierarchy of categories of feeling.

SECTION V

The reformed subjectivist principle adopted by the philosophy of organism is merely an alternative statement of the principle of relativity (the fourth Category of Explanation). This principle states that it belongs to the nature of a 'being' that it is a potential for every 'becoming.' Thus all things are to be conceived as qualifications of actual occasions. According to the ninth Category of Explanation, *how* an actual entity becomes constitutes *what* that actual entity is. This principle states that the *being* of a *res vera* is constituted by its 'becoming.' The way in which one actual entity is qualified by other actual entities is the 'experience' of the actual world enjoyed by that actual entity, as subject. The subjectivist principle** is that the whole universe consists of elements disclosed in the analysis of the experiences of subjects. Process is the becoming of experience. [253] It follows that the philosophy of organism entirely accepts the subjectivist bias of modern philosophy. It also accepts Hume's doctrine that nothing is to be received into the philosophical scheme which is not discoverable as an element in subjective experience. This is the ontological principle. Thus Hume's demand that causation be describable as an element in experience is, on these principles, entirely justifiable. The point of the criticisms of Hume's procedure is that we have direct intuition of inheritance and memory: thus the only problem is, so to describe the general character of experience that these intuitions may be included. It is here that Hume fails. Also those modern empiricists who substitute 'law' for 'causation' fail even worse than Hume. For 'law' no more satisfies Hume's tests than does 'causation.' There is no 'impression' of law, or of lawfulness. Even allowing memory, according to Humian principles what has happened in experience has happened in experience, and that is all that can be said. Everything else is bluff, combined with the fraudulent insertion of 'probability' into a conclusion which demands 'blank ignorance.'

The difficulties of all schools of modern philosophy lie in the fact that, having accepted the subjectivist principle,** they continue to use philosophical categories derived from another point of view. These categories are not wrong, but they deal with abstractions unsuitable for metaphysical use. It is for this reason that the notions of the 'extensive continuum' and of 'presentational† immediacy' require such careful discussion from every point of view. The notions of the 'green leaf' and of the 'round ball' are at the base of traditional metaphysics. They have generated two misconceptions: *one* is the concept of vacuous actuality, void of subjective experience; and the *other* is the concept of quality inherent in substance. In their proper character, as high abstractions, both of these notions are of the utmost pragmatic use. In fact, language has been formed chiefly to express such con [254] cepts. It is for this reason that language, in its ordinary usages, penetrates but a short distance into the principles of metaphysics. Finally, the reformed subjectivist principle must be repeated: that apart from the experiences of subjects there is nothing, nothing, nothing, bare nothingness.

It is now evident that the final analogy to philosophies of the Hegelian school, noted in the Preface, is not accidental. The universe is at once the multiplicity of *rēs veræ*† and the solidarity of *rēs veræ*. The solidarity is itself the efficiency of the macroscopic *res vera*, embodying the principle of unbounded permanence acquiring novelty through flux. The multiplicity is composed of microscopic *rēs veræ*, each embodying the principle of bounded flux acquiring 'everlasting' permanence. On one side, the one becomes many; and on the other side, the many become one. But *what* becomes is always a *res vera*, and the concrescence† of a *res vera* is the development of a subjective aim. This development is nothing else than the Hegelian development of an idea. The elaboration of this aspect of the philosophy of organism, with the purpose of obtaining an interpretation of the religious experience of mankind, is undertaken in Part V of these lectures.

Cosmological story, in every part and in every chapter, relates the interplay of the static vision and the dynamic history. But the whole story is comprised within the account of the subjective concrescence of *rēs veræ*.

CHAPTER VIII
SYMBOLIC REFERENCE
SECTION I

[255] THE pure mode of presentational immediacy gives no information as to the past or the future. It merely presents an illustrated portion of the presented duration. It thereby defines a cross-section of the universe: but does not in itself define on which side lies the past, and on which side the future. In order to solve such questions we now come to the interplay between the two pure modes. This mixed mode of perception is here named 'symbolic reference.' The failure to lay due emphasis on symbolic reference is one of the reasons for metaphysical difficulties; it has reduced the notion of 'meaning' to a mystery.

The first principle, explanatory of symbolic reference, is that for such reference a 'common ground' is required. By this necessity for a 'common ground' it is meant that there must be components in experience which are directly recognized as identical in each of the pure perceptive modes. In the transition to a higher phase of experience, there is a concrescence in which prehensions in the two modes are brought into a unity of feeling: this concrescent unity arises from a congruity of their subjective forms in virtue of the identity relation between the two prehensions, owing to some components in common. Thus the symbolic reference belongs to one of the later originative phases of experience. These later phases are distinguished by their new element of originative freedom. Accordingly, while the two pure perceptive modes are incapable of error, symbolic reference introduces this possibility. When human experience is in question, 'per- [256] ception' almost always means 'perception in the mixed mode of symbolic reference.' Thus, in general, human perception is subject to error, because, in respect to those components most clearly in consciousness, it is interpretative. In fact, error is the mark of the higher organisms, and is the schoolmaster by whose agency there is upward evolution. For example, the evolutionary use of intelligence is that it enables the individual to profit by error without being slaughtered by it. But at present, we are not considering conceptual or intellectual functioning.

One main element of common ground, shared between the two pure modes, is the presented locus. This locus enters subordinately into the perceptive mode of causal efficacy, vaguely exemplifying its participation in the general scheme of extensive interconnection, involved in the real

168

potentiality. It is not disclosed by that perceptive mode in any other way; at least it is not directly disclosed. The further disclosure must be indirect, since contemporary events are exactly those which are neither causing, nor caused by, the percipient actual occasion. Now, although the various causal pasts (i.e., 'actual worlds') of the contemporary actual occasions are not wholly identical with the causal past of the percipient actual occasion, yet, so far as important relevance is concerned, these causal pasts are practically identical. Thus there is, in the mode of causal efficacy, a direct perception of those antecedent actual occasions which are causally efficacious both for the percipient and for the relevant events in the presented locus. The percipient therefore, under the limitation of its own perspective, prehends the causal influences to which the presented locus in its important regions is subjected. This amounts to an indirect perception of this locus, a perception in which the direct components belong to the pure mode of causal efficacy. If we now turn to the perceptive mode of presentational immediacy, the regions, perceived by direct and indirect knowledge respectively, are inverted in comparison with the other mode. The presented locus is directly illus- [257] trated by the sensa; while the causal past, the causal future, and the other contemporary events, are only indirectly perceived by means of their extensive relations to the presented locus. It must be remembered that the presented locus has its fourth dimension of temporal thickness 'spatialized' as the specious present of the percipient. Thus the presented locus, with the animal body of the percipient as the region from which perspectives are focussed, is the regional origin by reference to which in this perceptive mode the complete scheme of extensive regions is rendered determinate. The respective rôles of the two perceptive modes in experience are aptly exemplified by the fact that all scientific observations, such as measurements, determinations of relative spatial position, determinations of sense-data such as colours, sounds, tastes, smells, temperature feelings, touch feelings, etc., are made in the perceptive mode of presentational immediacy; and that great care is exerted to keep this mode pure, that is to say, devoid of symbolic reference to causal efficacy. In this way accuracy is secured, in the sense that the direct observation is purged of all interpretation. On the other hand all scientific theory is stated in terms referring exclusively to the scheme of relatedness, which, so far as it is observed, involves the percepta in the pure mode of causal efficacy. It thus stands out at once, that what we want to know about, from the point of view either of curiosity or of technology, chiefly resides in those aspects of the world disclosed in causal efficacy: but that what we can distinctly register is chiefly to be found among the percepta in the mode of presentational immediacy.

The presented locus is a common ground for the symbolic reference, because it is directly and distinctly perceived in presentational immediacy, and is indistinctly and indirectly perceived in causal efficacy. In the latter mode, the indistinctness is such that the detailed geometrical relationships are, for the most part, incurably vague. Particular regions are, in this perceptive mode, [258] in general not distinguishable. In this respect, causal efficacy stands in contrast to presentational immediacy with its direct illustration of certain distinct regions.

But there are exceptions to this geometrical indistinctness of causal efficacy. In the first place, the separation of the potential extensive scheme into past and future lies with the mode of causal efficacy and not with that of presentational immediacy. The mathematical measurements, derivable from the latter, are indifferent to this distinction; whereas the physical theory, expressed in terms of the former, is wholly concerned with it. In the next place, the animal body of the percipient is a region for which causal efficacy acquires some accuracy in its distinction of regions—not all the distinctness of the other mode, but sufficient to allow of important identifications. For example, we see *with* our eyes, we taste *with* our palates, we touch *with* our hands, etc.: here the causal efficacy defines regions which are identified with themselves as perceived with greater distinctness by the other mode. To take one example, the slight eye-strain in the act of sight is an instance of regional definition by presentational immediacy. But in itself it is no more to be correlated with projected sight than is a contemporary stomach-ache, or a throb in the foot. The obvious correlation of the eye-strain with sight arises from the perception, in the other mode, of the *eye* as efficacious in sight. This correlation takes place in virtue of the identity of the two regions, the region of the eye-strain, and the region of eye-efficacy. But the eye-strain is so immeasurably the superior in its power of regional definition that, as usual, we depend upon it for explicit geometrical correlations with other parts of the body. In this way, the animal body is the great central ground underlying all symbolic reference. In respect to bodily perceptions the two modes achieve the maximum of symbolic reference, and pool their feelings referent to identical regions. Every statement about the geometrical relationships of physical bodies in the world is ultimately [259] referable to certain definite human bodies as origins of reference. A traveller, who has lost his way, should not ask, Where am I? What he really wants to know is, Where are the other places? He has got his own body, but he has lost them.

SECTION II

The second 'ground' for symbolic reference is the connection between the two modes effected by the identity of an eternal object ingredient in both of them. It will be remembered that the former 'ground' was the identity of the extensive region throughout such stages of direct perception and synthesis, when there was a diversity of eternal objects, for example, eye-region, visual sensa, eye-strain. But now we pass to a diversity of regions combined with an identity of the eternal object, for example, visual sensa given by efficacy of eye-region, and the region of the stone perceived in the mode of presentational immediacy under the illustration of the same visual sensa.† In this connection the 'make-believe' character of modern empiricism is well shown by putting into juxtaposition† two widely separated passages [1] from Hume's *Treatise*: "Impressions may be divided into two kinds, those of *sensation,* and those of *reflection.* The first kind arises in the soul originally, *from unknown causes.*" And "*If it be perceived by the eyes,* it must be a colour; . . ."

The earlier passage is Hume's make-believe, when he is thinking of his philosophical principles. He then refers the visual sensations 'in the soul' to 'unknown causes.' But in the second passage, the heat of argument elicits his real conviction—everybody's real conviction—that visual sensations arise '*by* the eyes.' The causes are not a bit 'unknown,' and among them there is usually to be found the efficacy of the eyes. If Hume had stopped to investigate the alternative causes for the occurrence of visual sensations—for example, eye-sight, or excessive consumption of alcohol— he might have hesitated in his [260] profession of ignorance. If the causes be indeed unknown, it is absurd to bother about eye-sight and intoxication. The reason for the existence of oculists and prohibitionists is that various causes *are* known.

We can now complete our account of presentational immediacy. In this perceptive mode the sensa are 'given' for the percipient, but this donation is not to be ascribed to the spatial object which is thereby presented, the stone, for example. Now it is a primary doctrine that what is 'given' is given by reason of objectifications of actual entities from the settled past. We therefore seek for the actual occasions to whose objectifications this donation is to be ascribed. In this procedure we are only agreeing with the *spirit* of Descartes' fifty-second principle (Part I): "For this reason, when we perceive any attribute, we therefore conclude that some existing thing or substance to which it may be attributed, is necessarily present." Common sense, physical theory, and physiological theory, combine to point out a historic route of inheritance, from actual occasion to succeeding actual occasion, first physically in the external environment, then physiologically—through the eyes in the case of visual data—up the nerves, into the brain. The donation—taking sight as an example—is not confined to definite sensa, such as shades of colour: it also includes geometrical relationships to the general environment. In this chain of inheritances, the eye is picked out to rise into perceptive prominence, because another historic route of physiological inheritance starts from it, whereby a later occasion (almost identical with the earlier) is illustrated by the sensum 'eyestrain' in the mode of presentational immediacy; but this eye-strain is another allied story. In the visual datum for the percipient there are first these components of colour-sensa combined with geometrical relationships to the external world of the settled past: secondly, there are also in the datum the general geometrical relationships forming the completion of this potential scheme into the contemporary world, and into [261] the future.

[1] Book I, Part I, Sects. II and VI (italics mine).*

The responsive phase absorbs these data as material for a subjective unity of feeling: the supplemental stage heightens the relevance of the colour-sensa, and supplements the geometrical relationships of the past by picking out the contemporary region of the stone to be the contemporary representative of the efficacious historic routes. There then results in the mode of presentational immediacy, the perception of the region illustrated by the sensum termed 'grey.' The term 'stone' is primarily applied to a certain historic route in the past, which is an efficacious element in this train of circumstance. It is only properly applied to the contemporary region illustrated by 'grey' on the assumption that this contemporary region is the prolongation, of that historic route, into the presented locus. This assumption may, or may not, be true. Further, the illustration of the contemporary region of 'grey' may be due to quite other efficacious historic routes—for example, to lighting effects arranged by theatrical producers—and in such a case, the term 'stone' may suggest an even more violent error than in the former example. What is directly perceived, certainly and without shadow of doubt, is a grey region of the presented locus. Any further interpretation, instinctive or by intellectual judgment, must be put down to symbolic reference.

This account makes it plain that the perceptive mode of presentational immediacy arises in the later, originative, integrative phases of the process of concrescence. The perceptive mode of causal efficacy is to be traced to the constitution of the datum by reason of which there is a concrete percipient entity. Thus we must assign the mode of causal efficacy to the fundamental constitution of an occasion so that in germ this mode belongs even to organisms of the lowest grade; while the mode of presentational immediacy requires the more sophistical activity of the later stages of process, so as to belong only to organisms of a relatively high grade. So far as we can judge, such high-grade organisms are relatively few, in [262] comparison with the whole number of organisms in our immediate environment. Presentational immediacy is an outgrowth from the complex datum implanted by causal efficacy. But, by the originative power of the supplemental phase, what was vague, ill defined, and hardly relevant in causal efficacy, becomes distinct, well defined, and importantly relevant in presentational immediacy. In the responsive phase, the grey colour,† and the geometrical relations between the efficacious, bodily routes and the contemporary occasions, were subjective sensations† associated with barely relevant geometrical relations: they represented the vivid sensational qualities in the enjoyment of which the percipient subject barely distinguished vague indirect relationships to the external world. The supplemental phase lifts the presented duration into vivid distinctness, so that the vague efficacy of the indistinct external world in the immediate past is precipitated upon the representative regions in the contemporary present. In the usual language, the sensations are projected. This phraseology is unfortunate; for there never were sensations apart from these geometrical relations.

Presentational immediacy is the enhancement of the importance of relationships which were already in the datum, vaguely and with slight relevance. This fact, that 'presentational immediacy' deals with the same datum as does 'causal efficacy,' gives the ultimate reason why there is a common 'ground' for 'symbolic reference.' The two modes express the same datum under different proportions of relevance. The two genetic processes involving presentational immediacy must be carefully distinguished. There is first the complex genetic process in which presentational immediacy originates. This process extends downwards even to occasions which belong to the historic routes of certain types of inorganic enduring objects, namely, to those enduring objects whose aggregates form the subject-matter of the science of Newtonian dynamics.† Secondly, prehensions in the mode of presentational immediacy are involved as components in [263] integration with other prehensions which are usually, though not always,† in other modes. These integrations often involve various types of 'symbolic reference.' This symbolic reference is the interpretative† element in human experience. Language almost exclusively refers to presentational immediacy as interpreted by symbolic reference. For example, we say that 'we see the *stone*' where *stone* is an interpretation of *stone-image*: also we say that 'we see the *stone-image* with our eyes'; this is an interpretation arising from the complex integration of (i) the causal efficacy of the antecedent eye in the vision, (ii) the presentational immediacy of the stone-image, (iii) the presentational immediacy of the eye-strain. When we say that 'we see the stone with our eyes,' the interpretations of these two examples are combined.

SECTION III

The discussion of the problem constituted by the connection between causation and perception† has been conducted by the various schools of thought derived from Hume and Kant under the misapprehension generated by an inversion of the true constitution of experience. The inversion was explicit in the writings of Hume and of Kant: for both of them presentational immediacy was the primary fact of perception, and any apprehension of causation was, somehow or other, to be elicited from this primary fact. This view of the relation between causation and perception, as items in experience, was not original to these great philosophers. It is to be found presupposed in Locke and Descartes; and they derived it from mediaeval predecessors. But the modern critical movement in philosophy arose when Hume and Kant emphasized the fundamental, inescapable, importance which this doctrine possesses for any philosophy admitting its truth. The philosophy of organism does not admit its truth, and thus rejects the touchstone which is the neolithic weapon of 'critical' philosophy. It must be remembered that clearness in consciousness is no evidence [264] for primitiveness in the genetic process: the opposite doctrine is more nearly true.

Owing to its long dominance, it has been usual to assume as an obvious fact the primacy of presentational immediacy. We open our eyes and our other sense-organs; we then survey the contemporary world decorated with sights, and sounds, and tastes; and then, by the sole aid of this information about the contemporary world, thus decorated, we draw what conclusions we can as to the actual world. No philosopher really holds that this is the sole source of information: Hume and his followers appeal vaguely to 'memory' and to 'practice,' in order to supplement their direct information; and Kant wrote other *Critiques*† in order to supplement his *Critique of Pure Reason*. But the general procedure of modern philosophical 'criticism' is to tie down opponents strictly to the front door of presentational immediacy as the sole source of information, while one's own philosophy makes its escape by a back door veiled under the ordinary usages of language.

If this 'Humian' doctrine be true, certain conclusions as to 'behaviour'† ought to follow—conclusions which, in the most striking way, are not verified. It is almost indecent to draw the attention of philosophers to the minor transactions of daily life, away from the classic sources of philosophic knowledge; but, after all, it is the empiricists who began this appeal to Caesar.

According to Hume, our behaviour presupposing causation is due to the repetition of associated presentational experiences. Thus the vivid presentment of the antecedent percepts should vividly generate the behaviour, in action or thought, towards the associated consequent. The clear, distinct, overwhelming perception of the one is the overwhelming reason for the subjective transition to the other. For behaviour, interpretable as implying causation, is on this theory the subjective response to presentational immediacy. According to Hume this subjective response is the beginning and the end of all that [265] there is to be said about causation. In Hume's theory the response is response to presentational immediacy, and to nothing else. Also the situation elicited in response is nothing but an immediate presentation, or the memory of one. Let us apply this explanation to reflex action: In the dark, the electric light is suddenly turned on and the man's eyes blink. There is a simple physiological explanation of this trifling incident.

But this physiological explanation is couched wholly in terms of causal efficacy: it is the conjectural record of the travel of a spasm of excitement along nerves to some nodal centre, and of the return spasm of contraction back to the eyelids. The correct technical phraseology would not alter the fact that the explanation does not involve any appeal to presentational immediacy either for actual occasions resident in the nerves, or for the man. At the most there is a tacit supposition as to what a physiologist, who in fact was not there, might have seen if he had been there, and if he could have vivisected the man without affecting these occurrences, and if he could have observed with a microscope which also in fact was absent.

Thus the physiological explanation remains, from the point of view of Hume's philosophy, a tissue of irrelevancies. It presupposes a side of the universe about which, on Hume's theory, we must remain in blank ignorance.

Let us now dismiss physiology and turn to the private experience of the blinking man. The sequence of percepts, in the mode of presentational immediacy, is† flash of light, feeling of eye-closure, instant of darkness. The three are practically simultaneous; though the flash maintains its priority over the other two, and these two latter percepts are indistinguishable as to priority. According to the philosophy of organism, the man also experiences another percept in the mode of causal efficacy. He feels that the experiences of the *eye* in the matter of the flash are causal of the blink. The man himself will have no doubt of it. In fact, it is the feeling [266] of causality which enables the man to distinguish the priority of the flash; and the inversion of the argument, whereby the temporal sequence 'flash to blink' is made the premise for the 'causality' belief, has its origin in pure theory. The man will explain his experience by saying, 'The flash made me blink'; and if his statement be doubted, he will reply, 'I know it, because I felt it.'

The philosophy of organism accepts the man's statement, that the flash *made* him blink. But Hume intervenes with another explanation. He first points out that in the mode of presentational immediacy there is no percept of the flash *making* the man blink. In this mode there are merely the two percepts—the flash and the blink—combining the two latter of the three percepts under the one term 'blink.' Hume refuses to admit the man's protestation, that the compulsion to blink is just what he did feel. The refusal is based on the dogma† that all percepts are in the mode of presentational immediacy—a dogma not to be upset by a mere appeal to direct experience. Besides,† Hume has another interpretation of the man's experience: what the man really felt was his *habit* of blinking after flashes. The word 'association' explains it all, according to Hume. But how can a 'habit' be felt, when a 'cause' cannot be felt? Is there any presentational immediacy in the feeling of a 'habit'? Hume by a sleight of hand confuses a 'habit of feeling blinks after flashes' with a '*feeling of the habit* of feeling blinks after flashes.'

We have here a perfect example of the practice of applying the test of presentational immediacy to procure the critical rejection of some doctrines, and of allowing other doctrines to slip out by a back door, so as to evade the test. The notion of causation arose because mankind lives amid experiences in the mode of causal efficacy.

SECTION IV

We will keep to the appeal to ordinary experience, and [267] consider another situation, which Hume's philosophy is ill equipped to explain.

The 'causal feeling' according to that doctrine arises from the long association of well-marked presentations of sensa, one precedent to the other. It would seem therefore that inhibitions of sensa, given in presentational immediacy, should be accompanied by a corresponding absence of 'causal feeling'; for the explanation of how there is 'causal feeling' presupposes the well-marked familiar sensa, in presentational immediacy. Unfortunately the contrary is the case. An inhibition of familiar sensa is very apt to leave us a prey to vague terrors respecting a circumambient world of causal operations. In the dark there are vague presences, doubtfully feared; in the silence, the irresistible causal efficacy of nature presses itself upon us; in the vagueness of the low hum of insects in an August woodland, the inflow into ourselves of feelings from enveloping nature overwhelms us; in the dim consciousness of half-sleep, the presentations of sense fade away, and we are left with the vague feeling of influences from vague things around us. It is quite untrue that the feelings of various types of influences are dependent upon the familiarity of well-marked sensa in immediate presentment. Every way of omitting the sensa still leaves us a prey to vague feelings of influence. Such feelings, divorced from immediate sensa, are pleasant, or unpleasant, according to mood; but they are always vague as to spatial and temporal definition, though their explicit dominance in experience may be heightened in the absence of sensa.

Further, our experiences† of our various bodily parts are primarily perceptions of them as *reasons* for 'projected' sensa: the *hand*† is the *reason* for the projected touch-sensum, the *eye* is the *reason* for the projected sight-sensum. Our bodily experience is primarily an experience of the dependence of presentational immediacy upon causal efficacy. Hume's doctrine inverts this relationship by making causal efficacy, as an experience, dependent upon presentational immediacy. This doc- [268] trine, whatever be its merits, is not based upon any appeal to experience.

Bodily experiences, in the mode of causal efficacy, are distinguished by their comparative accuracy of spatial definition. The causal influences from the body have lost the extreme vagueness of those which inflow from the external world. But, even for the body, causal efficacy is dogged with vagueness compared to presentational immediacy. These conclusions are confirmed if we descend‡ the scale of organic being. It does not seem to be the sense of causal awareness that the lower living things lack, so much as variety of sense-presentation, and then vivid distinctness of presentational immediacy. But animals, and even vegetables, in low forms of organism exhibit modes of behaviour directed towards self-preservation. There is every indication of a vague feeling of causal relationship with the external world, of some intensity, vaguely defined as to quality, and with some vague definition as to locality. A jellyfish advances and withdraws, and in so doing exhibits some perception of causal relationship with the world beyond itself; a plant grows downwards to the damp earth, and upwards towards the light. There is thus some direct reason for attributing dim, slow feelings of causal nexus, although we have no reason for any ascription of the definite percepts in the mode of presentational immediacy.

But the philosophy of organism attributes 'feeling' throughout the actual world. It bases this doctrine upon the directly observed fact that 'feeling' survives as a known element constitutive of the 'formal' existence of such actual entities as we can best observe. Also when we observe the causal nexus, devoid of interplay with sense-presentation, the influx of feeling with vague qualitative and 'vector' definition† is what we find. The dominance of the *scalar* physical quantity, inertia, in the Newtonian physics obscured the recognition of the truth that all fundamental physical quantities are *vector* and not *scalar*.

[269] When we pass to inorganic actual occasions, we have lost the two higher originative phases in the 'process,' namely, the 'supplemental' phase, and the 'mental' phase. They are lost in the sense that, so far as our observations go, they are negligible. The influx of objectifications of the actualities of the world as organized vehicles of feeling is responded to by a mere subjective appropriation of such elements of feeling in their received relevance. The inorganic occasions are merely what the causal past allows them to be.

As we pass to the inorganic world, causation never for a moment seems to lose its grip. What is lost is originativeness, and any evidence of immediate absorption in the present. So far as we can see, inorganic entities are vehicles for receiving, for storing in a napkin, and for restoring without loss or gain.

In the actual world we discern four grades of actual occasions, grades which are not to be sharply distinguished from each other. First, and lowest, there are the actual occasions in so-called 'empty space'; secondly, there are the actual occasions which are moments in the life-histories of enduring non-living objects, such as electrons or other primitive organisms; thirdly, there are the actual occasions which are moments in the life-histories of enduring living objects; fourthly, there are the actual occasions which are moments in the life-histories of enduring objects with conscious knowledge.

We may imaginatively conjecture that the first grade is to be identified with actual occasions for which 'presented durations' are negligible elements among their data, negligible by reason of negligible presentational immediacy. Thus no intelligible definition of rest and motion is possible for historic routes including them, because they correspond to no inherent spatialization† of the actual world.

The second grade is to be identified with actual occasions for which 'presented durations' are important elements in their data, but with a limitation only to be [270] observed in the lower moments of human experience. In such occasions the data of felt sensa, derived from the more primitive data of causal efficacy, are projected onto the contemporary 'presented locus' without any clear illustration of special regions in that locus. The past has been lifted into the present, but the vague differentiations in the past have not been transformed into any precise differentiations within the present. The enhancement of precision has not arrived.

The third grade is to be identified with occasions in which presentational immediacy has assumed some enhanced precision, so that 'symbolic transference' has lifted into importance precisely discriminated regions in the 'presented duration.' The delicate activities of self-preservation are now becoming possible by the transference of the vague message of the past onto the more precisely discriminated regions of the presented duration. Symbolic transference is dependent upon the flashes of conceptual originality constituting life.

The fourth grade is to be identified with the canalized importance of free conceptual functionings, whereby blind experience is analysed by comparison with the imaginative realization of mere potentiality. In this way, experience receives a reorganization in the relative importance of its components by the joint operation of imaginative enjoyment and of judgment. The growth of reason is the increasing importance of critical judgment in the discipline of imaginative enjoyment.

SECTION V

One reason for the philosophical difficulties over causation is that Hume, and subsequently Kant, conceived the causal nexus as, in its primary character, derived from the presupposed sequence of immediate presentations. But if we interrogate experience, the exact converse is the case; the perceptive mode of immediate presentation affords information about the percepta in the more aboriginal mode of causal efficacy.

[271] Thus symbolic reference, though in complex human experience it works both ways, is chiefly to be thought of as the elucidation of percepta in the mode of causal efficacy by the fluctuating intervention of percepta in the mode of presentational immediacy.

The former mode produces percepta which are vague, not to be controlled, heavy with emotion: it produces the sense of derivation from an immediate past, and of passage to an immediate future; a sense of emotional feeling, belonging to oneself in the past, passing into oneself in the present, and passing from oneself in the present towards oneself in the future; a sense of influx of influence from other vaguer presences in the past, localized and yet evading local definition, such influence modifying, enhancing, inhibiting, diverting, the stream of feeling which we are receiving, unifying, enjoying, and transmitting. This is our general sense of existence, as one item among others, in an efficacious actual world.

By diversion of attention we can inhibit its entry into consciousness; but, whether mentally analysed or no, it remains the given uncontrolled basis upon which our character weaves itself. Our bodies are largely contrivances whereby some central actual occasion may inherit these basic experiences of its antecedent parts. Thus organic bodies have their parts coordinated by a peculiar vividness in their mutual inheritance. In a sense, the difference between a living organism and the inorganic environment is only a question of degree; but it is a difference of degree which makes all the difference—in effect, it is a difference of quality.

The percepta in the mode of presentational immediacy have the con-verse characteristics. In comparison, they are distinct, definite, controllable, apt for immediate enjoyment, and with the minimum of reference to past, or to future. We are subject to our percepta in the mode of efficacy, we adjust our percepta in the mode of immediacy. But, in fact, our process of self-construction for the achievement of unified experience produces† a new [272] product, in which percepta in one mode, and percepta in the other mode, are synthesized into one subjective feeling. For example, we are perceiving before our eyes a grey stone.

We shall find that generally—though not always—the adjectival words express information derived from the mode of immediacy, while the sub-stantives convey our dim percepts in the mode of efficacy. For example, 'grey' refers to the grey shape immediately before our eyes: this percept is definite, limited, controllable, pleasant or unpleasant, and with no ref-erence to past or to future. It is this sort of percept which has led to Des-cartes' definition of substances as 'requiring nothing but themselves in order to exist,' and to his notion of 'extension' as the principal† attribute of a genus of substances. It has also led to Hume's notion of 'impressions of sensation'† arising from unknown sources, and in complete indepen-dence so far as any discernible† nexus is concerned. But the other element in the compound percept has a widely different character. The word 'stone' is selected, no doubt, because its dictionary meaning will afford some help in understanding the particular percepta meant. But the word is meant to refer to particular feelings of efficacy in the immediate past, combined with anticipations for the immediate future; this feeling is vaguely localized, and conjecturally† identified with the very definite localization of the 'grey' perceptum.

Thus, so far as concerns conscious judgment, the symbolic reference is the acceptance of the evidence of percepta, in the mode of immediacy, as evidence for the localization and discrimination of vague percepta in the mode of efficacy. So far as bodily feelings are concerned, there is some direct check on this procedure; but, beyond the body, the appeal is to the pragmatic consequences, involving some future state of bodily feelings which can be checked up.

But throughout this discussion of perception there has been excessive emphasis on the mental phase in the [273] experiential process. This is inevitable because we can only discuss experiences which have entered into conscious analysis. But perception is a feeling which has its seat in the two earlier phases of the experiential† process, namely, the 'responsive' phase, and the 'supplemental' phase. Perception, in these phases, is the appropriation of the datum by the subject, so as to transform the datum into a unity of subjective feeling. The mode of efficacy belongs to the responsive phase, in which the objectifications are felt according to their relevance in the datum: the mode of immediacy belongs to the supplemental phase in which the faint indirect relevance, in the datum, of relationships to regions of the presented locus is† lifted into distinct, prominent, relevance. The question as to which regions have their relatedness to other constituents of the datum—such as 'grey,' for instance—thus accentuated, depends upon the coordination of the bodily organs through which the routes of inheritance pass. In a fortunately construed** animal body, this selection is determined chiefly by the inheritance received by the superficial organs†—the skin, the eyes, etc.—from the external environment, and preserves the relevance of the vector character of that external inheritance. When this is the case, the perceptive mode of immediacy has definite relevance to the future efficacy of the external environment, and then indirectly illustrates the inheritance which the presented locus receives from the immediate past.

But this illustration does not gain its first importance from any rational analysis. The two modes are unified by a blind symbolic reference by which supplemental feelings derived from the intensive, but vague, mode of efficacy are precipitated upon the distinct regions illustrated in the mode of immediacy. The integration of the two modes in supplemental feeling makes what would have been vague to be distinct, and what would have been shallow to be intense. This is the perception of the grey stone, in the mixed mode of symbolic reference.

[274] Such perception can be erroneous, in the sense that the feeling associates regions in the presented locus with inheritances from the past, which in fact have not been thus transmitted into the present regions. In the mixed mode, the perceptive determination is purely due to the bodily organs, and thus there is a gap in the perceptive logic—so to speak. This gap is not due to any conceptual freedom on the part of the ultimate subject. It is not a mistake due to consciousness. It is due to the fact that the body, as an instrument for synthesizing and enhancing feelings, is faulty, in the sense that it produces feelings which have but slight reference to the real state of the presented duration.

SECTION VI

Symbolic reference between the two perceptive modes affords the main example of the principles which govern all symbolism. The requisites for symbolism are that there be two species of percepta; and that a perceptum of one species has some 'ground' in common with a perceptum of another species, so that a correlation between the pair of percepta is established.

The feelings, and emotions, and general characteristics associated with the members of one species are in some ways markedly diverse from those associated with the other species. Then there is 'symbolic reference' between the two species when the perception of a member of one species evokes its correlate in the other species, and precipitates upon this correlate the fusion of feelings, emotions, and derivate actions, which belong to either of the pair of correlates, and which are also enhanced by this correlation. The species from which the symbolic reference starts is called the 'species of symbols,' and the species witht which it ends is called the 'species of meanings.' In this way there can be symbolic reference between two species in the same perceptive mode: but the chief example of symbolism, upon which is based a great portion of the lives [275] of all high-grade animals, is that between the two perceptive modes.

Symbolism can be justified, or unjustified. The test of justification must always be pragmatic. In so far ast symbolism has led to a route of inheritance, along the percipient occasions forming the percipient 'person,' which constitutes a fortunate evolution, the symbolism is justified; and, in so far as the symbolism has led to an unfortunate evolution, it is unjustified. In a slightly narrower sense the symbolism can be right or wrong; and rightness or wrongness is also tested pragmatically. Along the 'historic route' there is the inheritance of feelings derived from symbolic reference: now, if feelings respecting some definite element in experience be due to two sources, one source being this inheritance, and the other source being direct perception in one of the pure modes, then, if the feelings from the two sources enhance each other by synthesis, the symbolic reference is right; but, if they are at variance so as to depress each other, the symbolic reference is wrong. The rightness, or wrongness, of symbolism is an instance of the symbolism being fortunate or unfortunate; but mere 'rectitude,' in the sense defined above, does not cover all that can be included in the more general concept of 'fortune.' So much of human experience is bound up with symbolic reference, that it is hardly an exaggeration to say that the very meaning of truth is pragmatic. But though this statement is *hardly* an exaggeration, still it *is* an exaggeration, for the pragmatic test can never work, unless on some occasion—in the future, or in the present—there is a definite determination of what is true on that occasion. Otherwise the poor pragmatist remains an intellectual Hamlet, perpetually adjourning decision of judgment to some later date. According to the doctrines here stated, the day of judgment arrives when the 'meaning' is sufficiently distinct and relevant, as a perceptum in its proper pure mode, to afford comparison with the precipitate of feeling derived [276] from symbolic reference. There is no inherent distinction between the sort of percepta which are symbolst and the sort of percepta which are meanings. When two species are correlated by a 'ground' of relatedness, it depends upon the experiential process, constituting the percipientt subject, as to which species is the group of symbols, and which is the group of meanings. Also it equally depends upon the percipient as to whether there is any symbolic reference at all.

Language is the example of symbolism which most naturally presents itself for consideration of the uses of symbolism. Its somewhat artificial character makes the various constitutive elements in symbolism to be the more evident. For the sake of simplicity, only spoken language will be considered here.

A single word is not one definite sound. Every instance of its utterance differs in some respect from every other instance: the pitch of the voice, the intonation, the accent, the quality of sound, the rhythmic relations of the component sounds, the intensity of sound, all vary. Thus a word is a species of sounds, with specific identity and individual differences. When we recognize the species, we have heard the word. But what we have heard is merely the sound—euphonious or harsh, concordant with or discordant with other accompanying sounds. The word is heard in the pure perceptive mode of immediacy, and primarily elicits merely the contrasts and identities with other percepta in that mode. So far there is no symbolic interplay.

If the meaning of the word be an event, then either that event is directly known, as a remembered perceptum in an earlier occasion of the percipient's life, or that event is only vaguely known by its dated spatio-temporal nexus with events which are directly known. Anyhow there is a chain of symbolic references (inherited along the historic route of the percipient's life, and reinforced by the production of novel and symbolic references at various occasions along that route) whereby in the datum [277] for the percipient occasion there is a faintly relevant nexus between the word in that occasion of utterance and the event. The sound of the word,† in presentational immediacy, by symbolic references elicits this nexus into important relevance, and thence precipitates feelings, and thoughts, upon the enhanced objectification of the event. Such enhanced relevance of the event may be unfortunate, or even unjustified; but it is the function of words to produce it. The discussion of mentality is reserved for Part III: it is a mistake to think of words as primarily the vehicle of thoughts.

Language also illustrates the doctrine that, in regard to a couple of properly correlated species of things, it depends upon the constitution of the percipient subject to assign which species is acting as 'symbol' and which as 'meaning.' The word 'forest' may suggest† memories of forests; but equally the sight of a forest, or memories of forests, may suggest the word 'forest.' Sometimes we are bothered because the immediate experience has not elicited the word we want. In such a case the word with the right sort of correlation with the experience has failed to become importantly relevant in the constitution of our experience.

But we do not usually think of the things as symbolizing the words correlated to them. This failure to invert our ideas arises from the most useful aspect of symbolism. In general the symbols are more handy elements in our experience than are the meanings. We can say the word 'forest' whenever we like; but only under certain conditions can we directly experience an existent forest. To procure such an experience usually involves a problem of transportation only possible on our holidays. Also it is not so easy even to remember forest scenes with any vividness; and we usually find that the immediate experience of the word 'forest' helps to elicit such recollections. In such ways language is handy as an instrument of communication along the successive occasions of the historic route forming the life of one individual. By an [278] extension of these same principles of behaviour, it communicates from the occasions of one individual to the succeeding occasions of another individual. The same means which are handy for procuring the immediate presentation of a word to oneself are equally effective for presenting it to another person. Thus we may have a two-way system of symbolic reference involving two persons, A and B. The forest, recollected by A, symbolizes the word 'forest' for A; then A, for his own sake and for B's sake, pronounces the word 'forest'; then by the efficacy of the environment and of B's bodily parts, and by the supplemental enhancement due to B's experiential process, the word 'forest' is perceived by B in the mode of immediacy; and, finally by symbolic reference, B recollects vaguely various forest scenes. In this use of language for communication between two persons, there is in principle nothing which differs from its use by one person for communication along the route of his own actual occasions.

This discussion shows that one essential purpose of symbols arises from their handiness. For this reason the Egyptian papyrus made ink-written language a more useful symbolism than the Babylonian language impressed on brick. It is easier to smell incense than to produce certain religious emotions; so, if the two can be correlated, incense is a suitable symbol for such emotions. Indeed, for many purposes, certain aesthetic experiences which are easy to produce make better symbols than do words, written or spoken. Quarrels over symbolism constitute one of the many causes of religious discord. One difficulty in symbolism is that the unhandy meanings are often vague. For instance, this is the case with the percepta in the mode of efficacy which are symbolized by percepta in the mode of immediacy: also, as another instance, the incense is definite, but the religious emotions are apt to be indefinite. The result is that the meanings are often shifting and indeterminate. This happens even in the case of words: other people misun- [279] derstand their import. Also, in the case of incense the exact religious emotions finally reached are very uncertain: perhaps we would prefer that some of them were never elicited.

Symbolism is essential for the higher grades of life; and the errors of symbolism can never be wholly avoided.

CHAPTER IX

THE PROPOSITIONS

SECTION I

[280] A LIVING occasion is characterized by a flash of novelty among the appetitions of its mental pole. Such 'appetitions,' i.e., 'conceptual prehensions,' can be 'pure' or 'impure.' An 'impure' prehension arises from the integration of a 'pure' conceptual prehension with a physical prehension originating in the physical pole. The datum of a pure conceptual prehension is an eternal object; the datum of an impure prehension is a proposition, otherwise termed a 'theory.'

The integration of a conceptual and physical prehension need not issue in an impure prehension: the eternal object as a mere potentiality, undetermined as to its physical realization, may lose its indetermination, i.e., its universality, by integration with itself as an element in the realized definiteness of the physical datum of the physical prehension. In this case we obtain what in Part III is termed a 'physical purpose.' In a physical purpose the subjective form has acquired a special appetition—adversion or aversion—in respect to that eternal object as a realized element of definiteness in that physical datum. This acquisition is derived from the conceptual prehension. The 'abruptness' of mental operations is here illustrated. The physical datum in itself illustrates an indefinite number of eternal objects. The 'physical purpose' has focussed appetition upon an abruptly selected eternal object.

But with the growth of intensity in the mental pole, evidenced by the flash of novelty in appetition, the appetition takes the form of a 'propositional prehension.' [281] These prehensions will be studied more particularly in Part III. They are the prehensions of 'theories.' It is evident, however, that the primary function of theories is as a lure for feeling, thereby providing immediacy of enjoyment and purpose. Unfortunately theories, under their name of 'propositions,' have been handed over to logicians, who have countenanced the doctrine that their one function is to be judged as to their truth or falsehood. Indeed Bradley does not mention 'propositions' in his *Logic*.† He writes only of 'judgments.' Other authors define propositions as a component in judgment. The doctrine here laid down is that, in the realization of propositions, 'judgment' is a† very rare component, and so is 'consciousness.' The existence of imaginative literature should have warned logicians that their narrow doctrine is absurd. It is difficult to believe that all logicians as they read Hamlet's speech, "To be, or not to be: . . ." commence by judging whether the initial proposition be true or false, and keep up the task of judgment throughout the whole thirty-five lines. Surely, at some point in the reading, judgment is eclipsed by aesthetic delight. The speech, for the theatre audience, is purely theoretical, a mere lure for feeling.

Again, consider strong religious emotion—consider a Christian meditating on the sayings in the Gospels. He is not judging 'true or false'; he is eliciting their value as elements in feeling. In fact, he may ground his judgment of truth upon his realization of value. But such a procedure is impossible, if the primary function of propositions is to be elements in judgments.

The 'lure for feeling' is the final cause guiding the concrescence of feelings. By this concrescence the multifold datum of the primary phase is gathered into the unity of the final satisfaction of feeling. The 'objective lure' is that discrimination among eternal objects introduced into the universe by the real internal constitutions of the actual occasions forming the datum of the concrescence under review. This discrimination also in- [282] volves eternal objects excluded from value in the temporal occasions of that datum, in addition to involving the eternal objects included for such occasions.

For example, consider the Battle of Waterloo. This battle resulted in the defeat of Napoleon, and in a constitution of our actual world grounded upon that defeat. But the abstract notions, expressing the possibilities of another course of history which would have followed upon his victory, are relevant to the facts which actually happened. We may not think it of practical importance that imaginative historians should dwell upon such hypothetical alternatives. But we confess their relevance in thinking about them at all, even to the extent of dismissing them. But some imaginative writers do not dismiss such ideas. Thus, in our actual world of today, there is a penumbra of eternal objects, constituted by relevance to the Battle of Waterloo. Some people do admit elements from this penumbral complex into effective feeling, and others wholly exclude them. Some are conscious of this internal decision of admission or rejection; for others the ideas float into their minds as day-dreams without consciousness of deliberate decision; for others, their emotional tone, of gratification or regret, of friendliness or hatred, is obscurely influenced by this penumbra of alternatives, without any conscious analysis of its content. The elements of this penumbra are propositional prehensions, and not pure conceptual prehensions; for their implication of the particular nexus which is† the Battle of Waterloo is an essential factor.

Thus an element in this penumbral complex is what is termed a 'proposition.' A proposition is a† new kind of entity. It is a hybrid between pure potentialities and actualities. A 'singular' proposition is the potentiality of an actual world including a definite set of actual entities in a nexus of reactions involving the hypothetical ingression of a definite set of eternal objects.

A 'general' proposition only differs from a 'singular' proposition by the generalization of 'one definite set of [283] actual entities' into 'any set belonging to a certain sort of sets.' If the sort of sets includes all sets with potentiality for that nexus of reactions, the proposition is called 'universal.'

For the sake of simplicity, we will confine attention to singular propositions; although a slight elaboration of explanation will easily extend the discussion to include general and universal propositions.

The definite set of actual entities involved are called the 'logical subjects of the proposition'; and the definite set of eternal objects involved are called the 'predicates of the proposition.' The predicates define a potentiality of relatedness for the subjects. The predicates form one complex eternal object: this is 'the complex predicate.' The 'singular' proposition is the potentiality of this complex predicate finding realization in the nexus of reactions between the logical subjects, with assigned stations in the pattern for the various logical subjects.

In a proposition the various logical subjects involved are impartially concerned. The proposition is no more about one logical subject than another logical subject. But according to the ontological principle, every proposition must be somewhere. The 'locus' of a proposition consists of those actual occasions whose actual worlds include the logical subjects of the proposition. When an actual entity belongs to the locus of a proposition, then conversely the proposition is an element in the lure for feeling of that actual entity. If by the decision of the concrescence, the proposition has been admitted into feeling, then the proposition constitutes *what* the feeling has felt. The proposition constitutes a lure for a member of its locus by reason of the germaneness of the complex predicate to the logical subjects, having regard to forms of definiteness in the actual world of that member, and to its antecedent phases of feeling.

The interest in logic, dominating overintellectualized philosophers, has obscured the main function of propositions in the nature of things. They are not primarily [284] for belief, but for feeling at the physical level of unconsciousness. They constitute a source for the origination of feeling which is not tied down to mere datum. A proposition is 'realized' by a member of its locus, when it is admitted into feeling.

There are two types of relationship between a proposition and the actual world of a member of its locus. The proposition may be conformal or non-conformal to the actual world, true or false.

When a conformal proposition is admitted into feeling, the reaction to the datum has simply resulted in the conformation of feeling to fact, with some emotional accession or diminution, by which the feelings inherent in alien fact are synthesized in a new individual valuation. The prehension of the proposition has abruptly emphasized one form of definiteness illustrated in fact.

When a non-conformal proposition is admitted into feeling, the reaction to the datum has resulted in the synthesis of fact with the alternative potentiality of the complex predicate. A novelty has emerged into creation. The novelty may promote or destroy order; it may be good or bad. But it is new, a new type of individual, and not merely a new intensity of individual feeling. That member of the locus has introduced a new form into the actual world; or,† at least, an old form in a new function.

The conception of propositions as merely material for judgments is fatal to any understanding of their rôle in the universe. In that purely logical aspect, non-conformal propositions are† merely wrong, and therefore worse than useless. But in their primary rôle, they pave the way along which the world advances into novelty. Error is the price which we pay for progress.

The term 'proposition' suits these hybrid entities,† provided that we substitute the broad notion of 'feeling' for the narrower notions of 'judgment' and 'belief.' A proposition is an element in the objective lure *proposed for feeling*, and when admitted into feeling it constitutes [285] *what is felt*. The 'imaginative' feeling (cf. Part III) of a proposition is one of the ways of feeling it; and intellectual belief is another way of† feeling the proposition, a way which presupposes imaginative feeling. Judgment is the decision admitting a proposition into intellectual belief.

Anyone who at bedtime consciously reviews the events of the day is subconsciously projecting them against the penumbral welter of alternatives. He is also unconsciously deciding feelings so as to maximize his primary feeling, and to secure its propagation beyond his immediate present occasion. In considering the life-history of occasions, forming the historic route of an enduring physical object, there are three possibilities as to the subjective aims which dominate the internal concrescence of the separate occasions. Either (i), the satisfactions† of the antecedent occasions may be uniform with each other, and each internally without discord or incitement to novelty. In such a case, apart from novel discordance introduced by the environment, there is the mere conformal transformation of the feeling belonging to the datum into the identical feeling belonging to the immediate subject. Such pure conformation involves the exclusion of all the contraries involved in the lure, with their various grades of proximity and remoteness. This is an absolute extreme of undifferentiated endurance, of which we have no direct evidence. In every instance for which we can analyse, however imperfectly, the formal constitutions of successive occasions, these constitutions are characterized by contraries supervening upon the aboriginal data, but† with a regularity of alternation which procures stability in the life-history. Contrast is thus gained. In physical science, this is 'vibration.' This is the main character of the life-histories of an inorganic physical object, stabilized in type.

Or (ii), there is a zest for the enhancement of some dominant element of feeling, received from the data, enhanced by decision admitting non-conformation of [286] conceptual feeling to other elements in the data, and culminating in a satisfaction transmitting enhancement of the dominant element by reason of novel contrasts and inhibitions. Such a life-history involves growth dominated by a single final end. This is the main character of a physical object in process of growth. Such physical objects are mainly 'organic,' so far as concerns our present knowledge of the world.

Or (iii), there is a zest for the elimination of all dominant elements of feeling, received from the data. In such a case, the route soon loses its historic individuality. It is the case of decay.

The first point to be noticed is that the admission of the selected elements in the lure, as felt contraries, primarily generates purpose; it then issues in satisfaction; and satisfaction qualifies the efficient causation. But a felt 'contrary' is consciousness in germ. When the contrasts and identities of such feelings are themselves felt, we have consciousness. It is the knowledge of ideas, in Locke's sense of that term. Consciousness requires more than the mere entertainment of theory. It is the feeling of the contrast of theory, as *mere* theory, with fact, as *mere* fact. This contrast holds whether or no the theory be correct.

A proposition, in abstraction from any particular actual entity which may be realizing it in feeling, is a manner of germaneness of a certain set of eternal objects to a certain set of actual entities. Every proposition presupposes those actual entities which are its logical subjects. It also presupposes certain definite actual entities, or a certain type of actual entities,† within a wide systematic nexus. In an extreme case, this nexus may comprise any actual entity whatsoever.

The presupposed logical subjects may not be in the actual world of some actual entity. In this case, the proposition does not exist for that actual entity. The pure concept of *such* a proposition refers in the hypothetical future beyond that actual entity. The propo- [287] sition itself awaits its logical subjects. Thus propositions grow with the creative advance of the world. They are neither pure potentials, nor pure actualities; they are a manner of potential nexus involving pure potentials and pure actualities. They are a new type of entities. Entities of this impure type presuppose the two pure types of entities.

The primary mode of realization of a proposition in an actual entity† is not by judgment, but by entertainment. A proposition is entertained when it is admitted into feeling. Horror, relief, purpose, are primarily feelings involving the entertainment of propositions.

In conclusion, there are four main types of entities in the universe, of which two are primary types and two are hybrid types. The primary types are actual entities and pure potentials (eternal objects); the hybrid types are feelings and propositions (theories). Feelings are the 'real' components of actual entities. Propositions are only realizable as one sort of 'objective' datum for feelings.

The primary element in the 'lure for feeling' is the subject's prehension of the primordial nature of God. Conceptual feelings are generated, and by integration with physical feelings a subsequent phase of propositional feelings supervenes. The lure for feeling develops with the concrescent phases of the subject in question. I have spoken of it elsewhere (cf. *Science and the† Modern World*, Ch. XI).

It is this realized extension of eternal relatedness beyond the mutual relatedness of the actual occasions which prehends into each occasion the full sweep of eternal relatedness. I term this *abrupt** realization the 'graded envisagement' which each occasion prehends into its synthesis. This graded† envisagement is how the actual includes what (in one sense) is 'not-being' as a positive factor in its own achievement. It is the source of error, of truth, of art, of ethics, and of religion. By it, fact is confronted with alternatives. [288]

SECTION II†

All metaphysical theories which admit a disjunction between the component elements of individual experience on the one hand,† and on the other hand the component elements of the external world, must inevitably run into difficulties over the truth and falsehood of propositions, and over the grounds for judgment. The former difficulty is metaphysical, the latter epistemological. But all difficulties as to first principles are only camouflaged metaphysical difficulties. Thus also the epistemological difficulty is only solvable by an appeal to ontology. The first difficulty poses the question as to the account of truth and falsehood, and the second difficulty poses the question as to the account of the intuitive perception of truth and falsehood. The former concerns propositions, the latter concerns judgments. There is a togetherness of the component elements in individual experience. This 'togetherness' has that special peculiar meaning of 'togetherness in experience.' It is a togetherness of its own kind, explicable by reference to nothing else. For the purpose of this discussion it is indifferent whether we speak of a 'stream' of experience, or of an 'occasion' of experience. With the former alternative there is togetherness in the stream, and with the latter alternative there is togetherness in the occasion. In either case, there is the unique 'experiential togetherness.'

The consideration of experiential togetherness raises the final metaphysical question: whether there is any other meaning of 'togetherness.' The denial of any alternative meaning, that is to say, of any meaning not abstracted from the experiential meaning, is the 'subjectivist' doctrine. This reformed version of the subjectivist doctrine is the doctrine of the philosophy of organism.

The contrary doctrine, that there is a 'togetherness' not derivative from experiential togetherness, leads to the disjunction of the components of subjective experience from the community of the external world. This dis- [289] junction creates the insurmountable difficulty for epistemology. For intuitive judgment is concerned with togetherness in experience, and there is no bridge between togetherness in experience, and togetherness of the non-experiential sort.

This difficulty is the point of Kant's 'transcendental' criticism. He adopted a subjectivist position, so that the temporal world was merely experienced. But according to his form of the subjectivist doctrine, in the *Critique of Pure Reason,* no element in the temporal world could itself be an experient. His temporal world, as in that *Critique,* was in its essence dead, phantasmal, phenomenal. Kant was a mathematical physicist, and his cosmological solution was sufficient for the abstractions to which mathematical physics is confined.

The difficulties of the subjectivist doctrine arise when it is combined with the 'sensationalist' doctrine concerning the analysis of the components which are together in experience. According to that analysis in such a component the only elements not stamped with the particularity of that individual 'occasion'—or 'stream'—of experience are universals such as 'redness' or 'shape.' With the sensationalist assumption, or with any generalization of that doctrine, so long as the elements in question are universals, the only alternatives are, either Bradley's doctrine of a single experient, the absolute, or Leibniz's doctrine of many windowless monads. Kant, in his final metaphysics, must either retreat to Leibniz, or advance to Bradley. Either alternative stamps experience with a certain air of illusoriness.† The Leibnizian solution can mitigate the illusoriness only by recourse to a pious dependence upon God. This principle was invoked by Descartes and by Leibniz, in order to help out their epistemology. It is a device very repugnant to a consistent rationality. The very possibility of knowledge should not be an accident of God's goodness; it should depend on the interwoven natures of things. After all, God's knowledge has equally to be explained.

[290] The philosophy of organism admits the subjectivist doctrine (as here stated), but rejects the sensationalist doctrine: hence its doctrine of the objectification of one actual occasion in the experience of another actual occasion. Each actual entity is a throb of experience including the actual world within its scope. The problems of efficient causation and of knowledge receive a common explanation by reference to the texture of actual occasions. The theory of judgment in the philosophy of organism can equally well be described as a 'correspondence' theory or as a 'coherence' theory. It is a correspondence theory, because it describes judgment as the subjective form of the integral prehension of the conformity, or of the non-conformity, of a† proposition and an objectified nexus. The prehension in question arises from the synthesis of two prehensions, one physical

and the other mental. The physical prehension is the prehension of the nexus of objectified actual occasions. The mental prehension is the prehension of the proposition. This latter prehension is necessarily 'impure,' and it arises from a history of antecedent synthesis whereby a pure conceptual prehension transfers its datum as a predicate of hypothetical relatedness for the actualities in the datum of some physical prehension (cf. Part III). But the origination of a propositional prehension does not concern us in this description of judgment. The sole point is the synthesis of a physical prehension and propositional prehension into an 'intellectual' prehension (cf. Part III) whose subjective form involves judgment.

This judgment is concerned with a conformity of two components within one experience. It is thus a 'coherence' theory. It is also concerned with the conformity of a proposition, not restricted to that individual experience, with a nexus whose relatedness is derived from the various experiences of its own members and not from that of the judging experient.† In this sense there is a 'correspondence' theory. But, at this point of the argument, a distinction must be made. We shall say that a [291] proposition can be *true* or *false*, and that a judgment can be *correct*, or *incorrect*, or *suspended*. With this distinction we see that there is a 'correspondence' theory of the truth and falsehood of propositions, and a 'coherence' theory of the correctness, incorrectness and suspension† of judgments.

In the 'organic' doctrine, a clear distinction between a judgment and a proposition has been made. A judgment is a feeling in the 'process' of the judging subject, and it is correct or incorrect respecting *that* subject. It enters, as a value, into the satisfaction of that subject; and it can only be criticized by the judgments of actual entities in the future. A judgment concerns the universe in process of prehension by the judging subject. It will primarily concern a definite selection of objectified actual entities, and of eternal objects; and it affirms the physical objectification—for the judging subject—of those actual entities by the ingression of those eternal objects; so that there is one objectified nexus of those actual entities, judged to be really interconnected, and qualified, by those eternal objects. This judgment affirms, correctly or incorrectly, a real fact in the constitution of the judging subject. Here there is no room for any qualification of the categorical character of the judgment. The judgment is made about itself by the judging subject, and is a† feeling in the constitution of the judging subject. The actual entities, with which the judgment is explicitly concerned, comprise the 'logical' subjects of the judgment, and the selected eternal objects form the 'qualities' and 'relations' which are affirmed of the logical subjects.

This affirmation about the logical subjects is obviously 'affirmation' in a sense derivative from the meaning of 'affirmation' about the judging subject. Identification of the two senses will lead to error. In the latter** sense there is abstraction from the judging subject. The subjectivist principle has been transcended, and the judgment has shifted its emphasis from the objectified nexus [292] to the truth-value of the proposition in question. Having regard to the fact that judgment concerns the subjective form of an impure feeling arising from the integration of simpler feelings, we note that judgments are divisible into two sorts. These are (i) intuitive judgments and (ii) derivative judgments. In an intuitive judgment the integration of the physical datum with the proposition elicits into feeling the full complex detail of the proposition in its comparison of identity, or diversity, in regard to the complex detail of the physical datum. The intuitive judgment is the consciousness of this complex detailed comparison involving identity and diversity. Such a judgment is in its nature correct. For it is the consciousness of *what is.*

In a derivative judgment the integration of the physical datum with the proposition elicits into feeling the full complex detail of the proposition, but does not elicit into feeling the full comparison of this detail with the complex detail of the physical fact. There is some comparison involving the remainder of the detail. But the subjective form embraces the totality of the proposition, instead of assuming a complex pattern which discriminates between the compared and the uncompared components. In derivative judgments there can be error. Logic is the analysis of the relationships between propositions in virtue of which derivative judgments will not introduce errors, other than those already attaching to the judgments in‡ the premises. Most judgments are derivative; such judgments illustrate the doctrine that the subjective form of a feeling is affected by the totality of the actual occasion. This has been termed the 'sensitivity' of feelings in one occasion. In an intuitive judgment the subjective form of assent or dissent has been restrained, so as to derive its character solely from the contrasts in the datum. Even in this case, the emotional force of the judgment, as it passes into purpose, is derived from the whole judging subject.

Further, the judging subject and the logical subjects [293] refer to a universe with the general metaphysical character which represents its 'patience' for those subjects, and also its 'patience' for those eternal objects. In each judgment the universe is ranged in a hierarchy of wider and wider societies, as explained above (cf. Part II, Ch. III). It follows that the distinction between the logical subjects, with their qualities and relations, and the universe as systematic background, is not quite so sharply defined as the previous explanation suggests. For it is a matter of convention as to which of the proximate societies are reckoned as logical subjects and which as background. Another way of stating this shading off of logical subjects into background† is to say that the patience of the universe for a real fact in a judging subject is a hierarchical patience involving systematic gradations of character. This discussion substantiates the statement made above (cf. Part I, Ch. I, Sect. V), that a verbal statement is never the full expression of a proposition.

We now recur to the distinction between a proposition and a judgment.

A proposition emerges in the analysis of a judgment; it is the datum of the judgment in abstraction from the judging subject and from the subjective form. A judgment [1] is a synthetic feeling, embracing two subordinate feelings in one unity of feeling. Of these subordinate feelings one is propositional, merely entertaining the proposition which is its datum. The same proposition can constitute the content of diverse judgments by diverse judging entities respectively. The possibility of diverse judgments by diverse actual entities, having the same content (of 'proposition' in contrast with 'nexus'), requires that the same complex of logical subjects, objectified via the same eternal objects, can enter as a partial constituent into the 'real' essences of diverse actual entities. The judgment is a decision of feeling, the proposition is what is felt; but it is only part of the datum felt.

But, since each actual world is relative to standpoint, [294] it is only some actual entities which will have the standpoints so as to include,† in their actual world, the actual entities which constitute the logical subjects of the proposition. Thus every proposition defines the judging subjects for which it is a proposition. Every proposition presupposes some definite settled actual entities in the actual world of its judging subject; and thus its possible judging subjects must have these actual entities in the actual world of each of them. All judgment requires knowledge of the presupposed actual entities. Thus in addition to the requisite composition of the actual world presupposed by a proposition, there must be the requisite knowledge of that world presupposed by a judgment, whether the judgment be correct or incorrect. For actual entities, whose actual worlds have not the requisite composition, the proposition is non-existent; for actual entities, without the requisite knowledge, the judgment is impossible. It is quite true that a more abstract proposition can be modelled on the lines of the original proposition, so as to avoid the presupposition of some or all of these settled actual entities which are the logical subjects in the original proposition. This new proposition will have meaning for a wider group of possible subjects than the original proposition. Some propositions seem to us to have meaning for all possible judging subjects. This may be the case; but I do not dare to affirm that our metaphysical capacities are sufficiently developed to warrant any certainty on this question. Perhaps we are always presupposing some wide society beyond which our imaginations cannot leap. But the vagueness of verbal statements is such that the same form of words is taken to represent a whole set of allied propositions of various grades of abstractness.

A judgment weakens or strengthens the decision whereby the judged proposition, as a constituent in the lure, is admitted as an efficient element in the concrescence, with the reinforcement of knowledge. A judgment is the critique of a lure for feeling.

[1] Cf. Part III, Ch. V.†

SECTION III

[295] It now remains to consider the sense in which the actual world, in some systematic aspect, enters into each proposition. This investigation is wholly concerned with the notion of the logical subjects of the proposition. These logical subjects are, in the old sense of the term, 'particulars.' They are not concepts in comparison with other concepts; they are particular facts in a potential pattern.

But particulars must be indicated; because the proposition concerns just those particulars and no others. Thus the indication belongs to the proposition; namely, 'Those particulars *as thus indicated* in such-and-such a predicative pattern' constitutes the proposition. Apart from the indication there is no proposition because there are no determinate particulars. Thus we have to study the theory of *indication*.

Some definitions are required:

A 'relation' between occasions is an eternal object illustrated in the complex of mutual prehensions by virtue of which those occasions constitute a nexus.

A relation is called a 'dual relation' when the nexus in which it is realized consists of two, and only two, actual occasions. It is a 'triple relation' when there are three occasions, and so on.

There will, in general, be an indefinite number of eternal objects thus illustrated in the mutual prehensions of the occasions of any one nexus; that is to say, there are an indefinite number of relations realized between the occasions of any particular nexus.

A 'general principle' is an eternal object which is only illustrated through its 'instances,' which are also eternal objects. Thus the realization of an instance is also the realization of the general principle of which that eternal object is an instance. But the converse is not true; namely, the realization of the general principle does not involve the realization of any particular instance, though [296] it does necessitate the realization of some instance. Thus the instances each involve the general principle, but the general principle only involves at least one instance. In general, the instances of a general principle are mutually exclusive, so that the realization of one instance involves the exclusion of the other instances. For example, colour is a general principle and colours are the instances. So if all sensible bodies exhibit the general principle, which is colour, each body exhibits some definite colour. Also each body exhibiting a definite colour is thereby 'coloured.'

A nexus exhibits an 'indicative system' of dual relations among its members, when (i) one, and only one, relation of the system relates each pair of its members; and (ii) these relations are instances of a general principle; and (iii) the relation (in the system) between any member A and any other member B does not also relate A and a member of the nexus other than B; and (iv) the relations (in the system) between A and B and between A and C suffice to define the relation (in the system) between B and C, where A, B, and C are any three members of the nexus.

Thus if A and X be any two members of the nexus, and if X has knowledge of A's systematic relation to it and also of A's systematic relations to B, C, and D, where B, C, and D are members of the nexus, then X has knowledge of its own systematic relations to B, C, and D, and of the mutual systematic relations between B, C, and D. Such a nexus admits of the precise indication of its members from the standpoint of any one of them. The relative 'where' presupposes a nexus exhibiting an indicative system. More complex types of indicative systems can be defined; but the simplest type suffices to illustrate the principle involved. We have been defining Aristotle's category of 'position.' It will be noticed that in a nexus with an indicative system of relations, the subjective aspect of experience can be eliminated from propositions involved. For a knowledge of B and C and D as from A [297] yields a proposition concerning C and D as from B. Thus the prevalent notion, that the particular subject of experience can, in the nature of the case, never be eliminated from the experienced fact, is quite untrue.

Every proposition presupposes some general nexus with an indicative relational system. This nexus includes its locus of judging subjects and also its logical subjects. This presupposition is part of the proposition, and the proposition cannot be entertained by any subject for which the presupposition is not valid. Thus in a proposition certain characteristics are presupposed for the judging subject and for the logical subjects. This presupposition of character can be carried further than the mere requirements of indication require. For example, in 'Socrates is mortal' the mere spatio-temporal indicative system may be sufficient to indicate 'Socrates.' But the proposition may mean 'The *man* Socrates is mortal,' or 'The *philosopher* Socrates is mortal.' The superfluous indication may be part of the proposition. Anyhow, the principle that a proposition presupposes the actual world as exhibiting some systematic aspect has now been explained.

This discussion can be illustrated by the proposition, 'Caesar has crossed the Rubicon.' This form of words symbolizes an indefinite number of diverse propositions. In its least abstract form 'Caesar' stands for a society of settled actual entities in the actual world from the standpoint of the judging subject, with their objectifications consciously perceived by the subject. The whole theory of perception will come up for further discussion in a later chapter (cf. Part III); at this point it can be assumed. The word 'Rubicon' is to be explained in the same way as the word 'Caesar.' The only points left ambiguous respecting 'Caesar' and 'Rubicon' are that these societies—either or both, and each with its defining characteristic—may be conjecturally supposed to be prolonged up to the world contemporary with the judging subject, or, even more conjecturally, into the future [298] world beyond the subject. The past tense of the word 'has' shows that this point of ambiguity is irrelevant, so that the proposition can be framed so as to ignore it. But it need not be so framed: one of Caesar's old soldiers may in later years have sat on the bank of the river and meditated on the assassination of Caesar, and on Caesar's passage over the little river tranquilly flowing before his gaze. This would have been a different proposition from the more direct one which I am now considering. Nothing could better illustrate the hopeless ambiguity of language; since both propositions fit the same verbal phraseology. There is yet a third proposition: a modern traveller sitting on the bank of the Rubicon, and meditating on his direct perceptions of actual occasions can locate, relatively to himself by spatio-temporal specifications, an event which inferentially and conjecturally he believes to include a portion of the past history of the Rubicon as directly known to him. He also, by an analogous process of inference and conjecture, and of spatio-temporal specification, locates relatively to himself another event which he believes to contain the life of Caesar of whom he has no direct knowledge. The proposition meditated on by this traveller sitting on the bank of the modern river is evidently a different proposition to that in the mind of Caesar's old soldier. Then there is the proposition which might have been in the mind of one of the crowd who listened to Antony's speech, a man who had seen Caesar and not the Rubicon.

It is obvious that in this way an indefinite number of highly special propositions can be produced, differing from each other by fine gradations. Everything depends upon the differences in direct perceptive knowledge which these various propositions presuppose for their subjects. But there are propositions of a† more general type, for which 'Caesar' and 'Rubicon' have more generalized, vaguer meanings. In these vaguer meanings, 'Caesar' and 'Rubicon' indicate the entities, if any, located by any one member of a *type* of routes, starting from a [299] certain *type* of inference and conjecture. Also there are some such propositions in which the fact of there being such entities, to be thus located, is part of the content whereby the judgment is true or false; and there are other propositions in which even this requisite is evaded, so far as truth or falsehood is concerned. It is by reason of these various types of more abstract propositions that we can conceive the hypothetical existence of the more special propositions which for some of us, as judging subjects, would be meaningless.

This discussion should show the futility of taking any verbal statement, such as 'Caesar has crossed the Rubicon,' and arguing about *the* meaning. Also any proposition, which satisfies the verbal form so as to be one of its possibilities of meaning, defines its own locus of subjects; and only for such subjects is there the possibility of a judgment whose content is that proposition.

A proposition is the potentiality of the objectification of certain presupposed actual entities via certain qualities and relations, the objectification being for some unspecified subject for which the presupposition has meaning in direct experience. The judgment is the conscious affirmation by a particular subject—for which the presupposition holds—that this potentiality is, or is not, realized for it. It must be noticed that 'realized' does not mean 'realized in direct conscious experience,' but does mean 'realized as being contributory to the datum out of which that judging subject originates.' Since direct† conscious experience is usually absent, a judgment can be erroneous.

Thus a proposition is an example of what Locke calls an 'idea determined to particular existences.' It is the potentiality of such an idea; the realized idea, admitted to decision in a given subject, is the judgment, which may be a true or false idea about the particular things. The discussion of this question must be resumed (cf. Part III) when conceptual activity is examined. But it is evident that a proposition is a complex entity which [300] stands between the eternal objects and the actual occasions. Compared to eternal objects a proposition shares in the concrete particularity of actual occasions; and compared to actual occasions a proposition shares in the abstract generality of eternal objects. Finally, it must be remembered that propositions enter into experience in other ways than through judgment-feelings.‡

SECTION IV

A metaphysical proposition—in the proper, general sense of the term† 'metaphysical'—signifies a proposition which (i) has meaning for any actual occasion, as a subject entertaining it, and (ii) is 'general,' in the sense that its predicate potentially relates any and every set of actual occasions, providing the suitable number of logical subjects for the predicative pattern, and (iii) has a 'uniform' truth-value, in the sense that, by reason of its form and scope, its truth-value is identical with the truth-value of each of the singular propositions to be obtained by restricting the application of the predicate to any one set of logical subjects. It is obvious that, if a metaphysical proposition be true, the third condition is unnecessary. For a general proposition can only be true if this condition be fulfilled. But if the general proposition be false, then it is only metaphysical when in addition each of the derivate singular propositions is false. The general proposition would be false, if any one of the derivate singular propositions were false. But the third condition is expressed in the proposition without any dependence upon the determination of the proposition's truth or falsehood.

There can be no cosmic epoch for which the singular propositions derived from a metaphysical proposition differ in truth-value† from those of any other cosmic epoch.

We certainly think that we entertain metaphysical propositions: but, having regard to the mistakes of the past respecting the principles of geometry, it is wise to [301] reserve some scepticism on this point. The propositions which seem to be most obviously metaphysical are the arithmetical theorems. I will therefore illustrate the justification both for the belief, and for the residual scepticism, by an examination of one of the simplest of such theorems: One and one make two.[2]

Certainly, this proposition, construed in the sense 'one entity and another entity make two entities,' seems to be properly metaphysical without any shadow of limitation upon its generality, or truth. But we must hesitate even here, when we notice that it is usually asserted, with equal confidence as to the generality of its metaphysical truth, in a sense which is certainly limited, and sometimes untrue. In our reference to the actual world, we rarely consider an individual actual entity. The objects of our thoughts are almost always societies, or looser groups of actual entities. Now, for the sake of simplicity, consider a society of the 'personal' type. Such a society will be a linear succession of actual occasions forming a historical route in which some defining characteristic is inherited by each occasion from its predecessors. A society of this sort is an 'enduring object.' Probably, a simple enduring object is simpler than anything which we ordinarily perceive or think about. It is the simplest type of society; and for any duration of its existence it requires that its environment be largely composed of analogous simple† enduring objects. What we normally consider is the wider society in which many strands of enduring objects are to be found, a 'corpuscular society.'

Now consider two distinct enduring objects. They will be easier to think about if their defining characteristics are different. We will call these defining characteristics a and b, and also will use these letters, a and b, as the names of the two enduring objects. Now the proposition 'one entity and another entity make two [302] entities' is usually construed in the sense that, given two enduring objects, any act of attention which consciously comprehends an actual occasion from each of the two historic routes will necessarily discover two actual occasions, one from each of the two distinct routes. For example, suppose that a cup and a saucer are two such enduring objects, which of course they are not; we always assume that, so long as they are both in existence and are sufficiently close to be seen in one glance, any act of attention, whereby we perceive the cup and perceive the saucer, will thereby involve the perception of two actual entities, one the cup in one occasion of its existence and the other the saucer in one occasion of its existence. There can be no reasonable doubt as to the truth of this assumption in this particular example. But in making it, we are very far from the metaphysical proposition from which we started. We are in fact stating a truth concerning the wide societies of entities amid which our lives are placed. It is a truth concerning this *cosmos*, but not a metaphysical truth.

Let us return to the two truly simple enduring objects, a and b. Also

[2] For the proof of this proposition, cf. *Principia Mathematica*, Vol. II, *110.643.

let us assume that their defining characteristics, *a* and *b*, are not contraries, so that both of them can qualify the same actual occasion. Then there is no general metaphysical reason why the distinct routes of *a* and *b* should not intersect in at least one actual occasion. Indeed, having regard to the extreme generality of the notion of a simple enduring object, it is practically certain that—with the proper choice for the defining characteristics, *a* and *b*—intersecting historic routes for *a* and *b* must have frequently come into existence. In such a contingency a being who could consciously distinguish the two distinct enduring objects *a* and *b*, so as to have knowledge of their distinct defining characteristics and their distinct historic routes, might find *a* and *b* exemplified in one actual entity. It is as though the cup and the saucer were at one instant identical; and then, later on, resumed their distinct existence.

[303] We hardly ever apply arithmetic in its pure metaphysical sense, without the addition of presumptions which depend for their truth on the character of the societies dominating the cosmic epoch in which we live. It is hardly necessary to draw attention to the fact, that ordinary verbal statements make no pretence of discriminating the different senses in which an arithmetical statement can be understood.

There is no difficulty in imagining a world—i.e., a cosmic epoch—in which arithmetic would be an interesting fanciful topic for dreamers, but useless for practical people engrossed in the business of life. In fact, we seem to have been only barely rescued from such a state of things. For amid the actual occasions located in the wilds of so-called 'empty space,' and well removed from the enduring objects which go to form the enduring material bodies, it is quite probable that the contemplation of arithmetic would not direct attention to any very important relations of things. It is, of course, a mere speculation that any actual entity, occurring in such an environment of faintly coordinated achievement, achieves the intricacy of constitution required for conscious mental operations.

SECTION V

We ask the metaphysical question, What is there in the nature of things, whereby an inductive inference, or a judgment of general truth, can be significantly termed 'correct' or 'incorrect'? For example, we believe now—July 1, 1927—that the railway time-tables for the United States, valid for the previous months of May and June, represent the facts as to the past running of the trains, within certain marginal limits of unpunctuality, and allowing for a few individual breakdowns. Also we believe that the current time-tables for July will be exemplified, subject to the same qualifications. On the evidence before us our beliefs are justified, provided that we introduce into our judgments some estimate of the [304] high probability which is all that we mean to affirm. If we are considering astronomical events, our affirmations will include an estimate of a higher probability. Though even here some margin of uncertainty may exist. The computers of some famous observatory may have made an unprecedented error; or some unknown physical law may have important relevance to the condition of the star mainly concerned, leading to its unexpected explosion.[3]

This astronomical contingency, and the beliefs which cluster round it, have been stated with some detail, because—as thus expressed—they illustrate the problem as it shapes itself in philosophy. Also the example of the railway time-tables illustrates another point. For it is possible momentarily, in Vermont on July 1, 1927, to forget that the unprecedented Mississippi floods happened during that May and June; so that although the estimate as to error in punctuality was justified by the evidence consciously before us, it did not in fact allow for the considerable derangement of the traffic in some states in the Union.[4] The point of this illustration from railway trains is that there is a conformity to matter of fact which these judgments exhibit, even if the events concerned have not happened, or will not happen. These considerations introduce the fundamental principle concerning 'judgment.' It is that all judgment is categorical; it concerns a proposition true or false in its application to the actual occasion which is the subject making the judgment. This doctrine is not so far from Bradley's doctrine of judgment, as explained in his *Logic*. According to Bradley, the ultimate subject of every judgment is the one ultimate substance, the absolute. Also, according to him, the judging subject is a mode of the absolute, self-contradictory if taken to be independently actual. For Bradley, the judging subject has only a [305] derivative actuality, which is the expression of its status as an affection of the absolute. Thus,† in Bradley's doctrine, a judgment is an operation by which the absolute, under the limitations of one of its affections, enjoys self-consciousness of its enjoyment of affections. It will be noticed that in this bald summary of Bradley's position, I am borrowing Spinoza's phrase, '*affectiones substantiae.*'

In the philosophy of organism, an actual occasion—as has been stated above—is the whole universe in process of attainment of a particular satisfaction. Bradley's doctrine of actuality is simply inverted. The final actuality is the particular process with its particular attainment of satisfaction. The actuality of the universe is merely derivative from its solidarity in each actual entity. It must be held that judgment concerns the universe as objectified from the standpoint of the judging subject. It concerns the universe through that subject.

With this doctrine in mind, we pass to the discussion of the sense in which probability can be a positive fact in an actual entity; so that a propo-

[3] Since this sentence was written in July, 1927, a star has unexpectedly split in two, in March, 1928.

[4] Still less, at the time of writing this sentence, were the Vermont floods of November, 1927, foreseen.

sition expressing the probability of some other proposition can in this respect agree or disagree with the constitution of the judging entity. The notion of 'probability,' in the widest sense of that term, presents a puzzling philosophical problem. The mathematical theory of probability is based upon certain statistical assumptions. When these assumptions hold, the meaning of probability is simple; and the only remaining difficulties are concerned with the technical mathematical development. But it is not easy to understand how the statistical theory can apply to all cases to which the notion of more or less probability is habitually applied. For example, when we consider—as we do consider—the probability of some scientific conjecture as to the internal constitution of the stars, or as to the future of human society after some unprecedented convulsion, we seem to be influenced by some analogy which it is very difficult to convert into an appeal to any definite statistical fact. We may consider that it is probable [306] that the judgment could be justified by some statistical appeal, if we only knew where to look. This is the belief that the statistical probability is itself probable. But here, evidently, there is an appeal to a wider meaning of probability in order to support the statistical probability applicable to the present case. It is arguable that this wider probability is itself another statistical probability as to the existence of the special statistics relevant to such types of scientific argument. But in this explanation puzzling questions are accumulating; and it is impossible to avoid the suspicion that we are being put off with one of those make-believe explanations, so useful to reasoners who are wedded to a theory. The philosophy of organism provides two distinct elements in the universe from which an intuition of probability can originate. One of them is statistical. In this and the next two sections,‡ an attempt will be made to justify the statistical theory. It is therefore the more imperative to survey carefully the difficulties which have to be met.

In the first place, probability is always relative‡ to evidence; so, on the statistical theory, the numerical probability will mean the numerical ratio of favourable to unfavourable cases in the particular class of 'cases' selected as the 'ground' for statistical comparison. But alternative 'grounds' certainly exist. Accordingly we must provide a reason,† not based upon 'probability,' why one 'ground' is selected rather than another. We may admit such a chain of vaguer and vaguer probabilities, in which our first ground is selected as statistically probable in respect to its superiority to other 'grounds' of other types. We are thus driven back to a second-order 'ground' of probability. We may logically proceed to third-order 'grounds,' and so on. But if the statistical theory is to be substantiated, after a finite number of steps we must reach a 'ground' which is not selected for any reason of probability. It must be selected because it is *the* 'ground' presupposed in all our reasonings. [307] Apart from some such ultimate 'ground,' the statistical theory, viewed as an ultimate explanation for all our uses of the notion of 'probability,' must inevitably fail. This failure arises by reason of the complete arbitrariness of the ultimate 'ground' upon which the whole estimate of probability finally rests.

Secondly, the primary requisite for a 'ground' suitable for statistical probability seems itself to appeal to probability. The members of the class, called the 'ground,' must themselves be 'cases of equal probability,' some favourable and some unfavourable, with the possibility of the limiting types of 'ground' in which all members are favourable, or all members are unfavourable. The proposition in question, whose probability is to be estimated, must be known to be a member of the 'ground'; but no other evidence, as to the set—favourable or unfavourable—to which† the proposition belongs, enters into consideration. It is evident that, for the ultimate ground, the phrase 'cases of equal probability' must be explicable without reference to any notion of probability. The principle of such an explanation is easily found by reference to the six faces of dice. A die is a given fact; and its faces do not differ, *qua* faces, in any circumstance relative to their fall with one face upwards or another face upwards. Also beyond this given fact, there is ignorance. Thus again we are driven to an ultimate fact: there must be an ultimate species, and the specific character must be irrelevant to the 'favourableness' or 'unfavourableness' of the members of the species in their capacity of cases. All this must be given in direct knowledge without any appeal to probability. Also there must be equally direct knowledge of the proportion of favourable or unfavourable cases within the species—at least within the limits of precision or vagueness presupposed in the conclusion.

Thirdly, it is another requisite for a 'ground' that the number of instances which it includes be finite. The whole theory of the ratios of cardinal numbers, on which [308] statistical probability depends, breaks down when the cardinal numbers are infinite.

Fourthly, the method of 'sampling' professes to evade two objections. One of them is the breakdown, mentioned above, when the number of cases in the 'ground' is infinite. The other objection, thus evaded, is that in practice the case in question is novel and does not belong to the 'ground' which is in fact examined. According to this second objection, unless there is some further evidence, the statistical state of the 'ground' is bogus evidence as to the probability of the case in question. To sum up: The method of sampling professes to overcome† (i) the difficulty arising from the infinity of the ground; and (ii) that arising from the novelty of the case in question, whereby it does not belong to the ground examined. In the discussion it must be remembered that we are considering that ultimate ground which must not require any appeal to probability beyond itself. Thus the statistical facts as to the ground† must be 'given' and not merely 'probable.'

(i) When we have an† infinite 'ground,' containing an infinite number of favourable cases and an infinite number of unfavourable cases, 'random' sampling can give no help towards the establishment of statistical probability; for one reason because no such notion of ratios can apply to these infinities; and for another reason, no sample is 'random'; it has only followed a complex method. A finite number of samples each following some method of its own, however complex each method may be, will give a statistical result entirely dependent upon those methods. In so far as repetitions of so-called random samplings give concordant results, the only conclusion to be drawn is that there is a relevant, though concealed, analogy between the 'random' methods. Thus a finite 'ground' is essential for statistical probability. It must be understood that this argument implies no criticism on a properly interpreted method of sampling applied to a finite 'ground.'

[309] (ii) When the 'case' in question does not belong to the ground examined, there† can, apart from further information, be no rational inference from the 'ground' to the novel case. If probability be in truth purely statistical, and if there be no additional information, there can be no escape from this conclusion. But we certainly do unhesitatingly argue from a 'ground' which does not include the case in question, to a probable conclusion concerning the case in question. Thus *either* such an inference is irrational, futile, useless; *or*, when there is justification, there is additional information. This is the famous dilemma which perplexes the theories of induction† and of probability.

SECTION VI

It is evident that the ultimate 'ground' to which all probable judgments must refer can be nothing else than the actual world as objectified in judging subjects. A judging subject is always passing a judgment upon its own data. Thus, if the statistical theory is to hold, the relations between the judging subject and its data must be such as to evade the difficulties which beset that theory.

Every actual entity is in its nature essentially social; and this in two ways. First, the outlines of its own character are determined by the data which its environment provides for its process of feeling. Secondly, these data are not extrinsic to the entity; they constitute that display of the universe which is inherent in the entity. Thus the data upon which the subject passes judgment are themselves components conditioning the character of the judging subject. It follows that any general presupposition as to the character of the experiencing subject also implies a general presupposition as to the social environment providing the display for that subject. In other words, a species of subject requires a species of data as its preliminary phase of concrescence. But such data are nothing but the social environment under the [310] abstraction effected by objectification. Also the character of the abstraction itself depends on the environment. The species of data requisite for the presumed judging subject presupposes an environment of a certain social character.

Thus, according to the philosophy of organism, inductive reasoning gains its validity by reason of a suppressed premise. This tacit presupposition is that the particular future which is the logical subject of the judgment, inductively justified, shall include actualities which have close analogy to some contemporary subject enjoying assigned experience; for example, an analogy to the judging subject in question, or to some sort of actuality presupposed as in the actual world which is the logical subject of the inductive judgment. It is also presumed that this future is derived from the present by a continuity of inheritance in which this condition is maintained. There is thus the presupposition of the maintenance of the general social environment—*either* by reference to judging subjects, *or* by more direct reference to the preservation of the general type of material world requisite for the presupposed character of one or more of the logical subjects of the proposition.

In this connection, I can only repeat, as a final summary, a paragraph from my *Science and the Modern World* (Ch. III):

You will observe that I do not hold induction to be in its essence the divination† of general laws. It is the derivation of some characteristics of a particular future from the known characteristics of a particular past. The wider assumption of general laws holding for all cognizable occasions appears a very unsafe addendum to attach to this limited knowledge. All we can ask of the present occasion is that it shall determine a particular community of occasions, which are in some respects mutually qualified by reason of their inclusion within that same community.

It is evident that, in this discussion of induction, the philosophy of organism [311] appears as an enlargement of the premise in ethical discussions: that man is a social animal. Analogously, every actual occasion is social, so that when we have presumed the existence of any persistent type of actual occasions, we have thereby made presumptions as to types of societies comprised in its environment. Another way of stating this explanation of the validity of induction is, that in every forecast there is a presupposition of a certain type of actual entities, and that the question then asked is, Under what circumstances will these entities find themselves? The reason that an answer can be given is that the presupposed type of entities requires a presupposed type of data for the primary phases of these actual entities; and that a presupposed type of data requires a presupposed type of social environment. But the laws of nature are the outcome of the social environment. Hence when we have presupposed a type of actual occasions, we have already some information as to the laws of nature in operation throughout the environment.

In every inductive judgment, there is therefore contained a presupposition of the maintenance of the general order of the immediate environment, so far as concerns actual entities within the scope of the induction. The inductive judgment has regard to the statistical probabilities inherent in this given order. The anticipations are devoid of meaning apart from the definite cosmic order which they presuppose. Also survival requires order, and to presuppose survival, apart from the type of order which that type of survival requires, is a contradiction. It is at this point that the organic philosophy differs from any form of Cartesian 'substance-philosophy.' For if a substance requires nothing but itself in order to exist, its survival can tell no tale as to the survival of order in its environment. Thus no conclusion can be drawn respecting the external relationships of the surviving substance to its future environment. For [312] the organic philosophy, anticipations as to the future of a piece of rock presuppose an environment with the type of order which that piece of rock requires. Thus the completely unknown environment never enters into an inductive judgment. The induction is about the statistical probabilities of this environment, or about the graded relevance to it of eternal objects.

Thus the appeal to the mere unknown is automatically ruled out. The question, as to what will happen to an unspecified entity in an unspecified environment, has no answer. Induction always concerns societies of actual entities which are important for the stability of the immediate environment.

SECTION VII

In the preceding section there has been a covert appeal to probability. It is the purpose of this section to explain how the probability, thus invoked, can be explained according to the statistical theory. First, we have to note exactly where this appeal to probability enters into the notion of induction. An inductive argument always includes a hypothesis, namely, that the environment which is the subject-matter considered contains a society of actual occasions analogous to a society in the present. But analogous societies require analogous data for their several occasions; and analogous data can be provided only by the objectifications provided by analogous environments. But the laws of nature are derived from the characters of the societies dominating the environment. Thus the laws of nature dominating the environment in question have some analogy to the laws of nature dominating the immediate environment.

Now the notions of 'analogy' and of 'dominance' both leave a margin of uncertainty. We can ask, How far analogous? and How far dominant? If there were exact analogy, and complete dominance, there would be a mixture of certainty as to general conditions and of complete ignorance as to specific details. But such a descrip- [313] tion does not apply either to our knowledge of the immediate present, or of the past, or to our inductive knowledge of the future. Our conscious experience involves a baffling mixture of certainty, ignorance, and probability.

Now it is evident that the theory of cosmic epochs, due to the dominance of societies of actual occasions, provides the basis for a statistical explanation of probability. In any one epoch there are a definite set of dominant societies in certain ordered interconnections. There is also an admixture of chaotic occasions which cannot be classified as belonging to any society. But, having regard to the enormous extension of any cosmic epoch, we are practically dealing with infinities, so that some method of sampling is required, rooted in the nature of the case and not arbitrarily adopted.

This natural method of sampling is provided by the data which form the primary phase of any one actual occasion. Each actual occasion objectifies the other actual occasions in its environment. This environment can be limited to the relevant portion of the cosmic epoch. It is a finite region of the extensive continuum, so far as adequate importance is concerned in respect to individual differences among actual occasions. Also, in respect to the importance of individual differences, we may assume that there is a lower limit to the extension of each relevant occasion within this region. With these two presumptions, it follows that the relevant objectifications, forming the relevant data for any one occasion, refer to a finite sample of actual occasions in the environment. Accordingly our knowledge of the external world, and of the conditions upon which its laws depend,† is, through and through, of that numerical character which a statistical theory of probability requires. Such a theory does not require that exact statistical calculations be† made. All that is meant by such a theory is that our probability judgments are ultimately derivable from vague estimates of 'more or less' in a numerical sense. [314] We have an unprecise intuition of the statistical basis of the sort of way in which things happen.

NOTE.—By far the best discussion of the philosophical theory of probability is to be found in Mr. J. Maynard Keynes' book, A *Treatise on Probability*. This treatise must long remain the standard work on the subject. My conclusions in this chapter do not seem to me to differ fundamentally from those of Mr. Keynes as set out towards the conclusion of his Chapter XXI. But Mr. Keynes here seems to revert to a view of probability very analogous to that form of the 'frequency theory' which, as suggested by me,† he criticized acutely (and rightly, so far as concerned that special form) in his Chapter VIII.

SECTION VIII

So far the argument of the three‡ preceding sections has been devoted to the explanation of the statistical ground for a probability judgment. But the same discussion also discloses an alternative non-statistical ground for such a judgment.

The main line of thought has been (i) that each actual occasion has at the base of its own constitution the environment from which it springs; (ii) that in this function of the environment abstraction has been made from its indefinite multiplicity of forms of definiteness, so as to obtain a concordant experience of the elements retained; (iii) that any actual occasion belonging to an assigned species requires an environment adapted to that species, so that the presupposition of a species involves a presupposition concerning the environment; (iv) that in every inductive judgment, and in every judgment of probability, there is a presupposition, implicit or explicit, of one, or more, species of actual occasions implicated in the situation considered, so that, by (iii),† there is a presupposition of some general type of environment.

Thus the basis of all probability and induction is the fact of analogy between an environment presupposed and an environment directly experienced.

The argument, as to the statistical basis of probability, then recurred to the doctrine of social order. According to this doctrine, all social order depends on the statistical dominance in the environment of occasions belonging [315] to the requisite societies. The laws of nature are statistical laws derived from this fact. Thus the judgment of probability can be derived from an intuition—in general vague and unprecise—as to the statistical basis of the presupposed environment. This judgment can be derived from the analogy with the experienced environment. There will be such factors in experience adequate to justify a judgment of the inductive type.

But there is another factor from which, in combination with the four premises, a non-statistical judgment of probability can be derived. The principle of the graduated 'intensive relevance' of eternal objects to the primary physical data of experience expresses a real fact as to the preferential adaptation of selected eternal objects to novel occasions originating from an assigned environment.

This principle expresses the prehension by every creature of the graduated order of appetitions constituting the primordial nature of God. There can thus be an intuition of an intrinsic suitability of some definite outcome from a presupposed situation. There will be nothing statistical in this suitability. It depends upon the fundamental graduation of appetitions which lies at the base of things, and which solves all indeterminations of transition.

In this way, there can be an intuition of probability respecting the origination of some novelty. It is evident that the statistical theory entirely fails to provide any basis for such judgments.

It must not be thought that these non-statistical judgments are in any sense religious. They lie at a far lower level of experience than do the religious emotions. The secularization of the concept of God's functions in the world is at least as urgent a requisite of thought as is the secularization of other elements in experience. The concept of God is certainly one essential element in religious feeling. But the converse is not true; the concept of religious feeling is not an essential element in the con- [316] cept of God's function in the universe. In this respect religious literature has been sadly misleading to philosophic theory, partly by attraction and partly by repulsion.

CHAPTER X
PROCESS

SECTION I

[317] THAT 'all things flow' is the first vague generalization which the unsystematized, barely analysed, intuition of men has produced. It is the theme of some of the best Hebrew poetry in the Psalms; it appears as one of the first generalizations of Greek philosophy in the form of the saying of Heraclitus; amid the later barbarism of Anglo-Saxon thought it reappears in the story of the sparrow flitting through the banqueting† hall of the Northumbrian king; and in all stages of civilization its recollection lends its pathos to poetry. Without doubt, if we are to go back to that ultimate, integral experience, unwarped by the sophistications of theory, that experience whose elucidation is the final aim of philosophy, the flux of things is one ultimate generalization around which we must weave our philosophical system.

At this point we have transformed the phrase, 'all things flow,' into the alternative phrase, 'the flux of things.' In so doing, the notion of the 'flux' has been held up before our thoughts as one primary notion for further analysis. But in the sentence 'all things flow,' there are three words—and we have started by isolating the last word of the three. We move backward to the next word 'things' and ask, What sort of things flow? Finally we reach the first word 'all' and ask, What is the meaning of the 'many' things engaged in this common flux, and in what sense, if any, can the word 'all' refer to a definitely indicated set of these many things?

The elucidation of meaning involved in the phrase 'all things flow'† is one chief task of metaphysics.

[318] But there is a rival notion, antithetical to the former. I cannot at the moment recall one immortal phrase which expresses it with the same completeness as that with which† the alternative notion has been rendered by Heraclitus. This other notion dwells on permanences of things—the solid earth, the mountains, the stones, the Egyptian Pyramids, the spirit of man, God.

The best rendering of integral experience, expressing its general form divested of irrelevant details, is often to be found in the utterances of religious aspiration. One of the reasons of the thinness of so much modern metaphysics is its neglect of this wealth of expression of ultimate feeling.

208

Accordingly we find in the first two lines of a famous hymn a full expression of the union of the two notions in one integral experience:

> Abide with me;
> Fast falls the eventide.

Here the first line expresses the permanences, 'abide,' 'me' and the 'Being' addressed; and the second line sets these permanences amid the inescapable flux. Here at length we find formulated the complete problem of metaphysics. Those philosophers who start with the first line have given us the metaphysics of 'substance'; and those who start with the second line have developed the metaphysics of 'flux.' But, in truth, the two lines cannot be torn apart in this way; and we find that a wavering balance between the two is a characteristic of the greater number of philosophers. Plato found his permanences in a static, spiritual heaven, and his flux in the entanglement of his forms amid the fluent imperfections of the physical world. Here I draw attention to the word 'imperfection.' In any assertion as to Plato I speak under correction; but I believe that Plato's authority can be claimed for the doctrine that the things that flow are imperfect in the sense of 'limited' and of 'definitely exclusive of much that they might be and are not.' The lines quoted from the hymn are an almost perfect expres- [319] sion of the direct intuition from which the main position of the Platonic philosophy is derived. Aristotle corrected his Platonism into a somewhat different† balance. He was the apostle of 'substance and attribute,' and of the classificatory logic which this notion suggests. But, on the other side, he makes a masterly analysis of the notion of 'generation.' Aristotle in his own person expressed a useful protest against the Platonic tendency to separate a static spiritual world from a fluent world of superficial experience. The later Platonic schools stressed this tendency: just as the mediaeval Aristotelian thought allowed the static notions of Aristotle's logic to formulate some of the main metaphysical problems in terms which have lasted till today.

On the whole, the history of philosophy supports Bergson's charge that the human intellect 'spatializes the universe'; that is to say, that it tends to ignore the fluency, and to analyse the world in terms of static categories. Indeed Bergson went further and conceived this tendency as an inherent necessity of the intellect. I do not believe this accusation; but I do hold that 'spatialization' is the shortest route to a clear-cut philosophy expressed in reasonably familiar language. Descartes gave an almost perfect example of such a system of thought. The difficulties of Cartesianism with its three clear-cut substances, and with its 'duration' and 'measured time' well in the background, illustrate the result of the subordination of fluency. This subordination is to be found in the unanalysed longing of the hymn, in Plato's vision of heavenly perfection, in Aristotle's logical concepts, and in Descartes' mathematical mentality. Newton, that Napoleon of the world of thought, brusquely ordered fluency back into the world, regimented into his 'absolute mathematical time, flowing equably without regard to anything external.' He also gave it a mathematical uniform in the shape of his Theory of Fluxions.

At this point the group of seventeenth- and eighteenth- [320] century philosophers practically made a discovery, which, although it lies on the surface of their writings, they only half-realized. The discovery is that there are two kinds of fluency. One kind is the *concrescence*† which, in Locke's language, is 'the real internal constitution of a particular existent.' The other kind is the *transition* from particular existent to particular existent. This transition, again in Locke's language, is the 'perpetually perishing' which is one aspect of the notion of time; and in another aspect the transition is the origination of the present in conformity with the 'power' of the past.

The phrase 'the real internal constitution of a particular existent,' the description of the human understanding as a process of reflection upon data, the phrase 'perpetually perishing,' and the word 'power' together with its elucidation are all to be found in Locke's *Essay*. Yet owing to the limited scope of his investigation Locke did not generalize or put his scattered ideas together. This implicit notion of the two kinds of flux finds further unconscious illustration in Hume. It is all but explicit in Kant, though—as I think—misdescribed. Finally, it is lost in the evolutionary monism of Hegel and of his derivative schools. With all his inconsistencies, Locke is the philosopher to whom it is most useful to recur, when we desire to make explicit the discovery of the two kinds of fluency, required for the description of the fluent world. One kind is the fluency inherent in the constitution of the particular existent. This kind I have called 'concrescence.' The other kind is the fluency whereby the perishing of the process, on the completion of the particular existent, constitutes that existent as an original element in the constitutions of other particular existents elicited by repetitions of process. This kind I have called 'transition.' Concrescence moves towards its final cause, which is its subjective aim; transition is the vehicle of the efficient cause, which is the immortal past.

The discussion of how the actual particular occasions become original elements for a new creation is termed [321] the theory of objectification. The objectified particular occasions together have the unity of a datum for the creative concrescence. But in acquiring this measure of connection, their inherent presuppositions of each other eliminate certain elements in their constitutions, and elicit into relevance other elements. Thus objectification is an operation of mutually adjusted abstraction, or elimination, whereby the many occasions of the actual world become one complex datum. This fact of the elimination by reason of synthesis is sometimes termed the perspective of the actual world from the standpoint of that concrescence. Each actual occasion defines its own actual world from which it originates. No two occasions can have identical actual worlds.

SECTION II

'Concrescence' is the name for the process in which the universe of many things acquires an individual unity in a determinate relegation of each item of the 'many' to its subordination in the constitution of the novel 'one.'

The most general term 'thing'—or, equivalently, 'entity'—means nothing else than to be one of the 'many' which find their niches in each instance of concrescence. Each instance of concrescence *is itself* the novel individual 'thing' in question. There are not 'the concrescence' *and* 'thet novel thing': when we analyse the novel thing we find nothing but the concrescence. 'Actuality' means nothing else than this ultimate entry into the concrete, in abstraction from which there is mere nonentity. In other words, abstraction from the notion of 'entry into the concrete' is a self-contradictory notion, since it asks us to conceive a thing as not a thing.

An instance of concrescence is termed an 'actual entity'—or, equivalently, an 'actual occasion.' There is not one completed set of things which are actual occasions. For the fundamental inescapable fact is the creativity [322] in virtue of which there can be no 'many things' which are not subordinated in a concrete unity. Thus a set of all actual occasions is by the nature of things a standpoint for another concrescence which elicits a concrete unity from those many actual occasions. Thus we can never survey the actual world except from the standpoint of an immediate concrescence which is falsifying the presupposed completion. The creativity in virtue of which any relative** complete actual world is, by the nature of things, the datum for a new concrescencet is termed 'transition.' Thus, by reason of transition, 'the actual world' is always a relative term, and refers to that basis of presupposed actual occasions which is a datum for the novel concrescence.

An actual occasion is analysable. The analysis discloses operations transforming entities which are individually alient into components of a complex which is concretely one. The term 'feeling' will be used as the generic description of such operations. We thus say that an actual occasion is a concrescence effected by a process of feelings.

A feeling can be considered in respect to (i) the actual occasions felt, (ii) the eternal objects felt, (iii) the feelings felt, and (iv) its own subjective forms of intensity. In the process of concrescence the diverse feelings pass on to wider generalities of integral feeling.

Such a wider generality is a feeling of a complex of feelings, including their specific elements of identity and contrast. This process of the integration of feeling proceeds until the concrete unity of feeling is obtained. In this concrete unity all indetermination as to the realization of possibilities has been eliminated. The many entities of the universe, including those originating in the concrescence itself, find their respective rôles in this final unity. This final unity is termed the 'satisfaction.' The 'satisfaction' is the culmination of the concrescence into a completely determinate matter of fact. In any of its antecedent stages the concrescence exhibits sheer inde- [323] termination as to the nexus between its many components.

SECTION III

An actual occasion is nothing but the unity to be ascribed to a particular instance of concrescence. This concrescence is thus nothing else than the 'real internal constitution' of the actual occasion in question. The analysis of the formal constitution of an actual entity has given three stages in the process of feeling: (i) the responsive phase, (ii) the supplemental stage, and (iii) the satisfaction.

The satisfaction is merely the culmination marking the evaporation of all indetermination; so that, in respect to all modes of feeling and to all entities in the universe, the satisfied actual entity embodies a determinate attitude of 'yes' or 'no.' Thus the satisfaction is the attainment of the private ideal which is the final cause of the concrescence. But the process itself lies in the two former phases. The first phase is the phase of pure reception of the actual world in its guise of objective datum for aesthetic synthesis. In this phase there is the mere reception of the actual world as a multiplicity of private centres of feeling, implicated in a nexus of mutual presupposition. The feelings are felt as belonging to the external centres, and are not absorbed into the private immediacy. The second stage is governed by the private ideal, gradually shaped in the process itself; whereby the many feelings, derivatively felt as alien, are transformed into a unity of aesthetic appreciation immediately felt as private. This is the incoming of 'appetition,' which in its higher exemplifications we term 'vision.' In the language of physical science, the 'scalar' form overwhelms the original 'vector' form: the origins become subordinate to the individual experience. The vector form is not lost, but is submerged as the foundation of the scalar superstructure.

In this second stage the feelings assume an emotional [324] character by reason of this influx of conceptual feelings. But the reason why the origins are not lost in the private emotion is that there is no element in the universe capable of pure privacy. If we could obtain a complete analysis of meaning, the notion of pure privacy would be seen to be self-contradictory. Emotional feeling is still subject to the third metaphysical principle,** that to be 'something' is 'to have the potentiality for acquiring real unity with other entities.' Hence, 'to be a real component of an actual entity' is in some way 'to realize this potentiality.' Thus 'emotion' is 'emotional feeling'; and 'what is felt' is the presupposed vector situation. In physical science this principle takes the form which should never be lost sight of in fundamental speculation, that scalar quantities are constructs derivative from vector quantities. In more familiar language, this principle can be expressed by the statement that the notion of 'passing on' is more fundamental than that of a private individual fact. In the abstract language here adopted for metaphysical statement, 'passing on' becomes 'creativity,' in the dictionary sense of the verb *creare*, 'to bring forth, beget, produce.' Thus, according to the third principle, no entity can be divorced from the notion of creativity. An entity is at least a particular form capable of infusing its own particularity into creativity. An actual entity, or a phase of an actual entity, is more than that; but, at least, it is that.

Locke's 'particular ideas' are merely the antecedent actual entities exercising their function of infusing with their own particularity the 'passing on,'† which is the primary phase of the 'real internal constitution' of the actual entity in question. In obedience to a prevalent misconception, Locke termed this latter entity the 'mind'; and discussed its 'furniture,' when he should have discussed 'mental operations' in their capacity of later phases in the constitutions of actual entities. Locke himself flittingly expresses this fundamental vector function of his 'ideas.' In a paragraph, forming a portion of a quotation already [325] made, he writes: "I confess power includes in it some kind of relation,—a relation to action or change; as, indeed, which of our ideas, of what kind soever, when attentively considered, does not?" [1]

SECTION IV

The second phase, that of supplementation, divides itself into two subordinate phases. Both of these phases may be trivial; also they are not truly separable, since they interfere with each other by intensification or inhibition. If both phases are trivial, the whole second phase is merely the definite negation of individual origination; and the process passes passively to its satisfaction. The actual entity is then the mere vehicle for the transference of inherited constitutions of feeling. Its private immediacy passes out of the picture. Of these two sub-phases, the former—so far as there is an order—is that of aesthetic supplement, and the latter is that of intellectual supplement.

In the aesthetic supplement there is an emotional appreciation of the contrasts and rhythms inherent in the unification of the objective content in the concrescence of one actual occasion. In this phase perception is heightened by its assumption of pain and pleasure, beauty and distaste. It is the phase of inhibitions and intensifications. It is the phase in which blue becomes more intense by reason of its contrasts, and shape acquires dominance by reason of its loveliness. What was received as alien, has been recreated as private. This is the phase of perceptivity, including emotional reactions to perceptivity. In this phase, private immediacy has welded the data into a new fact of blind feeling. Pure aesthetic supple-

[1] *Essay*, II, XXI, 3.†

ment has solved its problem. This phase requires an influx of conceptual feelings and their integration with the pure physical feelings.

But 'blindness' of the process, so far, retains an indetermination. There must be either a determinate nega- [326] tion of intellectual 'sight,' or an admittance of intellectual 'sight.' The negation† of intellectual sight is the dismissal into irrelevance† of eternal objects in their abstract status of pure potentials. 'What might be' has the capability of relevant contrast with 'what is.' If the pure potentials, in this abstract capacity, are dismissed from relevance, the second sub-phase is trivial. The process then constitutes a blind actual occasion, 'blind' in the sense that no intellectual operations are involved; though conceptual operations are always involved. Thus there is always mentality in the form of 'vision,' but not always mentality in the form of conscious 'intellectuality.'

But if some eternal objects, in their abstract capacity, are realized as relevant to actual fact, there is an actual occasion with intellectual operations. The complex of such intellectual operations is sometimes termed the 'mind' of the actual occasion; and the actual occasion is also termed 'conscious.' But the term 'mind' conveys the suggestion of independent substance. This is not meant here: a better term is the 'consciousness' belonging to the actual occasion.

An eternal object realized in respect to its pure potentiality as related to *determinate* logical subjects is termed a 'propositional feeling' in the mentality of the actual occasion in question. The consciousness belonging to an actual occasion is its sub-phase of intellectual supplementation, when that sub-phase is not purely trivial. This sub-phase is the eliciting, into feeling, of† the full contrast between mere propositional potentiality and realized fact.

SECTION V

To sum up: There are two species of process, macroscopic† process, and microscopic process. The macroscopic process is the transition from attained actuality to actuality in attainment; while the microscopic process is the conversion of conditions which are merely real into determinate actuality. The former process effects the [327] transition from the 'actual' to the 'merely real'; and the latter process effects the growth from the real to the actual. The former process is efficient; the latter process is† teleological. The future is merely real, without being actual; whereas the past is a nexus of actualities. The actualities are constituted by their real genetic phases. The present is the immediacy of teleological process whereby reality becomes actual. The former process provides the conditions which really govern attainment; whereas the latter process provides the ends actually attained. The notion of 'organism' is combined with that of 'process' in a twofold manner. The community of actual things is an organism; but it is not a static organism. It is an incompletion in process of production. Thus the expansion of the universe in respect to actual things is the first meaning of 'process'; and the universe in any stage of its expansion is the first meaning of 'organism.' In this sense, an organism is a nexus.

Secondly, each actual entity is itself only describable as an organic process. It repeats in microcosm what the universe is in macrocosm. It is a process proceeding from phase to phase, each phase being the real basis from which its successor proceeds towards the completion of the thing in question. Each actual entity bears in its constitution the 'reasons' why its conditions are what they are. These 'reasons' are the other actual entities objectified for it.

An 'object' is a transcendent element characterizing that *definiteness* to which our 'experience' has to conform. In this sense, the future has *objective* reality in the present, but no *formal* actuality. For it is inherent in the constitution of the immediate, present actuality that a future will supersede it. Also conditions to which that future must conform, including real relationships to the present, are really objective in the immediate actuality.

Thus each actual entity, although complete so far as concerns its microscopic process, is yet incomplete by reason of its objective inclusion of the macroscopic† [328] process. It really experiences a future which must be actual, although the completed actualities of that future are undetermined. In this sense, each actual occasion experiences its own objective immortality.

Note.—The function here ascribed to an 'object' is in general agreement with a paragraph (p. 249, 2nd† edition) in Professor Kemp Smith's *Commentary* on Kant's *Critique*, where he is considering Kant's 'Objective Deduction' as in the first edition of the *Critique*: "When we examine the objective, we find that the primary characteristic distinguishing it from the subjective is that it lays a compulsion upon our minds, constraining us to think about it in a certain way. By an object is meant something which will not allow us to think at haphazard."

There is of course the vital difference, among others, that where Kemp Smith, expounding Kant, writes 'thinking,' the philosophy of organism substitutes 'experiencing.'

PART III
THE THEORY OF PREHENSIONS

CHAPTER I

THE THEORY OF FEELINGS

SECTION I

[334] The philosophy of organism is a cell-theory of actuality. Each ultimate unit of fact is a cell-complex, not analysable into components with equivalent completeness of actuality.

The cell can be considered genetically and morphologically. The genetic theory† is considered in this part; [335] the morphological theory is considered in Part IV, under the title of the 'extensive analysis' of an actual entity.

In the genetic theory, the cell is exhibited as appropriating for the foundation of its own existence, the various elements of the universe out of which it arises. Each process of appropriation of a particular element is termed a prehension. The ultimate elements of the universe, thus appropriated, are the already constituted† actual entities, and the eternal objects. All the actual entities are positively prehended, but only a selection of the eternal objects. In the course of the integrations of these various prehensions, entities of other categoreal types become relevant; and some new entities of these types, such as novel propositions and generic contrasts, come into existence. These relevant entities of these other types are also prehended into the constitution of the concrescent cell. This genetic process has now to be traced in its main outlines.

An actual entity is a process in the course of which many operations with incomplete subjective unity terminate in a completed unity of operation, termed the 'satisfaction.' The 'satisfaction' is the contentment of the creative urge by the fulfilment of its categoreal demands. The analysis of these categories is one aim of metaphysics.

The process itself is the constitution of the actual entity; in Locke's phrase, it is the 'real internal constitution' of the actual entity. In the older phraseology employed by Descartes, the process is what the actual entity is in itself, *'formaliter.'* The terms 'formal' and 'formally' are here used in this sense.

The terminal unity of operation, here called the 'satisfaction,' embodies what the actual entity is beyond itself. In Locke's phraseology, the 'powers' of the actual entity are discovered in the analysis of the satisfaction. In Descartes' phraseology, the satisfaction is the actual entity considered as analysable in respect to its existence [336] *'objectivé.'*† It is the actual entity as a definite, determinate, settled fact, stubborn and with unavoidable consequences. The actual entity as described by the morphology of its satisfaction is the actual entity 'spatialized,' to use Bergson's term. The actual entity, thus spatialized, is a† given individual fact actuated by its own 'substantial form.' Its own process, which is its own internal existence, has evaporated, worn out and satisfied; but its effects are all to be described in terms of its 'satisfaction.' The 'effects' of an actual entity are its interventions in concrescent processes other than its own. Any entity, thus intervening in processes transcending itself, is said to be functioning as an 'object.' According to the fourth Category of Explanation it is the one general metaphysical character of all entities of all sorts, that they function as objects. It is this metaphysical character which constitutes the solidarity of the universe. The peculiarity of an actual entity is that it can be considered both 'objectively' and 'formally.' The 'objective' aspect is morphological so far as that actual entity is concerned: by this it is meant that the process involved is transcendent relatively to it, so that the *esse* of its satisfaction is *sentiri*. The 'formal' aspect is functional so far as that actual entity is concerned: by this it is meant that the process involved is immanent in it. But the objective consideration is pragmatic. It is the consideration of the actual entity in respect to its consequences. In the present chapter the emphasis is laid upon the formal consideration of an actual entity. But this formal consideration of one actual entity requires reference to the objective intervention of other actual entities. This objective intervention of other entities constitutes the creative character which conditions the concrescence in question. The satisfaction of each actual entity is an element in the givenness of the universe: it limits boundless, abstract possibility into the particular real potentiality from which each novel concrescence originates. The 'boundless, abstract possibility' means the creativity [337] considered solely in reference to the possibilities of the intervention of eternal objects, and in abstraction from the objective intervention of actual entities belonging to any definite actual world, including God among the actualities abstracted from.

SECTION II

The possibility of finite truths depends on the fact that the satisfaction of an actual entity is divisible into a variety of determinate operations. The operations are 'prehensions.' But the negative prehensions which consist of exclusions from contribution to the concrescence can be treated in their subordination to the positive prehensions. These positive prehensions are termed 'feelings.' The process of concrescence is divisible into an initial stage of many feelings, and a succession of subsequent phases of more complex feelings integrating the earlier simpler feelings, up to the satisfaction which is one complex unity of feeling. This is the 'genetic' analysis of the satisfaction. Its 'coordinate' analysis will be given later, in Part IV.

Thus a component feeling in the satisfaction is to be assigned, for its origination, to an earlier phase of the concrescence.

This is the general description of the divisible character of the satisfaction, from the genetic standpoint. The extensiveness which underlies the spatio-temporal relations of the universe is another outcome of this divisible character. Also the abstraction from its own full formal constitution involved in objectifications of one actual entity in the constitutions of other actual entities equally depends upon this same divisible character, whereby the actual entity is conveyed in the particularity of some one of its feelings. A feeling—i.e., a positive prehension—is essentially a transition effecting a concrescence. Its complex constitution is analysable into five factors which express what that transition consists of, and effects. The factors are: (i) the 'subject' which feels, (ii) the 'initial [338] data' which are to be felt, (iii) the 'elimination' in virtue of negative prehensions, (iv) the 'objective datum' which is felt, (v) the 'subjective form' which is *how* that subject feels that objective datum.

A feeling is in all respects determinate, with a determinate subject, determinate initial data, determinate negative prehensions, a determinate objective datum, and a determinate subjective form. There is a transition from the initial data to the objective datum effected by the elimination. The initial data constitute a 'multiplicity,' or merely one 'proper' entity, while the objective datum is a 'nexus,' a proposition, or a 'proper' entity of some categoreal type. There is a concrescence of the initial data into the objective datum, made possible by the elimination, and effected by the subjective form. The objective datum is the perspective of the initial data.† The subjective form receives its determination from the negative prehensions, the objective datum, and the conceptual origination of the subject. The negative prehensions are determined by the categoreal conditions governing feelings, by the subjective form, and by the initial data. This mutual determination of the elements involved in a feeling is one expression of the truth that the subject of the feeling is *causa sui*. The partial nature of a feeling, other than the complete satisfaction, is manifest by the impossibility of understanding its generation without recourse to the whole subject. There is a mutual sensitivity of feelings in one subject, governed by categoreal conditions. This mutual sensitivity expresses the notion of final causation in the guise of a pre-established harmony.

SECTION III

A feeling cannot be abstracted from the actual entity entertaining it. This actual entity is termed the 'subject' of the feeling. It is in virtue of its subject that the feeling is one thing. If we abstract the subject from the feeling we are left with many things. Thus a feeling is [339] a particular in the same sense in which each actual entity is a particular. It is one aspect of its own subject.

The term 'subject' has been retained because in this sense it is familiar in philosophy. But it is misleading. The term 'superject' would be better. The subject-superject is the purpose of the process originating the feelings. The feelings are inseparable from the end at which they aim; and this end is the feeler. The feelings aim at the feeler, as their final cause. The feelings are what they are in order that their subject may be what it is. Then transcendently, since the subject is what it is in virtue of its feelings, it is only by means of its feelings that the subject objectively conditions the creativity transcendent beyond itself. In our own relatively high grade of human existence, this doctrine of feelings and their subject is best illustrated by our notion of moral responsibility. The subject is responsible for being what it is in virtue of its feelings. It is also derivatively responsible for the consequences of its existence because they flow from its feelings.

If the subject-predicate form of statement be taken to be metaphysically ultimate, it is then impossible to express this doctrine of feelings and their superject. It is better to say that the feelings *aim at* their subject, than to say that they *are aimed at* their subject. For the latter mode of expression removes the subject from the scope of the feeling and assigns it to an external agency. Thus the feeling would be wrongly abstracted from its own final cause. This final cause is an inherent element in the feeling, constituting the unity of that feeling. An actual entity feels as it does feel in order to be the actual entity which it is. In this way an actual entity satisfies Spinoza's notion of substance: it is *causa sui*. The creativity is not an external agency with its own ulterior purposes. All actual entities share with God this characteristic of self-causation. For this reason every actual entity also shares with God the characteristic of transcending all other actual entities, including God. The [340] universe is thus a creative advance into novelty. The alternative to this doctrine is a static morphological universe.

SECTION IV

There are three main categoreal conditions which flow from the final nature of things. These three conditions are: (i) the Category of Subjective Unity, (ii) the Category of Objective Identity, and (iii) the Category of Objective Diversity. Later we shall isolate five** other categoreal conditions. But the three conditions mentioned above have an air of ultimate metaphysical generality.

The first category has to do with self-realization. Self-realization is the ultimate fact of facts. An actuality is self-realizing, and whatever is self-realizing is an actuality. An actual entity is at once the subject of self-realization, and the superject which is self-realized.

The second and third categories have to do with objective determination. All entities, including even other actual entities, enter into the self-realization of an actuality in the capacity of determinants of the definiteness of that actuality. By reason of this objective functioning of entities there is truth and falsehood. For every actuality is devoid of a shadow of ambiguity: it is exactly what it is, by reason of its objective definition at the hands of other entities. In abstraction from actualization, truth and falsehood are meaningless: we are in the region of nonsense, a limbo where nothing has any claim to existence. But definition is the soul of actuality: the attainment of a peculiar definiteness is the final cause which animates a particular process; and its attainment halts its process, so that by transcendence it passes into its objective immortality as a new objective condition added to the riches of definiteness attainable, the 'real potentiality' of the universe.

A distinction must here be made. Each task of creation is a social effort, employing the whole universe. Each novel actuality is a new partner adding a new con- [341] dition. Every new condition can be absorbed into additional fullness of attainment. On the other hand, each condition is exclusive, intolerant of diversities; except so far as it finds itself in a web of conditions which convert its exclusions into contrasts. A new actuality may appear in the wrong society, amid which its claims to efficacy act mainly as inhibitions. Then a weary task is set for creative function, by an epoch of new creations to remove the inhibition. Insistence on birth at the wrong season is the trick of evil. In other words, the novel fact may throw back, inhibit, and delay. But the advance, when it does arrive, will be richer in content, more fully conditioned, and more stable. For in its objective efficacy an actual entity can only inhibit by reason of its alternative positive contribution.

A chain of facts is like a barrier reef. On one side there is wreckage, and beyond it harbourage and safety. The categories governing the determination of things are the reasons why there should be evil; and are also the reasons why, in the advance of the world, particular evil facts are finally transcended.

SECTION V

Category I. The many feelings which belong to an incomplete phase in the process of an actual entity, though unintegrated by reason of the incompleteness of the phase, are compatible for synthesis by reason of the unity of their subject.

This is the Category of 'Subjective Unity.' This category is one expression of the general principle that the one subject is the final end which conditions each component feeling. Thus the superject is already present as a condition, determining how each feeling conducts its own process. Although in any incomplete phase there are many unsynthesized feelings, yet each of these feelings is conditioned by the other feelings. The process of each feeling is such as to render that feeling integrable with the other feelings.

[342] This Category of Subjective Unity is the reason why no feeling can

be abstracted from its subject. For the subject is at work in the feeling, in order that it may be the subject with that feeling. The feeling is an episode in self-production, and is referent to its aim. This aim is a certain definite unity with its companion feelings.

This doctrine of the inherence of the subject in the process of its production requires that in the primary phase of the subjective process there be a conceptual feeling of subjective aim: the physical and other feelings originate as steps towards realizing this conceptual aim through their treatment of initial data. This basic conceptual feeling suffers simplification in the successive phases of the concrescence. It starts with conditioned alternatives, and by successive decisions is reduced to coherence. The doctrine of responsibility is entirely concerned with this modification. In each phase the corresponding conceptual feeling is the 'subjective end' characteristic of that phase. The many feelings, in any incomplete phase, are necessarily compatible with each other by reason of their individual conformity to the subjective end evolved for that phase.

This Category of Subjective Unity is a doctrine of pre-established harmony, applied to the many feelings in an incomplete phase. If we recur therefore to the seven kinds of 'proper' entities, and ask how to classify an incomplete phase, we find that it has the unity of a proposition. In abstraction from the creative urge by which each such phase is merely an incident in a process, this phase is merely a proposition about its component feelings and their ultimate superject. The pre-established harmony is the self-consistency of this proposition, that is to say, its capacity for realization. But such abstraction from the process does violence to its nature; for the phase *is* an incident in the process. When we try to do justice to this aspect of the phase, we must say that it is a proposition seeking truth. It is a lure to the supervention of those integrating feelings by which the mere [343] potentiality of the proposition, with its outstanding indeterminations as to its setting amid the details of the universe, is converted into† the fully determinate actuality.

The ground, or origin, of the concrescent process† is the multiplicity of data in the universe, actual entities and eternal objects and propositions and nexūs. Each new phase in the concrescence means the retreat of mere propositional unity before the growing grasp of real unity of feeling. Each successive propositional phase is a lure to the creation of feelings which promote its realization. Each temporal entity, in one sense, originates from its mental pole, analogously to God himself. It derives from God its basic conceptual aim, relevant to its actual world, yet with indeterminations awaiting its own decisions. This subjective aim, in its successive modifications, remains the unifying factor governing the successive phases of interplay between physical and conceptual feelings. These decisions are impossible for the nascent creature antecedently to the novelties in the phases of its concrescence. But this statement in its turn requires amplification. With this amplification the doctrine, that the primary phase of a temporal actual entity is physical, is recovered. A 'physical feeling' is here defined to be the feeling of another actuality. If the other actuality be objectified by its conceptual feelings, the physical feeling of the subject in question is termed 'hybrid.' Thus the primary phase is a hybrid physical feeling of God, in respect to God's conceptual feeling which is immediately relevant to the universe 'given' for that concrescence. There is then, according to the Category of Conceptual Valuation, i.e., Categoreal Obligation IV, a derived conceptual feeling which reproduces for the subject the data and valuation of God's conceptual feeling. This conceptual feeling is the initial conceptual aim referred to in the preceding statement. In this sense, God can be termed the creator of each temporal actual entity. But the phrase is apt to be misleading by [344] its suggestion that the ultimate creativity of the universe is to be ascribed to God's volition. The true metaphysical position is that God is the aboriginal instance of this creativity, and is therefore the aboriginal condition which qualifies its action. It is the function of actuality to characterize the creativity, and God is the eternal primordial character. But,† of course, there is no meaning to 'creativity' apart from its 'creatures,' and no meaning to 'God' apart from the 'creativity' and the 'temporal creatures,' and no meaning to the 'temporal creatures'† apart from 'creativity' and 'God.'

Category II. There can be no duplication of any element in the objective datum of the satisfaction of an actual entity, so far as concerns the function of that element in that satisfaction.

This is the 'Category of Objective Identity.' This category asserts the essential self-identity of any entity as regards its status in each individualization of the universe. In such a concrescence one thing has one rôle, and cannot assume any duplicity. This is the very meaning of self-identity, that, in any actual confrontation of thing with thing, one thing cannot confront itself in alien rôles. Any one thing remains obstinately itself playing a part with self-consistent unity. This category is one ground of incompatibility.

Category III. There can be no 'coalescence' of diverse elements in the objective datum of an actual entity, so far as concerns the functions of those elements in that satisfaction.

This is the 'Category of Objective Diversity.' Here‡ the term 'coalescence' means the self-contradictory notion of diverse elements exercising an absolute identity of function, devoid of the contrasts inherent in their diversities. In other words, in a real complex unity each particular component imposes its own particularity on its status. No entity can have an abstract status in a real unity. Its status must be such that only it can fill and only that actuality can supply.

[345] The neglect of this category is a prevalent error in metaphysical reasoning. This category is another ground of incompatibility.

SECTION VI

The importance of these categories can only be understood by considering each actual world in the light of a 'medium' leading up to the concrescence of the actual entity in question. It will be remembered that the phrase 'actual world' has always reference to some one concrescence.

Any actual entity, which we will name A, feels other actual entities,† which we will name B, C, and D. Thus B, C, and D all lie in the actual world of A. But C and D may lie in the actual world of B, and are then felt by it; also D may lie in the actual world of C and be felt by it. This example might be simplified, or might be changed to one of any degree of complication. Now B, as an initial datum for A's feeling, also presents C and D for A to feel through its mediation. Also C, as an initial datum for A's feeling, also presents D for A to feel through its mediation. Thus, in this artificially simplified example, A has D presented for feeling through three distinct sources: (i) directly as a crude datum, (ii) by the mediation of B, and (iii) by the mediation of C. This threefold presentation is D, in its function of an initial datum for A's feeling of it, so far as concerns the mediation of B and C. But, of course, the artificial simplification of the medium to two intermediaries is very far from any real case. The medium between D and A consists of all those actual entities which lie in the actual world of A and not in the actual world of D. For the sake of simplicity the explanation will continue in terms of this threefold presentation.

There are thus three sources of feeling, D direct, D in its nexus with C, and D in its nexus with B. Thus in the basic phase of A's concrescence there arise three prehensions of the datum D. According to the first category [346] these prehensions are not independent. This subjective unity of the concrescence introduces negative prehensions, so that D in the direct feeling is not felt in its formal completeness, but objectified with the elimination of such of its prehensions as are inconsistent with D felt through the mediation of B, and through the mediation of C. Thus the three component feelings of the first phase† are consistent, so as to pass into the integration of the second phase in which there is A's one feeling of a coherent objectification of D. Since D is necessarily self-consistent, the inconsistencies must arise from the subjective forms of the prehensions of D by B directly, by C directly, and by A directly. These inconsistencies lead to the eliminations in A's total prehension of D.

In this process, the negative prehensions which effect the elimination are not merely negligible. The process through which a feeling passes in constituting itself† also records itself in the subjective form of the integral feeling. The negative prehensions have their own subjective forms which they contribute to the process. A feeling bears on itself the scars of its birth; it recollects as a subjective emotion its struggle for existence; it retains the impress of what it might have been, but is not. It is for this reason that what an actual entity has avoided as a datum for feeling may yet be an important part of its equipment. The actual cannot be reduced to mere matter of fact in divorce from the potential.

The same principle of explanation also holds in the case of a conceptual prehension, in which the datum is an eternal object. In the first phase of this conceptual prehension, there is this eternal object to be felt as a mere abstract capacity for giving definiteness to a physical feeling. But also there are the feelings of the objectifications of innumerable actual entities. Some of these physical feelings illustrate this same eternal object as an element providing their definiteness. There are in this way diverse prehensions of the same eternal object; and by the first category these various prehensions must be [347] consistent, so as to pass into the integration of the subsequent phase in which there is one coherent complex feeling, namely, a conceptual feeling of that eternal object. This subjective insistence on consistency may, from the beginning, replace the positive feelings by negative prehensions.

SECTION VII

In the explanations of the preceding section, only the first category has been explicitly alluded to. It must now be pointed out how the other categories have been tacitly presupposed.

The fact that there is integration at all arises from the condition expressed by the Category of Objective Identity. The same entity, be it actual entity or be it eternal object, cannot be felt twice in the formal constitution of one concrescence. The incomplete phases with their many feelings of one object are only to be interpreted in terms of the final satisfaction with its one feeling of that one object. Thus objective identity requires integration of the many feelings of one object into the one feeling of that object. The analysis of an actual entity is only intellectual, or, to speak with a wider scope, only objective. Each actual entity is a cell with atomic unity. But in analysis it can only be understood as a process; it can only be felt as a process, that is to say, as in passage. The actual entity is divisible; but is in fact undivided. The divisibility can thus only refer to its objectifications in which it transcends itself. But such transcendence is self-revelation.

[348] ‡The third category is concerned with the antithesis to oneness, namely, diversity. An actual entity is not merely one; it is also definitely complex. But, to be definitely complex is to include definite diverse elements in definite ways. The Category of Objective Diversity expresses the inexorable condition—that a complex unity must provide for each of its components a real diversity of status, with a reality which bears the same sense as its own reality and is peculiar to itself. In other words, a real unity cannot provide sham diversities of status for its diverse components.

This category is in truth only a particular application of the second category. For a 'status' is after all *something*; and, according to the Category of Objective Identity, it cannot duplicate its rôle. Thus if the 'status' be the status of *this*, it cannot in the same sense be the status of *that*. The prohibition of sham diversities of status sweeps away the 'class-theory't of particular substances, which was waveringly suggested by Locke (II, XXIII, 1), was more emphatically endorsed by Hume (*Treatise*, Bk. I,† Part I, Sect. 6), and has been adopted by Hume's followers. For the essence of a class is that it assigns no diversity of function to the members of its extension. The members of a class are diverse members in virtue of mere logical disjunction. The 'class,' thus appealed to, is a mere multiplicity. But in the prevalent discussion of classes, there are illegitimate transitions to the notions of a 'nexus' and of a 'proposition.' The appeal to a class to perform the services of a proper entity is exactly analogous to an appeal to an imaginary terrier to kill a real rat.

‡Thus the process of integration, which lies at the very heart of the concrescence, is the urge imposed on the concrescent unity of that universe by the three Categories of Subjective Unity, of Objective Identity, and of Objective Diversity. The oneness of the universe, and the oneness of each element in the universe, repeat themselves to the crack of doom in the creative advance from creature to creature, each creature including in itself the whole of history and exemplifying the self-identity of things and their mutual diversities.

SECTION VIII

This diversity of status, combined with the real unity of the components, means that the real synthesis of two component elements in the objective datum of a feeling [349] must be infected with the individual particularities of each of the relata. Thus the synthesis in its completeness expresses the joint particularities of that pair of relata, and can relate no others. A complex entity with this individual definiteness, arising out of determinateness of eternal objects, will be termed a 'contrast.' A contrast cannot be abstracted from the contrasted relata.

The most obvious examples of a contrast are to be found by confining attention purely to eternal objects. The contrast between blue and red cannot be repeated as *that* contrast between any other pair of colours, or any pair of sounds, or between a colour and a sound. It is just the contrast between blue and red, *that* and nothing else. Certain abstractions from that contrast, certain values inherent in it, can also be got from other contrasts. But they are *other* contrasts, and not *that* contrast; and the abstractions are not 'contrasts' of the same categoreal type.

In another sense, a 'nexus' falls under the meaning of the term 'contrast'; though we shall avoid this application of the term. What are ordinarily termed 'relations' are abstractions from contrasts. A relation can be found in many contrasts; and when it is so found, it is said to relate the things contrasted. The term 'multiple contrast' will be used when there are or may be more than two elements jointly contrasted, and it is desired to draw attention to that fact. A multiple contrast is analysable into component dual contrasts. But a multiple contrast is not a mere aggregation of dual contrasts. It is one contrast, over and above its component contrasts. This doctrine that a multiple contrast cannot be conceived as a mere disjunction of dual contrasts is the basis of the doctrine of emergent evolution. It is the doctrine of real unities being more than a mere collective disjunction of component elements. This doctrine has the same ground as the objection to the class-theory of particular substances. The doctrine is a commonplace of art.

Bradley's discussions of relations are confused by his [350] failure to distinguish between relations and contrasts. A relation is a genus of contrasts. He is then distressed—or would have been distressed if he had not been consoled by the notion of 'mereness' as in 'mere appearance'—to find that a relation will not do the work of a contrast. It fails to contrast. Thus Bradley's argument proves that relations, among other things, are 'mere'; that is to say, are indiscretions of the absolute, apings of reality without self-consistency.

SECTION IX

One use of the term 'contrast' is to mean that particularity of conjoint unity which arises from the realized togetherness of eternal objects. But there is another, and more usual, sense of 'particularity.' This is the sense in which the term 'particular' is applied to an actual entity.

One actual entity has a status among other actual entities, not expressible wholly in terms of contrasts between eternal objects. For example, the complex nexus of ancient imperial Rome to European history is not wholly expressible in universals. It is not merely the contrast of a sort of city, imperial, Roman, ancient, with a sort of history of a sort of continent, sea-indented, river-diversified, with alpine divisions, begirt by larger continental masses and oceanic wastes, civilized, barbarized, christianized, commercialized, industrialized. The nexus in question does involve such a complex contrast of universals. But it involves more. For it is the nexus of *that* Rome with *that* Europe. We cannot be conscious of this nexus purely by the aid of conceptual feelings. This nexus is implicit, below consciousness, in our physical feelings. In part we are conscious of such physical feelings, and of that particularity of the nexus between particular actual entities. This consciousness takes the form of our consciousness of particular spatial and temporal relations between things directly perceived. But, as in the case of Rome and Europe, so far as con- [351] cerns the mass of our far-reaching knowledge, the particular nexus between the particular actualities in question is† only indicated by constructive reference to the physical feelings of which we are conscious.

This peculiar particularity of the nexus between actual entities can be put in another way. Owing to the disastrous confusion, more especially by Hume, of conceptual feelings with perceptual feelings, the truism that we can only *conceive* in terms of universals has been stretched to mean that we can only *feel* in terms of universals. This is untrue. Our perceptual feelings feel particular existents; that is to say, a physical feeling, belonging to the percipient, feels the nexus between two other actualities, A and B. It feels feelings of A which feel B, and feels feelings of B which feel A. It integrates these feelings, so as to unify their identity of elements. These identical elements form the factor defining the nexus between A and B, a nexus also retaining the particular diversity of A and B in its uniting force.

Also the more complex multiple nexus between many actual entities in the actual world of a percipient is felt by that percipient. But this nexus, as thus felt, can be abstracted from that particular percipient. It is the same nexus for all percipients which include those actual entities in their actual worlds. The multiple nexus is how those actual entities are really together in all subsequent unifications of the universe, by reason of the objective immortality of their real mutual prehensions of each other.

We thus arrive at the notion of the actual world of any actual entity, as a nexus whose objectification constitutes the complete unity of ob-jective datum for the physical feeling of that actual entity. This actual entity is the original percipient of that nexus. But any other actual entity which includes in its own actual world that original percipient† also in-cludes that previous nexus as a portion of its own actual world. Thus each actual world is a nexus which in this sense is independent of its original [352] percipient. It enjoys an objective immortality in the future beyond itself.

Every nexus is a component nexus, first accomplished in some later phase of concrescence of an actual entity, and ever afterwards having its status in actual worlds as an unalterable fact, dated and located among the actual entities connected in itself. If in a nexus there be a realized con-trast of universals, this contrast is located in that actual entity to which it belongs as first originated in one of its integrative feelings. Thus every realized contrast has a location, which is particular with the particularity of actual entities. It is a particular complex matter of fact, realized; and, because of its reality, a standing condition in every subsequent actual world from which creative advance must originate.

It is this complete individual particularity of each actuality, and of each nexus, and of each realized contrast, which is the reason for the three Categoreal Conditions—of Subjective Unity, of Objective Identity, and of Objective Diversity. The word 'event' is used sometimes in the sense of a nexus of actual entities, and sometimes in the sense of a nexus as objecti-fied by universals. In either sense, it is a definite fact with a date.

The initial data of a complex feeling, as mere data, are many; though as felt they are one in the objective unity of a pattern. Thus a nexus is a realized pattern of the initial data; though this pattern is merely relative to the feeling, expressive of those factors in the many data by reason of which they can acquire their unity in the feeling. This is the second use of the term nexus, mentioned above.

Thus, just as the 'feeling as one' cannot bear the abstraction from it of the subject, so the 'data as one' cannot bear the abstraction from it of every feeling which feels it as such. According to the ontological principle, the impartial nexus is an objective datum in the consequent nature of God; since it is *somewhere* and yet not by any necessity of its own nature implicated in the [353] feelings of any determined actual entity of the actual world. The nexus involves realization somewhere. This is the first use of the term nexus.

In two extreme cases the initial data of a feeling have a unity of their own. In one case, the data reduce to a single actual entity, other than the subject of the feeling; and in the other case the data reduce to a single eternal object. These are called 'primary feelings.' A particular feeling divorced from its subject is nonsense.

There are thus two laws respecting the feelings constituting the complex satisfaction of an actual entity: (i) An entity can only be felt once, and (ii) the diverse feelings, in the same subject, of the same entity as datum which are to be unified into one feeling, must be compatible in their treatment of the entity felt. In conformity with this pre-established harmony, 'incompatibility' would have dictated from the beginning that some 'feeling' be replaced by a negative prehension.

SECTION X

The subjective forms of feelings are best discussed in connection with the different types of feelings which can arise. This classification into types has regard to the differences among feelings in respect to their initial data, their objective data, and their subjective forms. But these sources of difference cannot wholly be kept separate.

A feeling is the appropriation of some elements in the universe to be components in the real internal constitution of its subject. The elements are the initial data; they are what the feeling feels. But they are felt under an abstraction. The process of the feeling involves negative prehensions which effect elimination. Thus the initial data are felt under a 'perspective' which is the objective datum of the feeling.

In virtue of this elimination the components of the complex objective datum have become 'objects' intervening in the constitution of the subject of the feeling. In the phraseology of mathematical physics a feeling has a [354] 'vector' character. A feeling is the agency by which other things are built into the constitution of its one subject in process of concrescence. Feelings are constitutive of the nexus by reason of which the universe finds its unification ever renewed by novel concrescence. The universe is always one, since there is no surveying it except from an actual entity which unifies it. Also the universe is always new, since the immediate actual entity is the superject of feelings which are essentially novelties.

The essential novelty of a feeling attaches to its subjective form. The initial data, and even the nexus which is the objective datum, may have served other feelings with other subjects. But the subjective form is the immediate novelty; it is how *that* subject is feeling that objective datum. There is no tearing this subjective form from the novelty of this concrescence. It is enveloped in the immediacy of its immediate present. The fundamental example of the notion 'quality inhering in† particular substance' is afforded by 'subjective form inhering in feeling.' If we abstract the form from the feeling, we are left with an eternal object as the remnant of subjective form.

A feeling can be genetically described in terms of its process of origination, with its negative prehensions whereby its many initial data become its complex objective datum. In this process the subjective form originates, and carries into the feeling its own history transformed into the way in which the feeling feels. The way in which the feeling feels expresses how the feeling came into being. It expresses the purpose which urged it forward, and the obstacles which it encountered, and the indeterminations which were dissolved by the originative decisions of the subject.

There are an indefinite number of types of feeling according to the complexity of the initial data which the feeling integrates, and according to the complexity of the objective datum which it finally feels. But there are three primary types of feeling which enter into the forma- [355] tion of all the more complex feelings. These types are: (i) that of simple physical feelings, (ii) that of conceptual feelings, and (iii) that of transmuted feelings. In a simple physical feeling, the initial datum is a single actual entity; in a conceptual feeling, the objective datum is an eternal object;† in a transmuted feeling, the objective datum is a nexus of actual entities. Simple physical feelings and transmuted feelings make up the class of physical feelings.

In none of these feelings, taken in their original purity devoid of accretions from later integrations, does the subjective form involve consciousness. Although in a propositional feeling the subjective form may involve judgment, this element in the subjective form is not necessarily present.

One final remark must be added to the general description of a feeling. A feeling is a component in the concrescence of a novel actual entity. The feeling is always novel in reference to its data; since its subjective form, though it must always have reproductive reference to the data, is not wholly determined by them. The process of the concrescence is a progressive integration of feelings controlled by their subjective forms. In this synthesis, feelings of an earlier phase sink into the components of some more complex feeling of a later phase. Thus each phase adds its element of novelty, until the final phase in which the one complex 'satisfaction' is reached. Thus the actual entity, as viewed morphologically through its 'satisfaction,' is novel in reference to any one of its component feelings. It presupposes those feelings. But conversely, no feeling can be abstracted either from its data, or its subject. It is essentially a feeling aiming at that subject, and motivated by that aim. Thus the subjective form embodies the pragmatic aspect of the feeling; for the datum is felt with that subjective form in order that the subject may be the superject which it is.

In the analysis of a feeling, whatever presents itself as also *ante rem* is a datum, whatever presents itself as [356] exclusively *in re* is subjective form, whatever presents itself *in re* and *post rem* is 'subject-superject.' This doctrine of 'feeling' is the central doctrine respecting the becoming of an actual entity. In a feeling the actual world, selectively appropriated, is the presupposed datum, not formless but with its own realized form selectively germane, in other words 'objectified.' The subjective form is the ingression of novel form peculiar to the new particular fact, and with its peculiar mode of fusion with the objective datum. The subjective form in abstraction from the feeling is merely a complex eternal object. In the becoming, it meets the 'data' which are selected from the actual world. In other words, the data are already 'in being.' There the term 'in being' is for the moment used as equivalent to the term 'in realization.'

SECTION XI

**A subjective form has two factors, its qualitative pattern and its pattern of intensive quantity. But these two factors of pattern cannot wholly be considered in abstraction from each other. For the relative intensities of the qualitative elements in the qualitative pattern are among the relational factors which constitute that qualitative pattern. Also conversely, there are qualitative relations among the qualitative elements and they constitute an abstract qualitative pattern for the qualitative relations. The pattern of intensities is not only the variety of qualitative elements with such-and-such intensities; but it is also the variety of qualitative elements, as in such-and-such an abstract qualitative pattern, with such-and-such intensities. Thus the two patterns are not really separable. It is true that there is an abstract qualitative pattern, and an abstract intensive pattern; but in the fused pattern the abstract qualitative pattern lends itself† to the intensities, and the abstract intensive pattern lends itself to the qualities.

Further, the subjective form cannot be absolutely dis- [357] joined from the pattern of the objective datum. Some elements of the subjective form can be thus disjoined; and they form the subjective form as in abstraction from the patterns of the objective datum. But the full subjective form cannot be abstracted from the pattern of the objective datum. The intellectual disjunction is not a real separation. Also the subjective form, amid its own original elements, always involves reproduction of the pattern of the objective datum.

As a simple example of this description of a feeling, consider the audition of sound. In order to avoid unnecessary complexity, let the sound be one definite note. The audition of this note is a feeling. This feeling has first an auditor, who is the subject of the feeling. But the auditor would not be the auditor that he is apart from this feeling of his.

Secondly, there is the complex ordered environment composed of certain other actual entities which, however vaguely, is felt by reason of this audition. This environment is the datum of this feeling. It is the external world, as grasped systematically in this feeling. In this audition it is felt under the objectification of vague spatial relations, and as exhibiting musical qualities. But the analytic discrimination of this datum of the feeling is in part vague and conjectural, so far as consciousness is concerned: there is the antecedent physiological functioning of the human body, and the presentational immediacy of the presented locus.

There is also an emotional sensory pattern, the subjective form, which is more definite and more easily analysable. The note, in its capacity of a private sensation, has pitch, quality, and intensity. It is analysable into its fundamental tone, and a selection of its overtones. This analysis reveals an abstract qualitative pattern which is the complex relatedness of the fundamental tone-quality‡ with the tone-qualities of its select overtones. This qualitative pattern may, or may not, include relations of a spatial type, if some of the overtones come [358] from instruments spatially separate—† for example, from a spatial pattern of tuning forks.

The fundamental tone, and its overtones, have, each of them, their own intensities. This pattern of intensities can be analysed into the relative intensities of the various tones and the absolute intensity which is the total loudness. The scale of relative intensities enters into the final quality of the note, with some independence of its absolute loudness.

Also the spatial pattern of the tuning forks and the resonance of the music chamber enter into this quality. But these also concern the datum of the feeling. Also in this integration of feeling we must include the qualitative and quantitative auditory contributions derived from various nerve-routes of the body. In this way the animal body, as part of the external world, takes a particularly prominent place in the pattern of the datum of the feeling. Also in the subjective form we must reckon qualities of joy and distaste, of adversion and of aversion, which attach integrally to the audition, and also differentially to various elements of the audition. In an earlier phase of the auditor, there is audition divested of such joy and distaste. This earlier, bare audition does not in its own nature determine this additional qualification. It originates as the audition becomes an element in a higher synthesis, and yet it is an element in the final component feeling. Thus the audition gains complexity of subjective form by its integration with other feelings. Also, though we can discern three patterns, namely, the pattern of the datum, the pattern of emotional quality, and the pattern of emotional intensity, we cannot analyse either of the latter patterns in complete separation either from the pattern of the datum, or from each other.

The final concrete component in the satisfaction is the audition with its subject, its datum, and its emotional pattern as finally completed. It is a particular fact not to be torn away from any of its elements.

SECTION XII

[359] Prehensions are not atomic; they can be divided into other prehensions and combined into other prehensions. Also prehensions are not independent of each other. The relation between their subjective forms is constituted by the one subjective aim which guides their formation. This correlation of subjective forms is termed 'the mutual sensitivity' of prehensions (cf. Part I, Ch. II, Sect. III, Categoreal Obligation VII, 'The Category of Subjective Harmony').

The prehensions in disjunction are abstractions; each of them is its subject viewed in that abstract objectification. The actuality is the totality of prehensions with subjective unity in process of concrescence into concrete unity.

There are an indefinite number of prehensions, overlapping, subdividing, and supplementary to each other. The principle, according to which a prehension can be discovered, is to take any component in the objective datum of the satisfaction; in the complex pattern of the subjective form of the satisfaction there will be a component with direct relevance to this element in the datum. Then in the satisfaction, there is a prehension of this component of the objective datum with that component of the total subjective form as its subjective form.

The genetic growth of this prehension can then be traced by considering the transmission of the various elements of the datum from the actual world, and—in the case of eternal objects—their origination in the conceptual prehensions. There is then a growth of prehensions, with integrations, eliminations, and determination of subjective forms. But the determination† of successive phases of subjective forms, whereby the integrations have the characters that they do have, depends on the unity of the subject imposing a mutual sensitivity upon the prehensions. Thus a prehension, considered genetically, can never free itself from the incurable atomicity [360] of the actual entity to which it belongs. The selection of a subordinate prehension from the satisfaction—as described above—involves a hypothetical, propositional point of view. The fact is the satisfaction as one. There is some arbitrariness in taking a component from the datum with a component from the subjective form, and in considering them, on the ground of congruity, as forming a subordinate prehension. The justification is that the genetic process can be thereby analysed. If no such analysis of the growth of that subordinate prehension can be given, then there has been a faulty analysis of the satisfaction. This relation between the satisfaction and the genetic process is expressed in the eighth and ninth categories of explanation (cf. Part I, Ch. II, Sect. II).

CHAPTER II

THE PRIMARY FEELINGS

SECTION I

[361] A 'SIMPLE physical feeling' entertained in one subject is a feeling for which the initial datum is another single actual entity, and the objective datum is another feeling entertained by the latter actual entity.

Thus in a simple physical feeling there are two actual entities concerned. One of them is the subject of that feeling, and the other is the *initial* datum of the feeling. A second feeling is also concerned, namely, the *objective* datum of the simple physical feeling. This second feeling is the 'objectification' of *its* subject for the subject of the simple physical feeling. The initial datum is objectified as being the subject of the feeling which is the objective datum: the objectification is the 'perspective' of the initial datum.

A simple physical feeling is an act of causation. The actual entity which is the initial datum is the 'cause,' the simple physical feeling is the 'effect,' and the subject entertaining the simple physical feeling is the actual entity 'conditioned' by the effect. This 'conditioned' actual entity will also be called the 'effect.' All complex causal action can be reduced to a complex of such primary components. Therefore simple physical feelings will also be called 'causal' feelings.

But it is equally true to say that a simple physical feeling is the most primitive type of an act of perception, devoid of consciousness. The actual entity which is the initial datum is the actual entity perceived, the objective datum is the 'perspective' under which that actual entity is perceived, and the subject of the simple physical feeling [362] is the perceiver. This is not an example of conscious perception. For the subjective form of a simple physical feeling does not involve consciousness, unless acquired in subsequent phases of integration. It seems as though in practice, for human beings at least, only transmuted feelings acquire consciousness, never simple physical feelings. Consciousness originates in the higher phases of integration and illuminates those phases with the greater clarity and distinctness.

Thus a simple physical feeling is one feeling which feels another feeling. But the feeling felt has a subject diverse from the subject of the feeling which feels it. A multiplicity of simple physical feelings entering into the propositional unity of a phase constitutes the first phase in the concrescence of the actual entity which is the common subject of all these feelings. The limitation, whereby the actual entities felt are severally reduced to the perspective of one of their own feelings, is imposed by the Categoreal Condition of Subjective Unity, requiring a harmonious compatibility in the feelings of each incomplete phase. Thus the negative prehensions, involved in the production of any one feeling, are not independent of the other feelings. The subjective forms of feelings depend in part on the negative prehensions. This primary phase of simple physical feelings constitutes the machinery by reason of which the creativity transcends the world already actual, and yet remains conditioned by that actual world in its new impersonation.

Owing to the vagueness of our conscious analysis of complex feelings, perhaps we never consciously discriminate one simple physical feeling in isolation. But all our physical relationships are made up of such simple physical feelings, as their atomic bricks. Apart from inhibitions or additions, weakenings or intensifications, due to the history of its production, the subjective form of a physical feeling is re-enaction of the subjective form of the feeling felt. Thus the cause passes on its feeling to be reproduced by the new subject as its own, and yet [363] as inseparable from the cause. There is a flow of feeling. But the re-enaction is not perfect. The categoreal demands of the concrescence require adjustments of the pattern of emotional intensities. The cause is objectively in the constitution of the effect, in virtue of being the feeler of the feeling reproduced in the effect with partial equivalence of subjective form. Also the cause's feeling has its own objective datum, and its own initial datum. Thus this antecedent initial datum has now entered into the datum of the effect's feeling at second-hand through the mediation of the cause.

The reason why the cause is objectively in the effect† is that the cause's feeling cannot, as a feeling, be abstracted from its subject which is the cause. This passage of the cause into the effect is the cumulative character of time. The irreversibility of time depends on this character.

Note that in the 'satisfaction' there is an integration of simple physical feelings. No simple physical feeling need be distinguished in consciousness. Physical feelings may be merged with feelings of any type, and of whatever complexity. A simple physical feeling has the dual character of being the cause's feeling re-enacted for the effect as subject. But this transference of feeling effects a partial identification of cause with effect, and not a mere representation of the cause. It is the cumulation of the universe and not a stage-play about it. In a simple feeling there is a double particularity in reference to the actual world, the particular cause and the particular effect. In Locke's language (III, III, 6), and with his limitation of thought, a simple feeling is an idea in one mind 'determined to this or that particular existent.' Locke is here expressing what only metaphysicians can doubt.

By reason of this duplicity in a simple feeling there is a vector character which transfers the cause into the effect. It is a feeling *from* the cause which acquires the subjectivity of the new effect without loss of its original

[364] subjectivity in the cause. Simple physical feelings embody the reproductive character of nature, and also the objective immortality of the past. In virtue of these feelings time is the conformation of the immediate present to the past. Such feelings are 'conformal' feelings.

The novel actual entity, which is the effect, is the reproduction of the many actual entities of the past. But in this reproduction there is abstraction from their various totalities of feeling. This abstraction is required by the categoreal conditions for compatible synthesis in the novel unity. This abstractive 'objectification' is rendered possible by reason of the 'divisible' character of the satisfactions of actual entities. By reason of this 'divisible' character causation is the transfer of a feeling, and not of a total satisfaction. The other feelings are dismissed by negative prehensions, owing to their lack of compliance with categoreal demands.

A simple physical feeling enjoys a characteristic which has been variously described as 're-enaction,' 'reproduction,' and 'conformation.' This characteristic can be more accurately explained in terms of the eternal objects involved. There are eternal objects determinant of the definiteness of the objective datum which is the 'cause,' and eternal objects determinant of the definiteness of the subjective form belonging to the 'effect.' When there is re-enaction there is one eternal object with two-way functioning, namely, as partial determinant of the objective datum, and as partial determinant of the subjective form. In this two-way rôle, the eternal object is functioning relationally between the initial data on the one hand and the concrescent subject on the other. It is playing one self-consistent rôle in obedience to the Category of Objective Identity.

Physical science is the science investigating spatio-temporal and quantitative characteristics of simple physical feelings. The actual entities of the actual world are bound together in a nexus of these feelings. Also in the creative advance, the nexus proper to an antecedent [365] actual world is not destroyed. It is reproduced and added to, by the new bonds of feeling with the novel actualities which transcend it and include it. But these bonds have always their vector character. Accordingly the ultimate physical entities for physical science are always vectors indicating transference. In the world there is nothing static. But there is reproduction; and hence the permanence which is the result of order, and the cause of it. And yet there is always change; for time is cumulative as well as reproductive, and the cumulation of the many is not their reproduction as many.

This section on simple physical feelings lays the foundation of the treatment of cosmology in the philosophy of organism. It contains the discussion of the ultimate elements from which a more complete philosophical discussion of the physical world—that is to say, of nature—must be derived. In the first place an endeavour has been made to do justice alike to the aspect of the world emphasized by Descartes and to the atomism of the modern quantum theory. Descartes saw the natural world as an extensive spatial plenum, enduring through time. Modern physicists see energy transferred in definite quanta. This quantum theory also has analogues in recent neurology. Again fatigue is the expression of cumulation; it is physical memory. Further,† causation and physical memory spring from the same root: both of them are physical perception. Cosmology must do equal justice to atomism, to continuity, to causation, to memory, to perception, to qualitative and quantitative forms of energy, and to extension. But so far there has been no reference to the ultimate vibratory characters of organisms and to the 'potential' element in nature.

SECTION II

Conceptual feelings and simple causal feelings constitute the two main species of 'primary' feelings. All other feelings of whatever complexity arise out of a process of integration which starts with a phase of these [366] primary feelings. There is, however, a difference between the species. An actual entity in the actual world of a subject *must* enter into the concrescence of that subject by *some* simple causal feeling, however vague, trivial, and submerged. Negative prehensions may eliminate its distinctive importance. But in some way, by some trace of causal feeling, the remote actual entity is prehended positively. In the case of an eternal object, there is no such necessity. In any given concrescence, it may be included positively by means of a conceptual feeling; but it may be excluded by a negative prehension. The actualities *have* to be felt, while the pure potentials *can* be dismissed. So far as concerns their functionings as objects, this is the great distinction between an actual entity and an eternal object. The one is stubborn matter of fact; and the other never loses its 'accent' of potentiality.

In each concrescence there is a twofold aspect of the creative urge. In one aspect there is the origination of simple causal feelings; and in the other aspect there is the origination of conceptual feelings. These contrasted aspects will be called the physical and the mental poles of an actual entity. No actual entity is devoid of either pole; though their relative importance differs in different actual entities. Also conceptual feelings do not necessarily involve consciousness; though there can be no conscious feelings which do not involve conceptual feelings as elements in the synthesis.

Thus an actual entity is essentially dipolar, with its physical and mental poles; and even the physical world cannot be properly understood without reference to its other side, which is the complex of mental operations. The primary mental operations are conceptual feelings.

A conceptual feeling is feeling an eternal object in the primary metaphysical character of being an 'object,' that is to say, feeling its *capacity* for being a realized determinant of process. Immanence and transcendence are the characteristics of an object: as a realized determinant it [367] is immanent; as a capacity for determination it is transcendent; in both rôles it is relevant to something not itself. There is no character belonging to the actual apart from its exclusive determination by selected eternal objects. The definiteness of the actual arises from the exclusiveness of eternal objects in their function as determinants. If the actual entity be *this*, then by the nature of the case it is not *that* or *that*. The fact of incompatible alternatives is the ultimate fact in virtue of which there is definite character. A conceptual feeling is the feeling of an eternal object in respect to its general capacity as a determinant of character, including thereby its capacity of exclusiveness. In the technical phraseology of these lectures, a conceptual feeling is a feeling whose 'datum' is an eternal object. Analogously a negative prehension is termed 'conceptual't when its datum is an eternal object. In a conceptual feeling there is no necessary progress from the 'initial data' to the 'objective datum.' The two may be identical, except in so far as conceptual feelings with diverse sources of origination acquire integration.

Conceptual prehensions, positive or negative, constitute the primary operations among those belonging to the mental pole of an actual entity.

SECTION III

The subjective form of a conceptual feeling has the character of a 'valuation,' and this notion must now be explained.

A conceptual feeling arises in some incomplete phase of its subject and passes into a supervening phase in which it has found integration with other feelings. In this supervening phase, the eternal object, which is the datum of the conceptual feeling, is an ingredient in some sort of datum in which the other components are the objective data of other feelings in the earlier phase. This new datum is the integrated datum; it will be some sort of 'contrast.' By the first categoreal condition the feelings [368] of the earlier phase are compatible for integration. Thus the supervention of the later phase does not involve elimination by negative prehensions; such eliminations of positive prehensions in the concrescent subject would divide that subject into many subjects, and would divide these many subjects from the superject. But, though there can be no elimination from the supervening phase as a whole, there may be elimination from some new integral feeling which is merely one component of that phase.

But in the formation of this integrated datum there must be determination of exactly *how* this eternal object has ingress into that datum conjointly with the remaining eternal objects and actual entities derived from the other feelings. This determination is effected by the subjective forms of the component conceptual feelings. Again it is to be remembered that, by the first categoreal condition, this subjective form is not independent of the other feelings in the earlier phase, and thus is such as to effect this determination. Also the integral feeling has its subjective form with its pattern of intensiveness. This patterned intensiveness regulates the distinctive relative importance of each element of the datum as felt in that feeling. This intensive regulation of that eternal object,† as felt in the integrated datum, is determined by the subjective form of the conceptual feeling. Yet again, by reference to the first, and seventh, categoreal conditions, this intensive form of the conceptual feeling has dependence also in this respect on the other feelings of the earlier phase. Thus, according as the valuation of the conceptual feeling is a 'valuation up' or a 'valuation down,' the importance of the eternal object as felt in the integrated feeling is enhanced, or attenuated. Thus the valuation is both qualitative, determining how the eternal object is to be utilized, and is also intensive, determining what importance that utilization is to assume.

Thus a valuation has three characteristics:

(i) According to the Categories of Subjective Unity, and [369] of Subjective Harmony, the valuation is dependent on the other feelings in its phase of origination.

(ii) The valuation determines in what status the eternal object has ingression into the integrated nexus physically felt.

(iii) The valuation values up, or down, so as to determine the intensive importance accorded to the eternal object by the subjective form of the integral feeling.

These three characteristics of an integral feeling, derived from its conceptual components, are summed up in the term 'valuation.'

But though these three characteristics are included in a valuation, they are merely the outcome of the subjective aim of the subject, determining what it is itself integrally to be, in its own character of the superject of its own process.

SECTION IV

Consciousness concerns the subjective form of a feeling. But such a subjective form requires a certain type of objective datum. A subjective form in abstraction loses its reality, and sinks into an eternal object capable of determining a feeling into that distinctive type of definiteness. But when the eternal object 'informs' a feeling it can only so operate in virtue of its conformation to the other components which jointly constitute the definiteness of the feeling. The moral of this slight discussion must now be applied to the notion of 'consciousness.' Consciousness is an element in feeling which belongs to its subjective form. But there can only be that sort of subjective form when the objective datum has an adequate character. Further, the objective datum can only assume this character when it is derivate from initial data which carry in their individual selves the reciprocal possibilities of this objective synthesis.

A pure conceptual feeling in its first mode of origination never involves consciousness. In this respect a pure mental feeling, conceptual or propositional, is analogous [370] to a pure physical feeling. A primary feeling of either type, or a propositional feeling, can enrich its subjective form with consciousness only by means of its alliances.

Whenever there is consciousness there is some element of recollection. It recalls earlier phases from the dim recesses of the unconscious. Long ago this truth was asserted in Plato's doctrine of reminiscence. No doubt Plato was directly thinking of glimpses of eternal truths lingering in a soul derivate from a timeless heaven of pure form. Be that as it may, then in a wider sense consciousness enlightens experience which precedes it, and could be without it if considered as a mere datum.

Hume, with opposite limitations to his meaning, asserts the same doctrine. He maintains that we can never conceptually entertain what we have never antecedently experienced through impressions of sensation. The philosophy of organism generalizes the notion of 'impressions of sensation' into that of 'pure physical feeling.' Even then Hume's assertion is too unguarded according to Hume's own showing. But the immediate point is the deep-seated alliance of consciousness with recollection both for Plato and for Hume.

Here we maintain the doctrine that, in the analysis of the origination of any conscious feeling, some component physical feelings are to be found; and conversely, whenever there is consciousness, there is some component of conceptual functioning. For the abstract element in the concrete fact is exactly what provokes our consciousness. The consciousness is what arises in some process of synthesis of physical and mental operations. In his† doctrine of ideas, Locke goes further than Hume and is, as I think, more accurate in expressing the facts; though Hume adds something which Locke omits.

Locke upholds the direct conscious apprehension of 'things without' (e.g.,† *Essay*, II, XXI, 1), otherwise termed 'exterior things' (II, XXIII, 1), or 'this or that particular existence' (III, III, 6), and illustrated by an individual nurse and an individual mother (III, III, 7). [371] In the philosophy of organism the nexus, which is the basis for such direct apprehension, is provided by the physical feelings. The philosophy of organism here takes the opposite road to that taken alike by Descartes and by Kant. Both of these philosophers accepted (Descartes with hesitations, and Kant without question) the traditional subjectivist sensationalism, and assigned the intuition of 'things without' peculiarly to the intelligence.

Hume's addition consists in expressing and discussing, with the utmost clarity, the traditional sensationalist dogma. Thus for Hume, as for Locke when he remembers to speak in terms of this doctrine, an 'impression' is the conscious apprehension of a universal. For example, he writes (*Treatise*, Bk. I,† Part I, Ch. I), "That idea of red, which we form in the dark, and that impression which strikes our eyes in sunshine, differ only in degree, not in nature."† This means that a consistent sensationalism cannot distinguish between a percept and a concept. Hume had not in his mind (at least when philosophizing, though he admits it for other sorts of 'practice') the fourth category of explanation, that no entity can be abstracted from its capacity to function as an object in the process of the actual world. 'To function as an object' is 'to be a determinant of the definiteness of an actual occurrence.' According to the philosophy of organism, a pure concept does not involve consciousness, at least in our human experience. Consciousness arises when a synthetic feeling integrates physical and conceptual feelings. Traditional philosophy in its account of conscious perception has exclusively fixed attention on its pure conceptual side; and thereby has made difficulties for itself in the theory of knowledge. Locke, with his naïve good sense, assumes that perception involves more than this conceptual side; though he fails to grasp the inconsistency of this assumption with the extreme subjectivist sensational doctrine. Physical feelings form the non-conceptual element in our awareness of [372] nature.[1] Also, all awareness, even awareness of concepts, requires at least the synthesis of physical feelings with conceptual feeling. In awareness actuality, as a process in fact, is integrated with the potentialities which illustrate *either* what it is and might not be, *or* what it is not and might be. In other words, there is no consciousness without reference to definiteness, affirmation, and negation. Also affirmation involves its contrast with negation, and negation involves its contrast with affirmation. Further, affirmation and negation are alike meaningless apart from reference to the definiteness of particular actualities. Consciousness is how we feel the affirmation-negation contrast. Conceptual feeling is the feeling of an unqualified negation; that is to say, it is the feeling of a definite eternal object with the definite extrusion of any particular realization. Consciousness requires that the objective datum should involve (as one side of a contrast) a qualified negative determined to some definite situation. It will be found later (cf. Ch. IV) that this doctrine implies that there is no consciousness apart from propositions as one element in the objective datum.

[1] Cf. *The Concept of Nature*, Ch. I.

CHAPTER III

THE TRANSMISSION OF FEELINGS

SECTION I

[373] ACCORDING to the ontological principle there is nothing which floats into the world from nowhere. Everything in the actual world is referable to some actual entity. It is either transmitted from an actual entity in the past, or belongs to the subjective aim of the actual entity to whose concrescence it belongs. This subjective aim is both an example and a limitation of the ontological principle. It is an example, in that the principle is here applied to the immediacy of concrescent fact. The subject completes itself during the process of concrescence by a self-criticism of its own incomplete phases. In another sense the subjective aim limits the ontological principle by its own autonomy. But the initial stage of its aim is an endowment which the subject inherits from the inevitable ordering of things, conceptually realized in the nature of God. The immediacy of the concrescent subject is constituted by its living aim at its own self-constitution. Thus the initial stage of the aim is rooted in the nature of God, and its completion depends on the self-causation of the subject-superject. This function of God is analogous to the remorseless working of things in Greek and in Buddhist thought. The initial aim is the best for that *impasse*. But if the best be bad, then the ruthlessness of God can be personified as Atè, the goddess of mischief. The chaff is burnt. What is inexorable in God, is valuation as an aim towards 'order'; and 'order' means 'society permissive of actualities with patterned intensity of feeling arising from adjusted con- [374] trasts.'† In this sense God is the principle of concretion; namely, he is that actual entity from which each temporal concrescence receives that initial aim from which its self-causation starts. That aim determines the initial gradations of relevance of eternal objects for conceptual feeling; and constitutes the autonomous subject in its primary phase of feelings with its initial conceptual valuations, and with its initial physical purposes. Thus the transition of the creativity from an actual world to the correlate novel concrescence is conditioned by the relevance of God's all-embracing conceptual valuations to the particular possibilities of transmission from the actual world, and by its relevance to the various possibilities of initial subjective form available for the initial feelings. In this way there is constituted the concrescent subject in its primary phase with its dipolar constitution, physical and mental, indissoluble.

244

If we prefer the phraseology, we can say that God and the actual world jointly constitute the character of the creativity for the initial phase of the novel concrescence. The subject, thus constituted, is the autonomous master of its own concrescence into subject-superject. It passes from a subjective aim in concrescence into a superject with objective immortality. At any stage it is subject-superject. According to this explanation, self-determination is always imaginative in its origin. The deterministic efficient causation is the inflow of the actual world in its own proper character of its own feelings, with their own intensive strength, felt and re-enacted by the novel concrescent subject. But this re-enaction has a mere character of conformation to pattern. The subjective valuation is the work of novel conceptual feeling; and in proportion to its importance, acquired in complex processes of integration and reintegration, this autonomous conceptual element modifies the subjective forms throughout the whole range of feeling in that concrescence and thereby guides the integrations.

In so far as there is negligible autonomous energy, the [375] subject merely receives the physical feelings, confirms their valuations according to the 'order' of that epoch, and transmits by reason of its own objective immortality. Its own flash of autonomous individual experience is negligible for the science which is tracing transmissions up to the conscious experience of a final observer. But as soon as individual experience is not negligible, the autonomy of the subject in the modification of its initial subjective aim must be taken into account. Each creative act is the universe incarnating itself as one, and there is nothing above it by way of final condition.

SECTION II

The general doctrine of the previous section requires an examination of principles regulating the transmission of feelings into data for novel feelings in a new concrescence. Since no feeling can be abstracted from its subject, this transmission is merely another way of considering the objectification of actual entities. A feeling will be called 'physical' when its datum involves objectifications of other actual entities. In the previous chapter the special case of 'simple physical feelings' was discussed. A feeling belonging to this special case has as its datum only one actual entity, and this actual entity is objectified by one of its feelings. All the more complex kinds of physical feelings arise in subsequent phases of concrescence, in virtue of integrations of simpler physical feelings with each other and with conceptual feelings. But before proceeding to these more complex physical feelings, a subdivision of simple physical feelings must be considered. Such feelings are subdivided into 'pure physical feelings' and 'hybrid physical feelings.' In a 'pure physical feeling' the actual entity which is the datum is objectified by one of its own physical feelings. Thus having regard to the 're-enaction' which is characteristic of the subjective form of a simple physical feeling, we have—in the case of the simpler actual entities—an example of the transference of energy in the physical [376] world. When the datum is an actual entity of a highly complex grade, the physical feeling by which it is objectified as a datum may be of a highly complex character, and the simple notion of a transference of some form of energy to the new subject may entirely fail to exhaust the important aspects of the pure physical feeling in question.

In a 'hybrid physical feeling' the actual entity forming the datum is objectified by one of its own conceptual feelings. Thus having regard to the element of autonomy which is characteristic of the subjective form of a conceptual feeling, we have—in the case of the more complex actual entities—an example of the origination and direction of energy in the physical world. In general, this simplified aspect of a hybrid physical feeling does not exhaust its rôle in the concrescence of its subject.

The disastrous separation of body and mind, characteristic of philosophical systems which are in any important respect derived from Cartesianism, is avoided in the philosophy of organism by the doctrines of hybrid physical feelings and of the transmuted feelings. In these ways conceptual feelings pass into the category of physical feelings. Also conversely, physical feelings give rise to conceptual feelings, and conceptual feelings give rise to other conceptual feelings—according to the doctrines of the Categories of Conceptual Valuation (Category IV), and of Conceptual Reversion (Category V), to be discussed in the subsequent sections of this chapter.

One important characteristic of a hybrid feeling is the intensity of the conceptual feeling which originates from it, according to the Category of Subjective Valuation. In the next section, this Categoreal Condition of 'Conceptual Valuation' is considered in relation to all physical feelings, 'pure' and 'hybrid' alike. The present section will only anticipate that discussion so far as hybrid feelings are concerned. Thus the part of the general category now relevant can be formulated:

[377] A hybrid physical feeling originates for its subject a conceptual feeling with the same datum as that of the conceptual feeling of the antecedent subject. But the two conceptual feelings in the two subjects respectively may have different subjective forms.

There is an autonomy in the formation of the subjective forms of conceptual feelings, conditioned only by the unity of the subject as expressed in categoreal conditions I, VII, and VIII. These conditions for unity correlate the sympathetic subjective form of the hybrid feeling with the autonomous subjective form of the derivative conceptual feeling with the same subject.

There are evidently two sub-species of hybrid feelings: (i) those which feel the conceptual feelings of temporal actual entities, and (ii) those which feel the conceptual feelings of God.

The objectification of God in a temporal subject is effected by the hybrid feelings with God's conceptual feelings as data. Those of God's feelings which are positively prehended are those with some compatibility of contrast, or of identity, with physical feelings transmitted from the temporal world. But when we take God into account, then we can assert without any qualification Hume's principle, that all conceptual feelings are derived from physical feelings. The limitation of Hume's principle introduced by the consideration of the Category of Conceptual Reversion (cf. Sect. III of this chapter) is to be construed as referring merely to the transmission from the temporal world, leaving God out of account. Apart from the intervention of God, there could be nothing new in the world, and no order in the world. The course of creation would be a dead level of ineffectiveness, with all balance and intensity progressively excluded by the cross currents of incompatibility. The novel hybrid feelings derived from God, with the derivative sympathetic conceptual valuations, are the foundations of progress. [378]

SECTION III

Conceptual feelings are primarily derivate from physical feelings, and secondarily from each other. In this statement, the consideration of God's intervention is excluded. When this intervention is taken into account, all conceptual feelings must be derived from physical feelings. Unfettered conceptual valuation, 'infinite' in Spinoza's sense of that term, is only possible once in the universe; since that creative act is objectively immortal as an inescapable condition characterizing creative action.

But, unless otherwise stated, only the temporal entities of the actual world will be considered. We have to discuss the categoreal conditions for such derivation of conceptual feelings from the physical feelings relating to the temporal world. By the Categoreal Condition of Subjective Unity— Category I—the initial phase of physical feelings has the propositional unity of feelings compatible for integration into one feeling of the actual world. But the completed determination of the subjective form of this final 'satisfaction' awaits the origination of conceptual feelings whose subjective forms introduce the factor of 'valuation,' that is, 'valuation up' or 'valuation down.'

Thus a supplementary phase succeeds to the initial purely physical phase. This supplementary phase starts with two subordinate phases of conceptual origination, and then passes into phases of integration, and of reintegration, in which propositional feelings, and intellectual feelings, may emerge. In the present chapter we are concerned with the first two phases of merely conceptual origination. These are not phases of conceptual analysis, but of conceptual valuation. The subsequent analytic phases involve propositional feelings, and in certain circumstances issue in consciousness. But in this chapter† we are merely concerned with blind conceptual valuation, and with the effect of such valuation upon physical feel- [379] ings which lie in the future beyond the actual entities in which such valuations occur.

The initial problem is to discover the principles according to which some eternal objects are prehended positively and others are prehended negatively. Some are felt and others are eliminated.

In the solution of this problem five* additional categoreal conditions must be added to the three such conditions which have already been explained. The conditions have regard to the origination, and coordination, of conceptual feelings. They govern the general process of 'conceptual imagination,' so far as concerns its origination from physical experience.

Category IV. The Category of Conceptual Valuation. From each physical feeling there is the derivation of a purely conceptual feeling whose datum is the eternal object exemplified in the definiteness of the actual entity, or of† the nexus, physically felt.

This category maintains the old principle that mentality originates from sensitive experience. It lays down the principle that all sensitive experience originates mental operations. It does not, however, mean that there is no origination of other mental operations derivative from these primary mental operations. Nor does it mean that these mental operations involve consciousness, which is the product of intricate integration.

The mental pole originates as the conceptual counterpart of operations in the physical pole. The two poles are inseparable in their origination. The mental pole starts with the conceptual registration of the physical pole. This conceptual registration constitutes the sole datum of experience according to the sensationalist school. Writers of this school entirely neglect physical feelings, originating in the physical pole. Hume's 'impressions of sensation' and Kant's sensational data are considered in terms only applicable to conceptual registration. Hence Kant's notion of the chaos of such ulti- [380] mate data. Also Hume—at least, in his *Treatise*—can only find differences of 'force and vivacity.'

The subjective form of a conceptual feeling is valuation. These valuations are subject to the Category of Subjective Unity. Thus the conceptual registration is conceptual valuation; and conceptual valuation introduces creative purpose. The mental pole introduces the subject as a determinant of its own concrescence. The mental pole is the subject determining its own ideal of itself by reference to eternal principles of valuation autonomously modified in their application to its own physical objective datum. Every actual entity is 'in time' so far as its physical pole is concerned, and is 'out of time' so far as its mental pole is concerned. It is the union of two worlds, namely, the temporal world, and the world of autonomous valuation. The integration of each simple physical feeling with its conceptual counterpart produces in a subsequent phase a physical feeling whose subjective form of re-enaction has gained or lost subjective intensity according to the valuation up, or the valuation down, in the conceptual feeling. So far there is merely subjective readjustment of the subjective forms. This is the phase of physical purpose. The effect of the conceptual feeling is thus, so far, merely to provide that the modified subjective form is not merely derived from the re-enaction of the objectified actual entity. Also, in the complex subsequent integrations, we find that the conceptual counterpart has a rôle in detachment from the physical feeling out of which it originates.

Category V. The Category of Conceptual Reversion. There is secondary origination of conceptual feelings with data which are partially identical with, and partially diverse from, the eternal objects forming the data in the primary phase of the mental pole; the determination of identity and diversity depending on the subjective aim at attaining depth of intensity by reason of contrast.

Thus the first phase of the mental pole is conceptual [381] reproduction, and the second phase is a phase of conceptual reversion. In this second phase the proximate novelties are conceptually felt. This is the process by which the subsequent enrichment of subjective forms, both in qualitative pattern, and in intensity through contrast, is made possible by the positive conceptual prehension of relevant alternatives.[1] There is a conceptual contrast of physical incompatibles. This is the category which, as thus stated, seems to limit the strict application of Plato's principle of reminiscence, and of Hume's principle of recollection. Probably it does not contradict anything that Plato meant by his principle. But it does limit the rigid application of Hume's principle. Indeed Hume himself admitted exceptions. It is the category by which novelty enters the world; so that even amid stability there is never undifferentiated endurance. But, as the category states, reversion is always limited by the necessary inclusion of elements identical with elements in feelings of the antecedent phase. By the Category of Subjective Unity, and by the seventh Category of Subjective Harmony, to be explained later, all origination of feelings is governed by the subjective imposition of aptitude for final synthesis. Also by the Category of Objective Identity this aptitude always has its ground in the two-way functionings of self-identical elements. Then in synthesis there must always be a ground of identity and an aim at contrast. The aim at contrast arises from the depth of intensity promoted by contrast. The joint necessity of this ground of identity, and this aim at contrast, is partially expressed in this Category of Conceptual Reversion. This 'aim at contrast' is the expression of the ultimate creative purpose that each unification shall achieve some maximum depth of intensity of feeling, subject to the conditions of its concrescence. This ultimate purpose is formulated in Category VIII.

The question, how, and in what sense, one unrealized [382] eternal object can be more, or less, proximate to an eternal object in realized ingression—that is to say, in comparison with any other unfelt eternal object—

[1] For another discussion of this topic, cf. my Religion in the Making, Ch. III, Sect. VII.

is left unanswered by this Category of Reversion. In conformity with the ontological principle, this question can be answered only by reference to some actual entity. Every eternal object has entered into the conceptual feelings of God. Thus, a more fundamental account must ascribe the reverted conceptual feeling in a temporal subject to its conceptual feeling derived, according to Category IV, from the hybrid physical feeling of the relevancies conceptually ordered in God's experience. In this way, by the recognition of God's characterization of the creative act, a more complete rational explanation is attained. The Category of Reversion is then abolished;* and Hume's principle of the derivation of conceptual experience from physical experience remains without any exception.

SECTION IV

The two categories of the preceding section concerned the efficacy of physical feelings, pure or hybrid, for the origination of conceptual feelings in a later phase of their own subject. The present section considers analogous feelings with diverse subjects 'scattered' throughout members of a nexus. It considers a single subject, subsequent to the nexus, prehending this multiplicity of scattered feelings as the *data* for a corresponding multiplicity of its own simple physical feelings, some pure and some hybrid. It then formulates the process by which in that subject an analogy between these various feelings—constituted by one eternal object, of whatever complexity, implicated in the various analogous *data* of these feelings—is, by a supervening process of integration, converted into one feeling having for its datum the specific contrast between the nexus as one entity and that eternal object. This contrast is what is familiarly known as the qualification of the nexus by that eternal object. An inter- [383] mediate stage in this process of integration is the formation in the final subject of one conceptual feeling with that eternal object as its datum. This conceptual feeling has an impartial relevance to the above-mentioned various simple physical feelings of the various members of the nexus. It is this impartiality of the conceptual feeling which leads to the integration in which the many members of the nexus are collected into the one nexus which they form, and in which that nexus is set in contrast to the one eternal object which has emerged from their analogies.

Thus pure, and hybrid, physical feelings, issuing into a single conceptual feeling, constitute the preliminary phase of this transmutation in the prehending subject. The integration of these feelings in that subject leads to the transmuted physical feeling of a nexus as qualified by that eternal object which is the datum of the single conceptual feeling. In this way the world is physically felt as a unity, and is felt as divisible into parts which are unities, namely, nexūs. Each such unity has its own characteristics arising from the undiscriminated actual entities which are members of that nexus. In some cases objectification of the nexus has only indirect reference to the characteristics of its individual atomic actualities. In such a case the objectification may introduce new elements into the world, fortunate or unfortunate. Usually the objectification gives direct information, so that the prehending subject shapes itself as the direct outcome of the order prevalent in the prehended nexus. Transmutation is the way in which the actual world is felt as a community, and is so felt in virtue of its prevalent order. For it arises by reason of the analogies between the various members of the prehended nexus, and eliminates their differences. Apart from transmutation our feeble intellectual operations would fail to penetrate into the dominant characteristics of things. We can only understand by discarding. Transmutation depends upon a categoreal condition.

[384] *Category* VI. *The Category of Transmutation.* When (in accordance with Category IV, or with Categories IV and V) one and the samet conceptual feeling is derived impartially by a prehending subject from its analogous simple physical feelings of various actual entities, then in a subsequent phase of integration—of these simple physical feelings together with the derivate conceptual feeling—the prehending subject may transmute the datum of this conceptual feeling into a contrast with the nexus of those prehended actual entities, or of some part of that nexus; so that the nexus (or its part), thus qualified, is the objective datum of a feeling entertained by this prehending subject.

Such a transmutation of simple physical feelings of many actualities into one physical feeling of a nexus as one, is called a 'transmuted feeling.' The origination of such a feeling depends upon intensities, valuations, and eliminations conjointly favourable.

In order to understand this categoreal condition, it must be noted that the integration of simple physical feelings into a complex physical feeling only provides for the various actual entities of the nexus being felt as separate entities requiring each other. We have to account for the substitution of the one nexus in place of its component actual entities. This is Leibniz's problem which arises in his *Monadology*. He solves the problem by an unanalysed doctrine of 'confusion.' Some category is required to provide a physical feeling of a nexus as one entity with its own categoreal type of existence. This one physical feeling in the final subject is derived by transmutation from the various analogous physical feelings entertained by the various members of the nexus, together with their various analogous conceptual feelings (with these various members as subjects) originated from these physical feelings, *either* directly according to Category IV, *or* indirectly according to Category V. The analogy of the physical feelings consists in the fact that their definite character exhibits the same ingredient [385] eternal object. The analogy of the conceptual feelings consists in the fact that this one eternal object, or one reversion from this eternal object, is the datum for the various relevant conceptual feelings entertained respectively by members of the nexus. The final prehending subject prehends the members of the nexus, (i) by 'pure' physical feelings in which the members are severally objectified by these analogous physical feelings, and (ii) by hybrid physical feelings in which the members are severally objectified by these analogous conceptual feelings.

In the prehending subject, these analogous, pure physical feelings originate a conceptual feeling, according to Category IV; and, according to Category V, there may be a reverted conceptual feeling. There will be only one direct conceptual feeling; for the simple physical feelings (in the final subject) are analogous in the sense of exemplifying the same eternal object. (If there be no reversion, this analogy extends over the pure and the hybrid physical feelings. If there be important reversion, this analogy only extends over the hybrid feelings with the reverted conceptual feelings as data. This latter case is only important when the reverted feelings involve the predominantly intense valuation.) Thus these many physical feelings of diverse actualities originate in the final subject one conceptual feeling. This single conceptual feeling has therefore an impartial reference throughout the actualities of the nexus. Also reverted conceptual feelings in the nexus are, in this connection, negligible unless they preserved this impartiality of reference throughout the nexus. Excluding for the moment the consideration of reverted feelings in the actualities of the nexus, the hybrid physical feelings in the prehending subject also, by Category IV, generate one conceptual feeling with impartial reference; also it is the same conceptual feeling as that generated by the pure physical feelings (in the final subject). Thus (with no reversion) the influence of the hybrid physical feelings [386] is to enhance the intensity of the conceptual feeling derived from the pure physical feelings. But there may be reversions to be considered, that is to say, reversions with impartial reference throughout the nexus. The reversion may originate in the separate actualities of the nexus, or in the final prehending subject, or there may be a double reversion involving both sources. Thus we must allow for the possibility of diverse reverted feelings, each with impartial reference. In so far as there is concordance and the reversions are dominant, there will issue one conceptual feeling of enhanced intensity. When there is discordance among these various conceptual feelings, there will be elimination, and in general no transmutation. But when, from some (or all) of these sources of impartial conceptual feelings, one dominant impartial conceptual feeling emerges with adequate intensity, transmutation will supervene.

This impartiality of reference has then been transmuted into the physical feeling of that nexus, whole or partial, contrasted with some one eternal object. It will be noted that this one impartial conceptual feeling is an essential element of the process, whereby an impartial reference to the whole nexus is introduced. Otherwise there would be no element to transmute particular relevancies to the many members into general relevance to the whole.

The eternal object which characterizes the nexus in this physical feeling may be an eternal object characterizing the analogous physical feelings, belonging to all, or some, of the members of the nexus. In this case, the nexus as a whole derives a character which in some way belongs to its various members.

Again in the transmuted feeling only part of the original nexus may be objectified, and the eternal object may have been derived from members of the other part of the original nexus. This is the case for perception in the mode of 'presentational immediacy,' to be further discussed in a later chapter (Part IV, Ch. V; cf. also† [387] Part II, Ch. II, Sect. I, and Part II, Ch. IV, Sect. VII, and Part II, Ch. VIII).

Also the eternal object may be the datum of a reverted conceptual feeling, only indirectly derived from the members of the original nexus. In this case, the transmuted feeling of the nexus introduces novelty; and in unfortunate cases this novelty may be termed 'error.' But all the same, the transmuted feeling, whatever be its history of transmutation, is a definite physical fact whereby the final subject prehends the nexus. For example, considering the example of presentational immediacy, colour-blindness may be called 'error'; but nevertheless, it is a physical fact. A transmuted feeling comes under the definition of a physical feeling.

Our usual way of consciously prehending the world is by these transmuted physical feelings. It is only when we are consciously aware of alien mentalities that we even approximate to the conscious prehension of a single actual entity. It will be found that transmuted feelings are very analogous to propositional feelings, and to conscious perceptions and judgments in their sequence of integration. Vagueness has its origin in transmuted feelings. For a quality, characterizing the mutual prehensions of all the members of a nexus, is transmuted into a predicate of the nexus. The intensity arising from the force of repetition makes this transmuted perception to be the prominent type of those feelings which in further integrations acquire consciousness as an element in their subjective forms. It represents a simplification of physical feeling, effected in the course of integration.

According to this category the conceptual feelings entertained in any nexus modify the future rôle of that nexus as a physical objective datum. This category governs the transition from conceptual feelings in one actual entity to physical feelings either in a supervening phase of itself or in a later actual entity. What is conceptual earlier is felt physically later in an extended rôle. Thus, for instance, a new 'form' has its emergent ingression con- [388] ceptually by reversion, and receives delayed exemplification physically when the other categoreal conditions permit.

This joint operation of Categories IV and VI produces what has been termed 'adversion' and 'aversion.' For the conceptual feelings in the actualities of the nexus, produced according to Category IV, have data identical with the pattern exemplified in the objective data of the many physical feelings. If in the conceptual feelings there is valuation upward, then the physical feelings are transmitted† to the new concrescence with enhanced intensity in its subjective form. This is 'adversion.'

But if in the conceptual feelings there is valuation downward, then the physical feelings are (in the later concrescence) either eliminated, or are transmitted to it with attenuated intensity. This is 'aversion.' Thus 'adversion' and 'aversion' are types of 'decision.'

Thus the conceptual feeling with its valuation has primarily the character of purpose, since it is the agent whereby the decision is made as to the causal efficacy of its subject in its objectifications beyond itself. But it only achieves this character of purpose by its integration with the physical feeling from which it originates. This integration is considered in Chapter V on 'Comparative Feelings.'

It is evident that adversion and aversion, and also the Category of Transmutation, only have importance in the case of high-grade organisms. They constitute the first step towards intellectual mentality, though in themselves they do not amount to consciousness. But an actual entity which includes these operations must have an important intensity of conceptual feelings able to mask and fuse the simple physical feelings.

Also the examination of the Category of Transmutation shows that the approach to intellectuality consists in the gain of a power of abstraction. The irrelevant multiplicity of detail is eliminated, and emphasis is laid on the elements of systematic order in the actual world. In [389] so far as there is trivial order, there must be trivialized actual entities. The right coordination of the negative prehensions is one secret of mental progress; but unless some systematic scheme of relatedness characterizes the environment, there will be nothing left whereby to constitute vivid prehension of the world. The low-grade organism is merely the summation of the forms of energy which flow in upon it in all their multiplicity of detail. It receives, and it transmits; but it fails to simplify into intelligible system. The physical theory of the structural flow of energy has to do with the transmission of simple physical feelings from individual actuality to individual actuality. Thus some sort of quantum theory in physics, relevant to the existing type of cosmic order, is to be expected. The physical theory of alternative forms of energy, and of the transformation from one form to another form, ultimately depends upon transmission conditioned by some exemplification of the Categories of Transmutation and Reversion.

SECTION V

The seventh categoreal condition governs the efficacy of conceptual feelings both in the completion of their own subjects, and also in the objectifications of their subjects in subsequent concrescence. It is the Category of 'Subjective† Harmony.'

Category VII. The Category of Subjective Harmony. The valuations of conceptual feelings are mutually determined by their adaptation to be joint elements in a satisfaction aimed at by the subject.

This categoreal condition should be compared with the Category of 'Subjective Unity,' and also with the Category of 'Conceptual Reversion.' In the former category the intrinsic inconsistencies, termed 'logical,' are the formative conditions in the pre-established harmony. In this seventh category, and in the Category of Reversion, aesthetic adaptation for an end is the formative condition in the pre-established harmony. These three categories [390] express the ultimate particularity of feelings. For the superject which is their outcome is also the subject which is operative in their production. They are the creation of their own creature. The point to be noticed is that the actual entity, in a state of process during which it is not fully definite, determines its own ultimate definiteness. This is the whole point of moral responsibility. Such responsibility is conditioned by the limits of the data, and by the categoreal conditions of concrescence.

But autonomy is negligible unless the complexity is such that there is great energy in the production of conceptual feelings according to the Category of Reversion. This Category of Reversion has to be considered in connection with the Category of Aesthetic Harmony.** For the contrasts produced by reversion are contrasts required for the fulfillment of the aesthetic ideal. Unless there is complexity, ideal diversities lead to physical impossibilities, and thence to impoverishment. It requires a complex constitution to stage diversities as consistent contrasts.

It is only by reason of the Categories of Subjective Unity, and of Subjective Harmony, that the process constitutes the character of the product, and that conversely the analysis of the product discloses the process.‡

CHAPTER IV
PROPOSITIONS AND FEELINGS

SECTION I

[391] THE nature of consciousness has not yet been adequately analysed. The initial basic feelings, physical and conceptual, have been mentioned, and so also has the final synthesis into the affirmation-negation contrast. But between the beginning and the end of the integration into consciousness, there lies the origination of a 'propositional feeling.' A propositional feeling is a feeling whose objective datum is a proposition. Such a feeling does not in itself involve consciousness. But all forms of consciousness arise from ways of integration of propositional feelings with other feelings, either physical feelings or conceptual feelings. Consciousness belongs to the subjective forms of such feelings.

A proposition enters into experience as the entity forming the datum of a complex feeling derived from the integration of a physical feeling with a conceptual feeling.[1] Now a conceptual feeling does not refer to *the* actual world, in the sense that the history of *this* actual world has any peculiar relevance to its datum. This datum is an eternal object; and an eternal object refers only to the purely general *any* among undetermined actual entities. In itself an eternal object evades any selection among actualities or epochs. You cannot know what is red by merely thinking of redness. You can only find red things by adventuring amid physical experiences in *this* actual world. This doctrine is the ultimate ground of empiricism; namely, that eternal objects tell no tales as to their ingressions.

[392] But now a new kind of entity presents itself. Such entities are the tales that perhaps might be told about particular actualities. Such entities are neither actual entities, nor eternal objects, nor feelings. They are propositions. A proposition must be true or false. Herein a proposition differs from an eternal object; for no eternal object is ever true or false. This difference between propositions and eternal objects arises from the fact that truth and falsehood are always grounded upon a reason. But according to the ontological principle (the eighteenth† 'category of explanation'), a reason is always a reference to determinate actual entities. Now an eternal object, in itself, abstracts from all determinate actual entities, including even God. It is merely referent to *any* such entities, in the absolutely general sense of *any*. Then there can be no reason upon which to found

---

[1] Cf.† also 'Physical Purposes' considered in Ch. V.

the truth or falsehood of an eternal object. The very diversity of eternal objects has for its reason their diversity of functioning in *this* actual world.

Thus the endeavour to understand eternal objects in complete abstraction from the actual world results in reducing them to mere undifferentiated nonentities. This is an exemplification of the categoreal principle, that the general metaphysical character of being an entity is 'to be a determinant in the becoming of actualities.' Accordingly the differentiated relevance of eternal objects to each instance of the creative process requires their conceptual realization in the primordial nature of God. He does not create eternal objects; for his nature requires them in the same degree that they require him. This is an exemplification of the coherence of the categoreal types of existence. The general relationships of eternal objects to each other, relationships of diversity and of pattern, are their relationships in God's conceptual realization. Apart from this realization, there is mere isolation indistinguishable from nonentity.

But a proposition, while preserving the indeterminateness of an eternal object, makes an incomplete abstrac- [393] tion from determinate actual entities. It is a complex entity, with determinate actual entities among its components. These determinate actual entities, considered *formaliter* and not as in the abstraction of the proposition, do afford a reason determining the truth or falsehood of the proposition. But the proposition in itself, apart from recourse to these reasons, tells no tale about itself; and in this respect it is indeterminate like the eternal objects.

A propositional feeling (as has been stated) arises from a special type of integration synthesizing a physical feeling with a conceptual feeling. The objective datum of the physical feeling is either one actual entity, if the feeling be simple, or is a determinate nexus of actual entities, if the physical feeling be more complex. The datum of the conceptual feeling is an eternal object which is referent (*qua* possibility)‡ to any actual entities, where the *any* is absolutely general and devoid of selection. In the integrated objective datum the physical feeling provides its determinate set of actual entities, indicated by their felt physical relationships to the subject of the feeling. These actual entities are the logical subjects of the proposition. The absolute generality of the notion of *any*, inherent in an eternal object, is thus eliminated in the fusion. In the proposition, the eternal object, in respect to its possibilities as a determinant of nexūs,† is restricted to these logical subjects. The proposition may have the restricted generality of referring to *any* among these provided logical subjects; or it may have the singularity of referring to the complete set of provided logical subjects as potential relata, each with its assigned status, in the complex pattern which is the eternal object. The proposition is the potentiality of the eternal object, as a determinant of definiteness, in some determinate mode of restricted reference to the logical subjects. This eternal object is the 'predicative pattern' of the proposition. The set of logical subjects is *either* completely singled out as *these* logical subjects in *this* predicative pattern *or* is collec- [394] tively singled out as *any* of these logical subjects in *this* pattern, *or* as *some* of these logical subjects in *this* pattern. Thus the physical feeling indicates the logical subjects and provides them respectively with that individual definition necessary to assign the hypothetic status of each in the predicative pattern. The conceptual feeling provides the predicative pattern. Thus in a proposition the logical subjects are reduced to the status of food for a possibility. Their real rôle in actuality is abstracted from; they are no longer factors in fact, except for the purpose of their physical indication. Each logical subject becomes a bare '*it*' among actualities, with *its* assigned hypothetical relevance to the predicate.[2]

It is evident that the datum of the conceptual feeling reappears as the predicate in the proposition which is the datum of the integral, propositional feeling. In this synthesis the eternal object has suffered the elimination of its absolute generality of reference. The datum of the physical feeling has also suffered elimination. For the peculiar objectification of the actual entities, really effected in the physical feeling, is eliminated, except in so far as it is required for the services of the indication. The objectification remains only to indicate that definiteness which the logical subjects must have in order to be hypothetical food for that predicate. This necessary indication of the logical subjects requires the actual world as a systematic environment. For there can be no definite position in pure abstraction. The proposition is the possibility of *that* predicate applying in that assigned way to *those* logical subjects. In every proposition, as such and without going beyond it, there is complete indeterminateness so far as concerns its own realization in a propositional feeling, and as regards its own truth. The logical subjects are, nevertheless, in fact actual entities which are definite in their realized mutual relatedness. Thus the proposition is in fact true, or false. But its own [395] truth, or its own falsity, is no business of a proposition. That question concerns only a subject entertaining a propositional feeling with that proposition for its datum. Such an actual entity is termed a 'prehending subject' of the proposition. Even a prehending subject is not necessarily judging the proposition. That particular case has been discussed earlier in Chapter IX of Part II. In that chapter the term 'judging subject' was used in place of the wider term 'prehending subject.'

To summarize this discussion of the general nature of a proposition: A proposition shares with an eternal object the character of indeterminateness, in that both are definite potentialities *for* actuality with undetermined realization *in* actuality. But they differ in that an eternal object refers to actuality with absolute generality, whereas a proposition refers to indicated logical subjects. Truth and falsehood always require some element of sheer givenness. Eternal objects cannot demonstrate what they

---

[2] Cf. my *Concept of Nature*, Ch. I, for another exposition of this train of thought.

are except in some given fact. The logical subjects of a proposition supply the element of givenness requisite for truth and falsehood.

SECTION II

A proposition has neither the particularity of a feeling, nor the reality of a nexus. It is a† datum for feeling, awaiting a subject feeling it. Its relevance to the actual world by means of its logical subjects makes it a lure for feeling. In fact many subjects may feel it with diverse feelings, and with diverse sorts of feelings. The fact that propositions were first considered in connection with logic, and the moralistic preference for true propositions, have obscured the rôle of propositions in the actual world. Logicians only discuss the judgment of propositions. Indeed some philosophers fail to distinguish propositions from judgments; and most logicians consider propositions as merely appanages to judgments. The result is that false propositions have fared badly, thrown into the dust-heap, neglected. But in the real world it is more important [396] that a proposition be interesting than that it be true. The importance of truth is, that it adds to interest. The doctrine here maintained is that judgment-feelings form only one subdivision of propositional feelings; and arise from the special sort of integration of propositional feelings with other feelings. Propositional feelings are not, in their simplest examples, conscious feelings. Consciousness only arises in some integrations in which propositional feelings are among the components integrated. Another point to notice is that the physical feeling, which is always one component in the history of an integral propositional feeling, has no unique relation to the proposition in question, nor has the subject of that feeling, which is also a subject prehending the proposition. Any subject with any physical feeling which includes in its objective datum the requisite logical subjects† can in a supervening phase entertain a propositional feeling with that proposition as its datum. It has only to originate a conceptual feeling with the requisite predicative pattern as its datum, and then to integrate the two feelings into the required propositional feeling.

Evidently new propositions come into being with the creative advance of the world. For every proposition involves its logical subjects; and it cannot be the proposition which it is, unless those logical subjects are the actual entities which they are. Thus no actual entity can feel a proposition, if its actual world does not include the logical subjects of that proposition. The proposition 'Caesar crossed the Rubicon' could not be felt by Hannibal in any occasion of his existence on earth. Hannibal could feel propositions with certain analogies to this proposition, but not this proposition. It is, further, to be noticed that the form of words in which propositions are framed also includes an incitement to the origination of an affirmative judgment-feeling. In imaginative literature, this incitement is inhibited by the general context, and even by the form and make-up of the material book. Sometimes there is even a form of words designed [397] to inhibit the formation of a judgment-feeling, such as 'once upon a time.' The verbal statement also includes words and phrases to symbolize the sort of physical feelings necessary to indicate the logical subjects of the proposition. But language is always elliptical, and depends for its meaning upon the circumstances of its publication. For example, the word 'Caesar' may mean a puppy dog, or a negro slave, or the first Roman emperor.

The actual entities whose actual worlds include the logical subjects of a proposition will be said to fall within the 'locus' of that proposition. The proposition is prehensible by them. Of those actual entities which fall within the locus of a proposition, only some will prehend it positively. There are two kinds of pure propositional feelings, namely, 'imaginative feelings' and 'perceptive feelings.' These kinds are not sharply distinguished, but their extreme instances function very differently.

SECTION III

A propositional feeling can arise only in a late phase of the process of the prehending subject. For it requires, in earlier phases: (α) a physical feeling whose objective datum includes the requisite logical subjects; and (β) a physical feeling involving a certain eternal object among the determinants of the definiteness of its datum; and (γ) the conceptual feeling of this eternal object, necessarily derivate from the physical feeling under heading (β), according to categoreal condition IV; and *perhaps* (δ), some conceptual feeling which is a reversion from the former conceptual feeling, according to categoreal condition V, involving another eternal object as its datum.

The physical feeling under the heading (α) will be termed the 'indicative feeling'; the physical feeling under heading (β) will be called the 'physical recognition.' The physical recognition is the physical basis of the conceptual feeling which provides the predicative pattern.

[398] The 'predicative pattern' is *either* the eternal object which is the datum of the conceptual feeling under the heading (γ), *or* it is the eternal object which is the datum of the conceptual feeling under the heading (δ). In the former case, the second conceptual feeling, namely, that under the heading (δ), is irrelevant to the consideration of the propositional feeling. In either case, that conceptual feeling whose datum is the predicative pattern is called the 'predicative feeling.'

In this account of the origin of the predicative feeling, we are in general agreement with Locke and Hume, who hold that every conceptual feeling has a physical basis. But Hume lays down the principle that all eternal objects are first felt physically, and thus would only allow of the origination of the predicative feeling under heading (γ). However he makes two concessions which ruin his general principle. For he allows the independent origination of intermediate 'shades' in a scale of shades, and also of new 'manners' of pattern. Both of these cases are allowed for by the principle of 'reversion,' which is appealed to under heading (δ). The propositional feeling arises in the later phase in which there is integration of the 'indicative feeling' with the 'predicative feeling.' In this integration the two data are synthesized by a double elimination involving both data. The actual entities involved in the datum of the indicative feeling are reduced to a bare multiplicity in which each is a bare 'it' with the elimination of the eternal object really constituting the definiteness of that nexus. But the integration rescues them from this mere multiplicity by placing them in the unity of a proposition with the given predicative† pattern. Thus the actualities, which were first felt as sheer matter of fact, have been transformed into a set of logical subjects with the potentiality for realizing an assigned predicative pattern. The predicative pattern has also been limited by elimination. For as a datum in the conceptual feeling, it held its possibility for realization in respect to *absolutely any* actual entities; but in [399] the proposition its possibilities are limited to *just these* logical subjects.

The subjective form of the propositional feeling will depend on circumstances, according to categoreal condition VII. It may, or may not, involve consciousness; it may, or may not, involve judgment. It will involve aversion, or adversion, that is to say, decision. The subjective form will only involve consciousness when the 'affirmation-negation' contrast has entered into it. In other words, consciousness enters into the subjective forms of feelings, when those feelings are components in an integral feeling whose datum is the *contrast* between a nexus which *is*, and a proposition which in its own nature *negates* the decision of its truth or falsehood. The logical subjects of the proposition are the actual entities in the nexus. Consciousness is the way of feeling that particular real nexus, as in contrast with imaginative freedom about it. The consciousness may confer importance upon *what* the real thing is, or upon what the imagination is, or upon both.

SECTION IV

A proposition, as such, is impartial between its prehending subjects, and in its own nature it does not fully determine the subjective forms of such prehensions. But the different propositional feelings, with the same proposition as datum, in different prehending subjects, are widely different according to differences of their histories in these subjects. They can be divided into two main types, here termed, respectively, 'perceptive feelings' and 'imaginative feelings.' This difference is founded on the comparison between the 'indicative feeling' from which the logical subjects are derived, and the 'physical recognition' from which the predicative pattern is derived.

[400]‡ These physical feelings are either identical or different. If they

be one and the same feeling, the derived propositional feeling is here called a 'perceptive feeling.' For in this case, as will be seen, the proposition predicates of its logical subjects a character derived from the way in which they are physically felt by that prehending subject.

If the physical feelings be different, the derived propositional feeling is here called an 'imaginative feeling.' For in this case, as will be seen, the proposition predicates of its logical subjects a character without any guarantee of close relevance to the logical subjects. Since these physical feelings are complex, there are degrees of difference between them. Two physical feelings may be widely diverse or almost identical. Thus the distinction between the two types of propositional feelings is not as sharp-cut as it might be. This distinction is still further blurred by noting that three distinct cases arise which differentiate perceptive feelings into three species, which in their turn shade off into each other.

Since we are now dealing with perceptive feelings, we have on hand only one physical feeling which enjoys the rôle both of the indicative feeling, and of the physical recognition. In the first place, suppose that the predicative pattern is derived straight from the physical recognition under the heading (γ), so that there is no reversion and the heading (δ) is irrelevant. In this case the derived propositional feeling will be termed an 'authentic perceptive feeling.' Such a feeling, by virtue of its modes of origination, has as its datum a proposition whose predicate is in some way realized in the real nexus of its [401] logical subjects. Thus the proposition felt proposes a predicate derived from the real nexus, and not refracted by the prehending subject. But nevertheless the proposition need not be true, so far as concerns the way in which it implicates the logical subjects with the predicate. For the primary physical feeling of that nexus by the prehending subject may have involved 'transmutation' according to categoreal condition VI. In this case, the proposition ascribes to its logical subjects the *physical* enjoyment of a nexus with the definition of its predicate; whereas that predicate may have only been enjoyed *conceptually* by these logical subjects. Thus, what the proposition proposes as a physical fact in the nexus, was in truth only a mental fact. Unless it is understood for what it is, error arises. Such understanding belongs to the subjective form.

But if the primary physical feeling involves no reversion in any stage, then the predicate of the proposition is that eternal object which constitutes the definiteness of that nexus. In this case, the proposition is, without qualification, true. The authentic perceptive feeling will then be termed 'direct.' Thus there are 'indirect' perceptive feelings (when 're-version' is involved), and 'direct' perceptive feelings; and feelings of both these species are termed 'authentic.' In the case of these 'authentic' feelings, the predicate has realization in the nexus, physically or ideally, apart from any reference to the prehending subject.

‡Thirdly, and lastly, the predicative feeling may have arisen in the prehending subject by reversion, according to the heading (δ) of the previous

section. In this case the predicate has in it some elements which really contribute to the definiteness of the nexus; but it has also some elements which contrast with corresponding elements in the nexus. These latter elements have been introduced in the concrescence of the prehending subject. The predicate is thus distorted from the truth by the subjectivity of the prehending subject. Such a perceptive feeling will be termed 'unauthentic.'

Unauthentic feelings are feelings derived from a 'tied' imagination, in the sense that there is only one physical basis for the whole origination, namely, that physical feeling which is both the 'indicative' feeling† and the 'physical recognition.' The imagination is tied to one ultimate fact.

SECTION V

Imaginative feelings belong to the general case when the indicative feeling and the physical recognition differ. [402] But there are degrees of difference, which can vary from the case when the two nexūs, forming the objective data of the two feelings respectively, enjoy the extreme of remote disconnection, to the case at the other extreme when the two nexūs are almost identical. But in so far as there is diversity between the feelings, there is some trace of a free imagination. The proposition which is the objective datum of an imaginative feeling has a predicate derived, with or without reversions, from a nexus which in some respects differs from the nexus providing the logical subjects. Thus the proposition is felt as an imaginative notion concerning its logical subjects. The proposition in its own nature gives no suggestion as to how it should be felt. In one prehending subject it may be the datum of a perceptive feeling, and in another prehending subject it may be the datum of an imaginative feeling. But the subjective forms of the two feelings will differ according to the differences in the histories of the origination of those feelings in their respective subjects.

The subjective forms of propositional feelings are dominated by valuation, rather than by consciousness. In a pure propositional feeling the logical subjects have preserved their indicated particularity, but have lost their own real modes of objectification. The subjective form lies in the twilight zone between pure physical feeling and the clear consciousness which apprehends the contrast between physical feeling and imagined possibility. A propositional feeling is a lure to creative emergence in the transcendent future. When it is functioning as a lure, the propositional feeling about the logical subjects of the proposition may in some subsequent phase promote decision involving intensification of some physical feeling of those subjects in the nexus. Thus, according to the various categoreal conditions, propositions intensify, attenuate, inhibit, or transmute, without necessarily entering into clear consciousness, or encountering judgment.

It follows that in the pursuit of truth even physical [403] feelings must be criticized, since their evidence is not final apart from an analysis of their origination. This conclusion merely confirms what is a commonplace in all scientific investigation, that we can never start from dogmatic certainty. Such certainty is always an ideal to which we approximate as the result of critical analysis. When we have verified that we depend upon an authentic perceptive feeling, whose origination involves no reversions, then we know that the proposition which is the datum of that feeling is true. Thus there can be no immediate guarantee of the truth of a proposition, by reason of the mode of origination of the propositional feeling, apart from a critical scrutiny of that mode of origination.

The feeling has to be (i) perceptive, (ii) authentic, and (iii) direct, where a definite meaning has, in the preceding section, been assigned to each of these conditions.

‡There is, however, always this limitation to the security of direct knowledge, based on direct physical feeling, namely, that the creative emergence can import into the physical feelings of the actual world pseudo-determinants which arise from the concepts entertained in that actual world, and not from the physical feelings in that world.

This possibility of error is peculiarly evident in the case of that special class of physical feelings which belong to the mode of 'presentational immediacy.'

The proposition which is the datum of an imaginative feeling may be true. The two questions of the origination of consciousness in the subjective forms of feelings, and of the intuitive judgment of a proposition, apart from the mode of origination of the feeling of it, must now be considered.

SECTION VI

Language, as usual, is always ambiguous as to the exact proposition which it indicates. Spoken language is merely a series of squeaks. Its function is (α) to arouse in the prehending subject some physical feeling indicative of the logical subjects of the proposition, (β) to arouse in the prehending subject some physical feeling which plays the part of the 'physical recognition,' (γ) to promote the sublimation of the 'physical recognition' into the conceptual 'predicative feeling,' (δ) to promote the integration of the indicative feeling and the predicative feeling into the required propositional feeling. But in this complex function there is always a tacit reference to [404] the environment of the occasion of utterance. Consider the traditional example, 'Socrates is mortal.'

This proposition may mean 'It is mortal.' In this case the word 'Socrates' in the circumstances of its utterance merely promotes a physical feeling indicating the *it* which is mortal.

The proposition may mean 'It is Socratic and mortal'; where 'Socratic' is an additional element in the predicative pattern.

We now turn to the words denoting the predicative pattern, namely, *either* 'mortal,' *or* 'Socratic and mortal.' The slightest consideration discloses the fact that it is pure convention to suppose that there is only one logical subject to the proposition. The word 'mortal' means a certain relationship to the general nexus of actual entities in *this* world which is†possible for any one of the actual entities. 'Mortal' does not mean 'mortal in any possible world,' it means 'mortal in this world.' Thus there is a general reference to *this* actual world as exemplifying a scheme of things which render 'mortality' realizable in it.

The word 'Socratic' means 'realizing the Socratic predicate in Athenian society.' It does not mean 'Socratic, in any possible world'; nor does it mean 'Socratic, anywhere in this world': it means 'Socratic, in Athens.' Thus 'Socratic,' as here used, refers to a society of actual entities realizing certain general systematic properties such that the Socratic predicate is realizable in that environment. Also the 'Athenian society' requires that this actual world exemplifies a certain systematic scheme, amid which 'Athenianism' is realizable.

Thus in the one meaning of the phrase 'Socrates is mortal,' the logical subjects are one singular *It* (Socrates) and the actual entities of this actual world, forming a society amid which mortality is realizable and including the former '*It*.' In the other meaning, there are also included among the logical subjects the actual entities forming the Athenian society. These actual entities are [405] required for the realization of the predicative pattern 'Socratic and mortal' and are the definitely indicated logical subjects. They also require that the general scheme of *this* actual world be such as to support 'Athenianism' in conjunction with 'mortality.'‡

CHAPTER V

THE HIGHER PHASES OF EXPERIENCE

SECTION I

[406] 'COMPARATIVE feelings' are the result of integrations not yet considered: their data are generic contrasts. The infinite variety of the more complex feelings come under the heading 'comparative feelings.'

We have now to examine two simple types of comparative feelings. One type arises from the integration of a 'propositional feeling' with the 'indicative feeling' from which it is partly derived. Feelings of this type will be termed 'intellectual feelings.' This type of comparative feelings is subdivided into two species: one species consists of 'conscious perceptions'; and the other species consists of 'intuitive judgments.' The subjective forms of intuitive judgments also involve consciousness. Thus 'conscious perceptions' and 'intuitive judgments' are alike 'intellectual feelings.' Comparative feelings of the other type are termed 'physical purposes.' Such a feeling arises from the integration of a conceptual feeling with the basic physical feeling from which it is derived, either directly according to categoreal condition IV (the Category of Conceptual Valuation), or indirectly according to categoreal condition V (the Category of Conceptual Reversion). But this integration is a more primitive type of integration than that which produces, from the same basic physical feeling, the species of propositional feelings termed 'perceptive.' The subjective forms of these physical purposes are either 'adversions' or 'aversions.' The subjective forms of physical purposes do not involve consciousness unless these feelings acquire integration with conscious perceptions or intuitive judgments. [407]

SECTION II

In an intellectual feeling the datum is the generic contrast between a nexus of actual entities and a proposition with its logical subjects members of the nexus. In every generic contrast its unity arises from the two-way functioning of certain entities which are components in each of the contrasted factors. This unity expresses the conformation to the second categoreal condition (the Category of Objective Identity). The common 'subject' entertaining the two feelings effects an integration whereby each of these actual entities obtains its one rôle of a two-way functioning in the one generic contrast. As an element in the subject no objectified actual

266

entity can play two disconnected parts. There can only be one analysable part. Thus what in origination is describable as a pair of distinct ways of functioning of each actual entity in the two factors of the generic contrast respectively† is realized in the subject as one rôle with a two-way aspect. This two-way aspect is unified as 'contrast.' This one analysable part involves in itself the contrast between the sheer matter of fact, namely, what the objectified actual entity in question contributes to the objectified nexus in the physical feeling, and the mere potentiality of the same actual entity for playing its assigned part in the predicative pattern of the proposition, in the eventuality of the proposition's realization. This contrast is what has been termed the 'affirmation-negation contrast.' It is the contrast between the affirmation of objectified fact in the physical feeling, and the mere potentiality, which is the negation of such affirmation, in the propositional feeling. It is the contrast between 'in fact' and 'might be,' in respect to particular instances in *this* actual world. The subjective form of the feeling of this contrast is consciousness. Thus in experience, consciousness arises by reason of intellectual feelings, and in proportion to the variety and intensity of such feelings. But, in conformity with the seventh [408] categoreal condition (the Category of Subjective Harmony), subjective forms, which arise as factors in any feeling, are finally in the satisfaction shared in the unity of all feelings;† all feelings acquire their quota of irradiation in consciousness.

This account agrees with the plain facts of our conscious experience. Consciousness flickers; and even at its brightest, there is a small focal region of clear illumination, and a large penumbral region of experience which tells of intense experience in dim apprehension. The simplicity of clear consciousness is no measure of the complexity of complete experience. Also this character of our experience suggests that consciousness is the crown of experience, only occasionally attained, not its necessary base.

SECTION III

A feeling is termed a 'belief,' or is said to include an element of 'belief,' when its datum is a proposition, and its subjective form includes, as the defining element in its emotional pattern, a certain form, or eternal object, associated with some gradation of intensity. This eternal object is 'belief-character.' When this character enters into the emotional pattern, then, according to the intensity involved, the feeling, whatever else it be, is to some degree a belief.

This variation in the intensity of belief-character is insisted on by Locke in his *Essay*. He writes (IV, XV, 3):

The entertainment the mind gives this sort of propositions is called "belief," "assent," or "opinion," which is the admitting or receiving any proposition for true, upon arguments or proofs that are found to persuade us to receive it as true, without certain knowledge that it is so.

And herein lies the difference between probability and certainty, faith and knowledge, that in all thet parts of knowledge there is intuition; each immediate idea, each step has its visible and certain connection: in belief not so.

[409] Locke's distinction between certainty and uncertain belief is admirable. But it is not nearly so important as it looks. For it is not the immediate intuition that we are usually concerned with. We only have its recollection recorded in words. Whether the verbal record of a recollection recalls to our minds a true proposition must always be a matter of great uncertainty. Accordingly our attitude towards an immediate intuition must be that of the gladiators, *"morituri te salutamus,"* as we pass into the limbo where we rely upon the uncertain record. It must be understood that we are not speaking of the objective probability of a proposition, expressing its relation to certain other propositions. Comparative firmness of belief is a psychological fact which may, or may not, be justified by the objective evidence. This belief-character takes various forms from its fusion with consciousness derived from the various types of intellectual feelings.

SECTION IV

Conscious perception is the feeling of what is relevant to immediate fact in contrast with its potential irrelevance. This general description must now be explained in detail.

'Conscious perceptions' are of such importance that it is worth while to rehearse the whole sequence of their origination. It will be seen that alternative modes of origination are involved, and that some of these modes produce erroneous perceptions. Thus the criticism of conscious perceptions has the same importance as the criticism of judgments, intuitive and inferential.

In the first place, there is one basic physical feeling, from which the whole sequence of feelings originates for the 'subject' in question. From this physical feeling, the propositional feeling of the sort termed 'perceptive' arises. The conscious perception is the comparative feeling arising from the integration of the perceptive feeling with this original physical feeling.

[410] In the account of the origination of the 'perceptive' feeling (Part III, Ch. IV, Sect. IV), the various species of such feelings are analysed first into 'authentic' feelings and 'unauthentic' feelings; and secondly, 'authentic' feelings are analysed into 'direct' feelingst and 'indirect' feelings. Without qualification a direct perceptive feeling feels its logical subjects as potentially invested with a predicate expressing an intrinsic character of the nexus which is the initial datum of the physical feeling; with qualification this statement is also true of an indirect feeling. The qualification is that the secondary conceptual feelings, *entertained in the nexus*

by reason of reversion (cf. categoreal condition V), have been transmuted so as to be felt in the 'subject' (the final subject of the conscious perception) as if they had been physical facts in the nexus. Of course such transmutation of physical feeling only arises when no incompatibilities are involved.

Thus, in general, a transmuted physical feeling only arises as the outcome of a complex process of incompatibilities and inhibitions. Apart from exceptional circumstances only to be found in few high-grade organisms, transmutation only accounts for physical feelings of negligible intensity. It is, however, important to note that even authentic physical feelings can distort the character of the nexus felt by transmuting felt concept into felt physical fact. In this way authentic perceptive feelings can introduce error into thought; and transmuted physical feelings can introduce novelty into the physical world. Such novelty may be either fortunate or disastrous. But the point is that novelty in the physical world, and error in authentic perceptive feeling, arise by conceptual functioning, according to the Category of Reversion.

Putting aside the case when these transmuted perceptive feelings have importance, consider the prehending subject with its direct perceptive feeling. The subject has its concrescent phase involving two factors, the orig- [411] inal physical feeling, and the derived perceptive feeling. In the earlier factor the nexus, physically felt, is objectified through its own proper physical bonds. There are no incompatibilities between fact and reverted concept to produce attenuation. The objective datum is therefore felt with its own proper intensities, transmitted to the subjective form of the physical feeling. The other factor in the integration is the 'perceptive' feeling. The datum of this feeling is the proposition with the actual entities of the nexus as its logical subjects, and with its predicate also derived from the nexus. The whole origination of this perceptive feeling has its sole basis in the physical feeling, which plays the part both of 'indicative feeling' and of 'physical recognition' (cf. Part III, Ch. IV, Sect. III).

The integration of the two factors into the conscious perception thus confronts the nexus as fact, with the potentiality derived from itself, limited to itself, and exemplified in itself. This confrontation is the generic contrast which is the objective datum of the integral feeling. The subjective form thus assumes its vivid immediate consciousness of what the nexus really *is* in the way of potentiality realized. In Hume's phraseology, there is an 'impression' of the utmost 'force and vivacity.'

There are therefore two immediate guarantees of the correctness of a conscious perception: one is Hume's test of 'force and vivacity,' and the other is the illumination by consciousness of the various feelings involved in the process. Thus the fact, that the physical feeling has not transmuted concept into physical bond, lies open for inspection. Neither of these tests is infallible. There is also the delayed test, that the future conforms to expectations derived from this assumption. This latter test can be realized only by future occasions in the life of an enduring object, the enduring percipient.

It is to be observed that what is in doubt is not the immediate perception of a nexus which is a fragment of [412] the actual world. The dubitable element is the definition of this nexus by the observed predicate.

An unauthentic perceptive feeling arises in the subject when its own conceptual origination from its own basic physical feeling passed on to the secondary stage of producing a reverted conceptual feeling to play the part of predicative feeling. The physical feeling may, or may not, have also suffered loss of direct relevance by reason of derivation from conceptual reversions in the nexus. But anyhow the subject by its own process of reversion has produced for the logical subjects a predicate which has no immediate relevance to the nexus, either as physical fact or as conceptual functioning in the nexus. Thus the comparative feeling which integrates the physical feeling with the unauthentic perceptive feeling has for its datum the generic contrast of the nexus with a proposition, whose logical subjects comprise the actualities in the nexus, and whose predicate partly agrees with the complex pattern exemplified in the nexus and partly disagrees with it. This case is really the conscious perception of a proposition imaginatively arrived at, which concerns the nexus and disagrees with the facts. The case is in fact more analogous to intellectual feelings of the second species, namely, to intuitive judgments. But by reason of the use of one basic physical feeling, in the double function of indicative feeling and of physical recollection, the proposition in the comparative feeling will have some of the vivid relevance to the nexus in the same feeling, which arises in the case of authentic perceptions. Practically, however, this case is an intuitive judgment in which there is consciousness of a proposition as erroneous.

SECTION V

The term 'judgment' refers to three species among the comparative feelings with which we are concerned. In each of these feelings the datum is the generic contrast between an objectified nexus and a proposition whose logical subjects make up the nexus. The three species [413] are composed of (i) those feelings in the 'yes-form,' (ii) those feelings in the 'no-form,' and (iii) those feelings in the 'suspense-form.'

In all three species of felt contrast, the datum obtains its unity by reason of the objective identity of the actual entities on both sides of the contrast. In the 'yes-form' there is the further ground of unity by reason of the identity of the pattern of the objectified nexus with the predicate. In the 'no-form' this latter ground of unity is replaced by a contrast involving incompatible diversity. In the 'suspense-form'† the predicate is neither identical, nor incompatible, with the pattern. It is diverse from, and compatible with, the pattern in the nexus as objectified: the nexus, in its own 'formal' existence, may, or may not, in fact exemplify both the pattern and the predicate. In this species of comparative feeling there is therefore contrast between pattern and predicate, without incompatibility.

In intuitive judgments, as has been stated, the comparative feeling is the integration of the physical feeling of a nexus with a propositional feeling whose logical subjects are the actual entities in the nexus. So far as this general description is concerned intuitive judgments and conscious perceptions do not differ, and are therefore classed together as 'intellectual' feelings. But in the case of intuitive judgments there is a more complex process of origination. There are two distinct physical feelings, the indicative feeling and the physical recollection (Part III, Ch. IV, Sect. III). The predicative feeling originates from the physical recollection, either immediately according to categoreal condition IV or mediately according to categoreal condition V. The integration of the predicative feeling with the indicative feeling produces the 'imaginative feeling't (cf. Part III, Ch. IV, Sect. V). This is a propositional feeling with the logical subjects of its datum‡ derived from the indicative feeling† and with the predicative pattern derived from the† physical recollection. These two physical feelings may be relatively [414] disconnected in their origination. Thus the imaginative feeling may have in its subjective form no bias as to belief or disbelief; or, if there be such bias, the intensity of the emotion may be slight.

The intuitive judgment is the comparative feeling with its datum constituted by the generic contrast between the nexus involved in the indicative feeling and the proposition involved in the imaginative feeling. In this generic contrast each actual entity has its contrast of two-way functioning. One way is its functioning in the exemplified pattern of the nexus, and the other way is its functioning in the potential pattern of the proposition. If in addition to the contrast between exemplification and potentiality, there be identity as to pattern and predicate, then by the Category of Objective Unity there is also the single complex eternal object in its two-way functioning, namely, as exemplified and as potential. In this case, the proposition coheres with the nexus and this coherence is its truth. Thus 'truth' is the absence of incompatibility or of any 'material contrast' in the patterns of the nexus and of the proposition in their generic contrast. The sole contrast, involving the Category of Objective Diversity, is merely that between exemplification and potentiality, and in all other respects the coherence is governed by the Category of Objective Identity.

If a contrast arise in any respect other than that between exemplification and potentiality, then the two patterns are not identical. Then the proposition in some sense, important or unimportant, is not felt as true.

It will be noted that the intuitive judgment in its subjective form conforms to what there is to feel in its datum. Thus error cannot arise from the subjective form of the integration constituting the judgment. But it can arise because the indicative feeling, which is one of the factors integrated, may in its origin have involved [415] reversion. Thus error arises by reason of operations which lie below consciousness, though they may emerge into consciousness and lie open for criticism.

Finally, what differentiates an intuitive judgment from a conscious perception is that a conscious perception is the outcome of an originative process which has its closest possible restriction to the fact, thus consciously perceived. But the distinction between the two species is not absolute. Among the conscious perceptions we find transmutations by which concepts entertained in the nexus are transmuted into physical feelings in the nexus, and also the unauthentic propositional feelings in which a proposition with a 'reverted' predicate has arisen. These are cases in which conscious perceptions take on the general character of intuitive judgments. On the other hand the diversity between the two physical feelings—when they are diverse—may be trivial. The nexus which is the datum of the one may be practically identical with the nexus which is the datum of the other. In such a case an intuitive judgment approximates to a conscious perception.

The condensed analysis of the stages of origination of an intuitive judgment is (i) the 'physical recollection' and the 'indicative feeling,' (ii) the 'predicative feeling,' derived from the 'physical recollection,'† (iii) the 'imaginative feeling,'† derived by integration of the 'predicative feeling' with the 'indicative feeling,' (iv) the 'intuitive judgment,'† derived by integration of the 'imaginative feeling' with the 'indicative feeling.'†

It is a great mistake to describe the subjective form of an intuitive judgment as necessarily including definite belief or disbelief in the proposition. Three cases arise. The generic contrast which is the datum of the intuitive judgment may exhibit the predicate of the proposition as exemplified in the objectified nexus. In this case, the subjective form will include definite belief. Secondly, the predicate may be exhibited as incompatible with the [416] eternal objects exemplified in the objectified nexus. In this case, the subjective form will include definite disbelief. But there is a third case, which is in fact the more usual one: the predicate may be exhibited as irrelevant, wholly or partially, to the eternal objects exemplified in the objectified nexus. In this case, the subjective form need exhibit neither belief nor disbelief. It may include one or the other† of these decisions, but it need not do so. This third case will be termed the case of 'suspended judgment.' Thus an intuitive judgment may be a belief, or a disbelief, or a suspended judgment. It is the task of the inferential process sometimes to convert a suspended judgment into a belief, or a disbelief, so far as the final satisfaction is concerned.

But the main function of intellectual feelings is neither belief, nor disbelief, nor even suspension of judgment. The main function of these feelings is to heighten the emotional intensity accompanying the valuations in the conceptual feelings involved, and in the mere‡ physical purposes which are more primitive than any intellectual feelings. They perform this function by the sharp-cut way in which they limit abstract valuation to express possibilities relevant to definite logical subjects. In so far as these logical subjects, by reason of other prehensions, are topics of interest, the proposition becomes a lure for the conditioning of creative action. In other words, its prehension effects a modification of the subjective aim.

Intellectual feelings, in their primary function, are concentration of attention involving increase of importance. This concentration of attention also introduces the criticism of physical purposes, which is the intellectual judgment of truth or falsehood. But intellectual feelings are not to be understood unless it be remembered that they already find at work 'physical purposes' more primitive than themselves. Consciousness follows, and does not precede, the entry of the conceptual prehensions of the relevant universals. [417]

SECTION VI

It is evident that an affirmative intuitive judgment is very analogous to a conscious perception. A conscious perception is a very simplified type of affirmative intuitive judgment; and a direct affirmative intuitive judgment is a very sophisticated case of conscious perception. The difference between the two has its origin in the fact that one involves a perceptive feeling, and the other involves an imaginative feeling. Only one set of actual entities is involved in the formation of the perceptive feeling. These actual entities are the logical subjects of the proposition which is felt. But two sets of actual entities are involved in the formation of an imaginative feeling. Only one of these sets provides the logical subjects of the proposition which is felt; the other set is finally eliminated in the process of origination. The difference between the two feelings, the perceptive feeling and the imaginative feeling, does not therefore lie in the proposition which is felt. It lies in the emotional patterns of the two feelings. In either case this emotional pattern is derivative from the process of origination. In the case of the perceptive feeling, the emotional pattern reflects the close connection of the predicate with the logical subjects, throughout the process of origination. In the case of the imaginative feeling, this emotional pattern reflects the initial disconnection of the predicate from the logical subjects. This example illustrates that in the integration of feelings, components which are eliminated from the matter of the integral feeling may yet leave their mark on its emotional pattern. The triumph of consciousness comes with the negative intuitive judgment. In this case there is a conscious feeling of what might be, and is not. The feeling directly concerns the definite negative prehensions enjoyed by its subject. It is the feeling of absence, and it feels this absence as produced by the definite exclusiveness of what is really present. Thus, the explicitness of negation,

[*418*] which is the peculiar characteristic of consciousness, is here at its maximum.

The two cases of intuitive judgment, namely, the affirmative intuitive judgment and the negative intuitive judgment, are comparatively rare. These two cases of intuitive judgment, together with conscious perception, correspond to what Locke calls 'knowledge.' Locke's section (IV, XIV, 4) † on this subject is short enough to be quoted in full:

Judgment is the presuming things to be so without perceiving it.— Thus the mind has two faculties conversant about truth and falsehood,—

First, Knowledge, whereby it certainly perceives, and is undoubtedly satisfied of the agreement or disagreement of any ideas.

Secondly, Judgment, which is the putting ideas together, or separating them from one another in the mind, when their certain agreement or disagreement is not perceived, but presumed to be so; which is, as the word imports, taken to be so before it certainly appears. And if it so unites or separates them as in reality things are, it is right judgment.

What Locke calls 'judgment' is here termed 'inferential judgment.'

The process of origination of a suspended judgment consists in (i) the 'physical recollection' and the 'indicative feeling,' (ii) the 'conceptual imagination,' derivative from the 'physical recollection,' (iii) the 'propositional imagination,' derived by integration of the 'indicative feeling' with the 'conceptual imagination,' (iv) the 'suspended judgment,' derived by integration of the 'indicative feeling' with the 'propositional imagination,' the relation between the objectifying predicate and the imagined predicate‡ being such as to preclude either case of direct judgment.

The suspended judgment thus consists of the integration of the imaginative feeling with the indicative feeling, in the case where the imagined predicate fails to find identification with the objectifying predicate, or with [*419*] any part of it; but does find compatible contrast with it. It is the feeling of the contrast between what the logical subjects evidently *are*, and what the same subjects in addition *may be*. This suspended judgment is our consciousness of the limitations involved in objectification. If, in the comparison of an imaginative feeling with fact, we merely knew what *is* and what *is not*, then we should have no basis for discovering the work of objectification in effecting omissions from the formal constitutions of things. It is this additional knowledge of the compatibility of what we imagine with what we physically feel, that gives this information. We must not oversimplify the formal constitutions of the higher grade of acts of concrescence by construing a suspended judgment as though it were a negative judgment. Our whole progress in scientific theory, and even in subtility of direct observation, depends on the use of suspended judgments. It is to be noted that a suspended judgment is not a judgment of probability. It is a judgment of compatibility. The judgment tells us what *may* be additional information respecting the formal constitutions of the logical subjects, information which is neither included nor excluded by our direct perception. This is a judgment of fact concerning ourselves. Suspended judgments are weapons essential to scientific progress. But in intuitive judgments the emotional pattern may be dominated by indifference to truth or falsehood. We have then 'conscious imagination.' We are feeling the actual world with the conscious imputation of imagined predicates be they true or false.

When we compare these three cases of intuitive judgment (involving attention to truth) with conscious imagination (involving inattention to truth), that is to say, with 'imputative feeling,' we note that, except in the case of negative judgments, the datum of the conscious imagination is identical with the datum of the corresponding judgment. Nevertheless, the feelings are very different in their emotional patterns. One emotional [420] pattern is dominated by indifference to truth; and the other emotional pattern by attention to truth. This indifference to truth is otherwise to be expressed as readiness to eliminate the true objectifying pattern exemplified in the objective datum of the physical feeling in question; while the attention to truth is merely the refusal to eliminate this pattern. But these emotional elements in the subjective forms are not dictated by any diversity of data in the two feelings. For except in the case of the direct negative judgment, the datum is the same in both types of feeling. The emotional form of a feeling cannot be merely deduced from datum felt, though it has close relation to it. The emotional pattern in the subjective form of any one feeling arises from the subjective aim dominating the entire concrescent process. The other feelings of the subject may be conceived as catalytic agents. They are intellectually separable from the feeling in question. But that feeling is in fact the outcome of the subjective aim of the subject which is its locus; and the emotional pattern is the peculiar way in which the subject asserts itself in its feeling. This explanation of the status of the emotional pattern is merely an application of the doctrine that a feeling appropriates elements of the universe, which in themselves are other than the subject; and absorbs these elements into the real internal constitution of its subject by synthesizing them in the unity of an emotional pattern expressive of its own subjectivity.

This mutual dependence of the emotional pattern of a feeling on the other feelings of the same subject† may be termed the 'mutual sensitivity' of feelings. It is also one aspect of the incurable 'particularity' of a feeling, in the sense that no feeling can be abstracted from its subject.

SECTION VII

'Physical purposes' constitute a type of comparative feelings more primitive than the type of intellectual feel- [421] ings. In general, it seems as though intellectual feelings are negligible, so as only to obtain importance in exceptional actual entities. We have no means of testing this assumption in any crucial way. It is however the assumption usually made; and therefore it may be presumed that there is some evidence which persuades people to embrace the doctrine. But in fact no evidence, one way or the other, has ever been produced. We know that there are some few entities on the surface of this earth with intellectual feelings; and there our knowledge ends, so far as temporal entities are concerned.

In the more primitive type of comparative feelings indetermination as to its own ingressions—so prominent in intellectual feelings—is the aspect of the eternal object which is pushed into the background. In such a type of physical purposes the integration of a physical feeling and a conceptual feeling does not involve the reduction of the objective datum of the physical feeling to a multiplicity of bare logical subjects. The objective datum remains the nexus that it is, exemplifying the eternal objects whose ingression constitutes its definiteness. Also the indeterminateness as to its own ingressions is eliminated from the eternal object which is the datum of the conceptual‡ feeling. In the integral comparative feeling the datum is the contrast of the conceptual datum with the reality of the objectified nexus. The physical feeling is feeling a real fact; the conceptual feeling is valuing an abstract possibility. The new datum is the compatibility or incompatibility of the fact as felt with the eternal object as a datum in feeling. This synthesis of a pure abstraction with a real fact, as in feeling, is a generic contrast. In respect to physical purposes, the cosmological scheme which is here being developed requires† us to hold that all actual entities include physical purposes. The constancy of physical purposes explains the persistence of the order of nature, and in particular of 'enduring objects.'

[422] The chain of stages in which a physical purpose originates is simpler than in the case of intellectual feelings: (i) there is a physical feeling; (ii) the primary conceptual correlate of the physical feeling is generated, according to categoreal condition IV; (iii) this physical feeling is integrated with its conceptual correlate to form the physical purpose. Such physical purposes are called physical purposes of the first species.

In such a physical purpose, the datum is the generic contrast between the nexus, felt in the physical feeling, and the eternal object valued in the conceptual feeling. This eternal object is also exemplified as the pattern of the nexus. Thus the conceptual valuation now closes in upon the feeling of the nexus as it stands in the generic contrast, exemplifying the valued eternal object. This valuation accorded‡ to the physical feeling endows the transcendent creativity with the character of adversion, or of aversion. The character of adversion secures the reproduction of the physical feeling, as one element in the objectification of the subject beyond itself. Such reproduction may be thwarted by incompatible objectification derived from other feelings. But a physical feeling, whose valuation produces adversion, is thereby an element with some force of persistence into the future beyond its own subject. It is felt and re-enacted down a route of occasions forming an enduring object. Finally this chain of transmission meets with incompatibilities, and is attenuated, or modified, or eliminated from further endurance.

When there is aversion, instead of adversion, the transcendent creativity assumes the character that it inhibits, or attenuates, the objectification of that subject in the guise of that feeling. Thus aversion tends to eliminate one possibility by which the subject may itself be objectified in the future. Thus adversions promote stability; and aversions promote change without any indication of the sort of change. In itself an aversion [423] promotes the elimination of content, and the lapse into triviality.

The bare character of mere responsive re-enaction constituting the original physical feeling in its first phase† is enriched in the second phase by the valuation accruing from integration with the conceptual correlate. In this way, the dipolar character of concrescent experience provides in the physical pole for the objective side of experience, derivative from an external actual world, and provides in the mental pole for the subjective side of experience, derivative from the subjective conceptual valuations correlate to the physical feelings. The mental operations have a double office. They achieve, in the immediate subject, the subjective aim of that subject as to the satisfaction to be obtained from its own initial data. In this way the decision derived from the actual world, which is the efficient cause, is completed by the decision embodied in the subjective aim,† which is the final cause. Secondly, the physical purposes of a subject by their valuations determine the relative efficiency of the various feelings to enter into the objectifications of that subject in the creative advance beyond itself. In this function, the mental operations determine their subject in its character of an efficient cause. Thus the mental pole is the link whereby the creativity is endowed with the double character of final causation, and efficient causation. The mental pole is constituted by the decisions in virtue of which matters of fact enter into the character of the creativity. It has no necessary connection with consciousness; though, where there is origination of intellectual feelings, consciousness does in fact enter into the subjective forms.

SECTION VIII

The second species of physical purposes is due to the origination of reversions in the mental pole. It is due to this second species that vibration and rhythm have a [424] dominating importance in the physical world. Reversions are the conceptions which arise by reason of the lure of contrast, as a condition for intensity of experience. This lure is expressible as a categoreal condition.

Categoreal Condition VIII. The Category of Subjective Intensity. The subjective aim, whereby there is origination of conceptual feeling, is at‡ intensity of feeling (α) in the immediate subject, and (β) in the relevant future.

We first note (i) that intensity of feeling due to any realized ingression of an eternal object is heightened when that eternal object is one element in a realized contrast between eternal objects, and (ii) that two or more contrasts may be incompatible for joint ingression, *or* may jointly enter into a higher contrast.

It follows that balanced complexity is the outcome of this‡ Category of Subjective Aim. Here 'complexity' means the realization of contrasts, of contrasts of contrasts, and so on; and 'balance' means the absence of attenuations due to the elimination of contrasts which some elements in the pattern would introduce and other elements inhibit.

Thus there is the urge towards the realization of the maximum number of eternal objects subject to the restraint that they must be under conditions of contrast. But this limitation to 'conditions of contrast' is the demand for 'balance.' For 'balance' here means that no realized eternal object shall eliminate potential contrasts between other realized eternal objects. Such eliminations attenuate the intensities of feeling derivable from the ingressions of the various elements of the pattern. Thus so far as the immediate present subject is concerned, the origination of conceptual valuation according to Category IV is devoted to such a disposition of emphasis as to maximize the integral intensity derivable from the most favourable balance. The subjective aim is the selection of the balance amid the given materials. But one element in the immediate feelings of the concrescent [425] subject is comprised of the anticipatory feelings of the transcendent future in its relation to immediate fact. This is the feeling of the objective immortality inherent in the nature of actuality. Such anticipatory feelings involve realization of the relevance of eternal objects as decided in the primordial nature of God. In so far as these feelings in the higher organisms rise to important intensities there are effective feelings of the more remote alternative possibilities. Such feelings are the conceptual feelings which arise in accordance with the Category of Reversion (Category V†).

But there must be 'balance,' and 'balance' is the adjustment of identities and diversities for the introduction of contrast with the avoidance of inhibitions by incompatibilities. Thus this secondary phase, involving the future, introduces reversion and is subject to Category VIII.‡ Each reverted conceptual feeling has† its datum largely identical with that of its correlate primary feeling of the same pole. In this way, readiness for synthesis is promoted. But the introduction of contrast is obtained by the differences, or reversions, in some elements of the complex data. The category expresses the rule that what is identical, and what is reverted, are determined by the aim at a favourable balance. The reversion is due to the aim at complexity as one condition for intensity.

When this reverted conceptual feeling acquires a relatively high intensity of upward valuation in its subjective form, the resulting integration of physical feeling, primary conceptual feeling, and secondary conceptual feeling, produces a more complex physical purpose than in the former case when the reverted conceptual feeling was negligible. There is now the physical feeling as valued by its integration with the primary conceptual feeling, the integration with the contrasted secondary conceptual feeling, the heightening of the scale of subjective intensity by the introduction of conceptual contrast, and the concentration of this heightened intensity upon the reverted [426] feeling in virtue of its being the novel factor introducing the contrast. The physical purpose thus provides the creativity with a complex character, which is governed (i) by the Category of Conceptual Reversion, in virtue of which the secondary conceptual feeling arises, (ii) by the Category of Transmutation, in virtue of which conceptual feeling can be transmitted as physical feeling, (iii) by the Category of Subjective Harmony, in virtue of which the subjective forms of the two conceptual feelings are adjusted to procure the subjective aim, and (iv) by the Category of Subjective Intensity, in virtue of which the aim is determined to the attainment of balanced intensity from feelings integrated in virtue of near-identity, and contrasted in virtue of reversions.

Thus in the successive occasions of an enduring object in which the inheritance is governed by this complex physical purpose, the reverted conceptual feeling is transmitted into the next occasion as physical feeling, and the pattern of the original physical feeling now reappears as the datum in the reverted conceptual feeling. Thus along the route of the life-history there is a chain of contrasts in the physical feelings of the successive occasions. This chain is inherited as a vivid contrast of physical feelings, and in each occasion there is the physical feeling with its primary valuation in contrast with the reverted conceptual feeling.

Thus an enduring object gains the enhanced intensity of feeling arising from contrast between inheritance and novel effect, and also gains the enhanced intensity arising from the combined inheritance of its stable rhythmic character throughout its life-history. It has the weight of repetition, the intensity of contrast, and the balance between the two factors of the contrast. In this way the association of endurance with rhythm and physical vibration is† to be explained. They arise out of the conditions for intensity and stability. The subjective aim is seeking width with its contrasts, within the unity of a general design. An intense experience is an aesthetic fact, and [427] its categoreal conditions are to be generalized from aesthetic laws in particular arts.

The categoreal conditions, appealed to above, can be summarized thus: [1]

1. The novel consequent must be graded in relevance so as to preserve some identity of character with the ground.

2. The novel consequent must be graded in relevance so as to preserve some contrast with the ground in respect to that same identity of character.

[1] My *Religion in the Making*, Ch. III, Sect. VII.†

These two principles are derived from the doctrine that an actual fact is a fact of aesthetic experience. All aesthetic experience is feeling arising out of the realization of contrast under identity.

In the expansion of this account which has been given here, a third principle has been added, that new forms enter into positive realizations first as conceptual experience, and are then transmuted into physical experience. But conceptual experience does not in itself involve consciousness; its essence is valuation.

Between physical purposes and the conscious purposes introduced by the intellectual feelings there lie the propositional feelings which have not acquired consciousness in their subjective forms by association with intellectual feelings. Such propositional feelings mark a stage of existence intermediate between the purely physical stage and the stage of conscious intellectual operations. The propositions are lures for feelings, and give to feelings a definiteness of enjoyment and purpose which is absent in the blank evaluation of physical feeling into physical purpose. In this blank evaluation we have merely the determination of the comparative creative efficacies of the component feelings of actual entities. In a propositional feeling there is the 'hold up'—or, in its original sense, the epoch— of the valuation of the predicative pattern in its relevance to the definite logical subjects which are otherwise felt as definite elements in experience. [428] There is the arrest of the emotional pattern round this sheer fact as a possibility, with the corresponding gain in distinctness of its relevance to the future. The particular possibility for the transcendent creativity— in the sense of its advance from subject to subject—this particular possibility has been picked out, held up, and clothed with emotion. The stage of existence in which propositional feelings are important, apart from intellectual feelings, may be identified with Bergson's stage of pure and instinctive intuition. There are thus three stages, the stage of pure physical purpose, the stage of pure instinctive intuition, and the stage of intellectual feelings. But these stages are not sharply distinguished. There are stages in which there are propositional feelings with every degree of importance or of unimportance; there are stages in which there are intellectual feelings with every degree of importance or of unimportance. Also,† even in a higher stage, there are whole recesses of feeling which in the final satisfaction acquire merely the characteristics of their own proper stage, physical or propositional.

PART IV
THE THEORY OF EXTENSION

CHAPTER I

COORDINATE† DIVISION

SECTION I

[433] THERE are two distinct ways of 'dividing' the satisfaction of an actual entity into component feelings, genetically and coordinately. Genetic division is division of the concrescence; coordinate division is division of the concrete. In the 'genetic' mode, the prehensions are exhibited in their genetic relationship to each other. The actual entity is seen as a process; there is a growth from phase to phase; there are processes of integration and of [434] reintegration. At length a complex unity of objective datum is obtained, in the guise of a contrast of actual entities, eternal objects, and propositions, felt with corresponding complex unity of subjective form. This genetic passage from phase to phase is not in physical time: the exactly converse point of view expresses the relationship of concrescence to physical time. It can be put shortly by saying, that physical time expresses some features of the growth, but *not* the growth of the features. The final complete feeling is the 'satisfaction.'

Physical time makes its appearance in the 'coordinate' analysis of the 'satisfaction.' The actual entity is the enjoyment of a certain quantum of physical time. But the genetic process is not the temporal succession: such a view is exactly what is denied by the epochal theory of time. Each phase in the genetic process presupposes the entire quantum, and so does each feeling in each phase. The subjective unity dominating the process forbids the division of that extensive quantum which originates with the primary phase of the subjective aim. The problem dominating the concrescence is the actualization of the quantum *in solido.*† The quantum is that standpoint in the extensive continuum which is consonant with the subjective aim in its original derivation from God. Here 'God' is that actuality in the world, in virtue of which there is physical 'law.'

There is a spatial element in the quantum as well as a temporal element. Thus the quantum is an extensive region. This region is the determinate basis which the concrescence presupposes. This basis governs the objectifications of the actual world which are possible for the novel concrescence. The coordinate divisibility of the satisfaction is the 'satisfaction' considered in its relationship to the divisibility of this region.

The concrescence presupposes its basic region, and not the region its concrescence. Thus the subjective unity of the concrescence is irrelevant to the divisibility of the [435] region. In dividing the region we are ignoring the subjective unity which is inconsistent with such division. But the region is, after all, divisible, although in the genetic growth it is undivided.

So this divisible character of the undivided region is reflected into the character of the satisfaction. When we divide the satisfaction coordinately, we do not find feelings which *are* separate, but feelings which *might be* separate. In the same way, the divisions of the region are not divisions which *are*; they are divisions which *might be*. Each such mode of division of the extensive region yields 'extensive quanta': also an 'extensive quantum' has been termed a 'standpoint.' This notion of a 'standpoint' must now be briefly explained.

The notion has reference to three allied doctrines. First, there is the doctrine of 'the actual world' as receiving its definition from the immediate concrescent actuality in question. Each actual entity arises out of its own peculiar actual world. Secondly, there is the doctrine of each actual world as a 'medium.' According to this doctrine, if S be the concrescent subject in question, and A and B be two actual entities in its actual world, then either A is in the actual world of B, or B is in the actual world of A, or A and B are contemporaries. If, for example, A be in the actual world of B, then for the immediate subject S there are (1) the direct objectification of A in S, and (2) the indirect objectification by reason of the chain of objectification, A in B and B in S. Such chains can be extended to any length by the inclusion of many intermediate actualities between A and S.

Thirdly, it is to be noticed that 'decided' conditions are never such as to banish freedom. They only qualify it. There is always a contingency left open for immediate decision. This consideration is exemplified by an indetermination respecting '*the* actual world' which is to decide the conditions for an immediately novel concrescence. There are alternatives as to its determination, which are left over for immediate decision. Some actual [436] entities may be *either* in the settled past, *or* in the contemporary nexus, *or* even left to the undecided future, according to immediate decision. Also the indirect chains of successive objectifications will be modified according to such choice. These alternatives are represented by the indecision as to the particular quantum of extension to be chosen for the basis of the novel concrescence.

SECTION II

The sense in which the coordinate divisions of the satisfaction are 'feelings which might be separate'† has now to be discussed.

Each such coordinate division corresponds to a definite sub-region of the basic region. It expresses that component of the satisfaction which has the character of a unified feeling of the actual world from the standpoint of that sub-region. In so far as the objectification of the actual world from this restricted standpoint is concerned, there is nothing to distinguish this coordinate division from an actual entity. But it is only the physical pole of the actual entity which is thus divisible. The mental pole is incurably one. Thus the subjective form of this coordinate division is derived from the origination of conceptual feelings which have regard to the complete region, and are not restricted to the sub-region in question. In other words, the conceptual feelings have regard to the complete actual entity, and not to the coordinate division in question. Thus the whole course of the genetic derivation of the coordinate division is not explicable by reference to the categoreal conditions governing the concrescence of feeling arising from the mere physical feeling of the restricted objective datum. The originative energy of the mental pole constitutes the urge whereby its conceptual prehensions adjust and readjust subjective forms and thereby determine the specific modes of integration terminating in the 'satisfaction.'

It is obvious that in so far as the mental pole is trivial [437] as to originality, what is inexplicable in the coordinate division (taken as actually separate) becomes thereby trivial. Thus for many abstractions concerning low-grade actual entities, the coordinate divisions approach the character of being actual entities on the same level as the actual entity from which they are derived.

It is thus an empirical question to decide in relation to special topics, whether the distinction between a coordinate division and a true actual entity is, or is not, relevant. In so far as it is not relevant we are dealing with an indefinitely subdivisible extensive universe.

A coordinate division is thus to be classed as a generic contrast. The two components of the contrast are, (i) the parent actual entity, and (ii) the proposition which is the potentiality of that superject having arisen from the physical standpoint of the restricted sub-region. The proposition is thus the potentiality of eliminating from the physical pole of the parent entity all the objectified actual world, except those elements derivable from that standpoint; and yet retaining the relevant elements of the subjective form.

The unqualified proposition is false, because the mental pole, which is in fact operative, would not be the mental pole under the hypothesis of the proposition. But, for many purposes, the falsity of the proposition is irrelevant. The proposition is very complex; and with the relevant qualifications depending on the topic in question, it expresses the truth. In other words, the unqualified false proposition is a matrix from which an indefinite number of true qualified propositions can be derived. The requisite qualification depends on the special topic in question, and expresses the limits of the application of the unqualified proposition relevantly to that topic.

The unqualified proposition expresses the indefinite divisibility of the actual world; the qualifications express the features of the world which are lost sight of by the [438] unguarded use of this principle. The actual world is atomic; but in some senses it is indefinitely divisible.

SECTION III

The atomic actual entities individually express the genetic unity of the universe. The world expands through recurrent unifications of itself, each, by the addition of itself, automatically recreating the multiplicity anew.

The other type of indefinite multiplicity, introduced by the indefinite coordinate divisibility of each atomic actuality, seems to show that, at least for certain purposes, the actual world is to be conceived as a mere indefinite multiplicity.

But this conclusion is to be limited by the principle of 'extensive order' which steps in. The atomic unity of the world, expressed by a multiplicity of atoms, is now replaced by the solidarity of the extensive continuum. This solidarity embraces not only the coordinate divisions within each atomic actuality, but also exhibits the coordinate divisions of all atomic actualities from each other in one scheme of relationship.

In an earlier chapter (Part II, Ch. IV, Sects. IV to IX‡) the sense in which the world can be conceived as a medium for the transmission of influences† has been discussed. This orderly arrangement of a variety of routes of transmission, by which alternative objectifications of an antecedent actuality A can be indirectly received into the constitution of a subsequent actuality B, is the foundation of the extensive relationship among diverse actual entities. But this scheme of *external* extensive relationships links itself with the schemes of internal division which are *internal* to the several actual entities. There is, in this way, one basic scheme of extensive connection which expresses on one uniform plan† (i) the general conditions to which the bonds, uniting the atomic actualities into a nexus, conform, and (ii) the general conditions to which the bonds, uniting the infinite num- [439] ber of coordinate subdivisions of the satisfaction of any actual entity, conform.

As an example of (ii), suppose that P is a coordinate division of an actual occasion A. Then P can be conceived as an actual occasion with its own actual world forming its initial datum in its first phase of genetic origination. In fact, P is the hypothetical satisfaction of a hypothetical process of concrescence with this standpoint. The other coordinate divisions of A are *either* in the 'actual world' for P, *or* are contemporary with P, *or* are coordinate divisions of P, *or* have a complex relation to P expressed by the property that each one of them is coordinately divisible into prehensions $Q_1 \, Q_2 \ldots$, such that each of them has one or other† of the three above-mentioned relations to P.

Further, in addition to the merely potential subdivisions of a satisfaction into coordinate feelings, there is the merely potential aggregation of actual entities into a super-actuality in respect to which the true actualities play the part of coordinate subdivisions. In other words, just as,† for some purposes, one atomic actuality can be treated as though it were many coordinate actualities, in the same way, for other purposes,† a nexus of many actualities can be treated as though it were one actuality. This is what we habitually do in the case of the span of life of a molecule, or of a piece of rock, or of a human body.

This extensiveness is the pervading generic form to which the morphological structures† of the organisms of the world conform. These organisms are of two types: one type consists of the individual actual entities; the other type consists of nexūs of actual entities. Both types are correlated by their common extensiveness. If we confine our attention to the subdivision of an actual entity into coordinate parts, we shall conceive of extensiveness as purely derived from the notion of 'whole and part,' that is to say, 'extensive whole and extensive part.' This was the view taken by me in my† two earlier investigations of the [440] subject.[1] This defect of starting-point revenged itself in the fact that the 'method of extensive abstraction' developed in those works was unable to define a 'point'† without the intervention of the theory of 'duration.' Thus what should have been a *property* of 'durations' became the definition of a point. By this mode of approach the extensive relations of actual entities mutually external to each other were pushed into the background; though they are equally fundamental.

Since that date Professor T. de Laguna [2] has shown that the somewhat more general notion of 'extensive connection' can be adopted as the starting-point for the investigation of extension; and that the more limited notion of 'whole and part' can be defined in terms of it. In this way, as Professor de Laguna has shown, my difficulty in the definition of a point, without recourse to other considerations, can be overcome.

This whole question is investigated in the succeeding chapters of this Part.† Also I there give a definition of a straight line, and of 'flat' loci generally, in terms of purely extensive principles without reference to measurement or to durations.

SECTION IV

An actual entity, in its character of being a physical occasion, is an act of blind perceptivity of the other physical occasions of the actual world. When we consider such an occasion morphologically, as a given entity, its perceptive bonds are divisible by reason of the extensive divisibility of its own standpoints, and by reason of the extensive divisibility of the other actual occasions. Thus we reach perceptive bonds involving one sub-region of the basic region of the perceiver, and one subdivision of the basic region

[1] Cf. *The Principles of Natural Knowledge*, 1919, and *The Concept of Nature*, 1920, Cambridge University Press, England.

[2] Cf. Professor de Laguna's† three articles in the *Journal of Philosophy, Psychology, and Scientific Method*, Vol. XIX, 1922, especially the third article.

of the perceived. The relationship between these sub-regions involves the status of inter- [441] mediate regions functioning as agents in the process of transmission. In other words, the perspective of one sub-region from the other is dependent on the fact that the extensive relations express the conditions laid on the actual world in its function of a medium.

These extensive relations do not make determinate *what* is transmitted; but they do determine conditions to which all transmission must conform. They represent the systematic scheme which is involved in the real potentiality from which every actual occasion *arises*. This scheme is also involved in the attained fact which every actual occasion *is*. The 'extensive' scheme is nothing else than the generic morphology of the internal relations which bind the actual occasions into a nexus, and which bind the prehensions of any one actual occasion into a unity, coordinately divisible.

For Descartes the primary *attribute* of physical bodies is *extension*; for the philosophy of organism the primary *relationship* of physical occasions is *extensive connection*. This ultimate relationship is *sui generis*, and cannot be defined or explained. But its formal properties can be stated. Also,† in view of these formal properties, there are definable derivative notions which are of importance in expressing the morphological structure. Some general character of coordinate divisibility is probably an ultimate metaphysical character, persistent in every cosmic epoch of physical occasions. Thus some of the simpler characteristics of extensive connection, as here stated, are probably such ultimate metaphysical necessities.

But when we examine the characteristics considered in the next chapter, it is difficult to draw the line distinguishing characteristics so general that we cannot conceive any alternatives, from characteristics so special that we imagine them to belong merely to our cosmic epoch. Such an epoch may be, relatively to our powers, of immeasurable extent, temporally and spatially. But in reference to the ultimate nature of things, it is a limited nexus. Beyond that nexus, entities with new relationships, unrealized in our experiences and unforeseen by our imagi- [442] nations, will make their appearance, introducing into the universe new types of order.

But, for our epoch, extensive connection with its various characteristics is the fundamental organic relationship whereby the physical world is properly described as a community. There are no important physical relationships outside the extensive scheme. To be an actual occasion in the physical world means that the entity in question is a relatum in this scheme of extensive connection. In this epoch, the scheme defines what is physically actual.

The more ultimate side of this scheme, perhaps that side which is metaphysically necessary, is at once evident by the consideration of the mutual implication of extensive whole and extensive part. If you abolish the whole, you abolish its parts; and if you abolish any part, then *that* whole is abolished.

In this general description of the states of extension, nothing has been said about physical time or physical space, or of the more general notion of creative advance. These are notions which presuppose the more general relationship of extension. They express additional facts about the actual occasions. The extensiveness of space is really the spatialization of extension; and the extensiveness of time is really the temporalization of extension. Physical time expresses the reflection of genetic divisibility into coordinate divisibility.

So far as mere extensiveness is concerned, space might as well have three hundred and thirty-three dimensions, instead of the modest three dimensions of our present epoch. The three dimensions of space form an additional fact about the physical occasions. Indeed the sheer dimensionality of space, apart from the precise number of dimensions, is such an additional fact, not involved in the mere notion of extension. Also the seriality of time, unique or multiple, cannot be derived from the sole notion of extension.

[443] The notion of nature as an organic extensive community omits the equally essential point of view that nature is never complete. It is always passing beyond itself. This is the creative advance of nature. Here we come to the problem of time. The immediately relevant point to notice is that time and space are characteristics of nature which presuppose the scheme of extension. But extension does not in itself determine the special facts which are true respecting physical time and physical space.

SECTION V

The consideration of coordination and genesis raises a question wider than any yet discussed in this chapter.

The theory of 'prehensions' embodies a protest against the 'bifurcation' of nature. It embodies even more than that: its protest is against the bifurcation of actualities. In the analysis of actuality the antithesis between publicity and privacy obtrudes itself at every stage. There are elements only to be understood by reference to what is beyond the fact in question; and there are elements expressive of the immediate, private, personal, individuality of the fact in question. The former elements express the publicity of the world; the latter elements express the privacy of the individual.

An actual entity considered in reference to the publicity of things is a 'superject'; namely, it arises from the publicity which it finds, and it adds itself to the publicity which it transmits. It is a moment of passage from decided public facts to a novel public fact. Public facts are, in their nature, coordinate.

An actual entity considered in reference to the privacy of things is a 'subject'; namely, it is a moment of the genesis of self-enjoyment. It consists of a purposed self-creation out of materials which are at hand in virtue of their publicity.

Eternal objects have the same dual reference. An eternal object considered in reference to the publicity [*444*] of things is at 'universal'; namely, in its own nature it refers to the general public facts of the world without any disclosure of the empirical details of its own implication in them. Its own nature as an entity requires ingression—positive or negative —in every detailed actuality; but its nature does not disclose the private details of any actuality.

An eternal object considered in reference to the privacy of things is a 'quality' or 'characteristic'; namely, in its own nature, as exemplified in any actuality, it constitutes an element in the private definiteness of that actuality. It refers itself publicly; but it is enjoyed privately.

The theory of prehensions is founded upon the doctrine that there are no concrete facts which are merely public, or merely private. The distinction between publicity and privacy is a distinction of reason, and is not a distinction between mutually exclusive concrete facts. The sole concrete facts, in terms of which actualities can be analysed, are prehensions; and every prehension has its public side and its private side. Its public side is constituted by the complex datum prehended; and its private side is constituted by the subjective form through which a private quality is imposed on the public datum. The separations of perceptual fact from emotional fact; and of causal fact from emotional fact, and from perceptual fact;† and of perceptual fact, emotional fact, and causal fact, from purposive fact; have constituted a complex of bifurcations, fatal to a satisfactory cosmology. The facts of nature are the actualities; and the facts into which the actualities are divisible are their prehensions, with their public origins, their private forms, and their private aims. But the actualities are moments of passage into a novel stage of publicity; and the coordination of prehensions expresses the publicity of the world, so far as it can be considered in abstraction from private genesis. Prehensions have public careers, but they are born privately. [*445*]

SECTION VI

The antithesis between publicity and privacy is reflected in the classification of eternal objects according to their primary modes of ingression into actual entities. An eternal object can only function in the concrescence of an actual entity in one of three ways: (i) it can be an element in the definiteness of some objectified nexus, or of some single actual entity, which is the datum of a feeling; (ii) it can be an element in the definiteness of the subjective form of some feeling; or (iii) it can be an element in the datum of a conceptual, or propositional, feeling. All other modes of ingression arise from integrations which presuppose these modes.

Now the third mode is merely the conceptual valuation of the potential ingression in one of the other two modes. It is a real ingression into actuality; but it is a restricted ingression with mere potentiality withholding the immediate realization of its function of conferring definiteness.

The two former modes of ingression thus constitute the ways in which the functioning of an eternal object is unrestrictedly realized. But we now ask whether either mode is indifferently open to each eternal object. The answer is the classification of eternal objects into two species, the 'objective' species, and the 'subjective' species.

An eternal object of the objective species can only obtain ingression in the first mode, and never in the second mode. It is always, in its unrestricted realization, an element in the definiteness of an actual entity, or a nexus, which is the datum of a feeling belonging to the subject in question.

Thus a member of this species can only function relationally: by a necessity of its nature it is introducing one actual entity, or nexus, into the real internal constitution of another actual entity. Its sole avocation is to be an agent in objectification. It can never be an element in [446] the definiteness of a subjective form. The solidarity of the world rests upon the incurable objectivity of this species of eternal objects. A member of this species inevitably introduces into the immediate subject other actualities. The definiteness with which it invests the external world may, or may not, conform to the real internal constitutions of the actualities objectified. But conformably, or non-conformably, such is the character of that nexus for that actual entity. This is a real physical fact, with its physical consequences. Eternal objects of the objective species are the mathematical Platonic† forms. They concern the world as a medium.

But the description of sensa given above (Part II, Ch. IV,† Sect. III) will include some members of the subjective species.

A member of the subjective species is, in its primary character, an element in the definiteness of the subjective form of a feeling. It is a determinate way in which a feeling can feel. It is an emotion, or an intensity, or an adversion, or an aversion, or a pleasure, or a pain. It defines the subjective form of feeling of one actual entity. A_1 may be that component of A's constitution through which A is objectified for B. Thus when B feels A_1, it feels 'A with *that* feeling.' In this way, the eternal object which contributes to the definiteness of A's feeling becomes an eternal object contributing to the definiteness of A as an objective datum in B's prehension of A. The eternal object can then function both subjectively and relatively. It can be a private element in a subjective form, and also an agent in the objectification. In this latter character it may come under the operation of the Category of Transmutation and become a characteristic of a nexus as objectified for a percipient.

In the first stage of B's physical feeling, the subjective form of B's feeling is conformed to the subjective form of A's feeling. Thus this eternal object in B's experience will have a two-way mode of functioning. It will be among the determinants of A for B, and it will be among [447] the determinants of B's way of sympathy with A. The intensity of physical energy belongs to the subjective species of eternal objects, but the peculiar form of the flux of energy belongs to the objective species.

For example, 'redness' may first be the definiteness of an emotion which is a subjective form in the experience of A; it then becomes an agent whereby A is objectified for B, so that A is objectified in respect to its prehension with this emotion. But A may be only one occasion of a nexus, such that each of its members is objectified for B by a prehension with an analogous subjective form. Then by the operation of the Category of Transmutation, the nexus is objectified for B as illustrated by the characteristic 'redness.' The nexus will also be illustrated by its mathematical forms which are eternal objects of the objective species.

SECTION VII

The feelings—or, more accurately, the quasi-feelings—introduced by the coordinate division of actual entities eliminate the proper status of the subjects entertaining the feelings. For the subjective forms of feelings are only explicable by the categoreal demands arising from the unity of the subject. Thus the coordinate division of an actual entity produces feelings whose subjective forms are partially eliminated and partially inexplicable. But this mode of division preserves undistorted the elements of definiteness introduced by eternal objects of the objective species.

Thus in so far as the relationships of these feelings require an appeal to subjective forms for their explanation, the gap must be supplied by the introduction of arbitrary laws of nature regulating the relations of intensities. Alternatively, the subjective forms become arbitrary epiphenomenal facts, inoperative in physical nature, though claiming operative importance.

The order of nature, prevalent in the cosmic epoch in question, exhibits itself as a morphological scheme in- [448] volving eternal objects of the objective species. The most fundamental elements in this scheme are those eternal objects in terms of which the general principles of coordinate division itself are expressed. These eternal objects express the theory of extension in its most general aspect. In this theory the notion of the atomicity of actual entities, each with its concrescent privacy, has been entirely eliminated. We are left with the theory of extensive connection, of whole and part, of points, lines, and surfaces, and of straightness and flatness.

The substance of this chapter can be recapitulated in a summary: Genetic division is concerned with an actual occasion in its character of a concrescent immediacy. Coordinate division is concerned with an actual occasion in its character of a concrete object. Thus for genetic division the primary fact about an occasion is its initial 'dative' phase; for coordinate division the primary fact is the final 'satisfaction.' But with the attainment of the 'satisfaction,' the immediacy of final causation is lost, and the occasion passes into its objective immortality, in virtue of which efficient causation is constituted. Thus in coordinate division we are analysing the complexity of the occasion in its function of an efficient cause. It is in this connection that the morphological scheme of extensiveness attains its importance. In this way we obtain an analysis of the dative phase in terms of the 'satisfactions' of the past world. These satisfactions are systematically disposed in their relative status, according as *one* is, or is not, in the actual world of *another*. Also they are divisible into prehensions which can be treated as quasi-actualities with the same morphological system of relative status. This morphological system gains special order from the defining characteristic of the present cosmic epoch. The extensive continuum is this specialized ordering of the concrete occasions and of the prehensions into which they are divisible.

CHAPTER II
EXTENSIVE CONNECTION

SECTION I

[449] In this chapter we enumerate the chief characteristics of the physical relationship termed 'extensive connection.' We also enumerate the derivative notions which are of importance in our physical experience. This importance has its origin in the characteristics enumerated. The definitions of the derivative notions, as mere definitions, are equally applicable to any scheme of relationship whatever its characteristics. But they are only of importance when the relationship in question has the characteristics here enumerated for extensive connection.

No attempt will be made to reduce these enumerated characteristics to a logical minimum from which the remainder can be deduced by strict deduction. There is not a unique set of logical minima from which the rest can be deduced. There are many such sets. The investigation of such sets has great logical interest, and has an importance which extends beyond logic. But it is irrelevant for the purposes of this discussion.

For the sake of brevity the terms 'connection' and 'connected' will be used in the place of 'extensive connection' and 'extensively connected.' The term 'region' will be used for the relata which are involved in the scheme of 'extensive connection.' Thus, in the shortened phraseology, regions are the things which are connected.

A set of diagrams will illustrate the type of relationship meant by 'connection.' The two areas, A and B, in each diagram exhibit an instance of connection with each other.

[450] Such diagrams are apt to be misleading:† for one reason, because they introduce features as obvious, which it is our business to define in terms of our fundamental notion of 'connection'; for another reason, because they introduce features which are special to the two-dimensional, spatial extensiveness of a sheet of paper.

In the three diagrams of Set II, the areas, A and B, are *not* connected; but they are 'mediately' connected by the area C.

SECTION II

Definition 1.‡ Two regions are 'mediately' connected when they are both connected with a third region.

294

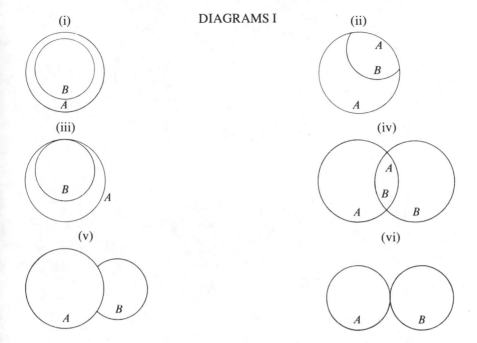

DIAGRAMS I

Assumption 1. Connection and mediate connection are both of them symmetrical relations; that is to say, if region A is connected, or mediately connected, with region B, then region B is connected, or mediately connected, with region A.

[451] It is obvious that the part of this assumption which concerns mediate connection can be proved from the terms of the definition. In the subsequent development of definitions and assumptions we shall not draw attention to such instances of the possibility of proof.

Assumption 2. No region is connected with all the other regions; and any two regions are mediately connected.

Assumption 3. Connection is not transitive; that is to say, if A be connected with B, and B with C, it does not thereby follow that A is connected with C; though in certain cases it does happen that A is connected with C.

Assumption 4. No region is connected, or mediately connected, with itself.

[452] This assumption is merely a convenient arrangement of nomenclature.

Definition 2. Region A is said to 'include' region B when every region connected with B is also connected with A. As an alternative nomenclature, region B will be said to be 'part' of region A.

This definition of 'inclusion' is due to Professor de Laguna; it constitutes an important addition to the theory of extension. In such investigations, as the present one, the definitions are the really vital portion of the subject.

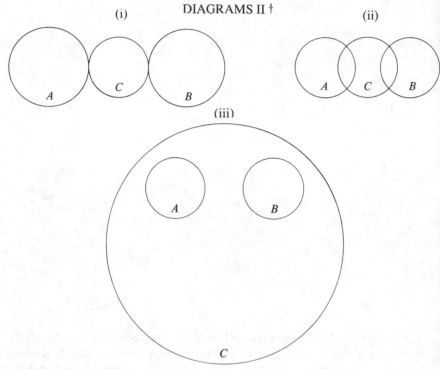

DIAGRAMS II †

Assumption 5. When one region includes another, the two regions are connected.

Assumption 6. The relation of inclusion is transitive.

Assumption 7. A region does not include itself.

Assumption 8. The relation of inclusion is asymmetrical; that is to say, if A includes B, then B does not include A.

Assumption 9. Every region includes other regions; and a pair of regions thus included in one region are not necessarily connected with each other. Such pairs can always be found, included in any given region.

Definition 3. Two regions are said to 'overlap,' when there is a third region which they both include.

Assumption 10. The relation of overlapping is symmetrical.

Assumption 11. If one region includes another region, the two regions overlap.

Assumption 12. Two regions which overlap are connected.

Definition 4. A 'dissection' of any given region A, is a set of regions, which is such that (i) all its members are included in A, (ii) no two of its members overlap, (iii) any region included in A, but not a member of the set, *either* is included in one member of the set, *or* overlaps more than one member of the set.

Assumption 13.† There are many dissections of any given region.

[453] *Assumption 14.*† A dissection of a region is not a dissection of any other region.

Definition 5. A region is called an 'intersect' of two overlapping regions, A and B, when (i) *either* it is included in both A and B, *or* it is one of the two regions and is included in the other, and (ii) no region, also included in both A and B, can overlap it without being included in it.

Definition 6.† If there be one, and only one, intersect of two regions, A and B, those regions are said to overlap with 'unique intersection'; if there be more than one intersect, they are said to overlap with 'multiple intersection.'

Assumption 15.† Any region included in both of two overlapping regions, and not itself an intersect, is included in one, and only one, intersect.

Assumption 16.† If A includes B, then B is the sole intersect of A and B.

Assumption 17.† An intersect of two regions, which is not one of the two regions, is included in both regions.

Assumption 18.† Each pair of overlapping regions has at least one intersect.

Definition 7. Two regions are 'externally' connected when (i) they are connected, and (ii) they do not overlap. The possibility of this definition is another of the advantages gained from the adoption of Professor de Laguna's starting-point, 'extensive connection,' over my original starting-point,[1] 'extensive whole and extensive part.' External connection is illustrated by diagrams (v) and (vi) in Set I of the diagrams. So far, we have not discriminated between the two cases illustrated respectively by these two diagrams. The notion of external connection is a long step towards the elaboration of the notion of a 'surface,' which has not yet been touched upon.

Definition 8. A region B is 'tangentially' included in a region A, when (i) B is included in A, and (ii) there are [454] regions which are externally connected with both A and B.

Definition 9. A region B is 'non-tangentially' included in a region A when (i) B is included in A, and (ii) there is no third region which is externally connected with both A and B.

The possibility, at this stage, of the three definitions 7, 8, and 9, constitutes the advantage to be gained by starting from Professor de Laguna's notion of 'extensive connection.' Non-tangential inclusion is illustrated by diagram (i) of the first set; and the two cases—as yet undiscriminated—of tangential inclusion are illustrated by diagrams (ii) and (iii).

SECTION III

Definition 10. A set of regions is called an 'abstractive set,' when (i) any two members of the set are such that one of them includes the other

[1] Cf. my *Principles of Natural Knowledge*, and *Concept of Nature*.

non-tangentially, and† (ii) there is no region included in every member of the set.

This definition practically limits abstractive sets to those sets which were termed 'simple abstractive sets' in my *Principles of Natural Knowledge* (paragraph 37.6). Since every region includes other regions, and since the relation of inclusion is transitive, it is evident that every abstractive set must be composed of an infinite number of members.

By reference to the particular case of three-dimensioned space, we see that abstractive sets can have different types of convergence. For in this case, an abstractive set can converge either to a point, or to a line, or to an area. But it is to be noted that we have not defined either points, or lines, or areas; and that we propose to define them in terms of abstractive sets. Thus we must define the various types of abstractive sets without reference to the notions, point, line, area.

Definition 11. An abstractive set α is said to 'cover' an [455] abstractive set β, when every member of the set α includes some members of the set β.

It is to be noticed that each abstractive set is to be conceived with its members in serial order, determined by the relation of inclusion. The series starts with a region of any size, and converges indefinitely towards smaller and smaller regions, without any limiting region. When the set α covers the set β, each member of α includes all the members of the convergent tail of β,† provided that we start far enough down in the serial arrangement of the set β. It will be found that, though an abstractive set must start with *some* region at its big end, these initial large-sized regions never enter into our reasoning. Attention is always fixed on what relations occur when we have proceeded *far enough down* the series. The only relations which are interesting are those which, if they commence anywhere, continue throughout the remainder of the infinite series.

Definition 12. Two abstractive sets are said to be 'equivalent' when each set covers the other.

Thus if α and β be the two equivalent abstractive sets, and A_1 be any member of α, there is some member of β, B_1 say, which is included in A_1;† also there is some member of α, A_2 say, which is included in B_1; also there is some member of β, B_2 say, which is included in A_2;† and so on indefinitely. Two equivalent abstractive sets are equivalent in respect to their convergence. But, in so far as the two sets are diverse, there will be relationships and characteristics in respect to which those sets are not equivalent, in a more general sense of the term 'equivalence.' The connection of this special sense of 'equivalence' to physical properties is explained more particularly in Chapter IV of the *Concept of Nature*.

Assumption 19.† An abstractive set is equivalent to itself. This assumption is merely a convenient arrangement of nomenclature. An abstractive set obviously satisfies the conditions for such reflexive equivalence.

Definition 13. A geometrical element is a complete [456] group of abstractive sets equivalent to each other, and not equivalent to any abstractive set outside the group.

Assumption 20.† The relation of equivalence is transitive and symmetrical.

Thus any two members of a geometrical element are equivalent to each other; and an abstractive set, not belonging to the geometrical element, is not equivalent to any member of that geometrical element. It is evident that each abstractive set belongs to one, and only one, geometrical element.

Definition 14. The geometrical element to which an abstractive set belongs† is called the geometrical element 'associated' with that abstractive set. Thus a geometrical element is 'associated' with each of its members.

Assumption 21.† Any abstractive set which covers any member of a geometrical element† also covers every member of that element.

Assumption 22.† An abstractive set which is covered by any member of a geometrical element† is also covered by every member of that element.

Assumption 23.† If *a* and *b* be two geometrical elements, *either* every member of *a* covers every member of *b, or* no member of *a* covers any member of *b.*

Definition 15. The geometrical element *a* is said to be 'incident' in the geometrical element *b,* when every member of *b* covers every member of *a,* but *a* and *b* are not identical.

Assumption 24.† A geometrical element is not incident in itself.

This assumption is merely a convenient arrangement of nomenclature.

When the geometrical element *a* is incident in the geometrical element *b,* the members of *a* will be said to have a 'sharper convergence' than those of *b.*

Definition 16. A geometrical element is called a 'point,' when there is no geometrical element incident in it. This definition of a 'point' is to be compared with Euclid's definition: 'A point is without parts.'

[457] *Definition 16.1.* The members of a geometrical element are said to be 'prime' in reference to assigned conditions, when (i) every member of that geometrical element satisfies† those conditions; (ii) if any abstractive set satisfies those conditions, every member of its associated geometrical element satisfies them; (iii) there is no geometrical element, with members satisfying those conditions, which is also incident in the given geometrical element.

The term 'prime' will also be applied to a geometrical element, when its members are 'prime' in the sense defined above.

It is obvious that a point is, in a sense, an 'absolute' prime. This is, in fact, the sense in which the definition† of a point, given here, conforms to Euclid's definition.

Definition 17. An abstractive set which is a member of a point will be called 'punctual.'

Definition 18. A geometrical element is called a 'segment between two points P and Q,' when its members are prime in reference to the condition that the points P and Q are incident in it.

Definition 19. When a geometrical element is a segment between two points, those points are called the 'end-points' of the segment.

Definition 20. An abstractive set which is a member of a segment is called 'segmental.'

Assumption 25.† There are many diverse segments with the same end-points;† but a segment has only one pair of end-points.

This assumption illustrates the fact that there can be many geometrical elements which are prime in reference to some given conditions. There are, however, conditions such that there is only one geometrical element prime to any one of them. For example, the set of points incident in one geometrical element uniquely defines that geometrical element. Also another instance of uniqueness is to be found in the theory of 'flat' geometrical elements, to be considered in the next chapter. A particular instance of such 'flat' elements is afforded [458] by straight lines. The whole theory of geometry depends upon the discovery of conditions which correspond to one, and only one, prime geometrical element. The Greeks, with their usual fortunate intuition, chanced upon such conditions in their notions of straight lines and planes. There is every reason, however, to believe that, in other epochs, widely different types of conditions with this property may be important—perhaps even in this epoch. The discovery of them is obviously of the first importance. It is possible that the modern Einsteinian reconstruction of physics is best conceived as the discovery of the interweaving in nature of different types of such conditions.

SECTION IV

Definition 21. A point is said to be 'situated' in a region, when the region is a member of one of the punctual abstractive sets which compose that point.

Assumption 26.† If a point be situated in a region, the regions, sufficiently far down the convergent tails of the various abstractive sets composing that point, are included in that region non-tangentially.

Definition 22. A point is said to be situated in the 'surface' of a region, when all the regions in which it is situated overlap that region but are not included in it.

Definition 23. A 'complete locus' is a set of points which compose *either* (i) all the points situated in a region, *or* (ii) all the points situated in the surface of a region, *or* (iii) all the points incident in a geometrical element.

A 'locus' always means a 'locus of points.'

Assumption 27.‡ A 'complete locus,' as defined in Definition 23, consists of an infinite number of points.

Definition 24. When a complete locus consists of all the points situated in a region, it is called the 'volume' of that region; when a complete locus consists of all the points in the surface of a region, the locus itself is called the 'surface' of that region; when a complete locus consists of all the points incident in a segment between end- [459] points, the locus is called a 'linear stretch' between those end-points.

Assumption 28.† There is a one-to-one correlation between volumes and regions, between surfaces and regions, and between linear stretches and segments, and between any geometrical element and the locus of points incident in it.

Assumption 29.† If two points lie in a given volume, there are linear stretches joining those two points, whose points all lie in that volume.

Assumption 30.† If two points lie in a given surface, there are linear stretches joining those two points, whose points all lie in that surface.

Assumption 31.† If two points lie in a given linear stretch, there is one, and only one, linear stretch with those points as end-points, whose points lie wholly in the given linear stretch.

It should be noted that the terms 'volume' and 'surface' are *not* meant to imply that volumes are three-dimensional, or that surfaces are two-dimensional. In the application of this theory of extension to the existing physical world of our epoch, volumes are four-dimensional, and surfaces are three-dimensional. But linear stretches are one-dimensional.

‡A sufficient number of assumptions, some provable and some axiomatic, have now been stated; so as to make clear the sort of development of the theory required for this stage of the definitions. In particular, the notion of the order of points in a linear stretch can now be elaborated from the definition of the notion of 'between.' But such investigations will lead us too far into the mathematical principles of geometry.‡

---

[546]‡ An explanatory paragraph is required at the end of this chapter to make clear the principle that a certain determinate boundedness is required for the notion of a region—i.e., for the notion of an extensive standpoint in the real potentiality for actualization. The inside of a region, its volume, has a complete boundedness denied to the extensive potentiality external to it. The boundedness applies both to the spatial and the temporal aspects of extension. Wherever there is ambiguity as to the contrast of boundedness between inside and outside, there is no proper region. In the next chapter all the ovals, members of one ovate class, preserve this property of boundedness, in the same sense for each of the ovals. Thus in the case of Elliptic Geometry (page 330) no oval can include half a straight line. On page 304, *Condition vii* has been expressed carelessly, so as to apply only to the case of infinite spatiality, i.e., to Euclidean and Hyperbolic Geometry.

CHAPTER III
FLAT LOCI

SECTION I

[460] Modern physical science, with its dependence on the exact notions of mathematics, began with the foundation of Greek Geometry. The first definition of Euclid's *Elements* runs,
"A point is that of which there is no part."
The second definition runs,
"A line is breadthless length."
The fourth definition runs,
"A straight line is any line which lies evenly with the points on itself."
These translations are taken from *Euclid In Greek, Book I*, edited with notes by Sir Thomas L. Heath, the greatest living authority on Euclid's *Elements*. Heath ascribes the second definition "to the Platonic school, if not to Plato himself."† For the Greek phrase translated 'evenly' Heath also suggests the alternatives 'on a footing of equality,' 'evenly placed,' 'without bias.'
Euclid's first 'postulate' is (Heath's translation):
"Let the following be postulated: to draw a straight line from any point to any point."
Heath points out that this postulate was meant to imply† *existence* and *uniqueness*.

As these statements occur in Greek science, a muddle arises between 'forms' and concrete physical things. Geometry starts with the purpose of investigating cer- [461] tain forms of physical things. But in its initial definitions of the 'point' and the 'line,' it seems immediately to postulate certain ultimate physical things of a very peculiar character. Plato himself appears to have had some suspicion of this confusion when (Heath, *loc. cit.*) he "objected to recognizing points as a separate class of things at all."† He ought to have gone further, and have made the same objection to all the geometrical entities, namely, points, lines, and surfaces. He wanted 'forms,' and he obtained new physical entities.

According to the previous chapter, 'extension' should be construed in terms of 'extensive connection'; that is to say, extension is a form of relationship between the actualities of a nexus. A point is a nexus of actual entities with a certain 'form'; and so is a 'segment.' Thus geometry is the investigation of the morphology of nexūs.

302

SECTION II

The weak point of the Euclidean definition of a straight line is, that nothing has been deduced from it. The notion expressed by the phrases 'evenly,' or 'evenly placed,' requires definition. The definition should be such that the uniqueness of the straight segment between two points can be deduced from it. Neither of these demands has ever been satisfied, with the result that in modern times the notion of 'straightness' has been based on that of measurement. A straight line has, in modern times, been defined as the shortest distance between two points. In the classic geometry, the converse procedure was adopted, and measurement presupposed straight lines. But, with the modern definition, the notion of the 'shortest distance' in its turn requires explanation.[1] This notion is practically defined to mean the line which is the route of certain physical occurrences.

In this section it will be shown that the gap in the old [462] classical theory can be remedied. Straight lines will be defined in terms of the extensive notions, developed in the preceding chapter; and the uniqueness of the straight line joining two points will be proved to follow from the terms of the definition.

A class of 'oval' regions must first be defined. Now the only weapon which we have for this definition is the notion of regions which overlap with a unique intersect (cf. Def. 6 of previous chapter). It is evidently a property of a pair of ovals that they can only overlap with a unique intersect. But it is equally evident that some regions which are not ovals also overlap with a unique intersect. However the *class* of ovals has the property that any region, not a member of it, intersects some ovals with multiple intersects. Also sub-sets of ovals can be found satisfying various conditions.

Thus we proceed to define a class whose region shall have those relations to each other, and to other regions, which we ascribe to the class of ovals. In other words,† we cannot define a single oval, but we can define a class of ovals. Such a class will be called 'ovate.' The definition of an ovate class proceeds by enumerating all those peculiar properties possessed by individual members of the class, or by sub-sets of members of the class. It will be found in the course of this enumeration that an extensive continuum which possesses an ovate class is dimensional in respect to that class. Thus existence of straight lines in an extensive continuum is bound up with the dimensional character of the continuum; and both characteristics are relative to a particular ovate class of regions in the continuum. It seems probable that an extensive continuum will possess only one ovate class. But I have not succeeded in proving that property; nor is it necessary for the argument.

A preliminary definition is convenient:

[1] Cf. Part IV, Ch. V, on 'Measurement.'

Definition 0.1. An 'ovate abstractive set' is an abstractive set whose members all belong to the complete ovate class under consideration.

[463] The characteristics of an ovate class will be divided into two groups: (a) the group of non-abstractive conditions, and (b) the group of abstractive conditions.

Definition 1. A class of regions is called 'ovate,' when it satisfies the conditions belonging to the two following groups, (a) and (b):

(a) *The Non-Abstractive Group*

(i) Any two overlapping regions of the ovate class have a unique intersect which also belongs to that ovate class.

(ii) Any region, not a member of the ovate class, overlaps some members of that class with 'multiple intersection' (cf. Def. 6 of previous chapter).

(iii) Any member of the ovate class overlaps some regions, not of that class, with multiple intersection.

(iv) Any pair of members of the ovate class, which are externally connected, have their surfaces touching either in a 'complete locus' of points (cf. Ch. II, Def. 23 and Ass. 27†), or in a single point.

(v) Any region, not belonging to the ovate class, is externally connected with some member of that class so that their surfaces touch in a set of points which does not form a 'complete locus.'

(vi) Any member of the ovate class is externally connected with some region not of that class so that their surfaces touch in a set of points which does not form a 'complete locus.'

(vii) Any finite number of regions are jointly included in some member of the ovate class.*

(viii) If A and B be members of the ovate class, and A include B, then there are members of the class which include B and are included in A.

(ix) There are dissections (cf. Def. 4 of the previous chapter) of every member of the ovate class, which consist wholly of members of that class; and there are dissections consisting wholly or partly of members not belonging to that class.

[464] (b) *The Abstractive Group*

(i) Among the members of any point, there are ovate abstractive sets.

(ii) If any set of two, or of three, or of four, points be considered, there are abstractive sets 'prime' in reference to the twofold condition, (*a*) of covering the points in question, and (*b*) of being equivalent to an ovate abstractive set.

(iii) There† are sets of five points such that *no* abstractive set exists prime in reference to the twofold condition, (*a*) of covering the points in question, and (*b*) of being equivalent to an ovate abstractive set.

By reason of the definitions of this latter group, the extensive continuum in question is called 'four-dimensional.' Analogously, an extensive continuum of any number of dimensions can be defined. The physical extensive continuum with which we are concerned in this cosmic epoch is four-dimensional. Notice that the property of being 'dimensional' is relative to a particular ovate class in the extensive continuum. There may be 'ovate' classes satisfying all the conditions with the exception of the 'dimensional' conditions. Also a continuum may have one number of dimensions relating to one ovate class, and another number of dimensions relating† to another ovate class.

Possibly physical laws, of the type presupposing continuity, depend on the interwoven properties of two, or more, distinct ovate classes.

SECTION III

Assumption 1. In the extensive continuum of the present epoch there is at least one ovate class, with the characteristics of the two groups, (a) and (b), of the previous section.

Definition 2. One such ovate class will be denoted by α: all definitions will be made relatively to this selected ovate class.

[465] It is indifferent to the argument whether or no there be an alternative ovate class. If there be, the derivative entities defined in reference to this alternative class are entirely different to those defined in reference to α. It is sufficient for us, that one such class interests us by the importance of its physical relations.

Assumption 2. If two abstractive sets are prime in reference to the same twofold condition, (a) of covering a *given* group of points, and (b) of being equivalent to *some* ovate abstractive set, then they are equivalent.

By reason of the importance of this proposition a proof is given.

Proof. The two abstractive sets are *either* equivalent to the same ovate abstractive set, *or* to different ovate abstractive sets. In the former alternative, the required conclusion is obvious. In the latter alternative, let μ and ν be the two different ovate abstractive sets. Each of these sets, μ and ν, satisfies the twofold condition. We have to prove that they are equivalent to each other. Let M and N be any regions belonging to μ and ν respectively. Then since the convergent portions of the abstractive sets belonging to the various points of the given group must ultimately consist of regions all lying in M and all lying in N, it follows that M and N intersect. But, being oval, M and N have only one intersect, and all the points in question must be situated in it. Also this intersect is oval. Hence, by selecting such intersects, a third abstractive set can be found which satisfies the twofold condition and is covered both by μ and by ν. But since μ and ν are prime in reference to this condition, they are both of them equivalent to this third abstractive class. Hence they are equivalent to each other. Q.E.D.

Corollary. It follows that all abstractive sets, prime with respect to the same twofold condition of this type, belong to one geometrical element.

Definition 3. The single geometrical element defined, as in the enunciation of Assumption 2, by a set of two points is called a 'straight' segment between those end- [466] points. If the set comprise more than two points, the geometrical element is called 'flat.' 'Straight' segments are also included under the designation 'flat geometrical elements.'

If a set of points define a flat geometrical element, as in the enunciation of Assumption 2, it may happen that the same geometrical element is defined by some sub-set of those points. Hence we have the following definition:

Definition 4. A set of points, defining a flat geometrical element, is said to be in its lowest terms when it contains no sub-set defining the same flat geometrical element.

Assumption 3. No two sets of a finite number of points, both in their lowest terms, define the same flat geometrical element.

Definition 5. The locus of points incident in a 'straight segment' is called the 'straight line' between the end-points of the segment.

Definition 6. The locus of points incident in a flat geometrical element is called the 'content' of that element. It is also called a 'flat locus.'

Assumption 4. If any sub-set of points lie† in a flat locus, that sub-set also defines a flat locus contained within the given locus.

Definition 6.1.† A complete straight line is a locus of points such that, (i) the straight line joining any two members of the locus lies wholly within the locus, (ii) every sub-set in the locus, which is in its lowest terms, consists of a pair of points, (iii) no points can be added to the locus without loss of one, or both, of the characteristics (i) and (ii).

Definition 7. A triangle is the flat locus defined by three points which are not collinear. The three points are the angular points of the triangle.

Definition 8. A plane is a locus of non-collinear points such that, (i) the triangle defined by any three non-collinear members of the locus lies wholly within the locus, [467] (ii) any finite number of points in the locus lie in some triangle wholly contained in the locus, (iii) no set of points can be added to the locus without loss of one, or both, of the characteristics (i) and (ii).

Definition 9. A tetrahedron is the flat locus defined by four points which are not coplanar. The four points are called the corners of the tetrahedron.

Definition 10. A three-dimensional flat space is a locus of non-coplanar points such that, (i) the tetrahedron defined by any four non-coplanar points of the locus lies wholly within the locus, (ii) any finite number of points in the locus lie† in some tetrahedron wholly contained in the locus, (iii) no set of points can be added to the locus without the loss of one, or both, of the characteristics (i) and (ii).

Any further development of definitions and propositions will lead to mathematical details irrelevant to our immediate purposes. It suffices to have proved that characteristic properties of straight lines, planes, and three-dimensional flat spaces are discoverable in the extensive continuum without any recourse to measurement. The systematic character of a continuum depends on its possession of one or more ovate classes. Here, the particular case of a 'dimensional' ovate class has been considered.

SECTION IV

The importance of the notion of 'external connection' requires further discussion.

First, there is a purely geometrical question to be noted. The theory of the external connection of oval regions throws light on the Euclidean concept of 'evenness.' A pair of ovals (cf. Sect. III) can only be externally connected in a 'complete locus,' or in a single point. We now consider that species of 'complete loci' which can be the points common to the surfaces of a pair of ovals externally connected. We exclude the case of one-point contact. The species seems to have what the [468] Greeks meant by their term 'even' (ἴσος). On either side of such a locus, there is the interior of one oval and the exterior of another oval, so that the locus is 'even' in respect to the contrasted notions of 'concavity' and 'convexity.' It is an extra 'assumption'—provable or otherwise according to the particular logical development of the subject which may have been adopted—that all 'even' loci are 'flat,' and that all 'flat' loci are 'even.'

The second question for discussion concerns the physical importance of 'external connection.' So long as the atomic character of actual entities is unrecognized, the application of Zeno's method of argument makes it difficult to understand the notion of continuous transmission which reigns in physical science. But the concept of 'actual occasions,' adopted in the philosophy of organism, allows of the following explanation of physical transmission.

Let two actual occasions be termed 'contiguous' when the regions constituting their 'standpoints' are externally connected. Then by reason of the absence of intermediate actual occasions, the objectification of the antecedent occasion in the later occasion is peculiarly complete. There will be a set of antecedent, contiguous occasions objectified in any given occasion; and the abstraction which attends every objectification will merely be due to the necessary harmonizations of these objectifications. The objectifications of the more distant past will be termed 'mediate'; the contiguous occasions will have 'immediate' objectification. The mediate objectifications will be transmitted through various routes of successive immediate objectifications. Thus the notion of continuous transmission in science must be replaced by the notion of immediate transmission through a route of successive quanta of extensiveness. These quanta of extensiveness are the basic regions of successive contiguous occasions. It is not necessary for the philosophy of organism entirely to deny that there [469] is direct objectification of one occasion in a later occasion which is not contiguous to it. Indeed, the contrary opinion would seem the more natural for this doctrine. Provided that physical science maintains its denial of 'action at a distance,' the safer guess is that direct objectification is practically negligible except for contiguous occasions; but that this practical negligibility is a characteristic of the present cosmic epoch, without any metaphysical generality. Also a further distinction should be introduced. Physical prehensions fall into two species, pure physical prehensions and hybrid physical prehensions. A pure physical prehension is a prehension whose datum is an antecedent occasion objectified in respect to one of its own *physical* prehensions. A hybrid prehension has as its datum an antecedent occasion objectified in respect to a *conceptual* prehension. Thus a pure physical prehension is the transmission of physical feeling, while hybrid prehension is the transmission of mental feeling.

There is no reason to assimilate the conditions for hybrid prehensions to those for pure physical prehensions. Indeed the contrary hypothesis is the more natural. For the conceptual pole does not share in the coordinate divisibility of the physical pole, and the extensive continuum is derived from this coordinate divisibility. Thus the doctrine of immediate objectification for the mental poles and of mediate objectification for the physical poles seems most consonant to the philosophy of organism in its application to the present cosmic epoch. This conclusion has some empirical support, both from the evidence for peculiar instances of telepathy, and from the instinctive apprehension of a tone of feeling in ordinary social intercourse.

But of course such immediate objectification is also reinforced, or weakened, by routes of mediate objectification. Also pure and hybrid prehensions are integrated and thus hopelessly intermixed. Hence it will only be in exceptional circumstances that an immediate hybrid [470] prehension has sufficient vivid definition to receive a subjective form of clear conscious attention.

SECTION V

We have now traced the main characteristics of that real potentiality from which the first phase of a physical occasion takes its rise. These characteristics remain inwoven in the constitution of the subject throughout its adventure of self-formation. The actual entity is the product of the interplay of physical pole with mental pole. In this way, potentiality passes into actuality, and extensive relations mould qualitative content and objectifications of other particulars into a coherent finite experience.

In general, consciousness is negligible; and even the approach to it in vivid propositional feelings has failed to attain importance. Blind physical purposes reign. It is now obvious that blind prehensions, physical and mental, are the ultimate bricks of the physical universe. They are bound together within each actuality by the subjective unity of aim which governs their allied genesis and their final concrescence. They are also bound together beyond the limits of their peculiar subjects by the way in which the prehension in one subject becomes† the objective datum for the prehension in a later subject, thus objectifying the earlier subject for the later subject. The two types of interconnection of prehensions are themselves bound together in one common scheme, the relationship of extension.

It is by means of 'extension' that the bonds between prehensions take on the dual aspect of internal relations, which are yet in a sense external relations. It is evident that if the solidarity of the physical world is to be relevant to the description of its individual actualities, it can only be by reason of the fundamental internality of the relationships in question. On the other hand, if the individual discreteness of the actualities is to have its weight, there must be an aspect in these relationships [471] from which they can be conceived as external, that is, as bonds between divided things. The extensive scheme serves this double purpose.

The Cartesian subjectivism in its application to physical science became Newton's assumption of individually existent physical bodies, with merely external relationships. We diverge from Descartes by holding that what he has described as primary *attributes* of physical bodies† are really the forms of internal relationships *between* actual occasions, and *within* actual occasions. Such a change of thought is the shift from materialism to organism, as the basic idea of physical science.

In the language of physical science, the change from materialism to 'organic realism'—as the new outlook may be termed—is the displacement of the notion of static stuff by the notion of fluent energy. Such energy has its structure of action and flow, and is inconceivable apart from such structure. It is also conditioned by 'quantum' requirements. These are the reflections into physical science of the individual prehensions, and of the individual actual entities to which these prehensions belong. Mathematical physics translates the saying of Heraclitus, 'All things flow,' into its own language. It then becomes, All things are vectors. Mathematical physics also accepts the atomistic doctrine of Democritus. It translates it into the phrase, All flow of energy obeys 'quantum' conditions.

But what has vanished from the field of ultimate scientific conceptions is the notion of vacuous material existence with passive endurance, with primary individual attributes, and with accidental adventures. Some features of the physical world can be expressed in that way. But the concept is useless as an ultimate notion in science, and in cosmology.

CHAPTER IV
STRAINS

SECTION I

[472] THERE is nothing in the real world which is merely an inert fact. Every reality is there for feeling: it promotes feeling; and it is felt. Also there is nothing which belongs merely to the privacy of feeling of one individual actuality. All origination is private. But what has been thus originated, publicly pervades the world. Thus the geometrical facts concerning straight and flat loci are public facts characterizing the feelings of actual entities. It so happens that in this epoch of the universe the feelings involving them are of dominating importance. A feeling in which the forms exemplified in the datum concern geometrical, straight, and flat loci will be called a 'strain.' In a strain qualitative elements, other than the geometrical forms, express themselves as qualities implicated in those forms; also the forms are the forms ingredient in particular nexūs forming the objective data of the physical feelings in question. It is to be remembered that two points determine a complete straight line, that three non-collinear points determine a complete plane, and that four non-coplanar points determine a complete three-dimensional flat locus.

Thus a strain has a complex distribution of geometrical significance. There is the geometrical 'seat' which is composed of a limited set of loci which are certain sets of points. These points belong to the volume defining the standpoint of the experient subject. A strain is a complex integration of simpler feelings; and it includes in its complex character simpler feelings in which the qualities concerned are more particularly associated with [473] this seat. But the geometrical interest which dominates the growth of a strain lifts into importance the complete lines, planes, and three-dimensional flats, which are defined by the seat of the strain. In the process of integration, these wider geometrical elements acquire implication with the qualities originated in the simpler stages. The process is an example of the Category of Transmutation; and is to be explained by the intervention of intermediate conceptual feelings. Thus extensive regions, which are penetrated by the geometrical elements concerned, acquire objectification by means of the qualities and geometrical relations derived from the simpler feelings. This type of objectification is characterized by the close association of qualities and definite geometrical relations. It is the basis of the so-called 'projection' of sensa. This projection of sensa in a strain takes many forms according to the differences among various strains.

Sometimes the 'seat' retains its individual importance; sometimes in the final synthesis it has been almost eliminated from the final synthesis of feelings into the one strain. Sometimes the whole extensive region indicated by the wider geometrical elements is only vaguely geometricized. In this case, there is feeble geometrical indication: the strain then takes the vague form of feeling certain qualities which are vaguely external. Sometimes the extensive region is geometricized without any corresponding elimination of importance from the seat. In this case,† there is a dual reference, to the seat *here*, and to some objectified region *there*. The *here* is usually some portion of an animal body; whereas the geometricized region may be within, or without, the animal body concerned.

It is obvious that important feelings of strain involve complex processes of concrescence. They are accordingly only to be found in comparatively high-grade actual entities. They do not in any respect necessarily involve consciousness, or even that approach to consciousness which we associate with life. But we shall find that the [474] behaviour of enduring physical objects is only explicable by reference to the peculiarities of their strains. On the other hand, the occurrences in empty space require less emphasis on any peculiar ordering of strains. But the growth of ordered physical complexity is dependent on the growth of ordered relationships among strains. Fundamental equations in mathematical physics, such as Maxwell's electromagnetic equations, are expressions of the ordering of strains throughout the physical universe.

SECTION II

Presentational immediacy is our perception of the contemporary world by means of the senses. It is a physical feeling. But it is a physical feeling of a complex type to the formation of which conceptual feelings, more primitive physical feelings, and transmutation have played their parts amid processes of integration. Its objective datum is a nexus of contemporary events, under the definite illustration of certain qualities and relations: these qualities and relations are prehended with the subjective form derived from the primitive physical feelings, thus becoming our 'private' sensations. Finally, as in the case of all physical feelings, this complex derivative physical feeling acquires integration with the valuation inherent in its conceptual realization† as a type of experience.

Naïve common sense insists, first, on the 'subject' entertaining this feeling; and, secondly, on the analytic components in the order: (i) region in contemporary world as datum, (ii) sensations as derivative from, and illustrative of, this datum, (iii) integral feeling involving these elements, (iv) appreciative subjective form, (v) interpretative subjective form, (vi) purposive subjective form. But this analysis of presentational immediacy has not exhausted the content of the feeling. For we feel *with the body*.

There may be some further specialization into a particular organ of sensation; but in any case the *'withness' of the body* is an ever-present, [475] though elusive, element in our perceptions of presentational immediacy. This 'withness' is the trace of the origination of the feeling concerned, enshrined by that feeling in its subjective form and in its objective datum. But in itself this 'withness of the body' can be isolated as a component feeling in the final 'satisfaction.' From this point of view, the body, or its organ of sensation, becomes the objective datum of a component feeling; and this feeling has its own subjective form. Also this feeling is physical, so that we must look for an eternal object, to be a determinant of the definiteness of the body, as objective datum. This component feeling will be called the feeling of bodily efficacy. It is more primitive than the feeling of presentational immediacy which issues from it. Both in common sense and in physiological theory, this bodily efficacy is a component presupposed by the presentational immediacy and leading up to it. Thus, in the immediate subject, the presentational immediacy is to be conceived as originated in a late phase, by the synthesis of the feeling of bodily efficacy with other feelings. We have now to consider the nature of the other feelings, and the complex eternal object concerned in the feeling of bodily efficacy.

In the first place, this eternal object must be partially identified with the eternal object in the final feeling of presentational immediacy. The whole point of the connection between the two feelings is that the presentational immediacy is derivative from the bodily efficacy. The present perception is strictly inherited from the antecedent bodily functioning, unless all physiological teaching is to be abandoned. Both eternal objects are highly complex; and the complex elements of the second eternal object must at least be involved in the complex elements of the former eternal object.

This complex eternal object is analysable into a sense-datum and a geometrical pattern. In physics, the geometrical pattern appears as a state of strain of that actual occasion in the body which is the subject of the [476] feeling. But this feeling of bodily efficacy in the final percipient is the reenaction of an antecedent feeling by an antecedent actual entity in the body. Thus in this antecedent entity there is a feeling concerned with the same sense-datum and a highly analogous state of strain. The feeling must be a 'strain' in the sense defined in the previous section. Now this strain involves a geometricized region, which in this case also involves a *'focal' region* as part of itself. This 'focal' region is a region of dense concurrence of straight lines defined by the 'seat.' It is the region onto which there is so-called 'projection.'

These lines enter into feeling through a process of integration of yet simpler feelings which primarily concern the 'seat' of the pattern. These lines have a twofold function as determinants of the feeling. They define the 'strain' of the feeler, and they define the focal region which they thus relate to the feeler. In so far as we are merely considering an abstract pattern, we are dealing with an abstract eternal object. But as a determinant of a concrete feeling in a concrete percipient, we are dealing with the feeling as relating its subject (which includes the 'seat' in its volume) to a definite spatial region (the focal region) external to itself. This definite contemporary focal region is a nexus which is part of the objective datum. Thus the feeling of bodily efficacy is the feeling of the sense-datum as generally implicated in the whole region (of antecedent 'seats' and focal regions) geometrically defined by the inherited strains. This patterned region is peculiarly dominated by the final 'seat' in the body of the feeler, and by the final 'focal' region. Thus the sense-datum has a general spatial relation, in which two spatial regions are dominant. Feelings of this sort are inherited by many strands from the antecedent bodily nerves. But in considering one definite feeling of presentational immediacy, these many strands of transmission of bodily efficacy, in their final deliverance to the ultimate percipient, converge upon the same focal region as picked out by the many bodily 'strains.'

[477] In the integration of these feelings a double act of transmutation is achieved. In each of the successive feelings transmitted along the successive actual entities of a bodily nervous strand there are two regions mainly concerned; and there is a relation between them constituted by intermediate regions picked out by the linkage of the pattern. One region is the focal region already discussed, the other region is the seat in the immediate subject, constituting its geometrical standpoint. The 'strain' of the final actual entity defines the 'seat' and the 'focal region' and the intermediary regions, and more vaguely the whole of a 'presented' space. This final feeling of bodily strain—in the sense of 'strain' defined in the previous section—is the last of a route of analogous feelings inherited one from the other along the series of bodily occasions along some nerve, or other path in the body. There will be parallel routes of such analogous feelings, which finally converge with concurrent reinforcement upon the single occasion, or route of occasions, which is the ultimate percipient.

Each of these bodily strain-feelings defines its own seat and its own focal region and intermediaries. The sense-datum is vaguely associated with the external world as thus felt and defined. But as such feelings are 'transmuted,' either gradually, or at critical nodes in the body, there is an increasing development of special emphasis. Now emphasis is valuation, and can only be changed by renewed valuation. But valuation arises in conceptual feelings. The conceptual counterpart of these physical feelings can be analysed into many conceptual feelings, associating the sense-datum with various regions defined by the strain. This conceptual feeling, by its reference to definite regions, belongs to the secondary type termed 'propositional feelings.' One subordinate propositional feeling associates the sense-datum with the 'seat' of the feeler, another with the 'focal' region of the feeler, another with the intermediary region of the feeler, another with the seats of the antecedent elements of the [478] nervous strand, and so on. The total association of the sense-datum with space-time is analysable into a bewildering variety of associations with definite regions, contemporary and antecedent. In general, and apart from high-grade organisms, this spatio-temporal association of the sense-datum is integrated into a vague sense of externality. The component valuations have in such cases failed to differentiate themselves into grades of intensity. But in high-grade† cases, in which presentational immediacy is prominent, one of three cases happens. Either (i) the association of the sense-datum with the seats of some antecedent sets of feelers is exclusively emphasized, or (ii) the association of the sense-datum with the focal region of the final percipient is exclusively emphasized, or (iii) the association of the sense-datum both with the seats of antecedent feelers and with the focal region of the immediate feeler is emphasized.

But these regions are not apprehended in abstraction from the general spatio-temporal continuum. The prehension of a region is always the prehension of systematic elements in the extensive relationship between the seat of the immediate feeler and the region concerned. When these valuations have been effected, the Category of Transmutation provides for the transmission to the succeeding subject of a feeling of these regions qualified by (i.e., contrasted with) that sense-datum. In the first case, there are purely bodily sensations; in the second case, there are 'projected' sensations, involving regions of contemporary space beyond the body; in the third case, there are both bodily feelings and sensations externally projected. Thus in the case of all sensory feeling, there is initial privacy of conceptual emphasis passing into publicity of physical feeling.

Thus, by the agency of the Category of Transmutation, there are two types of feelings, for which the objective datum is a nexus with undiscriminated actual entities. The feelings of the first type are feelings of 'causal efficacy'; and those of the second type are those of 'presenta- [479] tional immediacy.' In the first type, the analogous elements in the various feelings of the various actualities of the bodily nexus are transmuted into a feeling ascribed to the bodily nexus as one entity. In the second type, the transmutation is more elaborate and shifts the nexus concerned from the antecedent bodily nexus (i.e., the 'seat') to the contemporary focal nexus.

Both these types of feeling are the outcome of a complex process of massive simplification which is characteristic of higher grades of actual entities. They apparently have but slight importance in the constitutions of actual occasions in empty space; but they have dominating importance in the physical feelings belonging to the life-history† of enduring organisms —the inorganic and organic, alike.

In respect to the sensa concerned, there is a gradual transformation of their functions as they pass from occasion to occasion along a route of inheritance up to some final high-grade experient. In their most primitive form of functioning, a sensum is felt physically with emotional enjoyment of its sheer individual essence. For example, red is felt with emotional enjoyment of its sheer redness. In this primitive prehension we have aboriginal physical feeling in which the subject feels itself as enjoying redness. This is Hume's 'impression of sensation' stripped of all spatial relations with other such impressions. In so far as they spring up in this primitive, aboriginal way, they—in Hume's words—"arise in the soul from unknown causes." But in fact we can never isolate such ultimate irrationalities. In our experience, as in distinct analysis, physical feelings are always derived from some antecedent experient. Occasion B prehends occasion A as an antecedent subject experiencing a sensum with emotional intensity. Also B's subjective form of emotion is conformed to A's subjective form. Thus there is a vector transmission of emotional feeling of a sensum from A to B. In this way B feels the sensum as derived from A and feels it with an emotional form [480] also derived from A. This is the most primitive form of the feeling of causal efficacy. In physics it is the transmission of a form of energy. In the bodily transmission from occasion to occasion of a high-grade animal body, there is a gradual modification of these functions of sensa. In their most primitive functioning for the initial occasions within the animal body, they are qualifications of emotion—types of energy, in the language of physics;† in their final functioning for the high-grade experient occasion at the end of the route, they are qualities 'inherent' in a presented, contemporary nexus. In the final percipient any conscious feeling of the primitive emotional functioning of the sensum is often entirely absent. But this is not always the case; for example, the perception of a red cloak may often be associated with a feeling of red irritation.

To return to Hume's doctrine (cf. *Treatise*, Part III, Sect. V) of the origination of 'impressions of sensation' from unknown causes, it is first necessary to distinguish logical priority from physical priority. Undoubtedly an impression of sensation is logically the simplest of physical prehensions. It is the percipient occasion feeling the sensum as participating in its own concrescence. This is the enjoyment of a private sensation.

There is a logical simplicity about such a sensation which makes it the primitive, aboriginal type of physical feeling. But there are two objections to Hume's doctrine which assigns to them a physical priority. First, there is the empirical objection. Hume's theory of a complex of such impressions elaborated into a supposition of a common physical world is entirely contrary to naïve experience. We find ourselves in the double rôle of agents and patients in a common world, and the conscious recognition of impressions of sensation is the work of sophisticated elaboration. This is also Locke's doctrine in the third and fourth books of his *Essay*. The child first dimly elucidates the complex externality of particu- [481] lar things exhibiting a welter of forms of definiteness, and then disentangles his impressions of these forms in isolation. A young man does not initiate his experience by dancing with impressions of sensation, and then proceed to conjecture a partner. His experience takes the converse route. The un-empirical character of the philosophical school derived from Hume cannot be too often insisted upon. The true empirical doctrine is that physical feelings are in their origin vectors, and that the genetic process of concrescence introduces the elements which emphasize privacy.

Secondly, Hume's doctrine is necessarily irrational. For if the impressions of sensation arise from unknown causes (cf. Hume, *loc. cit.*) a stop is put to the rationalistic search for a rational cosmology. Such a cosmology requires that metaphysics shall provide a doctrine of relevance between a form and any occasion in which it participates. If there be no such doctrine, all hope of approximating to a rational view of the world vanishes.

Hume's doctrine has no recommendation except the pleasure which it gives to its adherents.

The philosophy of organism provides for this relevance by means of two doctrines, (i) the doctrine of God embodying a basic completeness of appetition, and (ii) the doctrine of each occasion effecting a concrescence of the universe, including God. Then, by the Category of Conceptual Reproduction, the vector prehensions of God's appetition, and of other occasions, issue in the mental pole of conceptual prehensions; and by integration of this pole with the pure physical prehensions there arise the primitive physical feelings of sensa, with their subjective forms,† emotional and purposive. These feelings, with their primitive simplicity, arise into distinctness by reason of the elimination effected by this integration of the vector prehensions with the conceptual appetitions. Such primitive feelings cannot be separated from their subjective forms. The subject never loses its triple character of recipient, patient, and agent. These primitive feel- [482] ings have already been considered under the name of 'physical purposes' (cf. Part III, Ch. V). They correspond to Hume's 'impressions of sensation.' But they do not originate the process of experience.

We see that a feeling of presentational immediacy comes into being by reason of an integration of a conceptual feeling drawn from bodily efficacy with a bare regional feeling which is also a component in a complex feeling of bodily efficacy. Also this bare regional feeling is reinforced with the general regional feeling which is the whole of our *direct* physical feeling of the contemporary world; and the conceptual feeling is reinforced by the generation of physical purpose. This integration takes the form of the creative imputation of the complex eternal object, ingredient in the bodily efficacy, onto some contemporary focal region felt in the strain-feeling. Also the subjective form is transmitted from the conceptual valuation and the derivate 'physical purpose.' But this subjective form is that suitable to the bodily efficacy out of which it has arisen. Thus the mere region with its imputed eternal object is felt as though there had been a feeling of *its* efficacy. But there is no mutual efficacy of contemporary regions. This transference of subjective form is termed 'symbolic transference.' [1]

An additional conceptual feeling, with its valuation, arises from this physical feeling of presentational immediacy. It is the conceptual feeling of *a* region *thus* characterized. This is the aesthetic valuation proper to the bare objective datum of the presentational immediacy. But this valuation is less primitive than that gained from the conceptual prehension by symbolic transference. The primitive subjective form includes a valuation *as though* the contemporary region, by its own proper constitution, were causally effective on the percipient sub- [483] ject. The secondary valuation is the aesthetic appreciation of the bare fact: this bare fact is merely *that* region, *thus* qualified. Thus the contemporary world, as felt through the senses, is valued for its own sake, by means of a later conceptual feeling; but it is also valued for its derivation from antecedent efficacy, by means of transmutation from earlier conceptual feeling combined with derivate 'physical purpose.'

But none of these operations can be segregated from nature into the subjective privacy of a mind. Mental and physical operations are incurably intertwined; and both issue into publicity, and are derived from publicity. The vector character of prehension is fundamental.

SECTION III

It is the mark of a high-grade organism to eliminate, by negative prehension, the irrelevant accidents in its environment, and to elicit massive attention to every variety of systematic order. For this purpose, the Category of Transmutation is the master-principle. By its operation each nexus can be prehended in terms of the analogies among its own members, or in terms of analogies among the members of other nexūs but yet relevant to it. In this way the organism in question suppresses the mere multiplicities of things, and designs its own contrasts. The canons of art are merely the expression, in specialized forms, of the requisites for depth of experience. The principles of morality are allied to the canons of art, in that they also express, in another connection, the same requisites. Owing to the principle that contemporary actual entities occur in relative independence, the nexūs of contemporary actual entities are peculiarly favourable for this transference of systematic qualities from other nexūs to themselves. For a difficulty arises in the operation of the Category of Transmutation, when a characteristic prevalent among the individual entities of one nexus is to be transferred to another nexus treated as a unity. The difficulty is that the individual actuali- [484] ties of the recipient nexus are also

[1] Cf. my three Barbour-Page lectures, *Symbolism*, at the University of Virginia (New York: Macmillan, 1927, and Cambridge University Press, 1928);† and also above, Part II, Ch. VIII.

respectively objectified in the percipient subject by systematic characteristics which equally demand the transference to their own nexus; but this
is the nexus which should be the recipient of the other transference. Thus
there are competing qualities struggling to effect the objectification of the
same nexus. The result is attenuation and elimination.

When the recipient nexus is composed of entities contemporary with
the percipient subject, this difficulty vanishes. For the contemporary entities do not enter into the constitution of the percipient subject by objectification through any of their own feelings. Thus their only direct connection with the subject is their implication in the same extensive scheme.
Thus a nexus of actual entities, contemporary with the percipient subject,
puts up no alternative characteristics to inhibit the transference to it of
characteristics from antecedent nexūs.

A high-grade percipient is necessarily an occasion in the historic route
of an enduring object. If this route is to propagate itself successfully into
the future, it is above all things necessary that its decisions in the immediate occasion should have the closest relevance to the concurrent happenings among contemporary occasions. For these contemporary entities
will, in the near future, form the 'immediate past' for the future embodiment of the enduring object. This 'immediate past' is of overwhelming influence; for all routes of transmission from the more remote past must
pass through it. Thus the contemporary occasions tell nothing; and yet
are of supreme importance for the survival of the enduring object.

This gap in the experience of the percipient subject is bridged by presentational immediacy. This type of experience is the lesson of the past reflected into the present. The more important contemporary occasions
are those in the near neighborhood. Their actual worlds [485] are practically identical with that of the percipient subject. The percipient prehends the nexūs of contemporary occasions by the mediation of eternal
objects which it inherits from its own past. Also it selects the contemporary
nexūs thus prehended by the efficacy of strains whose focal regions are
important elements in the past of those nexūs. Thus, for successful organisms, presentational immediacy—though it yields no direct experience
about the contemporary world, and though in unfortunate instances the
experience which it does yield may be irrelevant—does yield experience
which expresses how the contemporary world has in fact emerged from
its own past.

Presentational immediacy works on the principle that it is better to obtain information about the contemporary world, even if occasionally it be
misleading.

SECTION IV

Depth of experience is gained by concentrating emphasis on the systematic structural systems in the environment, and discarding individual
variations. Every element of systematic structure is emphasized, every in-

dividual aberration is pushed into the background. The variety sought is the variety of structures, and never the variety of individuals. For example,† we neglect empty space in comparison with the structural systematic nexus which is the historic route of an enduring object. In every possible way, the more advanced organisms simplify their experience so as to emphasize those nexūs with some element of tightness of systematic structure.

In pursuance of this principle, the regions, geometricized by the various strains in such an organism, not only lie in the contemporary world,† but they coalesce so as to emphasize one unified locus in the contemporary world. This selected locus is penetrated by the straight lines, the planes, and the three-dimensional flat loci associated with the strains. This is the 'strain-locus' belonging to an occasion in the history of an enduring object. [486] This occasion is the immediate percipient subject under consideration. Each such occasion has its one strain-locus which serves for all its strains. The focal regions of the various strains all lie within this strain-locus, and are in general distinct. But the strain-locus as a whole is common to all the strains. Each occasion lies in its own strain-locus.

The meaning of the term 'rest' is the relation of an occasion to its strain-locus, if there be one. An occasion with no unified strain-locus has no dominating locus with which it can have the relationship of 'rest.' An occasion 'rests' in its strain-locus. This is why it is nonsense to ask of an occasion in empty space whether it be 'at rest' in reference to some locus. For, since such occasions have no strain-loci, the relationship of 'rest' does not apply to them. The strain-locus is the locus which is thoroughly geometricized by the strain-feelings of the percipient occasion. It must have the property of being continent of straight lines, and of flat loci of all dimensions. Thus its boundaries will be three-dimensional† flat loci, non-intersecting. A strain-locus approximates to a three-dimensional flat locus; but in fact it is four-dimensional, with a time-thickness.

SECTION V

Reviewing the discussion in the preceding sections of this chapter and of Chapter IV of Part II, we note that, in reference to any one actual occasion M, seven (but cf. Section VIII†) distinct considerations define loci composed of other actual occasions. In the first place, there are three loci defined by causal efficacy, namely, the 'causal past' of M, the 'causal future' of M, and the 'contemporaries' of M. An actual occasion P, belonging to M's *causal past*, is objectified for M by a perspective representation of its own (i.e., P's) qualities of feeling and intensities of feeling. There is a quantitative and qualitative vector flow of feeling from P to M; and in this way, what P is subjectively, belongs to M objectively. An [487] actual occasion Q, belonging to M's *causal future*, is in the converse relation to M, compared to P's relation. For the causal future is composed of those actual occasions which will have M in their respective causal pasts.†

Actual occasions R and S,† which are *contemporary* with M, are those actual occasions which lie neither in M's causal past, nor in M's causal future. The peculiarity of the locus of contemporaries of M is that any two of its members, such as R and S, *need* not be contemporaries of each other. They *may* be mutually contemporaries, but not necessarily. It is evident from the form of the definition of 'contemporary,' that if R be contemporary with M, then M is contemporary with R. This peculiarity of the locus of M's contemporaries—that R and S may be both contemporaries of M, but not contemporaries of each other—points to another set of loci. A 'duration' is a locus of actual occasions, such that (α) any two members of the locus are contemporaries, and (β) that any actual occasion, not belonging to the duration, is in the causal past or causal future of some members of the duration.

A duration is a complete locus of actual occasions in 'unison of becoming,' or in 'concrescent unison.' It is the old-fashioned 'present state of the world.' In reference to a given duration, D, the actual world is divided into three mutually exclusive loci. One of these loci is the duration D itself. Another of these loci is composed of actual occasions which lie in the past of some members of D: this locus is the 'past of the duration D.' The remaining locus is composed of actual occasions which lie in the future of some members of D: this locus is the 'future of the duration D.'

By its definition, a duration which contains an occasion M† must lie within the locus of the contemporaries of M. According to the classical pre-relativistic notions of time, there would be only one duration including M, and it would contain all M's contemporaries. According to modern relativistic views,† we must admit that there are many durations including M—in fact, an infinite [488] number, so that no one of them contains all M's contemporaries.

Thus the past of a duration D includes the whole past of any actual occasion belonging to D, such as M for example, and it also includes *some* of M's contemporaries. Also the future of the duration D includes the whole future of M, and also includes *some* of M's contemporaries.

So far, starting from an actual occasion M, we find six loci, or types of loci, defined purely in terms of notions derived from 'causal efficacy.' These loci are, M's causal past, M's causal future, M's contemporaries, the set of durations defined by M; and finally, taking any one such duration which we call D as typical, there is D's past, and D's future. Thus there are the three definite loci, the causal past, the causal future,‡ and the contemporaries, which are defined uniquely by M; and there are the set of durations defined by M, and the set of 'durational pasts' and the set of 'durational futures.' The paradox which has been introduced by the modern theory of relativity is twofold. First, the actual occasion M does not, as a general characteristic of all actual occasions, define a unique duration; and secondly,† such a unique duration, if defined, does not include all the contemporaries of M.

But among the set of durations, there may be one with a unique association with M. For the mode of presentational immediacy objectifies for M† the actual occasions within one particular duration. This is the 'presented duration.' Such a presented duration is an inherent factor in the character of an 'enduring physical object.' It is practically identical with the strain-locus. This locus is the reason why there is a certain absoluteness in the notions of rest, velocity, and acceleration. For this presented duration is the spatialized world in which the physical object is *at rest*, at least momentarily for its occasion M. This spatialized world is objectified for M by M's own conditioned range of feeling-tones which have been inherited from the causal past of the actual occasion [489] in question, namely, of M. Thus the presented duration is with peculiar vividness part of the character of the actual occasion. A historic route of actual occasions,† each with its presented duration, constitutes a physical object.

Our partial consciousness of the objectifications of the presented duration constitutes our knowledge of the present world, so far as it is derived from the senses. Remembering that objectifications constitute the objective conditions from which an actual occasion (M) initiates its successive phases of feeling, we must admit that, in the most general sense, the objectifications express the causality by which the external world fashions the actual occasion in question. Thus the objectifications of the presented duration represent a recovery by its contemporaries of a very real efficacy in the determination of M. It is true that the eternal objects which effect this objectification belong to the feeling-tones which M derives from the past. But it is a past which is largely common to M and to the presented duration. Thus by the intermediacy of the past, the presented duration has its efficacy in the production of M. This efficacy does not derogate from the principle of the independence of contemporary occasions. For the contemporary occasions in the presented duration are only efficacious through the feeling-tones of their sources, and not through their own immediate feeling-tones.

Thus in so far as Bergson ascribes the 'spatialization' of the world to a distortion introduced by the intellect, he is in error. This spatialization is a real factor in the physical constitution of every actual occasion belonging to the life-history† of an enduring physical object. For actual occasions in so-called 'empty space,' there is no reason to believe that any duration has been singled out for spatialization; that is to say, that physical perception in the mode of presentational immediacy is negligible for such occasions. The reality of the rest and the motion of enduring physical objects depends on this spatializa- [490] tion for occasions in their historic routes. The presented duration is the duration in respect to which the enduring object is momentarily at rest. It is that duration which is the strain-locus of that occasion in the life-history of the enduring object.

CHAPTER V

MEASUREMENT

SECTION I

[491] THE identification of the strain-locus with a duration is only an approximation based upon empirical evidence. Their definitions are entirely different. A duration is a complete set of actual occasions, such that all the members are mutually contemporary one with the other. This property is expressed by the statement that the members enjoy 'unison of immediacy.' The completeness consists in the fact that no other actual occasion can be added to the set without loss of this unison of immediacy. Every occasion outside the set is in the past or in the future of some members of the set, and is contemporary with other members of the set. According as an occasion is in the past, or the future, of some members of a duration, the occasion is said to be in the past, or in the future, of that duration.

No occasion can be both in the past and in the future† of a duration. Thus a duration forms a barrier in the world between its past and its future. Any route of occasions, in which adjacent members are contiguous, and such that it includes members of the past, and members of the future, of a duration, must also include one or more members of that duration. This is the notion of a duration, which has already been explained (cf. Part II, Ch. IV, Sects. VIII and IX).

The definition of a strain-locus (cf. previous chapter) depends entirely on the geometrical elements which are the elements of geometric form in the objectification of a nexus including the experient occasion in question. These [492] elements are (i) a set of points, within the volume of the regional standpoint of the experient occasion, and (ii) the set of straight lines defined by all the pairs of these points. The set of points is the 'seat' of the strain; the set of straight lines is the set of 'projectors.' The complete region penetrated by the 'projectors' is the strain-locus. A strain-locus is bounded by two 'flat' three-dimensional surfaces. When some members of the seat have a special function in the strain-feeling, the projectors which join pairs of these points may define a subordinate region in the strain-locus; this subordinate region is termed the 'focal region.'

The strain-loci in the present epoch seem to be confined to the contemporaries of their experient occasions. In fact 'strain-loci' occur as essential components for perception in the mode of presentational immediacy.

In this mode of perception there is a unique strain-locus for each such experient. Rest and motion are definable by reference to real strain-loci, and to potential strain-loci. Thus the molecules, forming material bodies for which the science of dynamics is important, may be presumed to have unique strain-loci associated with their prehensions.

This recapitulation of the theories of durations and strain-loci brings out the entire disconnection of their definitions. There is no reason, derivable from these definitions, why there should be any close association between the strain-locus of an experient occasion and any duration including that occasion among its members. It is an empirical fact that mankind invariably conceives the presented world as consisting of such a duration. This is the contemporary world as immediately perceived by the senses. But close association does not necessarily involve unqualified identification. It is permissible, in framing a cosmology to accord with scientific theory, to assume that the associated pair, strain-locus and presented duration, do not involve one and the same extensive region. From the point of view of conscious per- [493] ception, the divergence may be negligible, though important for scientific theory.

SECTION II

The† notions which have led to the phraseology characterizing the 'projected' sensa as 'secondary qualities' arise out of a fundamental difference between 'strain-loci' and their associated 'presented durations.' A strain-locus is entirely determined by the experient in question. It extends beyond that experient indefinitely, although defined by geometrical elements entirely within the extensive region which is the standpoint of the experient. The 'seat' of the strain-locus, which is a set of points within this region, is sufficient to effect this definition of the complete strain-locus by the aid of the straight lines termed the 'projectors.' These straight lines are nexūs whose geometrical relations are forms ingredient in a strain-feeling with these nexūs as data. Presentational immediacy arises from the integration of a strain-feeling and a 'physical purpose,' so that, by the Category of Transmutation, the sensum involved in the 'physical purpose' is projected onto some external focal region defined by projectors.

It is to be noted that this doctrine of presentational immediacy and of the strain-locus entirely depends upon a definition of straight lines in terms of mere extensiveness. If the definition depends upon the actual physical occasions beyond the experient, the experient should find the actual physical structures of his environment a block, or an assistance, to his 'projection' to focal regions beyond them. The projection of sensa in presentational immediacy depends entirely upon the state of the brain and upon systematic geometrical relations characterizing the brain. How the brain is excited, whether by visual stimuli through the eye, or by auditory stimuli through the ear, or by the excessive consumption of alcohol, or by hysterical emotion, is completely indifferent; granted the proper excitement of the brain, the experient will per- [494] ceive some definite contemporary region illustrated by the projected sensa. The indifference of presentational immediacy to contemporary actualities in the environment cannot be exaggerated. It is only by reason of the fortunate dependence of the experient and of these contemporary actualities on a common past, that presentational immediacy is more than a barren aesthetic display. It does display something, namely, the real extensiveness of the contemporary world. It involves the contemporary actualities but only objectifies them as conditioned by extensive relations. It displays a system pervading the world, a world including and transcending the experient. It is a vivid display of systematic real potentiality, inclusive of the experient and reaching beyond it. In so far as straight lines can only be defined in terms of measurements, requiring particular actual occasions for their performance, the theory of geometry lacks the requisite disengagement from particular physical fact. The requisite geometrical forms can then only be introduced after examination of the particular actual occasions required for measurement. But the theory of 'projection,' explained above, requires that the definition of a complete straight line be logically prior to the particular actualities in the extensive environment. This requisite has been supplied by the preceding theory of straight lines (cf. Ch. III‡). The projectors do depend upon the one experient occasion. But even this dependence merely requires that component feelings of that occasion should participate in certain geometric elements, namely, a set of points, and the straight lines defined by them, among their data. Thus, according to this explanation, presentational immediacy is the mode in which vivid feelings of contemporary geometrical relations, with especial emphasis on certain 'focal' regions, enter into experience.

This doctrine is what common sense always assumes. When we see a coloured shape, it may be a real man, or a ghost, or an image behind a mirror, or a hallucination; [495] but whatever it be, *there* it *is*—exhibiting to us a certain region of external space. If we are gazing at a nebula, a thousand light-years away, we are not looking backward through a thousand years. Such ways of speaking are interpretative phrases, diverting attention from the primary fact of direct experience, observing the illumination of a contemporary patch of the heavens. In philosophy, it is of the utmost importance to beware of the interpretative vagaries of language. Further, the extent of the patch illuminated will depend entirely upon the magnifying power of the telescope used. The correlation of the patch, thus seen through the telescope, with a smaller patch, defined by direct 'projection' from the observer, is again a question of scientific interpretation. This smaller patch is what we are *said* to have seen 'magnified' by the use of the telescope. What we *do* see is the bigger patch, and we correlate it with the smaller patch by theoretical calculation. The scientific explanation neglects the telescope and the larger patch really seen, and considers them as merely instrumental intermediaries. It concentrates on the contemporary smaller patch, and finally deserts even that patch in favour of another region a thousand years in the past. This explanation is only one illustration of the way in which so-called statements of direct observation are, through and through, merely interpretative statements of simple direct experience. When we say that we have seen a man, we may mean that we have seen a patch which we believe to be a man. In this case, our total relevant experience may be more than that of bare sight. In Descartes' phraseology, our experience of the external world embraces not only an *'inspectio'* of the *'realitas objectiva'* in the prehensions in question, but also a *'judicium'* which calls into play the totality of our experience beyond those prehensions. The objection to this doctrine of 'presentational immediacy'—that it presupposes a definition of straight lines, freed from dependence on external actualities—has been removed by the production of such a definition in Ch. III.‡ [496] Of course the point of the definition is to demonstrate that the extensive continuum, apart from the particular actualities into which it is atomized, includes in its systematic structure the relationships of regions expressed by straight lines. These relationships are *there* for perception.

SECTION III

The Cartesian doctrine of the *'realitas objectiva'* attaching to presentational immediacy is entirely denied by the modern doctrine of private psychological fields. Locke's doctrine of 'secondary qualities' is a halfway house to the modern position, and indeed so is Descartes' own position considered as a whole. Descartes' doctrine on this point is obscure, and is interpretable as according with that of the philosophy of organism. But Locke conceives the sensa as purely mental additions to the facts of physical nature. Both philosophers conceive the physical world as in *essential* independence of the mental world, though the two worlds have ill-defined *accidental* relationships. According to the philosophy of organism, physical and mental operations are inextricably intertwined; also we find the sensa functioning as forms participating in the vector prehensions of one occasion by another; and finally in tracing the origin of presentational immediacy, we find mental operations transmuting the functions of sensa so as to transfer them from being participants in causal prehensions into participants in presentational† prehensions. But throughout the whole story, the sensa are participating in nature as much as anything else. It is the function of mentality to modify the physical participation of eternal objects: the case of presentational prehensions is only one conspicuous example. The whole doctrine of mentality—from the case of God downwards—is that it is a modifying agency. But Descartes and Locke abandon the *'realitas objectiva'* so far as sensa are concerned (but for Descartes, cf. *Meditation I*,† "it is certain all the same that the colours of [497] which this is composed are necessarily real"), and hope to save it so far as extensive relations are concerned. This is an impossible compromise. It was easily swept aside by Berkeley and Hume. (Cf. *Enquiry,* Sect. XII, Part I.† Hume,† with obvious truth, refers to Berkeley as the originator of this train of argument.) The modern doctrine of 'private psychological fields' is the logical result of Hume's doctrine, though it is a result which Hume 'as an agent' refused to accept. This modern doctrine raises a great difficulty in the interpretation of modern science. For all exact observation is made in these private psychological fields. It is then no use talking about instruments and laboratories and physical energy. What is really being observed are narrow bands of colour-sensa in the private psychological space of colour-vision. The impressions of sensation which collectively form this entirely private experience 'arise in the soul from unknown causes.' The spectroscope is a myth, the radiant energy is a myth, the observer's eye is a myth, the observer's brain is a myth, and the observer's record of his experiment on a sheet of paper is a myth. When,† some months later, he reads his notes to a learned society, he has a new visual experience of black marks on a white background in a new private psychological field. And again, these experiences arise in his soul 'from unknown causes.' It is merely 'custom' which leads him to connect his earlier with his later experiences.

All exact measurements are, on this theory, observations in such private psychological fields.

Hume himself 'as an agent' refused to accept this doctrine. The conclusion is that Hume's account of experience is unduly simplified. This is the conclusion adopted by the philosophy of organism.

But one important fact does emerge from the discussion: that all exact measurements concern perceptions in the mode of presentational immediacy; and that such observations purely concern the systematic geometric forms of the environment, forms defined by projectors [498] from the 'seat' of the strain and irrespective of the actualities which constitute the environment. The contemporary actualities of the world are irrelevant to these observations. All scientific measurements merely concern the systematic real potentiality out of which these actualities arise. This is the meaning of the doctrine that physical science is solely concerned with the mathematical relations of the world.

These mathematical relations belong to the systematic order of extensiveness which characterizes the cosmic epoch in which we live. The societies of enduring objects—electrons, protons, molecules, material bodies —at once sustain that order and arise out of it. The mathematical relations involved in presentational immediacy thus belong equally to the world perceived and to the nature† of the percipient. They are, at the same time, public fact and private experience.

The perceptive mode of presentational immediacy is in one sense barren. So far as—apart from symbolic transference—it discloses the contemporary world, that world, thus objectified, is devoid of all elements constitutive of subjective form, elements emotional, appreciative, purposive. The bonds of the objectified nexus only exhibit the definiteness of mathematical relations.

But in another sense this perceptive mode has overwhelming significance. It exhibits that complex of systematic mathematical relations which participate in all the nexūs of our cosmic epoch, in the widest meaning of that term. These relations only characterize the epoch by reason of their foundation in the immediate experience of the society of occasions dominating that epoch. Thus we find a special application of the doctrine of the interaction between societies of occasions and the laws of nature. The perceptive mode in presentational immediacy is one of the defining characteristics of the societies which constitute the nexūs termed material bodies. Also in some fainter intensity it belongs to the electromagnetic occasions in empty space. From the point of view of a [499] single experient, that mode discloses systematic relations which dominate the environment. But the environment is dominated by these relationships by reason of the experiences of the individual occasions constituting the societies.

It is by reason of this disclosure of ultimate system that an intellectual comprehension of the physical universe is possible. There is a systematic framework permeating all relevant fact. By reference to this framework the variant, various, vagrant, evanescent details of the abundant world can have their mutual relations exhibited by their correlation to the common terms of a universal system. Sounds differ qualitatively among themselves, sounds differ qualitatively from colours, colours differ qualitatively from the rhythmic throbs of emotion and of pain; yet all alike are periodic and have their spatial relations and their wave-lengths. The discovery of the true relevance of the mathematical relations disclosed in presentational immediacy was the first step in the intellectual conquest of nature. Accurate science was then born. Apart from these relations as facts in nature, such science is meaningless, a tale told by an idiot and credited by fools. For example, the conjecture by an eminent astronomer, based on measurements of photographic plates, that the period of the revolution of our galaxy of stars is about three hundred million years can only derive its meaning from the systematic geometrical relations which permeate the epoch. But he would have required the same reference to system, if he had made an analogous statement about the period of revolution of a child's top. Also the two periods are comparable in terms of the system.

SECTION IV

Measurement depends upon counting and upon permanence. The question is, what is counted, and what is permanent? The things that are counted are the inches on a straight metal rod, a yard-measure. Also the thing [500] that is permanent is this yard-measure in respect both to its internal relations and in respect to some of its extensive relations to the geometry of the world. In the first place, the rod is straight. Thus the measurement depends on the straightness and not the straightness upon the measurement. The modern answer to this statement is that the measurement is a comparison of infinitesimals, or of an approximation to infinitesimals. The answer to this answer is that there are no infinitesimals, and that therefore there can be no approximation to them. In mathematics,† all phraseology about infinitesimals is merely disguised statement about a class of finites. This doctrine has been conclusive mathematical theory since the time of Weierstrass in the middle of the nineteenth century. Also all the contortions of curvature are possible for a segment between any end-points.

Of course, in all measurement there is approximation in our suppositions as to the yard-measure.† But it is approximation to straightness. Also having regard to the systematic geometry of straight lines, and to the type of approximation exhibited by the rod, the smaller the portion used, the more negligible are the percentage errors introduced by the defects from straightness. But unless the notion of straightness has a definite meaning in reference to the extensive relations, this whole procedure in practical measurement is meaningless. There is nothing to distinguish one contorted segment between end-points from another contorted segment between those end-points. One is no straighter than another. Also any percentage differences between their lengths can exist.

Again, the inches are counted because they are congruent and are end-on along the straight rod. No one counts coincident inches. The counting essentially is concerned with non-coincident straight segments. The numerical measure of length is the indication of the fact that the yard-measure is a straight rod divisible into thirty-six congruent inch-long segments.

[501] There is a modern doctrine that 'congruence' *means* the possibility of coincidence. If this be the case, then the importance of congruence would arise when the possibility is realized. Alternatively, the possibility could be of importance as a lure entering into the subjective aim. If the latter alternative were true, congruence would play its part in the form of a tendency of congruent bodies to coalesce, or to resist coalescence. In fact, there would be adversion to, or aversion from,† coalescence. Of course the suggestion is fantastic. Recurring to the former alternative, the importance of the thirty-six inches along the yard-measure depends on the fact that they are *not* coincident and, until the destruction of the rod, never will be coincident. There is a realized property of the rod that it is thirty-six inches in length. Thus although 'coincidence' is used as a *test* of congruence, it is not the *meaning* of congruence.

We must now consider the use of 'coincidence' as a test. Congruence is tested either by the transference of a steel yard-measure from coincidence with one body to coincidence with another body, or by some optical means dependent on the use of an optical instrument and on the congruence of successive wave-lengths† in a train of waves, or by some other vibratory device dependent on analogous principles.

It is at once evident that all these tests are† dependent on a direct intuition of permanence. This 'permanence' means 'permanence in respect to congruence'† for the various instruments employed, namely, the yard-measure, or the optical instruments, or analogous instruments. For example, the yard-measure is assumed to remain congruent to its previous self, as it is transferred from one setting to another setting. It is not sufficient to intuit that it remains the same body. Substances that are very deformable preserve that sort of self-identity. The required property is that of self-congruence. Minute variations of physical conditions will make the rod vary slightly; also sense-perception is never absolutely exact. [502] But unless there be a meaning to 'exactitude,' the notions of a 'slight variation' and of a 'slight defect from exactitude' are nonsense. Apart from such a meaning the two occasions of the rod's existence are incomparable, except by another experiment depending upon the same principles. There can only be a finite number of such experiments; so ultimately we are reduced to these direct judgments.

However far the testing of instruments and the corrections for changes of physical factors, such as temperature, are carried, there is always a final dependence upon direct intuitions that relevant circumstances are unchanged. Instruments are used from minute to minute, from hour to hour, and from day to day, with the sole guarantee of antecedent tests and of the *appearance* of invariability of relevant circumstances.

This 'appearance' is always a perception in the mode of presentational immediacy. If such perception be in any sense 'private' in contradistinction to a correlative meaning for the term 'public,' then the perceptions, on which scientific measurement depends,† merely throw light upon the private psychology of the particular observer, and have no 'public' import.

Such a conclusion is so obviously inconsistent with our beliefs as to the intercommunication of real actualities in a public world, that it may be dismissed as a *reductio ad absurdum*, having regard to the groundwork of common experience which is the final test of all science and philosophy. A great deal of modern scientific philosophy consists in recurrence to the theory of 'privacy' when such statements seem to afford a short cut to simplicity of statement, and—on the other hand—of employment of the notion of observing a public world when that concept is essential for expressing the status of science in common experience. Science is *either* an important statement of systematic theory correlating observations of a common world, *or* is the daydream of a solitary intelligence with a taste for the daydream of publication. But [503] it is not philosophy to vacillate from one point of view to the other.

SECTION V

Finally, the† meaning of 'congruence' as a relation between two geometrical elements in a strain-locus must be considered. It will be sufficient to consider this meaning in reference to two segments of straight lines, and to treat all other meanings as derivative from this.

A strain-locus is defined by the 'projectors' which penetrate any one finite region within it. Such a locus is a systematic whole, independently of the actualities which may atomize it. In this it is to be distinguished from a 'duration' which does depend on its *physical content*. A strain-locus depends merely upon its *geometrical content*. This geometrical content is expressed by any adequate set of 'axioms' from which the systematic interconnections† of its included straight lines and points can be deduced. This conclusion requires the systematic uniformity of the geometry of a strain-locus, but refers to further empirical observation for the discovery of the particular character of this uniform system. For example, the question as to whether a complete straight line be a 'closed' serial locus of points or an 'open' serial locus, is entirely a question for such discovery. The only decision is to be found by comparing the rival theories in respect to their power of elucidating observed facts.

The only relevant properties of straight lines are (i) their completeness, (ii) their inclusion of points, (iii) their unique definition by any pair of included points, (iv) their possibility of mutual intersection in a single point. The additional axioms which express the systematic geometrical theory must not have reference to length or to congruence. For these notions are to be derived from the theory. Thus the axioms must have exclusive reference to the intersection of straight lines, and to their inclusion or exclusion of points indicated by the intersections of other lines. Such sets of axioms are [504] well known to mathematicians. There are many such sets which respectively constitute alternative geometrical theories. Also given one set of axioms constituting a definite geometrical theory, different sets of axioms can easily be obtained which are equivalent to each other in the sense that all the other sets can be deduced from any one of them. All such equivalent sets produce the same geometrical theory. Equivalent sets have their importance, but not for the present investigation. We can therefore neglect them, and *different* sets of axioms will mean sets of axioms which constitute *incompatible* geometrical theories.

There are many such sets, with a great variety of peculiar properties. There are, however, three such sets which combine a peculiar simplicity with a very general conformation to the observed facts. These sets give the non-metrical properties of the three geometrical theories respectively known to mathematicians as the theory of Elliptic Geometry, of Euclidean Geometry, and of Hyperbolic Geometry.* It will serve no purpose to give the three sets of axioms. But it is very easy to explain the main point of

difference between the theories, without being led too far from the philosophical discussion.

In the first place, a definition of a 'plane' can be given which is common to all the three theories. The definition already given in Chapter III
of this Part will suffice. But an alternative definition can be stated thus:
If A, B, C be any three non-collinear points, and AB, BC, CA denote the
three complete straight lines containing,† respectively, A and B, B and C,
C and A, then the straight lines which respectively intersect both members
of any pair of these three lines, not both lines at one of the corners A or
B or C, pass through all the points constituting one plane, and all their
incident points are incident in the plane.

Thus a plane is defined to be the locus of all the points incident in at
least one of such a group of straight lines. The axioms are such that this
definition is equivalent to [505] the definition in Chapter III. Also the
axioms secure that any straight line, passing through two points in a plane,
is itself† wholly incident in that plane. Also it follows from the definition
of a plane that a line l and a point P, not incident in l, are coplanar.

The distinction between the three geometrical theories can now be explained by the aid of such a triplet, a point P, a line l not passing through
P, and the plane π in which P and l are both incident. Consider all the
lines through P and incident in the plane π. Then in the Elliptic Geometrical Theory, all these lines intersect the line l; in the Euclidean Geometrical Theory, all these lines intersect the line l, with the exception of
one and only one line—the unique parallel to l through P; in the Hyperbolic Geometrical Theory the lines through P in the plane are divisible
into two classes, one class consisting of the lines intersecting l, the other
class consisting of the lines not intersecting l, and each class with an infinite number of members. Then it has been shown by Cayley and von
Staudt [1] that the congruence of segments and the numerical measures of
the distances involved are definable. The simplest case is that of Euclidean
Geometry. In that case the basic fact is that the opposite sides of parallelograms are equal. A further complication is required to define congruence
between segments which are not parallel. But it would serve no purpose to
enter into the detailed solutions of this mathematical problem.

But the illustration afforded by the particular case of the congruence of
the opposite sides of parallelograms† enables the general principle underlying the notion of congruence to be explained. Two segments are congruent when there is a certain analogy between their functions in a systematic
pattern of straight lines, which includes both of them.

The definition of this analogy is the definition of con- [506] gruence in
terms of non-metrical geometry. It is possible to discover diverse analogies
which give definitions of congruence which are inconsistent with each

[1] Cf. Cayley's "Sixth Memoir On Quantics," *Transactions of the Royal Society*, 1859; von† Staudt's *Geometrie der Lage*, 1847; and *Beiträge zur Geometrie der Lage*, 1856.

other. That definition which enters importantly into the internal constitutions of the dominating social entities is the important definition for the cosmic epoch in question.

Measurement is now possible throughout the extensive continuum. This measurement is a systematic procedure dependent on the dominant societies of the cosmic epoch. When one form of measurement has been given, alternative forms with assigned mathematical relations to the initial form can be defined. One such system is as good as any other, so far as mathematical procedure is concerned. The only point to be remembered is that each system of 'coordinates' must have its definable relation to the analogy which constitutes congruence.

SECTION VI

Physical measurement is now possible. The modern procedure, introduced by Einstein, is a generalization of the method of 'least action.' It consists in considering any continuous line between any two points in the spatio-temporal continuum and seeking to express the physical properties of the field as an integral along it. The measurements which are presupposed are the geometrical measurements constituting the coordinates of the various points involved. Various physical quantities enter as the 'constants' involved in the algebraic functions concerned. These constants depend on the actual occasions which atomize the extensive continuum. The physical properties of the medium are expressed by various conditions satisfied by this integral.

It is usual to term an 'infinitesimal' element of this integral by the name of an element of distance. But this name, though satisfactory as a technical phraseology, is entirely misleading. There can be no theory of the congruence of different elements of the path. The notion of coincidence does not apply. There is no systematic [507] theory possible, since the so-called 'infinitesimal' distance depends on the actual entities throughout the environment. The only way of expressing such so-called distance is to make use of the presupposed geometrical measurements. The mistake arises because, unconsciously, the minds of physicists are infected by a presupposition which comes down from Aristotle through Kant. Aristotle placed 'quantity' among his categories, and did not distinguish between extensive quantity and intensive quantity. Kant made this distinction, but considered both of them as categoreal notions. It follows from Cayley's and von Staudt's work (cf. *loc. cit.*) that extensive quantity is a construct. The current physical theory presupposes a comparison of so-called lengths among segments without any theory as to the basis on which this comparison is to be made, and in ignorance of the fact that all exact observation belongs to the mode of presentational immediacy. Further, the fact is neglected that there are no infinitesimals, and that a comparison of finite segments is thus required. For this reason, it would be better—so far as explanation is concerned—to abandon the term 'distance' for this integral, and to call it by some such name as 'impetus,' suggestive of its physical import.[2]

It is to be noted, however, that the conclusions of this discussion involve no objection to the modern treatment of ultimate physical laws in the guise of a problem in differential geometry. The integral impetus *is* an extensive quantity, a 'length.' The differential element of impetus is the differential element of systematic length weighted with the individual peculiarities of its relevant environment. The whole theory of the physical field is the interweaving of the individual peculiarities of actual occasions upon the background of systematic geometry. This systematic geometry expresses the most general 'substantial form' inherited throughout the vast cosmic society which [508] constitutes the primary real potentiality conditioning concrescence.[3] In this doctrine, the organic philosophy is very near to the philosophy of Descartes.

The whole argument can be summarized thus:

(i) Actual occasions are immovable, so that the doctrine of coincidence is nonsense.

(ii) Extensive quantity is a logical construct, expressing the number of congruent units which are (a) non-overlapping, and (b) exhaustive of the nexus in question.

(iii) Congruence is only definable as a certain definite analogy of function in a systematic complex which embraces both congruent elements.

(iv) That all experimental measurement involves ultimate intuitions of congruence between earlier and later states of the instruments employed.

(v) That all *exact* observation is made by perception in the mode of presentational immediacy.

(vi) That if such perception merely concerns a private psychological field, science is the daydream of an individual without any public import.

(vii) That perception in the mode of presentational immediacy solely depends upon the 'withness' of the 'body,' and only exhibits the external contemporary world in respect to its systematic geometrical relationship to the 'body.'

[2] Cf. my book, *The Principle of Relativity*, University Press, Cambridge, 1922.

[3] This theory of the derivation of the basic uniformity requisite for congruence, and thence for measurement, should be compared with that of two deeply interesting articles: (i) "The Theory of Relativity and The First Principles of Science," and (ii) "The Macroscopic Atomic Theory," *Journal of Philosophy*, Vol. XXV,† by Professor F. S. C. Northrop of Yale. I cannot adjust his doctrine of a 'macroscopic atom' to my cosmological outlook. Nor does this notion seem necessary if my doctrine of 'microscopic atomic occasions' be accepted. But Professor Northrop's theory does seem to be the only alternative if this doctrine be abandoned. I regret that the articles did not come under my notice till this work had been finally revised for publication.

PART V
FINAL INTERPRETATION

CHAPTER I

THE IDEAL OPPOSITES

SECTION I

[512] THE chief danger to philosophy is narrowness in the selection of evidence. This narrowness arises from the idiosyncrasies and timidities of particular authors, of particular social groups, of particular schools of thought, of particular epochs in the history of civilization. The evidence relied upon is arbitrarily biased by the temperaments of individuals, by the provincialities of groups, and by the limitations of schemes of thought.

The evil, resulting from this distortion of evidence, is at its worst in the consideration of the topic of the final part of this investigation—ultimate ideals. We must commence this topic by an endeavour to state impartially the general types of the great ideals which have prevailed at sundry seasons and places. Our test in the selection,† to be impartial, must be pragmatic: the chosen stage of exemplification must be such as to compel attention, by its own intrinsic interest, or by the intrinsic interest of the results which flow from it. For example, the stern self-restraint of the Roman farmers in the early history of the Republic issued in the great epoch of the Roman Empire; and the stern self-restraint of the early Puritans in New England issued in the flowering of New England culture. The epoch of the Covenanters has had for its issue the deep impression which modern civilization owes to Scotland. Neither the Roman farmers, nor the American Puritans, nor the Covenanters, can wholly command allegiance. Also they differ from each other. But in either case, there is greatness there, greatly exemplified. In contrast to this example, we find the flowering time of the aesthetic culture of ancient Greece, the Augustan epoch in Rome, the Italian Renaissance, the Elizabethan epoch in England, the Restoration epoch in England, [513] French and Teutonic civilization throughout the centuries of the modern world, Modern Paris, and Modern New York. Moralists have much to say about some of these societies. Yet, while there is any critical judgment in the lives of men, such achievements can never be forgotten. In the estimation of either type of these contrasted examples, sheer contempt betokens blindness. In each of these instances, there are elements which compel admiration. There is a greatness in the lives of those who build up religious systems, a greatness in action, in idea and in self-subordination, embodied in instance after instance through centuries of growth. There is a greatness in the rebels who destroy such systems:

337

they are the Titans who storm heaven, armed with passionate sincerity. It may be that the revolt is the mere assertion by youth of its right to its proper brilliance, to that final good of immediate joy. Philosophy may not neglect the multifariousness of the world—the fairies dance, and Christ is nailed to the cross.

SECTION II

There are various contrasted qualities of temperament, which control the formation of the mentalities of different epochs. In a previous chapter (Part II, Ch. X) attention has already been drawn to the sense of permanence dominating the invocation 'Abide with Me,' and the sense of flux dominating the sequel 'Fast Falls the Eventide.' Ideals fashion themselves round these two notions, permanence and flux. In the inescapable flux, there is something that abides; in the overwhelming permanence, there is an element that escapes into flux. Permanence can be snatched only out of flux; and the passing moment can find its adequate intensity only by its submission to permanence. Those who would disjoin the two elements can find no interpretation of patent facts.

The four symbolic figures in the Medici chapel in Florence—Michelangelo's masterpieces of statuary, Day [514] and Night, Evening and Dawn—exhibit the everlasting elements in the passage of fact. The figures stay there, reclining in their recurring sequence, forever showing the essences in the nature of things. The perfect realization is not merely the exemplification of what in abstraction is timeless. It does more: it implants timelessness on what in its essence is passing. The perfect moment is fadeless in the lapse of time. Time has then lost its character of 'perpetual perishing'; it becomes the 'moving image of eternity.'

SECTION III

Another contrast is equally essential for the understanding of ideals—the contrast between order as the condition for excellence, and order as stifling the freshness of living. This contrast is met with in the theory of education. The condition for excellence is a thorough training in technique. Sheer skill must pass out of the sphere of conscious exercise, and must have assumed the character of unconscious habit. The first, the second, and the third condition for high achievement is scholarship, in that enlarged sense including knowledge and acquired instinct controlling action.

The paradox which wrecks so many promising theories of education is that the training which produces skill is so very apt to stifle imaginative zest. Skill demands repetition, and imaginative zest is tinged with impulse. Up to a certain point each gain in skill opens new paths for the imagination. But in each individual formal training has its limit of usefulness. Beyond that limit there is degeneration: 'The lilies of the field toil not, neither do they spin.'

The social history of mankind exhibits great organizations in their alternating functions of conditions for progress, and of contrivances for stunting humanity. The history of the Mediterranean lands, and of western Europe, is the history of the blessing and the curse† of political organizations, of religious organizations, of [515] schemes of thought, of social agencies for large purposes. The moment of dominance, prayed for, worked for, sacrificed for, by generations of the noblest spirits, marks the turning point where the blessing passes into the curse. Some new principle of refreshment is required. The art of progress is to preserve order amid change, and to preserve change amid order. Life refuses to be embalmed alive. The more prolonged the halt in some unrelieved system of order, the greater the crash of the dead society.

The same principle is exhibited by the tedium arising from the unrelieved dominance of a fashion in art. Europe, having covered itself with treasures of Gothic architecture, entered upon generations of satiation. These jaded epochs seem to have lost all sense of that particular form of loveliness. It seems as though the last delicacies of feeling require some element of novelty to relieve their massive inheritance from bygone system. Order is not sufficient. What is required, is something much more complex. It is order entering upon novelty; so that the massiveness of order does not degenerate into mere repetition; and so that the novelty is always reflected upon a background of system.

But the two elements must not really be disjoined. It belongs to the goodness of the world, that its settled order should deal tenderly with the faint discordant light of the dawn of another age. Also order, as it sinks into the background before new conditions, has its requirements. The old dominance should be transformed into the firm foundations, upon which new feelings arise, drawing their intensities from delicacies of contrast between system and freshness. In either alternative of excess, whether the past be lost, or be dominant, the present is enfeebled. This is only an application of Aristotle's doctrine of the 'golden mean.' The lesson of the transmutation of causal efficacy into presentational immediacy is that great ends are reached by life in the present; life novel and immediate, but deriving its richness by its full inheritance from the rightly organized [516] animal body. It is by reason of the body, with its miracle of order, that the treasures of the past environment are poured into the living occasion. The final percipient route of occasions is perhaps some thread of happenings wandering in 'empty' space amid the interstices of the brain. It toils not, neither does it spin. It receives from the past; it lives in the present. It is shaken by its intensities of private feeling, adversion or aversion. In its turn, this culmination of bodily life transmits itself as an element of novelty throughout the avenues of the body. Its sole use to the body is its vivid originality: it is the organ of novelty.

SECTION IV

The world is thus faced by the paradox that, at least in its higher actualities, it craves for novelty and yet is haunted by terror at the loss of the past, with its familiarities and its loved ones. It seeks escape from time in its character of 'perpetually perishing.' Part of the joy of the new years is the hope of the old round of seasons, with their stable facts—of friendship, and love, and old association. Yet conjointly with this terror, the present as mere unrelieved preservation of the past assumes the character of a horror of the past, rejection of it, revolt:

> To die be given, or attain,
> Fierce work it were to do again.*   *Tennyson*

Each new epoch enters upon its career by waging unrelenting war upon the aesthetic gods of its immediate predecessor. Yet the culminating fact of conscious, rational life refuses to conceive itself as a transient enjoyment, transiently useful. In the order of the physical world its rôle is defined by its introduction of novelty. But, just as physical feelings are haunted by the vague insistence of causality, so the higher intellectual feelings are haunted by the vague insistence of another order, where there is no unrest, no travel, no shipwreck: 'There shall be no more sea.'

[517] This is the problem which gradually shapes itself as religion reaches its higher phases in civilized communities. The most general formulation of the religious problem is the question whether the process of the temporal world passes into the formation of other actualities, bound together in an order in which novelty does not mean loss.

The ultimate evil in the temporal world is deeper than any specific evil. It lies in the fact that the past fades, that time is a 'perpetual perishing.' Objectification involves elimination. The present fact has not the past fact with it in any full immediacy. The process of time veils the past below distinctive feeling. There is a unison of becoming among things in the present. Why should there not be novelty without loss of this direct unison of immediacy among things? In the temporal world, it is the empirical fact that process entails loss: the past is present under an abstraction. But there is no reason, of any ultimate metaphysical generality, why this should be the whole story. The nature of evil is that the characters of things are mutually obstructive. Thus the depths of life require a process of selection. But the selection is elimination as the first step towards another temporal order seeking to minimize obstructive modes. Selection is at once the measure of evil, and the process of its evasion. It means† discarding the element of obstructiveness in fact. No element in fact is ineffectual: thus the struggle with evil is a process of building up a mode of utilization by the provision of intermediate elements introducing a complex structure of harmony. The triviality in some initial reconstruction of order expresses the fact that actualities are being produced, which, trivial in their own proper character of immediate 'ends,' are proper 'means' for the emergence of a world at once lucid, and intrinsically of immediate worth.

The evil of the world is that those elements which are translucent so far as transmission is concerned, in themselves are of slight weight; and that those elements [518] with individual weight, by their discord, impose upon vivid immediacy the obligation that it fade into night. 'He giveth his be- *Shakespeare* loved—sleep.'

In our cosmological construction we are, therefore,† left with the final opposites, joy and sorrow, good and evil, disjunction and conjunction— that is to say, the many in one—flux and permanence, greatness and triviality, freedom and necessity, God and the World. In this list, the pairs of opposites are in experience with a certain ultimate directness of intuition, except in the case of the last pair. God and the World introduce the note of interpretation. They embody the interpretation of the cosmological problem in terms of a fundamental metaphysical doctrine as to the quality of creative origination, namely, conceptual appetition and physical realization. This topic constitutes the last chapter of Cosmology.

CHAPTER II

GOD AND THE WORLD

SECTION I†

[519] So long as the temporal world is conceived as a self-sufficient completion of the creative act, explicable by its derivation from an ultimate principle which is at once eminently real and the unmoved mover, from this conclusion there is no escape: the best that we can say of the turmoil is, 'For so he giveth his beloved—sleep.' This is the message of religions of the Buddhistic type, and in some sense it is true. In this final discussion we have to ask, whether metaphysical principles impose the belief that it is the whole truth. The complexity of the world must be reflected in the answer. It is childish to enter upon thought with the simple-minded question, What is the world made of? The task of reason is to fathom the deeper depths of the many-sidedness of things. We must not expect simple answers to far-reaching questions. However far our gaze penetrates, there are always heights beyond which block our vision.

The notion of God as the 'unmoved mover' is derived from Aristotle, at least so far as Western thought is concerned. The notion of God as 'eminently real' is a favourite doctrine of Christian theology. The combination of the two into the doctrine of an aboriginal, eminently real, transcendent creator, at whose fiat the world came into being, and whose imposed will it obeys, is the fallacy which has infused tragedy into the histories of Christianity and of Mahometanism.

When the Western world accepted Christianity, Caesar conquered; and the received text of Western theology was edited by his lawyers. The code of Justinian and the theology of Justinian are two volumes expressing [520] one movement of the human spirit. The brief Galilean vision of humility flickered throughout the ages, uncertainly. In the official formulation of the religion it has assumed the trivial form of the mere attribution to the Jews that they cherished a misconception about their Messiah. But the deeper idolatry, of the fashioning of God in the image of the Egyptian, Persian, and Roman imperial rulers, was retained. The Church gave unto God the attributes which belonged exclusively to Caesar.

In the great formative period of theistic philosophy, which ended with the rise of Mahometanism, after a continuance coeval with civilization, three strains of thought emerge which, amid many variations in detail, respectively fashion God in the image of an imperial ruler, God in the image of a personification of moral energy, God in the image of an ultimate philosophical principle. Hume's *Dialogues* criticize unanswerably these modes of explaining the system of the world.

The three schools of thought can be associated respectively with the divine Caesars, the Hebrew prophets, and Aristotle. But Aristotle was antedated by Indian, and Buddhistic, thought; the Hebrew prophets can be paralleled in traces of earlier thought; Mahometanism and the divine Caesars merely represent the most natural, obvious, idolatrous theistic‡ symbolism, at all epochs and places.

The history of theistic philosophy exhibits various stages of combination of these three diverse ways of entertaining the problem. There is, however, in the Galilean origin of Christianity yet another suggestion which does not fit very well with any of the three main strands of thought. It does not emphasize the ruling Caesar, or the ruthless moralist, or the unmoved mover. It dwells upon the tender elements in the world, which slowly and in quietness operate by love; and it finds purpose in the present immediacy of a kingdom not of this world. Love neither rules, nor is it unmoved; also it is [521] a little oblivious as to morals. It does not look to the future; for it finds its own reward in the immediate present.

SECTION II

Apart from any reference to existing religions as they are, or as they ought to be, we must investigate dispassionately what the metaphysical principles, here developed, require on these points, as to the nature of God. There is nothing here in the nature of proof. There is merely the confrontation of the theoretic system with a certain rendering of the facts. But the unsystematized report upon the facts is itself highly controversial, and the system is confessedly inadequate. The deductions from it in this particular sphere of thought cannot be looked upon as more than suggestions as to how the problem is transformed in the light of that system. What follows is merely an attempt to add another speaker to that masterpiece, Hume's *Dialogues Concerning Natural Religion*. Any cogency of argument entirely depends upon elucidation of somewhat exceptional elements in our conscious experience—those elements which may roughly be classed together as religious and moral intuitions.

In the first place, God is not to be treated as an exception to all metaphysical principles, invoked to save their collapse. He is their chief exemplification.

Viewed as primordial, he is the unlimited conceptual realization of the absolute wealth of potentiality. In this aspect, he is not *before* all creation, but *with* all creation. But, as primordial, so far is he from 'eminent reality,' that in this abstraction he is 'deficiently actual'—and this in two ways. His feelings are only conceptual and so lack the fulness of actuality. Secondly, conceptual feelings, apart from complex integration with physical feelings, are devoid of consciousness in their subjective forms.

Thus, when we make a distinction of reason, and con- [522] sider God in the abstraction of a primordial actuality, we must ascribe to him neither fulness of feeling, nor consciousness. He is the unconditioned actuality of conceptual feeling at the base of things; so that, by reason of this primordial actuality, there is an order in the relevance of eternal objects to the process of creation. His unity of conceptual operations is a free creative act, untrammelled by reference to any particular course of things. It is deflected neither by love, nor by hatred, for what in fact comes to pass. The *particularities* of the actual world presuppose *it*; while *it* merely presupposes the *general* metaphysical character of creative advance, of which it is the primordial exemplification. The primordial nature of God is the acquirement by creativity of a primordial character.

His conceptual actuality at once exemplifies and establishes the categoreal conditions. The conceptual feelings, which compose his primordial nature, exemplify in their subjective forms their mutual sensitivity and their subjective unity of subjective aim. These subjective forms are valuations determining the relative relevance of eternal objects for each occasion of actuality.

He is the lure for feeling, the eternal urge of desire. His particular relevance to each creative act,† as it arises from its own conditioned standpoint in the world, constitutes him the initial 'object of desire' establishing the initial phase of each subjective aim. A quotation from Aristotle's *Metaphysics* [1] expresses some analogies to, and some differences from, this line of thought:

> And since that which is moved and moves† is intermediate, there is something† which moves without being moved, being eternal, substance, and actuality. And the object of desire and the object of thought move in this way; they move without being moved. The primary objects of desire and of thought‡ are the same. For the apparent good is the object of appetite, and the real good is the primary object of rational wish.† But desire is conse- [523] quent on opinion rather than opinion on desire; for the thinking is the starting-point. And thought is moved by the object of thought, and one of the two columns† of opposites is in itself the object of thought; . . .

Aristotle had not made the distinction between conceptual feelings and the intellectual feelings which alone involve consciousness. But if 'conceptual feeling,' with its subjective form of valuation, be substituted for 'thought,' 'thinking,' and 'opinion,' in the above quotation, the agreement is exact.

SECTION III

There is another side to the nature of God which cannot be omitted. Throughout this exposition of the philosophy of organism we have been

---

[1] *Metaphysics* 1072a 23–32,† trans. by Professor W. D. Ross. My attention was called to the appositeness of this particular quotation by Mr. F. J. Carson.

considering the primary action of God on the world. From this point of view, he is the principle of concretion—the principle whereby there is initiated a definite outcome from a situation otherwise riddled with ambiguity. Thus, so far, the primordial side of the nature of God has alone been relevant.

But God, as well as being primordial, is also consequent. He is the beginning and the end. He is not the beginning in the sense of being in the past of all members. He is the presupposed actuality of conceptual operation, in unison of becoming with every other creative act. Thus,† by reason of the relativity of all things, there is a reaction of the world on God. The completion of God's nature into a fulness of physical feeling is derived from the objectification of the world in God. He shares with every new creation its actual world; and the concrescent creature is objectified in God as a novel element in God's objectification of that actual world. This prehension into God of each creature is directed with the subjective aim, and clothed with the subjective form, wholly derivative from his all-inclusive primordial valuation. God's conceptual nature is unchanged, by reason of its final completeness. But his derivative [524] nature is consequent upon the creative advance of the world.

Thus, analogously to all actual entities, the nature of God is dipolar. He has a primordial nature and a consequent nature. The consequent nature of God is conscious; and it is the realization of the actual world in the unity of his nature, and through the transformation of his wisdom. The primordial nature is conceptual, the consequent nature is the weaving of God's physical feelings upon his primordial concepts.

One side of God's nature is constituted by his conceptual experience. This experience is the primordial fact in the world, limited by no actuality which it presupposes. It is therefore infinite, devoid of all negative prehensions. This side of his nature is free, complete, primordial, eternal, actually deficient, and unconscious. The other side originates with physical experience derived from the temporal world, and then acquires integration with the primordial side. It is determined, incomplete, consequent, 'everlasting,' fully actual, and conscious. His necessary goodness expresses the determination of his consequent nature.

Conceptual experience can be infinite, but it belongs to the nature of physical experience that it is finite. An actual entity in the temporal world is to be conceived as originated by physical experience with its process of completion motivated by consequent, conceptual experience initially derived from God. God is to be conceived as originated by conceptual experience with his process of completion motivated by consequent, physical experience, initially derived from the temporal world.

SECTION IV

The perfection of God's subjective aim, derived from the completeness of his primordial nature, issues into the character of his consequent nature.

In it there is no loss, no obstruction. The world is felt in a unison of immediacy. The property of combining creative advance with [525] the retention of mutual immediacy is what in the previous section is meant by the term 'everlasting.'

The wisdom of subjective aim prehends every actuality for what it can be in such a perfected system—its sufferings, its sorrows, its failures, its triumphs, its immediacies of joy—woven by rightness of feeling into the harmony of the universal feeling, which is always immediate, always many, always one, always with novel advance, moving onward and never perishing. The revolts of destructive evil, purely self-regarding, are dismissed into their triviality of merely individual facts; and yet the good they did achieve in individual joy, in individual sorrow, in the introduction of needed contrast, is yet saved by its relation to the completed whole. The image—and it is but an image—the image under which this operative growth of God's nature is best conceived, is that of a tender care that nothing be lost.

The consequent nature of God is his judgment on the world. He saves the world as it passes into the immediacy of his own life. It is the judgment of a tenderness which loses nothing that can be saved. It is also the judgment of a wisdom which uses what in the temporal world is mere wreckage.

Another image which is also required to understand his consequent nature† is that of his infinite patience. The universe includes a threefold creative act composed of (i) the one infinite conceptual realization, (ii) the multiple solidarity of free physical realizations in the temporal world, (iii) the ultimate unity of the multiplicity of actual fact with the primordial conceptual fact. If we conceive the first term and the last term in their unity over against the intermediate multiple freedom of physical realizations in the temporal world, we conceive of the patience of God, tenderly saving the turmoil of the intermediate world by the completion of his own nature. The sheer force of things lies in the intermediate physical process: this is the energy of physical production. God's rôle is not the combat of productive force [526] with productive force, of destructive force with destructive force; it lies in the patient operation of the overpowering rationality of his conceptual harmonization. He does not create the world, he saves it: or, more accurately, he is the poet of the world, with tender patience leading** it by his vision of truth, beauty, and goodness.

SECTION V

The vicious separation of the flux from the permanence leads to the concept of an entirely static God, with eminent reality, in relation to an entirely fluent world, with deficient reality. But if the opposites, static and fluent, have once been so explained as separately to characterize diverse actualities, the interplay between the thing which is static and the things which are fluent involves contradiction at every step in its explanation. Such philosophies must include the notion of 'illusion' as a fundamental

principle—the notion of 'mere appearance.' This is the final Platonic†
problem.

Undoubtedly, the intuitions of Greek, Hebrew, and Christian thought
have alike embodied the notions of a static God condescending to the
world, and of a world either thoroughly fluent, or accidentally static, but
finally fluent—'heaven and earth shall pass away.' In some schools of
thought, the fluency of the world is mitigated by the assumption that
selected components in the world are exempt from this final fluency, and
achieve a static survival. Such components are not separated by any decisive line from analogous components for which the assumption is not
made. Further, the survival is construed in terms of a final pair of opposites, happiness for some, torture for others.

Such systems have the common character of starting with a fundamental
intuition which we do mean to express, and of entangling themselves in
verbal expressions, which carry consequences at variance with the initial
intuition of permanence in fluency and of fluency in permanence.

[527] But civilized intuition has always, although obscurely, grasped the
problem as double and not as single. There is not the mere problem of
fluency and permanence. There is the double problem: actuality with
permanence, requiring fluency as its completion; and actuality with fluency, requiring permanence as its completion. The first half of the problem
concerns the completion of God's primordial nature by the derivation of
his consequent nature from the temporal world. The second half of the
problem concerns the completion of each fluent actual occasion by its
function of objective immortality, devoid of 'perpetual perishing,' that is
to say, 'everlasting.'

This double problem cannot be separated into two distinct problems.
Either side can only be explained in terms of the other. The consequent
nature of God is the fluent world become 'everlasting' by its objective immortality in God. Also the objective immortality of actual occasions requires the primordial permanence of God, whereby the creative advance
ever re-establishes itself endowed with initial subjective aim derived from
the relevance of God to the evolving world.

But objective immortality within the temporal world does not solve the
problem set by the penetration of the finer religious intuition. 'Everlastingness' has been lost; and 'everlastingness' is the content of that vision upon
which the finer religions are built—the 'many' absorbed everlastingly in
the final unity. The problems of the fluency of God and of the everlastingness of passing experience are solved by the same factor in the universe.
This factor is the temporal world perfected by its reception and its re-
formation, as a fulfilment of the primordial appetition which is the basis of
all order. In this way God is completed by the individual, fluent satisfactions of finite fact, and the temporal occasions are completed by their
everlasting union with their transformed selves, purged into conformation
with the eternal order which is the final absolute 'wisdom.' The final sum-

mary can [528] only be expressed in terms of a group of antitheses, whose apparent self-contradictions depend† on neglect of the diverse categories of existence. In each antithesis there is a shift of meaning which converts the opposition into a contrast.

It is as true to say that God is permanent and the World fluent, as that the World is permanent and God is fluent.

It is as true to say that God is one and the World many, as that the World is one and God many.

It is as true to say that, in comparison with the World, God is actual eminently, as that, in comparison with God, the World is actual eminently.

It is as true to say that the World is immanent in God, as that God is immanent in the World.

It is as true to say that God transcends the World, as that the World transcends God.

It is as true to say that God creates the World, as that the World creates God.

God and the World are the contrasted opposites in terms of which Creativity achieves its supreme task of transforming disjoined multiplicity, with its diversities in opposition, into concrescent unity, with its diversities in contrast. In each actuality there† are two concrescent poles of realization—'enjoyment' and 'appetition,' that is, the 'physical' and the 'conceptual.' For God the conceptual is prior to the physical, for the World the physical poles are prior to the conceptual poles.

A physical pole is in its own nature exclusive, bounded by contradiction: a conceptual pole is in its own nature all-embracing, unbounded by contradiction. The former derives its share of infinity from the infinity of appetition; the latter derives its share of limitation from the exclusiveness of enjoyment. Thus, by reason of his priority of appetition, there can be but one primordial nature for God; and, by reason of their priority of enjoyment, there must be one history of many actualities in the physical world.

[529] God and the World stand over against each other, expressing the final metaphysical truth that appetitive vision and physical enjoyment have equal claim to priority in creation. But no two actualities can be torn apart: each is all in all. Thus each temporal occasion embodies God, and is embodied in God. In God's nature, permanence is primordial and flux is derivative from the World: in the World's nature, flux is primordial and permanence is derivative from God. Also the World's nature is a primordial datum for God; and God's nature is a primordial datum for the World. Creation achieves the reconciliation of permanence and flux when it has reached its final term which is everlastingness—the Apotheosis of the World.

Opposed elements stand to each other in mutual requirement. In their unity, they inhibit or contrast. God and the World stand to each other in this opposed requirement. God is the infinite ground of all mentality, the unity of vision seeking physical multiplicity. The World is the multiplicity of finites, actualities seeking a perfected unity. Neither God, nor the World, reaches static completion. Both are in the grip of the ultimate metaphysical ground, the creative advance into novelty. Either of them, God and the World, is the instrument of novelty for the other.

In every respect God and the World move conversely to each other in respect to their process. God is primordially one, namely, he is the primordial unity of relevance of the many potential forms;† in the process he acquires a consequent multiplicity, which the primordial character absorbs into its own unity. The World is primordially many, namely, the many actual occasions with their physical finitude; in the process it acquires a consequent unity, which is a novel occasion and is absorbed into the multiplicity of the primordial character. Thus God is to be conceived as one and as many in the converse sense in which the World is to be conceived as many and as one. The theme of Cosmology, which is the basis of all reli- [530] gions, is the story of the dynamic effort of the World passing into everlasting unity, and of the static majesty of God's vision, accomplishing its purpose of completion by absorption of the World's multiplicity of effort.

SECTION VI

The consequent nature of God is the fulfilment of his experience by his reception of the multiple freedom of actuality into the harmony of his own actualization. It is God as really actual, completing the deficiency of his mere conceptual actuality.

Every categoreal type of existence in the world presupposes the other types in terms of which it is explained. Thus the many eternal objects conceived in their bare isolated multiplicity lack any existent character. They require the transition to the conception of them as efficaciously existent by reason of God's conceptual realization of them.

But God's conceptual realization is nonsense if thought of under the guise of a barren, eternal hypothesis. It is God's conceptual realization performing an efficacious rôle in multiple unifications of the universe, which are free creations of actualities arising out of decided situations. Again this discordant multiplicity of actual things, requiring each other and neglecting each other, utilizing and discarding, perishing and yet claiming life as obstinate matter of fact, requires an enlargement of the understanding to the comprehension of another phase in the nature of things. In this later phase, the many actualities are one actuality, and the one actuality is many actualities. Each actuality has its present life and its immediate passage into novelty; but its passage is not its death. This final phase of passage in God's nature is ever enlarging itself. In it the complete adjustment of the immediacy of joy and suffering reaches the final end of creation. This end is existence in the perfect unity of adjustment as means, and in the perfect multiplicity of the attainment of individual types of [531] self-existence. The function of being a means is not disjoined from the function of being an end. The sense of worth beyond itself is immediately enjoyed as an overpowering element in the individual self-attainment. It is in this way that the immediacy of sorrow and pain is transformed into an element of triumph. This is the notion of redemption through suffering† which haunts the world. It is the generalization of its very minor exemplification as the aesthetic value of discords in art.

Thus the universe is to be conceived as attaining the active self-expression of its own variety of opposites—of its own freedom and its own necessity, of its own multiplicity and its own unity, of its own imperfection and its own perfection. All the 'opposites' are elements in the nature of things, and are incorrigibly there. The concept of 'God' is the way in which we understand this incredible fact—that what cannot be, yet is.

SECTION VII

Thus the consequent nature of God is composed of a multiplicity of elements with individual self-realization. It is just as much a multiplicity as it is a unity; it is just as much one immediate fact as it is an unresting advance beyond itself. Thus the actuality of God must also be understood as a multiplicity of actual components in process of creation. This is God in his function of the kingdom of heaven.

Each actuality in the temporal world has its reception into God's nature. The corresponding element in God's nature is not temporal actuality, but is the transmutation of that temporal actuality into a living, ever-present fact. An enduring personality in the temporal world is a route of occasions in which the successors with some peculiar completeness sum up their predecessors. The correlate fact in God's nature is an even more complete unity of life in a chain of elements for which succession does not mean loss of immediate unison. This element in God's nature inherits from the temporal counterpart [532] according to the same principle as in the temporal world the future inherits from the past. Thus in the sense in which the present occasion is the person *now*, and yet with his own past, so the counterpart in God is that person in God.

But the principle of universal relativity is not to be stopped at the consequent nature of God. This nature itself passes into the temporal world according to its gradation of relevance to the various concrescent occasions. There are thus four creative phases in which the universe accomplishes its actuality. There is first the phase of conceptual origination, deficient in actuality, but infinite in its adjustment of valuation. Secondly, there is the temporal phase of physical origination, with its multiplicity of actualities. In this phase full actuality is attained; but there is deficiency in the solidarity of individuals with each other. This phase derives its determinate conditions from the first phase. Thirdly, there is the phase of perfected actuality, in which the many are one everlastingly, without the qualification of any loss either of individual identity or of completeness of unity. In everlastingness, immediacy is reconciled with objective immortality. This phase derives the conditions of its being from the two antecedent phases. In the fourth phase, the creative action completes itself. For the perfected actuality passes back into the temporal world, and qualifies this world so that each temporal actuality includes it as an immediate fact of relevant experience. For the kingdom of heaven is with us today. The action of the fourth phase is the love of God for the world. It is the particular providence for particular occasions. What is done in the world is transformed into a reality in heaven, and the reality in heaven passes back into the world. By reason of this reciprocal relation, the love in the world passes into the love in heaven, and floods back again into the world. In this sense, God is the great companion—the fellow-sufferer who understands.

[533] We find here the final application of the doctrine of objective immortality. Throughout the perishing occasions in the life of each temporal Creature, the inward source of distaste or of refreshment, the judge arising out of the very nature of things, redeemer or goddess of mischief, is the transformation of Itself, everlasting in the Being of God. In this way, the insistent craving is justified—the insistent craving that zest for existence be refreshed by the ever-present, unfading importance of our immediate actions, which perish and yet live for evermore.

INDEX

INDEX

Prepared by David Ray Griffin

Notes: (1) After terms which are modified, page references sometimes precede the modifications. These are of two types: single-page references are to occurrences which are trivial and/or do not fit under any of the modifications; multiple-page references are usually to extended discussions. (2) The Table of Contents is not indexed.

Abruptness, 184, 187, 189

Absolute: idealism, xiii, 7, 116, 200; God as, 7; qualified by universals, 43; self-realization, 51, 60; duration and place, 70–72; and phenomenal world, 116; freedom, 132; of Bradley, 190, 200; and relations, 229; motion, 321

Abstraction(s), 3, 6, 7, 16–17, 18, 20, 22, 28, 30, 63, 73, 75, 93, 97, 101, 116, 133, 146, 160, 162, 163, 167, 203, 210, 220, 231, 235, 238, 254, 287, 307

Abstractive set, 297–333

Acceleration, 101, 321

Accidents, 7, 55, 78

Act: of experience, 40, 68, 75, 155–56, 157; of becoming, 69; of causation, 236; of perception, 236

Action, 49, 78, 104, 142, 181; at a distance, 308

Actual entity: synonym for actual occasion, 18, 22, 73, 77, 141, 211; primordial, 40, 65, 75, 86; non-temporal, 46; normally excludes God, 88; conditioned, 88

Actual entity(-ies), occasion(s): present in others, 7, 41, 48, 50, 56, 145, 149, 291; formative elements of, 15; grades (species) of, 15, 18, 98, 108, 110, 111, 115, 116, 119–20, 148, 149, 177–78, 239; finality of, 18, 22, 24, 158, 219; plurality of, 18; interdependence of, 18, 59; one genus of, 18, 77, 110; metaphysical characteristics of, 18–19, 88–89, 90, 110; examples of, 19, 91; and eternal objects, 22, 25, 158, 219,

220, 239; functioning of, 25; definition of, 25, 41, 212; prehending thing, 41; as dipolar, 45, 108, 239; in and for itself, 51, 88; specified and unspecified, 60; as somewhere, 59, 67; atomize continuum, 62, 72, 77, 80; as everywhere, 67; as extensive, 67, 77; and societies, 72, 73; as ego, soul, mind, 75, 141; and endurance, 78, 136; as new (creation), 80, 210, 232–33, 238; as creator, 85, 255; threefold character of, 87; as feeler, 88; as molecular, 94–95; living, 102, 104, 109, 184; capacities of, 110, 112; simplest elements of, 115; not sum of parts, 140; completion of, 214–15; past, 219, 244; as effects, 220, 236; particularity of, 221, 230; as reproduction of many, 238; as union of two worlds, 248; two-way functioning of, 271. *See also* Occasions

Actuality: and the ultimate, 7; non-derivative, 32; and potentiality, 40; of the temporal, 40; meaning of, 43, 56, 75, 80, 211; as stubborn fact, 43; efficacy of, 46; human being as, 47; particularity of, 55; as atomic, 61, 62; prehended by God, 88; Descartes' view of, 144–45; standard of, 145; substance-quality notion of, 145, 156; as general term, 147; as process, 200, 243; future, 215; as self-realizing, 222; definition as soul of, 223; characterizes creativity, 225; super-, 286; quasi-, 293; as means and end, 340–41; as dipolar, 348; as all in all, 348

Actual occasion: synonym for actual en-

355

EDITORS' NOTES

EDITORS' NOTES

All divergencies (or, in some instances, *types* of divergencies) from one or both of the two original editions are signaled in the text by either a single obelisk (†) or a double obelisk (‡). *Single obelisks* indicate changes which are usually obvious and often trivial. *Double obelisks* indicate two sorts of changes: (1) they indicate changes which are not so obvious and which may affect the sense of the text, and (2) they are used to flag the first occurrences of changes which are very trivial and have been changed subsequently without further notation—changes such as inserting hyphens in words which had been hyphenated in only some of their occurrences.

A note is provided below for each obelisk; it describes the change made, indicates whether the divergence is from only one edition or both, and, where this was deemed appropriate, provides justification for the change. (We have not noted those divergencies from the Cambridge edition which merely reflect such American editorial conventions as putting periods and commas inside rather than outside quotation marks.)

There are also notes for some passages where no changes have been made. These notes are signaled in the text by either a single asterisk (*) or a double asterisk (**). *Single asterisks* indicate comments which are non-controversial, as, for example, when we indicate marginalia found in Whitehead's personal copies of *Process and Reality*. *Double asterisks* indicate comments about other possible readings of the text; these often reflect actual suggestions for changes made by Whitehead scholars.

Some of the notes do not quite fit neatly into one or another of these four classes, but by and large they do, and this system tells the reader which notes are most worthwhile consulting. It would probably make sense for the general reader to ignore notes indicated by single obelisks.

Where a change from the Macmillan edition is involved, the letter "M," followed by the page and line of the passage in Macmillan, is placed in parentheses after the description of the change; where a change from the Cambridge edition is involved, the same is done with the letter "C." For example, "(M 42.4)" means page 42, line 4 of the Macmillan edition. (In counting the lines on a page, section and chapter headings have been counted, but running heads at the tops of pages have not.) Very often a note is followed by both an M reference and a C reference; this indicates that the present text deviates from both original editions, which, unless we indicate otherwise, had the same reading. In many places, however, the two original editions diverged. *A note followed by a reference to only one edition signifies that only the edition referenced was modified and that this corrected text therefore follows the reading of the unmentioned edition.* For example, the note "changed 'nation' to 'notion' (M 51.9)" indicates that the word "notion" was misspelled in only the

391

Macmillan edition. In such a case *we* have not actually introduced a change, but have simply made this new edition conform to one of the original editions (in this case Cambridge).

The external sources cited as the basis for some of the changes have been identified in the Editors' Preface.

* xi.2   The bracketed number in the text indicates the exact place at which the corresponding page began in the 1929 Macmillan edition.

† xi.14   inserted 'the' before 'scheme' (M v.17)—As explained above, the fact that there is a reference to only the Macmillan edition (M) means that this corrected edition follows Cambridge at this point.

‡ xi.16   inserted comma after 'part' (M v.20) to conform to parallels in the previous and following paragraphs (as Cambridge did)—Series of introductory phrases (e.g., "In the first case, . . . in the second case, . . .") were quite often punctuated inconsistently. We have made the punctuation consistent at these points without further notation.

* xi fn.1   Whitehead used the thirtieth edition of Locke's *Essay*, which was printed for Thomas Tegg in London in 1846 by James Nichols. In the "Advertisement" at the front, Nichols says that this edition "is nearly an exact reprint of the sixth"; however, he also says that the sixth edition was "carelessly executed," and that in his edition "considerable pains have been bestowed on the punctuation." The punctuation of this edition differs considerably from that of the editions preferred today. In those few places where the quotations in Cambridge and Macmillan differed from this edition, we have brought them into conformity with it.

† xii.8   deleted comma after 'cosmology' (M vi.25; C vi.15); changed 'bring' to 'brings' (M vi.26; C vi.16)

† xii.25   changed 'them' to 'their' (M vii.10)

† xiv.20   decapitalized 'the' (M x.3)

‡ xvii.26   decapitalized 'between' (M 3.22; C v.25)—We have made the capitalization in the Table of Contents consistent without further notation.

† xviii.18   inserted comma after 'namely' (M 4.8; C xii.7)

† xviii.37   changed 'Giveness' to 'Givenness' (M 57.11)

† xix.10   inserted comma after 'Determined' (M 57.20)

† xix.22   italicized '*Essay*' (M 57.32; C xiii.1)

** xx.11   It might be supposed that 'Lure of Feeling' is an error, since Whitehead usually writes 'lure *for* feeling'; however, the text corresponding to this entry in the Table of Contents has 'lures of feeling' (88.3).

† xx.13   inserted comma after 'Environment' (M 58.29)

† xx.32   changed 'Trivialty' here and in following line to 'Triviality' (M 59.8, 9)

‡ xx.35   changed 'Co-ordination' to 'Coordination' (C xiv.11)—Macmillan usually did not hyphenate 'coordination' and 'coordinate'; Cambridge always did. We have, usually without further notation, written these words without the hyphen.

† xxi.7   changed 'Amplifyer' to 'Amplifier' (M 59.23)

† xxii.23   changed comma after 'Feeling' to colon (M 60.40; C xv.37)

† xxii.31   changed semicolon after 'Misconceptions' to colon (M 61.8)

† xxiii.5   changed 'Propositions' to 'The Propositions' (M 61.23)

* xxiii.29   'Samples' is evidently used here as a verb.

† xxiii.35   changed comma after 'Spatialization' to semicolon and comma after 'Fluency' to colon (M 62.14; C xvii.3)

† xxiv.6   changed 'Feelings' to 'The Theory of Feelings' (M 331.2)

† xxiv.10   changed '*Objectivè*' to '*Objectivé*' (M 331.7)

† xxiv.30   decapitalized and italicized '(*continued*)' (M 331.27)

† xxvi.17   italicized '*be*' (M 333.13; C xix.12)

† xxvi.32   changed colon after 'Perceptive Feelings' to semicolon (M 333.28; C xix.29)

† xxvi.42   changed 'Functon' to 'Function' (M 333.39)

† xxvii.17   deleted 'In Suspense Form Diversity and Incompatibility' before 'In Suspense-Form' and inserted hyphen in 'Suspense-Form' (M 334.13–14; C xx.9–10)

‡ xxviii.23   inserted commas after both instances of 'i.e.' (M 431.31; C xxi.18)—Cambridge printed 'i.e.' and 'e.g.' in most cases without commas following them; Macmillan had commas in many instances. We have always, without further notation, put commas after these abbreviations.

† xxix.15   changed semicolon after 'Involved' to colon (M 432.26; C xxii.5)

† xxx.8   changed comma after 'Geometries' to colon (M 433.19; C xxii.40)

† xxx.21   changed semicolon after 'Opposites' to colon (M 511.5; C xxx.5)

† xxx.29   changed comma after 'Paradox' to colon (M 511.12; C xxiii.13)

† xxx.31   changed comma after 'Opposites' to colon (M 511.14; C xxiii.15)

† xxx.38   changed comma after 'God' to colon (M 511.21; C xxiii.22)

† xxx.40   changed '*On*' to '*Concerning*' (M 511.23; C xxiii.24)

‡ 4.28   inserted hyphen in 'starting-point' (M 6.28)—Macmillan did not hyphenate this expression; Cambridge always did. We have followed Cambridge's practice without further notation.

† 6.12   inserted comma after 'mathematics' (M 9.7; C 7.19)

† 6.39   inserted comma after 'But' (M 10.4)

† 6.43   deleted heading '§ III' (C 8.20)—Cf. the note for 7.30.

* 7.22   In his Macmillan copy, Whitehead underlined 'non-temporal accident' and wrote "*non-historical*" in the margin.

† 7.30   inserted 'SECTION III' (M 11.13; C 9.23)—This change was made by Whitehead in his Macmillan copy. Cf. the note for 6.43.

† 7.39   inserted comma after 'termed' (M 11.24)

† 9.14   changed 'in' to 'with' (M 13.26)

† 11.1   changed 'Leibnitz' to 'Leibniz' (M 16.10; C 14.13)

* 11.24   In his Macmillan copy, Whitehead underlined 'proposing a fact' and wrote "careless" in the margin.

‡ 12.5   changed parentheses to brackets (M 17.31; C 15.32)—There are many places where Whitehead's own insertions into direct quotations were enclosed in parentheses instead of brackets; we have introduced brackets in these places without further notation.

‡ 12.7   replaced semicolon after 'distinguished' with comma (M 17.34; C 15.34)—The punctuation, including italics, in direct quotations sometimes did not correspond exactly to that in the original sources. We have made corrections without further notation.

‡ 12 fn.4   deleted 'Cf.' at the beginning of the footnote (M 18 fn.4; C 16 fn.1)—A directly-quoted passage is being identified. Similar occurrences of 'Cf.' have been deleted without further notation.

† 16.36   changed 'generalizaing' to 'generalizing' (M 24.36–37)

‡ 17.6   inserted hyphen in 'subject-matter' (M 25.18)—Macmillan often did not hyphenate this expression; Cambridge always did. We have followed Cambridge's practice without further notation.

† 17.12   deleted comma after 'society' (M 25.26)—This is one of many places where Cambridge deleted a comma between the subject and the verb.

‡ 18.2   While correcting proofs, Whitehead changed the title of this chapter from "The Categorical Scheme" to "The Categoreal Scheme." Macmillan, unlike Cambridge, did not change the running heads accordingly. We have made these changes without further notation.

† 18.32   capitalized 'Cartesian' (M 28.11)

† 18.34   Macmillan inserted the abbreviations 'Bk.,' 'Ch.' and 'Sect.' into this reference, the first one to Locke's *Essay* within the body of the work (C 25.8). For the edition used, see the note for xi fn.1.

† 18.35   put quoted words in double instead of single quotation marks (M 28.14–15; C 25.8–9)

‡ 19.40   changed '*Monodology*' to '*Monadology*' (M 29.28; C 26.19)—This change was made by Whitehead throughout his Macmillan copy. We have incorporated this correction without further notation.

† 20 fn.2   added 'Press' (M 30 fn.2)

‡ 21.1   capitalized 'Category' (M 31.8)—Both editions were hopelessly inconsistent in the matter of capitalizing references to particular categories. There are three major types of references involved: (1) Expressions such as 'fourth category of explanation' and 'ninth categoreal obligation' were usually not capitalized, but occasionally were—e.g., 'fourth Category of Explanation.' (2) Whitehead often used Roman numerals to refer to the categoreal obligations. Such references in the present chapter were uncapitalized—e.g., 'category (iv)'—in conformity with the fact that the Roman numerals were not capitalized in the initial listing of the categoreal obligations in this chapter. Later in the book, the Roman numerals were capitalized, in conformity with the presentation of the categoreal obligations in Part III. The word 'category' preceding the Roman numeral was also capitalized—e.g., 'Category IV.' However, when the term 'categoreal condition' was used, it was left uncapitalized, even though the Roman numeral was capitalized— e.g., 'categoreal condition IV.' (3) In references to 'the Category of the Ultimate,' and to particular categoreal obligations which designate them by name (e.g., 'the Category of Transmutation'), either the name of the category, or both it and the term 'category' (or 'categoreal condition'), were very frequently capitalized. In a couple of places (here and 247.27), Cambridge capitalized the entire reference which Macmillan had left partially or wholly uncapitalized. On the basis of these precedents, and of the high frequency with which instances of this third type were already capitalized, we capitalized (without further notation) the remaining instances of this third type. However, there was no similar justification for bringing consistency into the references of the first and second types.

* 21.14   In the margin of his Macmillan copy, Whitehead wrote: " 'Potentiality' is closely allied to 'disjunctive diversity.' "

* 21.18   In the margin of his Macmillan copy, Whitehead wrote: "cf. p. 47." The reference is to 31.29 of this corrected edition.

‡ 22.17   changed period after 'Prehension' in previous line to comma and inserted '*or Patterned Entities.*' (M 33.6; C 29.28)—This change was made by Whitehead in his Macmillan copy.

‡ 22.29   inserted 'in disjunctive diversity' (M 33.21; C 30.7)—This change was made by Whitehead in his Macmillan copy.

* 22.35   In the margin of his Macmillan copy, Whitehead wrote: "cf. Plato's *Sophist* 247 i.e. disjunctive diversity is potentiality."

† 22.36   deleted comma after 'actuality' (M 33.30; C 30.15)

† 23.4   deleted comma after 'concrescence' (M 34.7; C 30.27)

‡ 23.27　took semicolon after '*is*' out of italics (M 34.37)—Macmillan frequently italicized a colon or semicolon following an italicized word; Cambridge, never. We have followed Cambridge's convention without further notation.

† 24.36　deleted comma after 'instance' (M 36.33; C 33.10)

† 25.27　changed 'definitness' to 'definiteness' (M 38.7)—This change was made by Whitehead in his Macmillan copy.

* 26.37　In the margin of his Macmillan copy, Whitehead wrote: "cf. p. 382." The reference is to 250.9–10 of this corrected edition.

† 27.2　changed parentheses around 'v' and both instances of 'iv' to brackets (C 36.23)

† 27.4　deleted commas after 'analogous' and 'simple' (M 40.16–17; C 36.25) to conform to the identical passage at 251.15

‡ 27.31　changed 'is an intensity of feeling' to 'is at intensity of feeling' (C 37.22–23)—Evidently here the Cambridge editor, not understanding Whitehead's thought, "miscorrected" the text; cf. the note for 277.42.

† 28.9　deleted 'subsequent' before 'discussion' (M 42.4)

* 29.17　The first printing of the Macmillan edition had: "But subject-superject, and neither half of this description can of 'subject-superject.'" Whitehead wrote the correct sentence in his Macmillan copy. This sentence was correctly written in the first printing of the Cambridge edition and in subsequent printings of the Macmillan edition.

† 29.23　changed '2d' to '2nd' (M 44.3)

† 30.1　changed 'are multiplicities' to 'is a multiplicity' (M 44.33; C 40.35)

** 31.16　It has been suggested that 'actual occasions' should read 'actual entities,' since Whitehead has God's agency in view here and yet says elsewhere that the term 'actual occasions' excludes God (88.29–30). It is possible that, when writing the present passage, Whitehead had not yet settled upon this distinction between the two terms.

* 31.29　In the margin of his Macmillan copy, Whitehead wrote: "cf. p. 31." The reference is to 21.18 of this corrected edition.

† 32.14　inserted comma after 'example' (M 47.33)

† 33.8　put 'impure' in quotation marks (M 49.8; C 44.37)

† 33.22　put 'intuition' in quotation marks (M 49.26; C 45.17)

† 33.26　changed 'Obligations' to 'Obligation' (C 45.21)

† 33.34　inserted 'of' before 'evil' (M 50.4; C 45.31) to agree with the quotation two sentences below

† 33.39　changed 'appetion' to 'appetition' (M 50.11–12)—This change was included on the list entitled "Misprints."

* 34.20　In the quotation of this passage in *Adventures of Ideas* (Macmillan, 1933, p. 261), 'positive feelings involving that' was substituted for 'positive feelings of that.'

† 34.21　changed 'nation' to 'notion' (M 51.9)—This change was made by Whitehead in his Macmillan copy.

† 34.22　inserted 'of' after 'notion' (M 51.10)

‡ 34.39　took 's' after '*B*' out of italics (M 51.32)—Macmillan italicized the 's' in such instances; Cambridge did not. We have followed Cambridge's convention without further notation.

* 36.1　In his Macmillan copy, Whitehead underlined 'not' and put two question marks in the margin, with "cf. p. 173" written above them. The reference is to 113.20 of this corrected edition; cf. the note for that passage.

† 36.4　deleted comma after 'complexity' (M 53.19)

† 36.9　inserted 'a' before 'wave front' (M 53.25; C 49.12)

† 36.39   took 'Parts' out of single quotation marks (M 54.28; C 50.11)

† 39.13   inserted 'the' before 'European' (M 63.3; C 53.15)

† 39.28   changed 'writing' to 'writings' (M 63.23)

** 40.13   It has been suggested that 'orderings' should read 'ordering.' Evidence for this is provided by the fact that the Table of Contents has it in the singular. However, the content of the previous sentence in the text, along with the use of 'such' (which normally takes a plural noun), supports the text as it is.

* 40 fn.1   Whitehead would have, of course, been using their 1911–12 translation, not their 1931 corrected edition, which most scholars today use.

† 41 fn.6   took 'for' out of italics (M 65 fn.6)

† 42.1   changed 'from' to 'form' (M 66.35)—This change was included on the list entitled "Misprints."

† 42.7   deleted comma after 'theory' (M 67.4; C 57.10)

* 42 fn.7   The quotation is from p. 455.

** 43.23   It has been suggested that 'decision' should read 'decisions.'

* 43.29   In British usage, 'eat' can express the past tense.

† 44.24   changed 'be' to 'the' (M 70.24)

‡ 44.25   decapitalized 'he' (C 60.27)—Cambridge capitalized occurrences of 'he' and 'him' referring to God; Macmillan did not. We have followed Macmillan's convention without further notation.

* 44.32   In the margin of his Cambridge copy, Whitehead wrote: "Thus consciousness is a factor in the subjective form of the prehension of data as given. Cf. pp. 344, 369, on the 'affirmation-negation contrast.'" These pages correspond to pp. 371–72 and 399 of the Macmillan edition and to pp. 243 and 261 of this corrected edition.

* 44.39   In the margin of his Cambridge copy, Whitehead wrote: "Law of Excluded Middle."

* 45.28   In the margin of his Cambridge copy, Whitehead wrote: "i.e. the 'Satisfaction' is always objective. It never feels itself."

† 46.12   inserted closing quotation mark after 'God' (M 73.12)

‡ 46.15   changed 'efficacity' to 'efficacy' (M 73.16; C 63.12)—Both editions sometimes had the archaic form 'efficacity' instead of 'efficacy.' The list entitled "Misprints" drew attention to this discrepancy in reference to Macmillan 184 (120 of this corrected edition); Cambridge changed 'efficacity' to 'efficacy' at 316.39. We have changed the remaining instances to 'efficacy' without further notation.

† 46.24   put quotation mark before 'the' here and in preceding line instead of before 'multiplicity' and 'class' (M 73.28–29)

‡ 47.17   deleted 'only' after 'illustrated' (M 74.38; C 64.31)—The presence of 'only' produced a contradiction between this sentence and the following one. This 'only' was perhaps transposed by the typist from the following sentence.

† 49.33   italicized '*Meditations II*' and '*III*' (M 78.24)

* 50.4   The quotation is from Shakespeare's *A Midsummer-Night's Dream*, Act III.

† 50.6   changed 'commonsense' to 'common sense' (M 79.3)

† 50.28   deleted parentheses around 'A substance' (M 79.30; C 69.16)— They (or brackets) are not needed, since this is not a direct quotation.

* 50 fn.13   As stated in the note for 40 fn.1, Whitehead was using the 1911–12 Haldane and Ross translation; this sentence was completely retranslated in their 1931 corrected edition.

† 51.5   changed 'on' to '*Concerning*' (M 80.17; C 70.2)

† 51.28   capitalized '*Concerning*' (M 81.9; C 70.29)

† 51.33   capitalized 'Concerning' (C 70.35)

† 52.23   changed 'I, I, 1' to 'II, I, 1' (M 82.20–21; C 72.2)

† 52.27   inserted 'are' after 'as' (M 82.25; C 72.6)

† 52.30   deleted comma after 'later' (M 82.28)

† 53.11   changed 'Section 3' to 'Section 4' (M 83.23; C 73.3)

† 53.16   changed 'parts' to 'sorts' (M 83.29; C 73.9)

† 53.39   changed 'Section 13' to 'Section 15' (M 84.24; C 74.4)

† 54.4   changed 'entities. Though' to 'entities, though' (M 84.30)

† 54.14   inserted comma after 'cited' (M 85.4)

† 54.17   changed 'illusioriness' to 'illusoriness' (M 85.9)

† 54.27   inserted 'the' before 'exception' (M 85.20; C 74.37)

† 55.43   changed 'or' to 'of' (M 87.24; C 76.36)

† 56.12   inserted comma after 'that' (M 88.4; C 77.15)

‡ 56.18   changed 'an' to 'a' before 'historic' (M 88.11; C 77.22)—Both editions alternated between 'a' and 'an' before words beginning with 'h.' We have changed each such instance of 'an' to 'a' without further notation.

† 57.22   changed '1' to '1–3' (M 89.37; C 79.8–9)

† 57.31   changed 'thing' to 'things' (M 90.10; C 79.19)

† 57.36   inserted 'the' before 'like' (M 90.16; C 79.24)

* 57.41   'Power' begins the quotation from Section 2.

* 57.43   'I confess' begins the quotation from Section 3.

† 59.20   changed 'these' to 'those' (M 92.31; C 81.30)

† 59.23   changed 'thus' to 'this' (M 92.35)

† 59.24   inserted 'most' (M 92.36; C 81.34)

† 59.33   Although 'coexisting' was hyphenated in the above quotation from Locke, we followed Macmillan, as against Cambridge, in printing Whitehead's own use of the word without the hyphen (C 82.7).

† 60.26   changed 'B II, C XIV, D 1' to 'II, XIV, 1' (M 94.20)

† 61.17   changed 'physcial' to 'physical' (M 95.22)

† 61.23   inserted hyphen in 'sense-data' (M 96.2–3; C 84.28) to conform to the usual practice of both editions

† 62.30   deleted comma after 'eternal objects' (M 97.21; C 86.12)—The comma made the sentence erroneously suggest that all eternal objects are sense-data; cf. 64.28, where the same expression was written without the comma.

† 64.28   deleted comma after 'sense-data' (M 100.17)

‡ 68.31   changed 'earlier' to 'indicated' (M 106.25; C 95.2)—Only with this change does the sentence make sense; perhaps the typist transposed 'earlier creature' from the previous line.

† 68 fn.4   changed '*in*' to '*of*' in '*Some Problems of Philosophy*' (M 106 fn.4; C 94 fn.3); decapitalized 'the' (M 106 fn.4)

† 69.12   inserted comma after 'successor' (M 107.15; C 95.27)

† 70.32   inserted 'the' before 'means' (M 109.26; C 97.31)

‡ 71.4   inserted 'sucession; and in space as to order of' (M 110.6–7; C 98.8–9)

† 72.11   put quotation mark before 'the' instead of 'vulgar' here and at 72.28 (M 111.34, 112.16; C 99.25–26, 100.9)

† 73.5   put passage in double instead of single quotation marks (M 113.7–9; C 100.36–101.1)

† 73.8   changed 'epistomological' to 'epistemological' (M 113.12)

† 74.12   inserted 'the' after 'any' (M 115.1; C 102.25)

‡ 75.9   changed 'III' to 'IV' (M 116.13; C 103.31)—Perhaps the first paragraph of Section IV was originally part of Section III.

† 75.21   changed period after 'conceive it' to comma (M 116.29; C 104.9)

† 76.9   changed 'well' to 'dwell' (M 117.31)—This change was made by Whitehead in his Macmillan copy.

† 76.9   put both passages in double instead of single quotation marks (M 117.29–31; C 105.7–9)

† 76.41   changed 'exemplication' to 'exemplification' (M 118.33)

† 76 fn.8   decapitalized *'the'* (M 118 fn.8; C 105 fn.1)

† 77.18   changed 'synonomously' to 'synonymously' (M 119.23)

† 78.34   changed 'adventure' to 'adventures' (M 121.23; C 108.35)

† 80.1   changed 'substance' to *'substances'* (M 123.19; C 110.28)—This, incidentally, is a place where correcting the punctuation in quoted material required adding italics.

† 80.5   inserted comma after 'substance' (M 123.25)

† 80.24   put 'nexus' in single instead of double quotation marks (M 124.13)

† 82.8   changed 'the' to 'a' (M 126.31; C 114.2)

† 82 fn.9   inserted '28A'; changed *'the'* to *'Plato's'* (M 126 fn.9; C 113 fn.1)

† 83.17   changed comma before 'disorder' to semicolon (M 127.21; C 115.20)

† 84.15   put 'final causes' in quotation marks (M 128.36; C 116.28)

† 85.9   changed double to single quotation marks (M 130.12–13; C 118.2) —This is not a direct quotation: 'It' is not in the quoted passage.

† 85 fn.1   inserted '10' after 'xxxvii' (M 131 fn.1; C 118 fn.1)

* 86.15   Whitehead used *The Philosophical Works of David Hume*, in four volumes, published in 1854 by Little, Brown and Company, Boston, and by Adam and Charles Black, Edinburgh. The punctuation of the *Treatise* in this edition differs considerably from that in editions of the *Treatise* which are now more commonly used. In those few places where the quotations in Cambridge and Macmillan differed from this edition, we have brought them into conformity with it.

† 86.30   changed 'of' to 'or' (M 132.25)

† 86.38   changed 'has never' to 'never has' (M 132.34; C 120.17)

† 86.42   changed 'between' to 'betwixt' (M 133.3; C 120.22)

† 86.44   deleted 'to' before 'raise' (M 133.6; C 120.24)

† 87.4   changed 'instances' to 'instance' (M 133.11)

† 87.35   deleted hyphen in 'threefold' (M 134.15)

† 87.45   changed 'an unity' to 'a unity' (M 134.28)

* 88.3   See the note for xx.11.

‡ 88.6   changed 'This' to 'His' (M 134.35; C 122.9)—Whitehead's hand-written 'H' is such that it could appear to a typist to be 'Th'; cf. the notes for 139.34 and 225.36.

† 88.9   put closing quotation mark after 'nature' instead of after 'superjective' (M 135.2; C 122.13) to conform to parallels above

‡ 88.13   changed 'goal' to 'goad' (M 135.8; C 122.18)—In agreement with most other scholars consulted, we do not think that the expression 'goal towards novelty' makes sense. Also, the presence of 'goal' in the text is easily intelligible as a mistranscription of Whitehead's handwriting. An objection to this change might be that the use of the word 'goad' in this context is incompatible with Whitehead's conception as to how God influences the world, i.e., by presenting ideals which serve as lures for feeling. It is, however, quite normal to say that one person goads another to action when the former insistently presents the latter with an attractive ideal.

** 89.35   It has been suggested that 'a' should be inserted before 'man.'

† 89 fn.2   deleted comma after 'Cf.' (M 136 fn.2); deleted 'and' before '*The Order of Nature*' and changed 'both' to 'all' (M 136 fn.2; C 123 fn.1)

† 89 fn.3   deleted comma after 'cf.' (M 136 fn.3)

† 93 fn.6   decapitalized '*the*' (M 143 fn.6; C 129 fn.1)

‡ 95.12   changed 'quantum-theory' to 'quantum theory' (M 145.26–27; C 132.16)—Both editions occasionally printed this expression with the hyphen. We have, without further notation, deleted the hyphen in all such instances.

† 96.6   capitalized 'Night' (M 146.32; C 133.21)

† 97 fn.11   changed 'Ch.' here and in following footnote to 'Chs.' (M 148 fns.11, 12)

† 97 fn.13   changed '*Sixth Memoir on Quantities*' to ' "Sixth Memoir on Quantics" ' (M 149 fn.13; C 136 fn.1); changed 'R.S., Trans. 1859' (M 149 fn.13) and 'R.S. Trans. 1859' (C 136 fn.1) to '*Transactions of the Royal Society*'

† 98 fn.14   inserted hyphen in 'congruence-definition' (M 149 fn.14)

† 99.6   deleted comma after 'inter-relations' (M 151.7; C 137.27)

† 99.22   changed 'it' to 'itself' (M 151.29; C 138.11)

† 100.5   changed 'difference' to 'differences' (M 152.25; C 139.5)

† 100.18   inserted period after 'components' (M 153.4)

† 100.33   deleted comma after 'features' (M 153.23; C 140.1)

† 101.2   changed 'members. Whereas' to 'members, whereas' (M 154.3)

† 101.6   changed 'problems' to 'problem' (M 154.8)—This change was included on the list entitled "Misprints."

† 101.33   decapitalized 'dynamics' (M 155.6; C 141.18) to conform to the usual practice of both editions

† 101 fn.15   capitalized 'Part' and took it out of single quotation marks (M 155 fn.1)

† 102.13   inserted comma after 'organisms' (M 155.35; C 142.9)

‡ 103.15   changed 'eternal' to 'external' (M 157.21; C 143.28)—This change was made by Whitehead in his Macmillan copy.

† 103.21   changed 'reaction' to 'reactions' (M 157.30)

† 103.34   inserted comma after 'nexūs' (M 158.9)

† 104.10   changed question mark after 'order' to period (M 158.33; C 145.2)

† 106.33   changed 'intersticial' to 'interstitial' (M 162.31)

‡ 108.6   changed 'structural' to 'structured' (M 164.32; C 150.28)

‡ 108.12   changed 'casual' to 'causal' (M 165.5; C 150.35)—We believe that a change from 'causal' to 'casual'—one of the most common typographical errors—occurred here. The context shows that Whitehead had in view the problem of interaction between two different types of substances, which is a problem of causality.

‡ 108.16   changed 'partly conformed to, and partly introductory of, a' to 'partly conformed to it, and partly introductory of a' (M 165.10–11; C 151.5–6)—It is hard to see how a conceptual reaction could be partly conformed to a relevant novel contrast; it *involves* a relevant novel contrast. What it is "partly conformed to" is the physical inheritance.

† 109.14   deleted comma after 'not' (M 166.30; C 152.22)

† 109.25   changed 'body' to 'bodily' (M 167.7; C 152.34)—This change was made by Whitehead in both of his copies.

† 111.13   changed 'that' to 'one' (M 169.34; C 155.26)—The last two lines of Tennyson's *In Memoriam* begin: "And one far-off divine event. . . ." This is probably an instance of Whitehead's quoting a passage from memory.

† 111.42   changed semicolon after 'character' to comma (M 170.35)

† 113.6   changed 'experiental' to 'experiential' (M 172.27); deleted comma after 'attained' (M 172.27; C 158.16)

‡ 113.11   deleted 'as' after 'aesthetic' (M 172.33)—This occurrence of 'transcendental aesthetic,' unlike the other two in the immediate context, was neither capitalized nor put in quotes. The other two clearly name a part of the *Critique,* whereas this occurrence can be regarded as a reference to its content. On this reading, it is possible that the deleted 'as' was a mistranscription from an 's' originally completing the word 'aesthetics.'

* 113.20   In his Macmillan copy, Whitehead underlined 'responsive conformity of feeling' and wrote "cf. p. 53" in the margin. The reference is to pp. 35–36 of this corrected edition; cf. the note for 36.1.

† 113.34   deleted comma after 'question' (M 173.25; C 159.12)

† 114.24   changed 'for' to 'from' (M 174.34)

† 114.42   changed 'show' to 'shows' (M 175.20; C 161.5)

† 115.34   deleted comma after 'feelings' (M 176.29; C 162.11)

† 116.41   changed 'experiment' to 'experient' (M 178.20–21; C 163.37)

† 117.35   changed 'anything' to 'any thing' (M 179.33; C 165.10)

‡ 117 fn.1   inserted 'Bk.I,' (M 179 fn.1; C 165 fn.1)—The references to the *Treatise* were not uniform: sometimes '*Treatise*' was omitted; sometimes the Part; and always the Book. We have, without further notation, brought all footnote references to the *Treatise* into standard form.

* 117 fn.2   The italics in this quotation were also (as in the one before it) not in the original.

† 118.8   inserted hyphens in 'such-and-such' here (M 180.14–15; C 165.25–26) and in lines 10 and 18 (M 180.16–17 & 27–28; C 165.28, 166.2)

† 118.11   changed 'though' to 'through' (M 180.19)—This change was included on the list entitled "Misprints."

† 118.23   deleted comma after 'conclusion' (C 166.9)

† 118.29   inserted 'to us' (M 181.4; C 166.13)

† 119.36   changed 'nexus' to 'nexūs' (M 182.32; C 168.2)—This change was made by Whitehead in his Macmillan copy.

† 120.1   changed 'gives' to 'give' (M 183.6; C 168.11)

† 120.6   changed 'vector-character' to 'vector character' (M 183.12–13; C 168.17) to conform to the usual spelling

† 120.19   changed 'S,' (M 183.29) and 'S' (C 168.35) to 'S₁'—This change was made by Whitehead in his Macmillan copy.

‡ 121.11   changed 'be' to 'have been' and inserted 'a' before 'missile' (M 185.1; C 170.6)

† 121.30   inserted dash after 'immediacy' (M 185.27)

† 121 fn.4   changed 'of' to 'cf.' (M 185 fn.4; C 170 fn.1)—This change was made by Whitehead in his Macmillan copy.

‡ 121 fn.5   changed '*Meaning and Importance*' to '*Meaning and Effect*'; changed 'Macmillan' to '(New York: Macmillan, 1927; Cambridge University Press, 1928)' (M 185 fn.5; C 170 fn.2)—Parentheses were introduced to distinguish clearly the data relating to the lectures from that referring to the publications. It might be inferred that '*Meaning and Importance*' was used in the title of the lectures; however, Whitehead's letter to the University, and the announcement in the University's newspaper, had the following as the announced topic: "Symbolic Expression, Its Function for the Individual and for Society."

‡ 123.42   changed 'ways' to 'way' (M 189.5; C 174.2)—The following sen-

tences in the text show that Whitehead has in mind only two ways of obtaining loci; hence the mode of causal efficacy is *one* way.

† 124.32   deleted comma after 'sensa' (M 190.11; C 175.6)

† 125.16   changed 'congredient' to 'cogredient' (M 191.12; C 176.5)

† 125.42   changed comma after 'M' to semicolon (M 192.9; C 177.1)

‡ 126.13   inserted hyphen in 'strain-loci' (M 192.28; C 177.18)—Both editions consistently hyphenated this expression in Part IV; we have brought the few occurrences in the present chapter into accord with that practice without further notation.

† 127.2   deleted comma after 'say' (M 193.32; C 178.20)

** 127.3   In both of his copies, Whitehead crossed out 'of' and inserted 'in.' However, we did not change the text, since it is doubtful that the resulting expression, 'in terms in which,' would make sense. It is possible that Whitehead also meant to cross out 'in terms.' But, especially since Whitehead crossed out only the one word in both editions, we did not find that additional change justifiable. Hence, it seemed best simply to leave the text in its original condition and to alert the reader to Whitehead's marking.

** 127.32   It is possible that this is another place (like 108.12) where 'causal' was corrupted to 'casual.' However, either word makes sense in this context, and substituting one for the other would make no difference to Whitehead's main point.

† 127.38   changed 'depend' to 'depends' (M 195.3)

† 127.44   changed 'these' to 'there' (M 195.10)—This change was made by Whitehead in his Macmillan copy.

† 128.26   changed 'and' after 'societies' to comma (C 180.29)

** 128.41   It has been suggested that 'microscopic' and 'macroscopic' in this paragraph and elsewhere should be changed to 'microcosmic' and 'macrocosmic,' respectively. The doctrinal arguments are too complex to consider here. The textual arguments supporting the change might be (1) that the '-scopic' ending was introduced inadvertently by Whitehead or in the production process, or (2) that Whitehead later decided to use '-cosmic' instead of '-scopic' but did not go back and change all the occurrences of that ending. Evidence that '-cosmic' was his later preference might be provided by the fact that Macmillan indexed all the occurrences of 'macroscopic' and 'microscopic' under 'macrocosmic' and 'microcosmic,' since this might reflect Whitehead's own choice of words to be indexed. However, there are several textual considerations that, at the very least, make these possibilities remote: (1) the '-scopic' ending is used several more times than the '-cosmic' (cf. Ch. X of the Table of Contents as well as the Index); (2) it was also used in the summary of the Gifford Lectures; (3) the '-scopic' ending is used in the same context in which the words 'macrocosm' and 'microcosm' are used (pp. 214–15); (4) Whitehead did not change 'macroscopic' when it was called to his attention, due to a misspelling, after the book was printed (see the note for 214.29); (5) in a footnote (p. 333) written after the book "had been finally revised for publication," Whitehead spoke of his "doctrine of 'microscopic atomic occasions'" in reference to Northrop's notion of a "macroscopic atom'; (6) finally, we do not know how much attention, if any, Whitehead gave to the Index. His letter to his son (mentioned in the Editors' Preface) says only: "At last I have got through with my Gifford Lectures—final proofs corrected, Index Printed, and the last corrections put in." But, whoever was responsible for the Index, it was not done with great care—e.g., the important footnote on p. 333 was not indexed. Also, it is noteworthy that the Cambridge edition had the '-scopic' and '-cosmic' occurrences correctly indexed.

† 131.21   changed 'colored' to 'coloured' (M 200.2)

† 131.24   changed 'change' to 'chance' (M 200.4; C 183.34)

† 131.25   changed 'would' to 'should' (M 200.5; C 183.35)

† 132.1   changed 'the' before 'substance' to 'a' (M 200.25; C 184.19)

* 132 fn.7   For the edition quoted, see the note for 86.15.

† 133.10   deleted comma after 'freedom' (M 202.19; C 186.5)

* 133.16   The italics are Whitehead's.

† 134.27   deleted 'that' before 'this' (M 204.17; C 187.37)

† 134.29   changed single to double quotation marks (M 204.20–21; C 187. 40–188.1)

* 134.41   These latter italics are also Hume's.

† 135.3   deleted 'by' before 'the nature' (M 205.5; C 188.19)

† 135.29   changed single to double quotation marks; changed 'Ideas' to 'the Idea'; and decapitalized 'external' (M 206.5–6; C 189.18–19)

* 135 fn.9   The passage to which Whitehead refers does not come at the end of the Appendix in some editions of the *Treatise*, e.g., that of Selby–Bigge, but is followed by other material. The last three sentences of the edition Whitehead used (see the note for 86.15) read: "The second error may be found in [Bk.I, Part III, Sect. VII], where I say, that two ideas of the same object can only be different by their different degrees of force and vivacity. I believe there are other differences among ideas, which cannot properly be comprehended under these terms. Had I said, that two ideas of the same object can only be different by their different *feeling*, I should have been nearer the truth."

† 137.7   moved closing bracket from after 'time' to after 'such' (M 208.2; C 191.13)

† 137.20   changed 'endeavor' to 'endeavour' (M 208.20)

* 138.15   Whitehead used an edition (cf. the note for xi fn.1) based on Locke's English arrangement of the introductory material, not one based on Coste's French translation. In editions following Coste's arrangement, such as that of Campbell Fraser, the reference here would be 'Introduction, 8.'

† 138.18   changed '6 and 7' to '6' (M 209.36; C 193.8)—Although the quoted material is only from Sect. 6, Whitehead perhaps wanted to draw attention to some material in Sect. 7.

* 138 fn.13   Whitehead means that the italics throughout the remainder of this paragraph are his.

‡ 139.34   changed 'thence' to 'hence' (M 212.1); changed 'This' to 'His' (M 212.2; C 195.7)—Cf. the note for 88.6.

† 139 fn.15   changed footnote to its present reading from 'Cf. *Treatise*, Bk. III, Sects. V and VI' (M 211 fn.15; C 194 fn.1)

† 139 fn.16   put 'Transcendental Logic' in quotation marks and changed 'Intro. I' to 'Introduction, Sect. I' (M 211 fn.16; C 195 fn.1) for the sake of consistency

‡ 140.38   changed 'founded in' (M 213.25) and 'founded on' (C 196.27) to 'found in'

† 141.8   changed 'reflections' to 'reflection' (M 214.2–3)

* 142.23   The quotation is from *Scepticism and Animal Faith*, Ch. 7.

† 142.27   changed 'in' to 'is' (M 216.11)

† 143.3   decapitalized 'books' (M 216.35; C 199.29)—References elsewhere to the books of Locke's *Essay* are not capitalized.

† 144.4   inserted 'the' before 'different' (M 218.4; C 200.4)
† 144.27   inserted comma after 'qualities' (M 219.2)
† 144.32   deleted comma after 'another' (M 219.9)
† 145.2   inserted commas after 'is' and 'however' (M 219.19)
† 145.25   changed 'experiences' to 'experience' (M 220.11); put 'self-enjoy-ment . . . by ideas' in quotation marks (M 220.11–13; C 202.4–5)
† 146.9   changed 'preceptions' to 'perceptions' (M 221.9)
† 146.36   changed 'analysis' to 'analyse' (M 222.6)—This change was in-cluded on the list entitled "Misprints."
† 147.10   deleted comma after 'idea' (M 222.32; C 204.20)
† 148.7   changed 'are constituents' to 'is a constituent' (M 224.9; C 205.29–30)
† 149.4   inserted hyphen in 'successor-phase' (M 225.27)
† 149.32   changed 'limitations' to 'limitation' (M 226.30; C 208.9)
† 149 fn.4 inserted comma after 'Soc.' (C 207 fn.1)
† 151.15   inserted comma after 'efficient cause' (M 229.7; C 210.18) to con-form to parallel in previous clause
† 151.38   inserted comma after 'impressions' (M 229.37; C 211.11)
† 152.19   deleted comma after 'world' (M 230.31; C 212.3)
† 152.27   changed 'from' to 'for' (M 231.4)—This change was made by Whitehead in his Macmillan copy.
‡ 153.17   changed 'critical' to 'uncritical' (M 232.11; C 213.18)—This change was made by Whitehead in both of his copies.
† 154.1   put 'Transcendental Aesthetic' in quotation marks (M 233.7; C 214.12–13)
† 154.10   deleted 'is' after 'which' (M 233.18)—This change was included on the list entitled "Misprints."
* 154.21   In his Macmillan copy, Whitehead underlined 'individuality' and wrote in the margin: "= subjective form"; cf. the note for 154.37.
‡ 154.22   italicized *'qua'* (M 233.33)—Macmillan often left *'qua'* without italics; Cambridge always italicized it. We have followed Cambridge's practice without further notation.
† 154.24   deleted comma after 'rejects' (M 233.37)
† 154.28   inserted comma after 'data' (M 234.3)
* 154.37   In his Macmillan copy, Whitehead underlined 'individualization' and 'subjective side'; cf. the note for 154.21.
† 155.34   capitalized *'Materie'* (M 235.30)
† 155 fn.6 changed 'Sinnlickkert' to 'Sinnlichkeit'; changed 'Anschanungen' to 'Anschauungen' (M 235 fn.6)—The quotation is from the 'Trans-cendental Aesthetic,' A 19 B 33.
† 155 fn.7 changed *'Transcendal'* to 'Transcendental' in fns. 7 and 8 (M 235 fn.7, M 236 fn.8); took names of parts out of italics and put in quotation marks (M 235 fn.7, M 236 fn.8; C 216 fn.2, 217 fn.1)—The reference in fn. 7 is to A 86 B 118.
* 155 fn.8 The reference is to A 51 B 75. As Whitehead has indicated, the previous two quotations are taken from Max Müller's translation. This third quotation, however, corresponds to Kemp Smith's trans-lation. (Müller has the sentence italicized and translates 'Inhalt' as 'contents.')
† 157.14   changed 'II' to 'V' (M 238.17; C 219.16)
‡ 158.13   changed 'sensationalist' to 'subjectivist' (M 239.35; C 220.28)—The issue in this paragraph is *not* whether the initial entertainment of the datum of experience is devoid of subjective form of reception, which is what the "sensationalist principle" affirms. Rather, the issue is whether this datum involves actual entities; it is the denial that it does—

which is the "subjectivist principle"—which is "mitigated" by Descartes' use of *"realitas objectiva."* We could have achieved the same effect by changing 'sensationalist principle' to 'sensationalist doctrine,' since the sensationalist doctrine *includes* the subjectivist principle and hence would likewise be mitigated by one who sometimes referred to real objects. But we thought it more likely that Whitehead intended 'subjectivist principle.' For one thing, that is the term used in the previous sentence. Also, the inadvertent substitution of 'sensationalist' for 'subjectivist' seems more likely than the substitution of 'principle' for 'doctrine,' especially given the previous paragraphs.

† 158.29   changed 'generalization' to 'generalizations' (M 240.17; C 221.9) to conform to the following sentence and to 159.17

† 158.43   inserted comma after 'is' (M 240.36)

† 159.10   deleted comma after 'experiences' (M 241.14; C 222.4)

† 159.36   inserted comma after 'muddle' (M 242.10)

† 159.42   inserted single quotation mark before *'realitas'* (M 242.17)

† 160.6   deleted comma after 'mind' (M 242.30; C 223.19)

† 160.9   changed 'an' to 'a' (M 242.33)

* 160.19   The quotation is from the *Treatise*, Bk. I, Part I, Sect. I.

† 160.26   moved comma from outside to inside the quotation marks (M 243.17)

† 161.29   changed exclamation point to question mark (M 245.2)

† 161.37   inserted 'in' after 'is' (M 245.13)

† 162.6   changed comma to semicolon (M 245.28)

† 163.2   changed 'feelings' to 'feeling' (M 247.6)

† 163.4   inserted comma after 'world' (M 247.8)

† 163.22   changed 'are' to 'is' (M 247.32)

† 164.4   inserted comma after 'prehensions' (M 248.27; C 229.9)

† 164.27   put 'conformal' in quotation marks (M 249.19; C 230.3)

‡ 164.35   changed 'earlier' to 'latter' (M 249.29; C 230.12)—'Latter' is used instead of 'later' to conform to 165.36 and 166.5.

† 165.14   inserted comma after 'example' (M 250.22)

† 166.2   changed 'synthetized' to 'synthesized' (M 251.28)

** 166.36   This is clearly *not* a reference to the "subjectivist principle" as defined in the opening section of this chapter at 157.28–29; the same is true of the reference at 167.13. For one thing, the definition on 157 is of a principle which Whitehead rejects, whereas these latter two references are to a principle which he accepts.

** 167.13   See the note for 166.36.

† 167.17   changed 'presentation' to 'presentational' (M 253.29)

† 167.31   changed all four instances of *'rēs veroe'* on this page to *'res verae'* (M 254.10, 14, 28)

† 167.37   changed 'conscresence' to 'concrescence' (M 254.18)

† 171.2   changed 'sense' to 'sensa' (M 259.19; C 240.13)

† 171.3   changed 'justaposition' to 'juxtaposition' (M 259.20–21)

* 171 fn.1   The words *'sensation'* and *'reflection'* were italicized in the original.

† 172.35   changed 'grey-colour' to 'grey colour' (M 262.8)

† 172.37   changed 'sensation' to 'sensations' (M 262.10–11)

† 173.12   decapitalized 'dynamics' (M 262.37; C 243.27)

† 173.15   inserted comma after 'always' (M 263.2)

† 173.16   changed 'interpretive' to 'interpretative' (M 263.4)

† 173.28   deleted commas after 'problem' and 'perception' (M 263.17–18)

† 174.9   took *'Critiques'* out of single quotation marks and italicized it (M 264.14; C 245.2) for the sake of consistency

† 174.15 changed 'behavior' to 'behaviour' (M 264.22) to conform to the usual spelling of both editions

† 175.7 changed 'are' to 'is' (M 265.29; C 246.15)

† 175.27 deleted comma after 'dogma' (M 266.19)

† 175.29 inserted comma after 'Besides' (M 266.21)

† 176.22 changed 'experience' to 'experiences' (M 267.30)

† 176.23 italicized *'hand'* (M 267.32; C 248.15) to correspond to *'eye'*

‡ 176.35 deleted 'to' after 'descend' (M 268.10; C 248.29)—The discussion was already about 'organic being.'

† 177.9 deleted comma after 'definition' (M 268.34)

† 177.40 changed 'spatiatization' to 'spatialization' (M 269.34)

† 179.12 changed 'produce' to 'produces' (M 271.38)—This change was included on the list entitled "Misprints."

† 179.23 changed 'principle' to 'principal' (M 272.15)

† 179.25 changed 'sensations' to 'sensation' (M 272.16–17; C 252.32)

† 179.26 changed 'discernable' to 'discernible' (M 272.18)

† 179.32 changed 'conjectually' to 'conjecturally' (M 272.26)

† 179.45 changed 'experiental' to 'experiential' (M 273.4)

† 180.7 changed 'are' to 'is' (M 273.13; C 253.27)

** 180.11 Some have suggested that 'construed' should be changed to 'constructed,' but we believe that the text is correct as it stands.

† 180.13 deleted comma after 'organs' (M 273.21; C 253.34)

† 181.9 inserted 'with' before 'which' (M 274.32)

† 181.15 inserted 'as' after 'far' (M 275.4)

† 181.42 changed 'percept' to 'percepta' and deleted comma after 'symbols' (M 276.2)—The first change was made by Whitehead in his Macmillan copy.

† 181.44 changed 'precipient' to 'percipient' (M 276.6)

† 182.28 inserted comma after 'word' (M 277.3)

† 182.38 deleted 'of' after 'suggest' (M 277.16)

† 184.33 italicized *'Logic'* (M 281.10)

† 184.35 inserted 'a' after 'is' (M 281.13)

† 185.42 changed 'in' to 'is' (M 282.29)

† 185.44 inserted 'a' before 'new' (M 282.31)

† 187.10 inserted comma after 'or' (M 284.25)

† 187.13 changed 'a non-conformal proposition is' to 'non-conformal propositions are' (M 284.29–30)—As usual, the change made by Cambridge was an improvement, since the following sentence uses the plural pronoun.

† 187.17 inserted comma after 'entities' (M 284.34; C 264.26)

† 187.22 inserted 'of' before 'feeling' (M 285.3)

† 187.32 inserted '(i),' after 'Either' and changed 'satisfaction' to 'satisfactions' (M 285.16)

† 187.43 changed 'data. But' to 'data, but' (M 285.31)

† 188.27 inserted comma after 'entities' (M 286.31)

† 188.39 deleted comma after 'entity' (M 287.9; C 266.34)

† 189.9 decapitalized 'the' (M 287.27; C 267.14)

* 189.12 The word *'abrupt'* was not italicized in *Science and the Modern World,* but Whitehead evidently wanted it stressed here.

† 189.14 inserted 'graded' before 'envisagement' (M 287.34; C 267.19)

† 189.18 changed 'VI' to 'II' (M 288.1)

† 189.20 inserted comma after 'hand' (M 288.4; C 267.25)

† 190.27 changed both instances of 'illusioriness' to 'illusoriness' (M 289.30, 31)

† 190.44 inserted 'a' before 'proposition' (M 290.14; C 269.34)

† 191.15　changed 'experiment' to 'experient' (M 290.36; C 270.18)

† 191.21　deleted comma after 'suspension' (M 291.5)

† 191.36　inserted 'a' before 'feeling' (M 291.26; C 271.6)

** 191.43　Whitehead's sentence can lead to confusion as to which of the two senses is the 'latter.' Some scholars have thought a change to be necessary. But we believe that the text is correct, with the 'latter' sense being the one introduced second in the previous paragraph, i.e., in the sentence at 191.37–40.

‡ 192.22　changed 'on' to 'in' (M 292.28; C 272.7)

† 192.40　deleted comma after 'background' (M 293.13; C 272.28)

† 193.15　inserted comma after 'include' (M 294.2)

† 193 fn.1　changed 'Ch. VI' to 'Ch. V' (M 293 fn.1; C 273 fn.1)

† 196.26　inserted 'a' between 'of' and 'more' (M 298.34; C 278.6)

† 197.6　deleted comma after 'direct' (M 299.28)

‡ 197.19　inserted hyphen in 'judgment-feelings' (M 300.7; C 279.14)— Cambridge always printed this expression without the hyphen; Macmillan sometimes inserted it. In bringing consistency into the text, which we have done without further notation, we chose to use the hyphen, since 'judgment' is not an adjective.

† 197.21　changed 'terms' to 'term' (M 300.10)

† 197.39　inserted hyphen in 'truth-value' (M 300.33)

† 198.20　deleted commas after 'analogous' and 'simple' (M 301.27; C 280.31–32) to conform to similar passages

* 198 fn.2　The asterisk in this footnote is not ours, but is part of the reference to *Principia*.

† 200.27　inserted comma after 'Thus' (M 305.2)

‡ 201.27　changed 'next section' to 'next two sections' (M 306.17; C 285.13) —Whitehead evidently added one more section than he had intended when writing this passage; cf. the note for 206.35.

‡ 201.30　changed 'relevant' to 'relative' (M 306.21; C 285.16)

† 201.34　inserted comma after 'reason' (M 306.27)

† 202.10　changed 'as to which set—favourable or unfavourable—the proposition belongs' to the present reading (M 307.16–17)

† 202.36　deleted comma after 'overcome' (M 308.12)

† 202.41　deleted comma after 'ground' (M 308.19)

† 202.43　inserted 'an' after 'have' (M 308.21; C 287.13)

† 203.13　changed 'these' to 'there' (M 309.2)

† 203.21　deleted comma after 'induction' (M 309.13)

† 204.18　changed 'derivation' to 'divination' (M 310.28; C 289.15)

† 206.19　inserted comma after 'depend' (M 313.32)

† 206.21　changed 'require that exact statistical calculations are' (M 313.35) and 'require exact statistical calculations to be' (C 292.14) to the present reading

† 206.32　deleted comma after 'theory' and inserted commas after 'which' and 'me' (M 314.10)

‡ 206.35　changed 'two' to 'three' (M 314.13; C 292.29)—Cf. the note for 201.27.

† 207.5　changed brackets around 'by (iii)' to commas (M 314.31; C 293.8)

† 208.9　changed 'banquetting' to 'banqueting' (M 317.11; C 295.10)

† 208.25　deleted comma after 'flow' (M 317.32; C 295.31)

† 208.29　inserted 'that with which' after 'as' (M 318.3)

† 209.22　changed 'difference' to 'different' (M 319.3)

† 210.7　italicized *'concrescence'* (M 320.4; C 297.36)—It is parallel with

'*transition*' (and both terms are put in quotation marks in the following paragraph).

† 211.9   put quotation mark before 'the' instead of before 'novel' (M 321.26)

** 211.24   It has been suggested that 'relative' ought to read 'relatively,' but we believe that this change would be incorrect.

† 211.25   deleted comma after 'concrescence' (M 322.10; C 300.1)

† 211.30   deleted comma after 'alien' (M 322.17; C 300.7)—This change was made by Whitehead in his Macmillan copy.

** 212.37   It might be thought that the twofold reference in this paragraph to the 'principle of relativity,' which is the *fourth* category of explanation (and is often referred to as such), as the *third* metaphysical principle is erroneous. However, it is possible that this paragraph was incorporated from Whitehead's Gifford Lectures (which were greatly revised and expanded for publication), and that this reference reflects a numbering used therein for some of his metaphysical principles, such as the ontological principle, and the principles of process and of relativity; compare 22.35–40, 23.26–29, and 24.35–39 with 149.37–40 and 166.27–42.

† 213.11   inserted closing quotation mark after 'passing on' (M 324.30)

† 213 fn.1   changed 'II, XXI, 1' to '*Essay*, II, XXI, 3' (M 325 fn.1; C 302 fn.1)

† 214.5   changed 'negations' to 'negation' (M 326.2)

† 214.6   deleted comma after 'irrelevance' (M 326.3)

† 214.26   inserted 'of' before 'the full' (M 326.28; C 304.14)

† 214.29   changed 'mascroscopic' to 'macroscopic' (M 326.32)—This change was included on the list entitled "Misprints."

† 214.35   changed 'in' to 'is' (M 327.4)

† 215.21   changed 'mascroscopic' to 'macroscopic' (M 327.38)

† 215.26   changed '2d' to '2nd' (M 328.6)

† 219.8   changed 'genetic-theory' to 'genetic theory' here and in line 11 (M 334.38, 335.4)

† 219.15   changed 'already-constituted' to 'already constituted' (M 335.9)

† 219.37   changed 'objectivè' to 'objectivé' (M 336.1)

† 220.3   inserted 'a' before 'given' (M 336.6; C 310.13)

† 221.25   changed 'datum' to 'data' (M 338.16; C 312.20)

** 222.35   When Whitehead was writing this material he evidently had not yet formulated the *ninth* categoreal condition, that of 'Freedom and Determination' (cf. 27.41). However, although there are six categoreal conditions beyond the three discussed in the present chapter, we have let 'five' stand, since 'Freedom and Determination' is not discussed as a categoreal condition in the following material; cf. 248.6 and the note for 278.6.

† 224.31   changed 'in' to 'into' (M 343.3; C 317.3)

† 224.32   deleted comma after 'process' (M 343.5; C 317.5)

† 225.18   inserted comma after 'But' (M 344.8)

† 225.21   put 'creativity' on previous line in quotation marks (M 344.9); put 'temporal creatures' in quotation marks (M 344.10; C 318.8)

‡ 225.36   changed 'There' to 'Here' (M 344.30; C 318.25)—Cf. the note for 88.6.

† 226.6   inserted comma after 'entities' (M 345.12; C 319.8)

† 226.32   changed 'phrase' to 'phase' (M 346.8)

† 226.40   deleted comma after 'itself' (M 346.17; C 320.11)

‡ 227.36   This paragraph was originally preceded by the paragraph which now closes this section.

† 228.5   inserted hyphen in 'class-theory' (M 348.20)

† 228.7   inserted 'Bk.I,' (M 348.23; C 322.14)

‡ 228.16   This paragraph originally appeared two paragraphs higher, i.e., prior to the paragraph beginning 'The third category. . . .'

† 229.43   changed 'are' to 'is' (M 351.3; C 324.28)

† 230.24   deleted comma after 'percipient' (M 351.36; C 325.23)

† 231.39   changed 'constitutions' to 'constitution' (M 353.36; C 327.21)

‡ 232.10   changed 'is' (M 354.18) and 'in a' (C 328.4) to 'in'—This is a place where the Cambridge editor "miscorrected" the text; Whitehead uses this and similar expressions (i.e., without an article) several times, e.g., in the latter part of the same sentence.

† 232.29   changed commas after 'entity' and 'object' to semicolons (M 355.5, 6)

** 233.22   Many scholars have thought that some of the instances of 'qualitative' in this paragraph should have been 'quantitative,' but we believe the text to be correct. To see how *two* types of pattern are involved, the reader will be aided by mentally inserting 'quantitative' before each 'intensive.'

† 233.34   changed 'iself' to 'itself' (M 356.35)

‡ 234.19   inserted 'is' after 'which' (M 357.35; C 331.16); deleted 'displays' after 'tone quality' (C 331.17)—This is another place at which the Cambridge editor "miscorrected" the text.

† 234.21   changed comma after 'separate' to dash (M 358.1; C 331.19)

† 235.29   changed 'determinations' to 'determination' (M 359.33; C 333.10)

† 237.27   deleted comma after 'effect' (M 363.12; C 336.5)

† 239.3   inserted comma after 'Further' (M 365.25)

† 240.11   deleted comma after 'conceptual' (M 367.16; C 340.2)

† 241.2   inserted comma after 'object' (M 368.24)

† 242.23   changed 'this' to 'his' (M 370.30; C 343.13)

† 242.27   took 'e.g.' out of italics (M 370.35)

† 242.41   inserted 'Bk.I,' (M 371.15; C 343.32–33)

† 242.43   changed single to double quotation marks (M 371.15–18)

† 244.25   moved take-out quotation mark from after 'society' (M 373.29; C 344.29) to end of sentence

† 245.37   deleted comma after 'simple' (M 375.26; C 347.19)

† 247.42   deleted comma after 'chapter' (M 378.34)

* 248.6   Cf. the notes for 222.35 and 278.6.

† 248.14   inserted 'of' before 'the nexus' (M 379.18; C 351.2)—Cf. 26.36.

* 250.10   In his Macmillan copy, Whitehead underlined 'The Category of Reversion is then abolished' and wrote "cf. p. 40" in the margin. The reference is to p. 26 of this corrected edition.

† 251.13   deleted commas after 'one' and 'same' (M 384.3; C 355.15–16)

† 253.9   changed 'cf. Ch.V, and also' to 'Ch.V; cf. also' (M 386.38; C 358.8)

† 254.2   changed 'transmuted' to 'transmitted' (M 388.11; C 359.15)

† 254.42   changed 'subject' to 'subjective' (M 389.25)

** 255.19   It has been suggested that 'Aesthetic Harmony' should be changed to 'Subjective Harmony,' but this expression seems to be simply an alternative way of referring to Categoreal Obligation VII. (This is one of the places where we added the capitalization; cf. the note for 21.1.)

‡ 255.26   This paragraph was originally followed by the two paragraphs which now appear prior to the last paragraph of Section V of the following chapter; cf. the note for 264.15.

† 256.32   changed 'seventeenth' to 'eighteenth' (M 392.10–11; C 363.6)

† 256 fn.1   deleted comma after 'Cf.' (M 391 fn.1)

‡ 257.29   In his Cambridge copy, Whitehead indicated that '(*qua* possibility)' should be inserted in the text after 'referent' (M 393.17; C 364.9).

† 257.36   inserted comma after 'eternal object' (M 393.25; C 364.17); changed 'nexus' to 'nexūs' (M 393.26; C 364.18)

† 259.5   inserted 'a' before 'datum' (M 395.24; C 366.13)

† 259.27   deleted comma after 'subjects' (M 396.16; C 367.4)

† 261.10   changed 'predicate' to 'predicative' (M 398.31; C 369.16)

‡ 261.43   This paragraph was originally preceded by the paragraph which now appears prior to the last paragraph of this section.

‡ 262.44   This paragraph originally appeared as the second paragraph of this section.

† 263.10   deleted comma after 'feeling' (M 401.32; C 372.11)

‡ 264.15   This and the following paragraph originally appeared at the end of Chapter III of this Part. The correct location of these two paragraphs is less obvious than that of those moved in Section VII of Chapter I and Section IV of Chapter IV, but they seem to fit here better than anywhere else.

† 265.5   changed 'are' to 'is' (M 404.16; C 374.26)

‡ 265.26   deleted 'as well as "immortality," and' after 'Athenianism' and put 'mortality' in quotation marks (M 405.5, 6; C 375.16, 17)—The deletion was made by Whitehead in his Cambridge copy.

† 267.4   deleted comma after 'respectively' (M 407.18; C 377.16)

† 267.21   changed comma after first 'feelings' to semicolon (M 408.4; C 378.1) —This change was included on the list entitled "Misprints."

† 268.2   inserted 'the' after 'all' (M 408.34; C 378.28)

† 268.37   deleted comma after 'feelings' (M 410.5; C 379.33)

† 270.42   put 'suspense-form' in quotation marks (M 413.11; C 382.32)

† 271.16   changed 'imaginative feelings' to 'imaginative feeling' (M 413.34; C 383.18)

‡ 271.18   changed 'doctrine' to 'datum' (M 413.36; C 383.19)—The datum of a propositional feeling is a proposition, and a proposition is what is constituted by logical subjects and a predicative pattern. This is one of those errors most easily explainable as due to the typist's misreading of Whitehead's handwriting.

† 271.18   changed 'indicative feelings' to 'indicative feeling' (M 413.36; C 383.20)

† 271.19   inserted 'the' before 'physical' (M 413.37; C 383.21)

† 272.21   put 'physical recollection' in quotation marks (M 415.25; C 385.3)

† 272.22   inserted comma after 'imaginative feeling' (M 415.26; C 385.3)

† 272.23   put 'intuitive judgment' in quotation marks (M 415.27–28; C 385.5)

† 272.24   put 'indicative feeling' in quotation marks (M 415.29)

† 272.36   deleted comma after 'other' (M 416.8)

‡ 272.45   changed 'more' to 'mere' (M 416.19; C 385.33)

† 274.6   deleted comma after parentheses (M 418.8)

‡ 274.27   changed 'practice' to 'predicate' (M 418.33; C 388.4)

† 275.36   deleted comma after 'subject' (M 420.30; C 389.34)

‡ 276.16   changed 'physical' to 'conceptual' (M 421.25; C 390.25)

† 276.23   deleted comma after 'developed' and changed 'required' to 'requires' (M 421.34; C 390.34)

‡ 276.38   changed 'according' to 'accorded' (M 422.16; C 391.16)—The

word 'according' would suggest, contrary to Whitehead's position, that the conceptual valuation is completely determined by the physical feeling. It would also prevent this sentence from speaking to the issue that dominates the rest of the paragraph, which is how, in a physical purpose, the fate of a physical feeling is determined by the conceptual valuation given (accorded) to it. Whitehead does, in other places, stress that the conceptual valuation is *partly* determined by the physical feeling; but that is not the topic of this paragraph.

† 277.12   deleted comma after 'phase' (M 423.3; C 392.1)

† 277.22   inserted comma after 'subjective aim' (M 423.18; C 392.15) to conform to the parallel in the first part of the sentence and to avoid the false suggestion that there might be a subjective aim which is *not* "the final cause"

‡ 277.42   changed 'subject' to 'subjective' and inserted 'at' before 'intensity' (M 424.6 & 7; C 393.2 & 3) to conform to 27.30–31

‡ 278.6   deleted 'final' after 'this' (M 424.17; C 393.11)—As mentioned in the note for 222.35, Whitehead evidently added the ninth category after writing this section; cf. also the note for 278.35.

† 278.31   changed 'Category IV' to 'Category V' (M 425.11; C 394.4)

‡ 278.35   changed 'this final category' to 'Category VIII' (M 425.16–17; C 394.9)—Cf. the note for 278.6.

† 278.36   changed 'had' to 'has' (M 425.17; C 394.10)

† 279.33   changed 'are' to 'is' (M 426.35; C 393.23)

† 279 fn.1   inserted 'Sect. VII' (M 427 fn.1; C 395 fn.1)

† 280.34   inserted comma after 'Also' (M 428.17)

† 283.2   changed 'CO-ORDINATE' to 'COORDINATE (C 401.2)—Cf. the note for xx.35.

† 283.26   changed '*solído*' to '*solido*' (M 434.23)

† 284.39   deleted comma after 'separate' (M 436.10; C 403.21)

‡ 286.17   changed 'Ch. VIII, Sects. IV to IX' (M 438.22–23) and 'Ch. VIII, §§ IV to VI' (C 405.28) to 'Ch. IV, Sects. IV to IX'—Chapter VIII has only six sections, so the Macmillan reference is clearly erroneous, and the subject at issue is not discussed in the sections cited by Cambridge.

† 286.19   deleted commas after 'sense' and 'influences' (M 438.23–24; C 405.29–30)

† 286.26   deleted comma after 'plan' (M 438.34)

† 286.39   italicized '$Q_1 Q_2$' and changed 'either' to 'other' (M 439.13–14)

† 287.1   inserted comma after 'as' (M 439.21)

† 287.3   changed 'purpose' to 'purposes' (M 439.23)

† 287.8   inserted 'the' before 'morphological' and changed 'structure' to 'structures' (M 439.29; C 406.32–33)

† 287.15   changed 'taken in by my' to 'taken by me in my' (M 439.38)

† 287.17   deleted comma after 'point' (M 440.3; C 407.8)

† 287.30   capitalized 'Part' (M 440.19; C 407.23)

† 287 fn.2   changed 'Lajuna's' to 'Laguna's' (M 440 fn.2)

† 288.17   inserted comma after 'Also' (M 441.22)

† 290.2   changed 'an' to 'a' (M 444.1)

† 290.22   changed comma after 'fact' to semicolon (M 444.27)

† 291.25   capitalized 'Platonic' (M 446.11; C 413.7)

† 291.26   changed 'VIII' to 'IV' (M 446.14; C 413.9)

† 294.26   changed semicolon to colon (C 416.31)

‡ 294.34   We have followed Macmillan, as against Cambridge, in italicizing the numbers of *Definitions* and *Assumptions* here (C 417.6) and below.

† 296.1 These diagrams were on p. 451 of the Macmillan edition.
† 296.22 changed '*15*' to '*13*' (M 452.37)
† 297.1 changed '*16*' to '*14*' (M 453.1)
† 297.7 deleted '1.' after '*Definition 6.*' (M 453.9; C 419.34)
† 297.11 changed '*17*' to '*15*' (M 453.14)
† 297.14 changed '*18*' to '*16*' (M 453.17)
† 297.15 changed '*19*' to '*17*' (M 453.19)
† 297.17 changed '*20*' to '*18*' (M 453.21)
† 298.1 inserted 'and' before '(ii)' (M 454.18–19; C 421.4)
† 298.23 changed period after '*B*' to comma (M 455.9)
† 298.33 changed comma after 'A_1' to semicolon (M 455.23; C 422.7)
† 298.35 changed comma after 'A_2' to semicolon (M 455.25; C 422.9)
† 298.42 changed '*21*' to '*19*' (M 455.34)
† 299.3 changed '*22*' to '*20*' (M 456.3)
† 299.10 deleted comma after 'belongs' (M 456.12; C 422.32)
† 299.13 changed '*23*' to '*21*' (M 456.15)
† 299.14 deleted comma after 'element' (M 456.16; C 422.36)
† 299.15 changed '*24*' to '*22*' (M 456.18)
† 299.16 deleted comma after 'element' (M 456.19; C 432.2)
† 299.17 changed '*25*' to '*23*' (M 456.21)
† 299.23 changed '*26*' to '*24*' (M 456.28)
† 299.33 changed 'satisfied' to 'satisfies' (M 457.3–4)
† 299.41 changed 'definitions' to 'definition' (M 457.13)
† 300.7 changed '*27*' to '*25*' (M 457.26)
† 300.8 changed colon after 'end-points' to semicolon (M 457.27; C 424.10)
† 300.30 changed '*28*' to '*26*' (M 458.18)
‡ 300.40 changed '*33*' (M 459.33) and '*31*' (C 426.11) to '*27*'—This Assumption appears to have been added after the text was otherwise completed; it came at the very end of the chapter in both editions. Since it refers explicitly to *Definition 23*, it has been relocated directly after this Definition.
† 301.4 changed '*29*' (M 459.3) and '*27*' (C 425.20) to '*28*'
† 301.8 changed '*30*' (M 459.8) and '*28*' (C 425.24) to '*29*'
† 301.10 changed '*31*' (M 459.11) and '*29*' (C 425.27) to '*30*'
† 301.12 changed '*32*' (M 459.14) and '*30*' (C 425.30) to '*31*'
‡ 301.20 Neither edition had a new paragraph at this point (M 459.25; C 426.3), but it is clearly desirable.
‡ 301.25 This paragraph was originally followed by *Assumption 33*, which has been changed to *Assumption 27* and moved to the appropriate place.
‡ 301.26 Whereas Cambridge placed this paragraph at this point in the text, Macmillan had it (under the heading "Corrigenda") at the very back of the book, after the Index, with an indication that it belonged on page 459. The page references in the paragraph were to 504 and 463 of the Macmillan edition. We took each 'i.e.' out of italics (M 544.5, 19).
† 302.12 changed single to double quotation marks (M 460.17–18; C 427.16–17)
† 302.18 deleted comma after 'imply' (M 460.25)
† 302.27 changed single to double quotation marks (M 461.6–7; C 427.32–33)
† 303.30 inserted comma after 'words' (M 462.19)
† 304.17 changed 'Ch. III' to 'Ch. II' (M 463.18); changed 'Ass. 33' (M 463.19) and 'Ass. 31' (C 430.8) to 'Ass. 27'
* 304.25 See the added paragraph on p. 301.
† 304.38 changed 'These' to 'There' (M 464.9)

† 305.8   changed 'relatively' to 'relating' (M 464.24)
† 306.19   changed 'lies' to 'lie' (C 433.7)—Whitehead has consistently been using the subjunctive.
† 306.21   changed '6' to '6.1' (M 466.26)
† 306.39   changed 'lies' to 'lie' (C 433.32)
† 309.2   changed 'become' to 'becomes' (M 470.23)
† 309.18   deleted comma after 'bodies' (M 471.8; C 437.21)
† 311.8   inserted comma after 'case' (M 473.28; C 440.22) to conform to parallel two sentences above
† 311.35   changed 'realisation' to 'realization' (M 474.24)
† 314.7   inserted hyphen in 'high-grade' (M 478.9)
† 314.39   inserted hyphen in 'life-history' (M 479.14; C 446.4) to conform to other occurrences
† 315.20   changed colon after 'physics' to semicolon (M 480.8; C 446.35)
† 316.22   inserted comma after 'forms' (M 481.32; C 448.18)
† 317 fn.1   placed commas around '*Symbolism*' in place of Cambridge's parentheses; changed comma after 'New York' to colon; added '1928'; and put publication data in parentheses (M 482 fn.1; C 449 fn.1)—Cf. the note for 121 fn.5.
† 319.2   inserted comma after 'example' (M 485.24)
† 319.8   changed semicolon after 'world' to comma (M 485.38)
† 319.27   changed '-dimensioned' to '-dimensional' (M 486.20)
† 319.33   took reference out of italics (M 486.28); changed 'VI' to 'VIII' (M 486.28; C 453.10)—The reference is to Part II, Ch. IV, Sect. VIII.
† 319.43   changed 'parts' to 'pasts' (M 487.4; C 453.23)
† 320.1   deleted comma after 'occasions' (M 487.5; C 453.23); inserted comma after 'S' (M 487.5)
† 320.22   deleted comma after 'M' (M 487.33; C 454.14)
† 320.26   inserted comma after 'views' (M 487.37)
‡ 320.38   changed 'present' to 'future' (M 488.15; C 454.33)
† 320.44   inserted comma after 'secondly' (M 488.22; C 455.2)
† 321.3   deleted comma after 'M' (M 488.26)
† 321.13   inserted comma after 'occasions' (M 489.3)
† 321.35   inserted hyphen in 'life-history' (M 489.31)
† 322.16   deleted comma after 'future' (M 491.19)
† 323.20   changed 'THE' to 'The' (M 493.4)
‡ 324.21   changed 'previous chapter' to 'Ch. III' (M 494.26; C 460.16)—Whitehead evidently ended up with one more chapter in Part IV than he had intended when writing this passage.
‡ 325.15   changed 'the previous chapter' to 'Ch. III' (M 495.38; C 461.27)—Cf. the note for 324.21.
† 325.36   changed 'presentation' to 'presentational' (M 496.28)
† 325.43   italicized '*Meditation I*' (M 496.36–37)
† 326.3   changed 'Part I, Sect. XII' to 'Sect. XII, Part I' (M 497.4; C 462.29)
† 326.4   inserted comma after 'Hume' (M 497.5)
† 326.16   inserted comma after 'When' (M 497.21)
† 326.42   changed 'natures' to 'nature' (M 498.16; C 464.2)
† 328.8   changed 'In-mathematics' to 'In mathematics' (M 500.10–11)
† 328.14   inserted hyphen in 'yard-measure' here, at 328.27, and at 329.8 & 9 (M 500.18 & 37; M 501.29 & 31)
† 328.36   inserted comma after 'from' (M 501.9; C 466.29)
† 329.3   inserted hyphen in 'wave-lengths' (M 501.23)
† 329.5   inserted 'are' after 'tests' (M 501.26)—This change was included on the list entitled "Misprints."

† 329.7   deleted comma after 'congruence' (M 501.28; C 467.9)

† 329.30   changed 'depend' to 'depends' (M 502.21)

† 330.2   inserted 'the' before 'meaning' (M 503.4; C 468.21)

† 330.12   changed 'inter-connections' to 'interconnections' (M 503.16)

* 330.42   See the added paragraph on p. 301.

† 331.7   inserted comma after 'containing' (M 504.29)

† 331.16   deleted comma after 'line' and changed 'itself is' to 'is itself' (M 505.2-3)

† 331.36   deleted comma after 'parallelograms' (M 505.29; C 471.7)

† 331 fn.1   took 'Sixth Memoir on Quantics' out of italics and put it in quotation marks; changed 'Trans. R.S.' to '*Transactions of the Royal Society*'; and decapitalized 'von' (M 505 fn.1; C 470 fn.1)

† 333 fn.3   inserted comma after 'measurement' in second line (M 508 fn.3); changed 'Vol. XXIV' to 'Vol. XXV' (M 508 fn.3; C 473 fn.1)

† 337.14   inserted comma after 'selection' (M 512.17; C 477.17)

† 339.6   deleted comma after 'curse' (M 514.36; C 479.33)

* 340.11   Mathew Arnold's poem, "Resignation," which was written as advice to his sister, begins with the following two lines in italics:
To die be given us, or attain!
Fierce work it were, to do again.
These lines are presented as sentiments expressed by pilgrims on the way to Mecca. Whitehead evidently quoted these lines (imperfectly) from memory, and they clearly conveyed a different message to him from the one implied by the title of Arnold's poem.

† 340.38   deleted 'the' after 'means' (M 517.26; C 482.20)

† 341.8   inserted comma after 'therefore' (M 518.4)

† 342.3   inserted 'SECTION I' (M 519.3)

‡ 343.9   changed 'theistic idolatrous' to 'idolatrous theistic' (M 520.26; C 485.21)

† 344.20   inserted comma after 'creative act' (M 522.24)

† 344.25   changed 'mover' to 'moves' (M 522.30; C 487.23)

† 344.26   changed ' a mover' to 'something' (M 522.31; C 487.24)

‡ 344.29   inserted 'move in this way; they move without being moved. The primary objects of desire and of thought' (M 522.33; C 487.26)

† 344.31   changed 'desire' to 'wish' (M 522.35; C 487.28)

† 344.33   deleted 'side' after 'one' and changed 'list' to 'two columns' (M 523.3; C 487.30)

† 344 fn.1   changed '1072' to '1072a 23-32' (M 522 fn.1; C 487 fn.1)

† 345.9   inserted comma after 'Thus' (M 523.26)

† 346.21   deleted comma after 'nature' (M 525.25; C 490.10)

** 346.35   In his Macmillan copy, Whitehead crossed out 'leading' and wrote both "persuading" and "swaying" in the margin. No change was made in the text, partly because Whitehead did not clearly specify a substitute.

† 347.1   capitalized 'Platonic' (M 526.18; C 491.3)

† 348.2   changed 'self-contradiction' to 'self-contradictions' (M 528.2); changed 'depends' to 'depend' (C 492.21)

† 348.20   changed 'these' to 'there' (M 528.24)

† 349.7   changed colon after 'forms' to semicolon (M 529.29; C 494.7)

† 350.6   deleted comma after 'suffering' (M 531.7; C 495.20)—This change was made by Whitehead on Mrs. Greene's typescript.